I0147157

Taming The Lion

1 Peter 5:8

Cephas

Cephas Ministry Inc. Publishing, Denver CO U.S.A.

Taming The Lion

Taming The Lion

Table of Contents

Taming The Lion

INTRODUCTION

To read this book requires love for the Gospel, if you don't you might as well put it away because you'll simply think it foolishness. The book proves that biblical truth is indeed truth that sustains us. No matter what happens to us we land on our feet and move on knowing we are only passing through. The world is irrelevant. What is relevant is our eternal life, where we'll spend it in heaven or hell. All human beings have eternal life but where they will spend it is the question.

This book will reveal the resistance we are up against in our enemy Satan who only works to undermine believers in Christ Jesus because Satan knows where he is going and wants all of humanity to join him. Those who already have sworn their allegiance to Satan are no problem to him. Like Jesus Christ, who preached only three years, was crucified because Satan hated Him, we become the object of Satan's hatred as well. Had Jesus weakened and let Satan tempt Him, He would have been King of this world for a season and the whole world would have ended up in hell forever.

Every man, woman, and child's salvation hung on one man. To prove to us that we can depend on Him forever, He weakened Himself by fasting 40 days before He was confronted with the offer to possess the whole world. If He was 100% human and 100% Spirit, He experienced everything humans do, yet gave Himself to be humiliated, be bled and died for our sakes who are completely undeserving as you will see in this book.

God knows our lot, that we have no chance of making it to Heaven on our own. We can try as hard as we want; Satan derails us at every turn without God's intervention. Most of us believe that we are good people and would not hurt anyone, go to church on Sunday and earn our wages by the sweat of our brow. That is well and good, but we tend to be rebels spiritually. We want to do it our way instead of studying the Bible we read other books and listen to evangelists

4

in the hope that's going to get us to heaven. Nothing could be further from the truth.

In my case raised in an affluent household I never thought I'd be confronted with utter poverty like I was. God is love and since we are in the likeness of God we all have love inherent in us. Some are aware of it and others not. Love and hate are parallel and if you have ever noticed it is very easy to go from love to hate. Love is God and hate is Satan. The minute we have unmet needs, Satan is going to be there with his solutions. Both God and Satan have a price for their services. When we reach out to God for help, the price is to know His Word enough so we apply it correctly and reap the benefits. We also have to learn to listen to the still small voice of the Holy Spirit. He is in believers and signals to us when we need to deal with an issue and immediately act on it or we lose. It takes practice and we learn by trial and error like a baby that skins its knees learning how to walk.

Satan's price is violating the Word of God. Satan expects us to engage in behavior that grieves God. When we participate in Satan's tools we reap God's wrath. The Bible warns that we can even lose our souls.

When we engage in activity that seems to be godly and are too ignorant to see the problem God has given us a way out because Satan is too cunning for those who do not read or understand the Bible. I found that I wanted to read the Bible but it seemed cryptic to me, I could not make head or tail out of it. My sister said, to her the Old Testament stories were simply romantic stories. She couldn't figure out what she was supposed to learn from it.

Until we truly receive the Holy Spirit we cannot understand the Bible. It is veiled to people who are not committed to Jesus Christ like a Bride is committed to her Bridegroom. That is not just casual but a deep relationship that lasts forever. Why? The relationship is based on unconditional love. When there are no conditions to be filled in a relationship, there are no disappointments and it lasts forever. There is no sin in that kind of a relationship because Jesus died for every sin that was ever committed. If we continue to sin deliberately we do not have the Holy Spirit in us and are not part of the Bride of Christ. We know when we have the Holy Spirit because He controls our behavior.

The Apostle Paul shared: **"But we have this treasure in earthen vessels, that the excellency of the power may be of God, and not of us."** (2 Corinthians 4:7 KJV) **"For ye see your calling, brethren, how that not many wise men after the flesh, not many mighty, not many noble, are called: But God hath chosen the foolish things of the world to confound the wise; and God hath chosen the weak things of the world to confound the things which are mighty; And base things of the world, and things which are despised, hath God chosen, yea, and things which are not, to bring to nought things that are: That no flesh should glory in his presence."** (1 Corinthians 1:26-29 KJV)

This book is meant for readers who want to know the truth, which rests in the reality of Jesus Christ. The book is not to be viewed as an attack on segments of society, but is meant to hold suggestions as to how Christians can exist and live their faith within today's pagan society. It proves that endurance to the end should be a top priority. Complacency is Satan's favorite playground to bring Jesus Christ down in us. Every person is in the Book of Life until they deny or reject Jesus Christ's existence; only then is their name blotted out.

During my travel through life, I met few people who truly had a testimony of Jesus Christ. That realization motivated me to share my discoveries. The devil's focal point is to destroy Jesus Christ in us and he has thousands of devices to get the job done. We cannot come to Christ Jesus without the knowledge that He really exists. It takes believing that Christ Jesus is God's Word that became flesh. He is our creator. Jesus Christ is God's first begotten Son and that He, Jesus Christ; God the Father and God the Holy Spirit, are One God in three persons. See: John 1:1-4; 10-14; 1 John 5:7 (KJV)

Remember that only the Body of Christ Jesus has the one and only God in three persons. All other denominations and religions are monotheists. That is going to be extremely good to know since major movements are destroying the Biblical concepts today.

The history of creation has been removed and replaced by evolution. Evolution has been proven to be an impossibility mathematically and so far people have not come up with an alternative teaching to avoid bringing the history of creation back into the schools. This faulty teaching has had the most devastating effects on today's society.

From my own life, I realized the importance of discovering God in my heart early in life, to develop that personal relationship that became the guiding hand so essential through perilous times. Relying on preachers to share the true history of humanity was wrong on my part. The truth did not penetrate until I studied it myself. The Scriptures are a God breathed history and prophecy of God's promises and their fulfillment daily. We can prove its authenticity by applying biblical principles to our every day life. They work. God teaches us through His Son, prophets and apostles how to resist the devil.

The circumstances I grew up under gave me an unusual awareness and made me dig for answers of what life was all about. It didn't make much sense to me. God performed a miraculous victory in my case considering where I came from and what I had to work through. I could not have maintained on my own. The story will bear that out. We plan our course, but God determines the steps and often derails what we set out to do unless our plans line up with His. **"It is a fearful thing to fall into the hands of the living God. But call to remembrance the former days, in which, after ye were illuminated, ye endured a great fight of afflictions;"** (Hebrews 10:31-32 KJV)

Christians may object to the handling of this life. It will test Christian's understanding of God's methods of administering discipline. God has to tame (temper, mellow, soften us) to bring us into line with His will for us and His will is to become a harvester of souls, a fisher of men and women by allowing the Holy Spirit to indwell us and use our bodies for His purposes. That is why Jesus taught the following:

Blessed are the poor in spirit: for theirs is the kingdom of heaven.

Blessed are they that mourn: for they shall be comforted. Blessed are the meek: for they shall inherit the earth.

Blessed are they which do hunger and thirst after righteousness: for they shall be filled.

Blessed are the merciful: for they shall obtain mercy.

Blessed are the pure in heart: for they shall see God.

Blessed are the peacemakers: for they shall be called the children of God.

Blessed are they which are persecuted for righteousness' sake: for theirs is the kingdom of heaven.

Blessed are ye, when men shall revile you, and persecute you, and shall say all manner of evil against you falsely, for my sake.

Rejoice, and be exceeding glad: for great is your reward in heaven: for so persecuted they the prophets which were before you. Ye are the salt of the earth: but if the salt have lost his savour, wherewith shall it be salted? it is thenceforth good for nothing, but to be cast out, and to be trodden under foot of men. Ye are the light of the world. A city that is set on a hill cannot be hid. Neither do men light a candle, and put it under a bushel, but on a candlestick; and it giveth light unto all that are in the house. Let your light so shine before men, that they may see your good works, and glorify your Father which is in heaven." (Matthew 5:3-16 KJV)

Evangelists persuade the public to be born again with the conviction; once saved, always saved and the new Christian becomes a victim of the diabolic devices of Satan unless he or she begins a daily disciplined walk of Bible study. Becoming a disciple of Christ Jesus is not about just following Him and telling others about it. "The word disciple is derived from 'dis', - apart, and 'cipere' to hold, to take, to seize. 1. A 'pupil' follower of Jesus. The word disciple comes from the word discipline: 1. A branch of knowledge or learning; 2. Training that develops self- control, character, or orderliness and efficiency; 3. The result of such training; 4. Acceptance of or submission to authority and control (in our case as Christians, submission to the Holy Spirit, Who is part of the God head)" – The source of the explanations is Strong's Exhaustive Concordance of the Bible

This account is about false teachers who appeal to our sinful nature and entice us who are just barely escaping from those who live in error. They promise freedom, while they themselves are slaves to depravity. A man is a slave to whatever has mastered him as the apostle Paul states in 2 Peter 2:17-22. If we have escaped the corruption of the world by knowing our Lord and Savior Jesus Christ and are again entangled in it and overcome by it, we are worse off at the end then we were at the beginning and a fool like me repeated that folly over and over until I did what God asks of all of us, study the Word of God to understand my plight from a spiritual perspective. I couldn't win without first doing that.

There is a judgment for believers as well as unbelievers. Believers are judged for how they spend their time. God expects us to dedicate a reasonable amount of time to Him. Believers will not be in the final judgment, the second Resurrection. Believers are raised into eternal life in heaven at the First Resurrection / Rapture.

The future of unbelievers according to 2 Peter 3:7,8 is: **"But the heavens and the earth, which are now, by the same word are kept in store, reserved unto fire against the day of judgment and perdition of ungodly men. But, beloved, be not ignorant of this one thing, that one day is with the Lord as a thousand years, and a thousand years as one day."**

The 'Day of Judgment' is coming when the earth will be destroyed by fire after the devil and those who are ungodly and do

Taming The Lion

not wish to go to heaven will be placed in the lake of fire forever. **"And death and hell were cast into the lake of fire. This is the second death. And whosoever was not found written in the book of life was cast into the lake of fire."** (Revelation 20:14-15 KJV)

There are some who teach that the lake of fire is a temporary state and that after cremation of bodies takes place, they simply become ashes. Nothing is further from the truth. Scripture states that the 'last enemy that shall be destroyed is death.' Death is also thrown into the lake of fire; in other words, it ceases to exist.. That proves that the lake of fire is eternal. This event is called the 'second death.' In the second death there is no separation of soul and body as in the case of the first death. That means there will be full awareness of the condition that the body is in. Obviously the suffering will be eternally excruciating. We certainly do not wish to see our loved ones in this situation.

Death, in any form, is the penalty of law. It is attended with pain. It cuts off from hope, from friends, from enjoyment. It subjects him or her who dies to a much-dreaded condition. In all these respects it was proper to call the final condition of the wicked death, even though their soul would live. There is no evidence that John om the Book of John, meant to affirm that the second death would imply an extinction of existence. See "death and hell" Hosea 13:14; 1 Corinthians 15:26,54; "lake of fire" Matthew 25:41

This day is the last day of the `Lord's Day'. Our only opportunity to bypass the final judgment completely is this moment. We may die in the next moment. By just believing that Jesus is the Christ, the first begotten Son of God, who shed His blood out of His Body from the cross to literally wash 'our' sins away into the sea of forgetfulness, that He resurrected on the third day and gave His Holy Spirit Who set about to gather all who wish to go to heaven back to our Lord and Savior Christ Jesus. When we are confronted with this event and say "yes Lord, I wish to be Your Bride" the Holy Spirit takes residence in our hearts and begins to bring us into awareness of our sinful nature and helplessness and makes us realize that our only hope is Christ Jesus. Depending on how we have lived to this point, we begin to feel sorrow about our past and wish that we had done this long ago. Repentance is to stop doing things that grieve the Holy Spirit.

Because the Holy Spirit begins to coach us, our lives change. Our lives are now under attack by Satan and we become aware of the Holy Spirit in us because He empowers us to overcome the world. When we don't heed Him we will know because doing it in the physical without Him is to fail every time.

The journey was long and tedious and often discouraging, but His promises are in the Bible and only those who endure to the end will get the ring. An awareness of the empty space inside that yearns for this loving Holy Spirit to enter is for real. Then when He lives in that space it is filled with the peace that is beyond all understanding. When it first happens the joy is as indescribable as falling in love with the man or woman of one's dreams. There comes a desire to shout it from the rooftop that never leaves. The joy calms down like it does in marriage when the daily routine sets in of being married to man or woman, as well as Jesus Christ.

When I got to that point, God had a whole agenda ready to go which has not stopped to this day. It was shock and awe to say the least that God had been in my life really all my life preparing me for that day. I had all the skills I needed, the equipment necessary to go public and the funding from my own past to keep the balls in the air. He had led me through many facets in society that are satanic to share with others so they could be set free as I had.

I knew all my life at some point I would be doing what I am doing today but it took many years before God opened the door for me to actually do it. Had I run ahead of Him, heresy is what I would have been teaching. We definitely have to have patience and wait on God. He is working on us as in Isaiah 64:8 **"But now, O LORD, thou art our father; we are the clay, and thou our potter; and we all are the work of thy hand."**

The `Lord's Day' is described in 2 Peter 3:8 to be equivalent to a 1000 years in God's mind. This day includes the dreaded seven-year tribulation, which hangs over civilization suspended without dates. Because God's patience is incredible, He does not want anyone to perish, but everyone to come to repentance. He is waiting as long as He possibly can. But in Luke 12:39, He shares with us that He will suddenly come like a thief in the night at an hour when we least expect it and warns us in Luke 21:34-36 **"And take heed to yourselves, lest at any time your hearts be overcharged with surfeiting, and drunkenness, and cares of this life, and so that day come upon you unawares. For as a snare shall it come on all them that dwell on the face of the whole earth. Watch ye therefore, and pray always, that ye may be accounted worthy to escape all these things that shall come to pass, and to stand before the Son of man." "Take ye heed, watch and pray: for ye know not when the time is."** *(*Mark 13:33 KJV)

When I read Luke 21:36 I question the word 'accounted worthy'. What does Luke refer to since we are saved by the mere fact that we believe that Jesus Christ is God Himself in flesh and that He died for our sins. The Jamieson-Fausset- Brown Commentary explains this verse 36 to mean: "Watch . . . pray, the two great duties which in prospect of trial are constantly enjoined. These warnings, suggested by the need of preparedness for the tremendous calamities approaching, and the total wreck of the existing state of things, are the general improvement of the whole discourse, carrying the mind forward to Judgment and Vengeance of another kind and on a grander and more awful scale--not ecclesiastical or political but personal, not temporal but eternal--when all safety and blessedness will be found to lie in being able to "STAND BEFORE THE SON OF MAN" in the glory of His personal appearing."

We stand before Jesus Christ with His righteousness, rather than our own, which was imputed to us when we came to Him in repentance. The Bible describes this event as the wedding between the bride of Christ, His church, and Jesus Christ. Anyone who attends this wedding in a wedding dress that is incorrect is told to leave. The wedding dress is the righteousness of Jesus Christ. We can't lose if we have the Word in us and understand the truth.

Taming The Lion

During the tribulation discussed in the final pages of this book, the heavens disappear with a roar, elements will be destroyed by fire. Christians are looking forward to a new heaven and a new earth. The corruption described in the following pages caused by evil desires of people will come to a climax when the Antichrist becomes the only world leader.

Jesus taught two simple commandments, which covers all requirements of us: **"Jesus said unto him, Thou shalt love the Lord thy God with all thy heart, and with all thy soul, and with all thy mind. This is the first and great commandment. And the second is like unto it, Thou shalt love thy neighbour as thyself. On these two commandments hang all the law and the prophets."** (Matthew 22:37-40 KJV)

To escape this wrath and to make our calling and election sure and preventing us from falling, we must do what He tells us to in 2 Peter 1:1-14 **"Simon Peter, a servant and an apostle of Jesus Christ, to them that have obtained like precious faith with us through the righteousness of God and our Saviour Jesus Christ: Grace and peace be multiplied unto you through the knowledge of God, and of Jesus our Lord, According as his divine power hath given unto us all things that pertain unto life and godliness, through the knowledge of him that hath called us to glory and virtue: Whereby are given unto us exceeding great and precious promises: that by these ye might be partakers of the divine nature, having escaped the corruption that is in the world through lust. And beside this, giving all diligence, add to your faith virtue; and to virtue knowledge; And to knowledge temperance; and to temperance patience; and to patience godliness; And to godliness brotherly kindness; and to brotherly kindness charity.**

"For if these things be in you, and abound, they make you that ye shall neither be barren nor unfruitful in the knowledge of our Lord Jesus Christ. But he that lacketh these things is blind, and cannot see afar off, and hath forgotten that he was purged from his old sins.

Taming The Lion

"Wherefore the rather, brethren, give diligence to make your calling and election sure: for if ye do these things, ye shall never fall: For so an entrance shall be ministered unto you abundantly into the everlasting kingdom of our Lord and Saviour Jesus Christ. Wherefore I will not be negligent to put you always in remembrance of these things, though ye know them, and be established in the present truth. Yea, I think it meet, as long as I am in this tabernacle, to stir you up by putting you in remembrance; Knowing that shortly I must put off this my tabernacle, even as our Lord Jesus Christ hath shewed me."

The confession in the following chapters proves that whoever lives by the truth comes into the light, so that it may be seen plainly that the Holy Spirit produced the victory. **"No man, when he hath lighted a candle, putteth it in a secret place, neither under a bushel, but on a candlestick, that they which come in may see the light."** (Luke 11:33 KJV)

Names are left out to protect the innocent. The historical background is documented and confirmed in a bibliography. Research was done in Europe as well as the United States. The book required a lived life. It was in production three years. Information was gathered and formulated in written form.

The struggle between principalities becomes clearly evident and will bring the reader's memories into focus in relation to God and our adversary and shed light on those episodes. What became clear while writing was our three dimensional existence: the flesh, the soul (mind) and the spirit. Our soul is our awareness of this physical existence in our environment, which can be called our horizontal view. The vertical awareness only comes by accepting the Word of God as truth. We can only acknowledge that when we have the Holy Spirit who witnesses to our spirit and empowers us to communicate with God. God is Spirit. These two perceptions make up the cross. **"Then said Jesus unto his disciples, If any man will come after me, let him deny himself, and take up his cross, and follow me. For whosoever will save his life shall lose it: and whosoever will lose his life for my sake shall find it."** - (Matthew 16:24-25 KJV)

14

Taming The Lion

The direct spiritual growth came by continuously contending for the faith no matter what was happening. The discoveries that the Bible is true come by comparing the circumstances with the Bible. The realization that the encounters are natural was a byproduct. The goal was to be obedient but ignorance spawned continuous obstacles. The writer really had no plans of her own other than just getting through on God's terms. She knew God and trusted Him every step of the way. **"Or what man is there of you, whom if his son ask bread, will he give him a stone?"**(Matthew 7:9 KJV)

Since we are vessels on a potter's wheel, the process does not feel very comfortable. Life often does not make sense, because we do not know God's goal for us. If God were to tell us what He is going to do with us, we would probably resign on the spot. Like physical marriage, spiritual marriage is much the same. God keeps us from the truth so nature can take its course. Then one day the truth becomes a reality in Christ Jesus when He reveals Himself. Our worship of Him then becomes sharing the good news that He is forever faithful. **"Jesus saith unto him, I am the way, the truth, and the life: no man cometh unto the Father, but by me."** (John 14:6 KJV)

A hymn from John Newton that was given to John by a Jewish friend in London in 1946, sums up what this story is about. The old hymns characterize not only profound theology, but also a logical progression from the first verse through the end.

"I ask the Lord that I might grow
in wisdom, love and every grace,
 might of His salvation know,
seek more earnestly His face.

T'was He who taught me thus to pray
and He I trust has answered prayer,
but it has been in such a way
it almost drove me to despair.

Taming The Lion

I thought that in some favorite hour
at once he'd answer my request,
and by his love's sustaining power
subdue my sins, and give me rest.

Instead of this He made me feel
the hidden evils of my heart
and let the angry powers of hell
assault my soul in every part.

Nay more with His own hand he seemed
intent to aggravate my vow
broke all the fair designs I schemed
blasted my gourds and laid me low,

Lord why is this I trembling cried
wilt thou pursue thy worm to death?
T'is in this way the Lord replied
I answer prayer for grace and faith.

These inward struggles I employ
from self in pride to set thee free
and break thy schemes of earthly joy
that thou mayest find thy all in me."

Taming The Lion

CHAPTER 1

GOD IS DEPENDABLE

Understanding the reality of the biblical teachings comes by implementing Bible principles. "Pick up your cross and follow me," means just that. Faith in God develops from trust in God. Trust in God comes from confirmation that the Bible is true. Truthfulness of the scriptures comes from putting it through the test. The test is: does the application of principles preserve the Christian's life and bring the blessings God promises?

Many Christians believe this is just about prayer. Too often there is no fulfillment without the Life of Christ. Unfulfilled prayer makes many disbelievers. God only responds to prayers that correspond with His will and our prayers may not be what He deems good for us. His love does not mean fulfilling our whims. He is what they call today 'tough love'. His love is what He believes makes us grow into Him so we can become what He wants us to be not what we want to be. And what would that be about? A life that runs smoothly with a fun job, a good husband, lovely kids and enough money to take care of vacations? If all were taken care of we would not need God.

Many evangelists teach the prosperity Gospel, if you just give to us, all blessings will flow to you. That is not God's message. God is raising sons and daughters in the likeness of Jesus Christ, able to do God's will in the face of the devil.

Transplanted as an American citizen to Germany in 1933 to live through the Nazi regime it describes it from a German's perspective that is rare and often misunderstood. I contend that Hitler was the devil's instrument perpetrating his agenda to overthrow Bible prophecy.

In some respects the devil made huge inroads on God's plans for a family for Himself. Not only did millions lose access to their bodies but also spiritual effects after it was over were devastating. The depth of human depravity revealed publicly caused many people to give up on God since He was the creator of human beings and people like to believe that people are basically good because God is a good God. How could He create such monsters and how could He allow the killing of millions of not only Jews but all other nationalities. The casualties of that particular war, WWII, including the camps, approached a hundred million. Stalin, a Jew, drug millions of Germans to slave camps in Siberia and many died on route. They walked on dirt roads in freezing temperatures not meant for human existent. Cities in Germany and Britain were under constant attacks by air for years.

Had people read the Bible, they would have understood that the events related to the Old Testament and prophecies of the future in the New Testament. God makes his thoughts very clear through His prophets. On the other hand many came and are still coming to Christ because WWII revealed that the Bible is a prophecy that will be completely fulfilled soon. On the other hand people like myself had to go on living when there seemed to be no reason to if that was what life was all about. The fear of a rerun of that disaster seemed eminent. People like myself had to be motivated some other way to continue living. Houses and material things had lost their meaning since they could so easily be ripped out from under a person. There had to be more to life than that. I took to reading and listening to people to see how they coped and that eventually led to God. To tell you the truth, I was nine years old when my life began to experience the effects of war and I'm still putting the puzzle together of what it is all about and it is close to seventy years later today. The struggle for the truth is like mining for gold. You find a nugget here and a nugget there. The rest of the information is lie upon lie upon lie.

Even though there are documentaries about Hitler's demise from people who were there supposedly, somehow people have come up with a number of stories that cannot be verified. Stalin insisted that he had examined Hitler's skull since the death occurred in the Russian occupied Berlin. Some believe that the man in the bunker in Berlin found dead with Eva Brown supposedly, was an impostor, that Hitler used underground tunnels to get away and died in Spain in 1950. Others swear that he was brought to South America and died there. Others believe that he is still alive there. So one can take their pick basically. Like Elvis, who pops up here and there supposedly alive. They simply can't give him up.

To answer the question why Jews were singled out of all the nations on earth to be pursued to their death can only be found in the Bible. Sometimes it occurs to me that Jesus, a Jew, represented TRUTH that couldn't be tolerated because He represented the fact that God exists. **"Jesus saith unto him, I am the way, the TRUTH, and the life: no man cometh unto the Father, but by me."** (John 14:6) To get rid of Jesus it would get rid of Romans 1:18 **"For the wrath of God is revealed from heaven against all ungodliness and unrighteousness of men, who hold the truth in unrighteousness;"** They nailed Jesus to the cross.

As long as there are Jews, there are reminders of the truth of the Bible, which simply cannot be tolerated. It seems that they must be eradicated. In other words truth cannot be tolerated. **"And this is the condemnation, that light is come into the world, and men loved darkness rather than light, because their deeds were evil."** (John 3:19)

There is no excuse. Many believers believe that they have been especially selected which is heresy considering the facts in 1 Timothy 2:4 **"Who will have all men to be saved, and to come unto the knowledge of the truth."** God is not a respecter of persons. He gave all human beings the option by giving them the Light to begin with. See John 1

What we need is the love of truth. **"And with all deceivableness of unrighteousness in them that perish; because they received not the love of the truth, that they might be saved. That they all might be damned who believed not the truth, but had pleasure in unrighteousness But we are bound to give thanks alway to God for you, brethren beloved of the Lord, because God hath**

from the beginning chosen you to salvation through sanctification of the Spirit and belief of the truth: " *(2* Thessalonians 2:10,12,13)

Speaking of the Spirit, the Holy Spirit, Whose dispensation this is. Jesus sent Him after He returned to His Father, to represent Jesus Christ and gather His Church to Himself: **"Howbeit when he, the Spirit of truth, is come, he will guide you into all truth: for he shall not speak of himself; but whatsoever he shall hear, that shall he speak: and he will shew you things to come."** (John 16:13)

Again to those who prefer darkness realize your lot before it is too late. **"For the wrath of God is revealed from heaven against all ungodliness and unrighteousness of men, who hold the truth in unrighteousness;"** (Romans 1:18)

The underlying secret about Jews is just now coming to light as well and reveals what really happened. The Bible relates to our character often as metals or clay. Metal is tempered with heat and tools that shape it and clay is a mixture of water and clay placed on a potter's wheel to shape containers that hold something in them. In even other Scriptures we are likened to wine bottles that hold old or new wine. God has to relate to us in words that we understand and we have to realize that they symbolize what God is doing with us. It is not to be interpreted literally. For me to understand what God is talking about I went through many books over my lifetime before I got to the Bible. To find truth we have to have patience and endurance that turn out to be qualities that the Holy Spirit seeks to develop in us.

To understand how Satan operates I passed through his ranks and saw the reality of it. This book is an actual account and witness of mechanisms in place to lead Christians to loose their souls. What I discovered was that Christianity is not an automatic, natural occurrence. Adam and Eve gave dominion to the father of lies at the beginning and still do today. It is not safe to assume that all is well.

Taming The Lion

The apostle Paul wrote this about himself: **"But what things were gain to me, those I counted loss for Christ. Yea doubtless, and I count all things but loss for the excellency of the knowledge of Christ Jesus my Lord: for whom I have suffered the loss of all things, and do count them but dung, that I may win Christ, And be found in him, not having mine own righteousness, which is of the law, but that which is through the faith of Christ, the righteousness which is of God by faith: That I may know him, and the power of his resurrection, and the fellowship of his sufferings, being made conformable unto his death; If by any means I might attain unto the resurrection of the dead. Not as though I had already attained, either were already perfect: but I follow after, if that I may apprehend that for which also I am apprehended of Christ Jesus. Brethren, I count not myself to have apprehended: but this one thing I do, forgetting those things which are behind, and reaching forth unto those things which are before, I press toward the mark for the prize of the high calling of God in Christ Jesus."** *(*Philippians 3:7-14)

Paul asked for His Scriptures during His final days to insure His communication line with God was in tact.

If the Bible is true, everything in it is true. The reason many are going to perish is the fact that laborers are few. **"Then saith He unto His disciples, The harvest truly is plenteous, but the labourers are few;"** (Matthew 9:37). Two faithful believers send their monthly love gift are a powerful testimony to me that there are others who feel like I do about the Gospel. That is what it is about. We can only be a light if we participate doing the Gospel in the name of Jesus Christ.

There is no desire to frighten Christians but to bring the good news that God is dependable and the final result will be the fulfillment of the following scripture: **"Now the God of hope fill you with all joy and peace in believing, that ye may abound in hope, through the power of the Holy Ghost."** (Romans 15:13)

Taming The Lion

Since a great deal of this book deals with cults, even Hitler was a cult leader; Christians need to understand what cults are willing to do to get new members. Their expertise knows no restraint. Financially, they have access to most sophisticated sales techniques through the media and missionaries. They are applied without shame. The Bible Answer Man said "If Christians would do what cult members do for their cults, we would all be converted to Christianity. "

The first question from people's lips was always, "how did you get into this situation?" There was no simple answer. If you read the book it will answer that question clearly.

In making the Bible one's focal point, it becomes obvious that God is not a formula. He is drawing us in the way He sees fit. Every life has a different calling and experience. It is meant to fit a certain need in the Body of Christ. God expects to exert control over our natural sin nature by the Holy Spirit. The life of Christ is lived in the spiritual realm and not accessible by physical means. That is why it is indestructible. It can only be received from the realm either from God or the devil. Satan is a spirit being and has that kind of influence as well and many are open to Satan and don't realize that Satan is out to destroy their souls. Most hard rock concerts portray the evilness of hell.

The gospel is simple. Our answer has to be: yes or no. There is no gray area. Being undecided is to leave the door open to the devil. God tells us to contend for the faith. It means struggle for the faith. He has the right to expect us to love Him above all and back it up with our tangible witness. It is futile for men or women to think that we can compare ourselves to the Glory of God although at some point in our existence we will receive a glorified body that is incorruptible and eternal just as Jesus did.

The more forgiveness we need, the greater our appreciation for God. To think God gave His human body's life for our sins is simply awesome. He set us free from our sinful nature and opted not to remember our past. If He had created robots, He would not have come to earth in person and put Himself on the cross. We would have been his perfect little children. Satan creates robots to use for his own purposes. He throws them away when the youth and vigor departs. There is no advantage to serving him, outside of worldly substance. What happens when death knocks on the door? It is over and too late to start thinking about eternity.

Looking at the decline of the world, it becomes obvious with all the knowledge available to man in many forms, such as sciences, religions and philosophies; solutions to man's condition are not forthcoming. To get rid of the problem, man again has decided that there are too many people on this planet and too much diversity. The motto over the past fifty years, 'Let us come together' as one body and by depopulation show progress as an alternative to self-destruction.

"But as many as received him [Jesus Christ], to them gave he power to become the sons of God, even to them that believe on his name: Which were born, not of blood, nor of the will of the flesh, nor of the will of man, but of God. And the Word was made flesh, and dwelt among us, (and we beheld his glory, the glory as of the only begotten of the Father), full of grace and truth." (John 1:12-14)

It is most difficult for adults to hear Jesus when He said the following: **"And said, Verily I say unto you, Except ye be converted, and become as little children, ye shall not enter into the kingdom of heaven ."** (Matthew 18:3) Why is that? You might ask.

God expects us to lay down the very accomplishments we have worked so hard to achieve and start over. God uses a child's attitude. To come to the truth one has to keep digging. There is a tendency to come to a plateau and stop. We think all is well, when we may be far from it.

A child keeps exploring, learning, growing and loving all that it meets. It loves intensely without restraint, but also hurts intensely when it fails to achieve its goal. Father or mother is close to sooth the pain. This is where God wants us to be in our lives. He wishes to be the caring Father. God revealed Himself in the most unexpected form of experiences most of the time by using believers. It is much easier to allow Him to solve our problems. We as human beings can't compete with God because of His all-knowingness, His access to people and His unconditional love.

The timing of events, the uniqueness of the experience, not written anywhere nor channeled, nor suggested and the end product confirms His Word, **"And we know that all things work together for good to them that love God, to them who are the called according to his purpose."** (Romans 8:28). Even when Satan thought he had the upper hand, he found himself defeated.

"He that covereth his sins shall not prosper: but whoso confesseth and forsaketh them shall have mercy. (Proverbs 28:13) - If we claim to be without sin, we deceive ourselves and the truth is not in us. See 1 John 1:8-9. **"Confess your faults one to another, and pray one for another, that ye may be healed. The effectual fervent prayer of a righteous man availeth much."** (James 5:16) **"Casting all your care upon him; for he careth for you."** (1 Peter 5:7)

"That the trial of your faith, being much more precious than of gold that perisheth, though it be tried with fire, might be found unto praise and honour and glory at the appearing of Jesus Christ:" (1 Peter 1:7)

The book proves that we cannot overcome Satan without God and that is the essence of our walk here. People who opt to live life on their own terms find themselves defeated sooner or later.

"Psalms 119:91-96: **"They continue this day according to thine ordinances: for all are thy servants. Unless thy law had been my delights, I should then have perished in mine affliction. I will never forget thy precepts: for with them thou hast quickened me. I am thine, save me; for I have sought thy precepts. The wicked have waited for me to destroy me: but I will consider thy** testimonies. I have seen an end of all perfection: but thy commandment is exceeding broad."

"Your word, O LORD, is eternal; it stands firm in the heavens. Your faithfulness continues through all generations; you established the earth, and it endures. Your laws endure to this day, for all things serve you. If your law had not been my delight, I would have perished in my affliction. I will never forget your precepts, for by them you have preserved my life. Save me, for I am yours; I have sought out your precepts. The wicked are waiting to destroy me, but I will ponder your statutes. To all perfection I see a limit; but your commands are boundless." Psalms 119:89-96. "One generation shall praise thy works to another, and shall declare thy mighty acts." (Psalms 145:4).

Who is our teacher, but the Holy Spirit. "But the anointing which ye have received of Him abideth in you, and ye need not that any man teach you: but as the same anointing teacheth you of all things, and is truth, and is no lie, and even as it hath taught you, ye shall abide in him." (1 John 2:27)

A Psalm of David: "...Hear me when I call, O God of my righteousness: thou hast enlarged me when I was in distress; have mercy upon me, and hear my prayer." (Psalms 4:1).

"It is sown in dishonour; it is raised in glory: it is sown in weakness; it is raised in power: It is sown a natural body; it is raised a spiritual body. There is a natural body, and there is a spiritual body. And so it is written, The first man Adam was made a living soul; the last Adam was made a quickening spirit. Howbeit that was not first which is spiritual, but that which is natural; and afterward that which is spiritual. The first man is of the earth, earthy: the second man is the Lord from heaven. As is the earthy, such are they also that are earthy: and as is the heavenly, such are they also that are heavenly." (1 Corinthians 15:43-48).

Taming The Lion

"Grace be to you and peace from God the Father, and from our Lord Jesus Christ, Who gave himself for our sins, that he might deliver us from this present evil world, according to the will of God and our Father: To whom be glory for ever and ever. Amen." (Galatians 1:3-5)

Taming The Lion

CHAPTER 2

THE RISE OF AN ADAM GOD

Seasick on a bunk in a room with thirty-four other women, I was trying to talk myself into calming down. "Biting off more than I could chew" was my middle name already then. The large troopship I had boarded in Bremerhaven, Germany was climbing twenty foot waves maneuvering through the foamy saltwater. It was January of 1947 and freezing cold in the middle of the Atlantic. Two weeks it was going to last, before we would anchor in New York. The oily odor mixed with the smell of fish and cigarette smoke was causing my stomach to rise every time I attempted to get on deck to satisfy my curiosity. Incapacitated from experiencing the joy of adventure, I laid there wondering what to do about my condition. No one was chaperoning me. Help did not seem within reach, because I was shy and just sixteen. The ship was pointing west cutting through the ocean.

A whole new life was about to begin for me. My family had lived in Niagara Falls by Buffalo, New York for seven years and returned to Germany in 1933, a year well remembered by millions. Adolf Hitler came into power 1933 and we as a family were about to experience Nazism then quite different from the American life style.

There were three little girls. One of the sisters had to stay behind in New York. She was an invalid. As it turned out in Germany it was an intuitive decision, which saved my sister's life. Invalids had no place in Hitler's society. Remaining in the U.S. allowed her to live to the age of 15.

My family planned to come back to New York but life has a way of taking controls out of our hands and going off in other directions.

My dad began building his own business and became quite successful under the Hitler Regime without having to join the party and that wasn't so easy. To get privileges one would usually have to

Taming The Lion

join. In my mother and dad's case good family names gained them many privileges that were not available in the U.S.

Adolf Hitler was an occultist, which had effects on many years of my life. Martin Luther the reformer was the only theologian I grew up with. I was always an activist and my curiosity knows no limits. It is extraordinary where it led me over time.

The first thing the family, grandparents, insisted on when my family arrived back in Germany was baptism. I was three and needed to get baptized according to the Lutheran belief. At fourteen in the Lutheran teachings is confirmation. At the parish we attended two years of classes to make us eligible for confirmation. Religion was part of the public school curriculum. Hitler was supposedly a Christian like many politicians to get elected.

There were no child labor laws in Germany. In fact Hitler encouraged the Hitler Youth to work to help farmers since the men were all drafted in 1939 to go to war. The women had to take the place of their men at home. Our business had to continue without my father.

Just remember now when I share this that I was an innocent child at six when two major events happened. They were first grade and the Hitler Youth. I still remember how I was looking forward to wearing a sport shirt with the swastika on the breast area It is amazing that Hitler could not wait to hang his evil symbols on all his German folk including the children. Does it remind you of the Mark of the Beast? The fact that I was looking forward to it shows indoctrination had taken place. In the U.S. we call it fads. In raising kids you get it when they get into school. They won't wear clothing that is out of style. It has a tendency to unify people. Hitler's focus was on unity of the Fatherland and they were all to be purebred Germans.

I later traced my roots in Germany and found it still had a caste system, which I traced back to the twelve hundreds when Freemasonry became a means of segregating people into groups of similar professions, interests, political persuasions and wealth.

28

Taming The Lion

One's future depended on the segment of society one was born into. In one sense it was protective but in another restricting. People had to stay in their own levels. In our case we were independent business people in the hotel business.

My parents were not only perfectly suited to each other, but also very much in love. My mother insisted my father was her one and only. Families in Europe families stay in the same locations for hundreds of years. Family names are just about the most important possession a male can have. Females marry, but men have to watch over their surname carefully. Honoring one's name was a high priority. The whole family depended on it. A worthy name meant a good credit rating automatically. Fortunately, my family line was such. My mother and father's families had lived in the same location for hundreds of years.

In Europe, young people began thinking about marriage at fourteen. Matchmaking often came through parents especially when there were businesses involved. Having them and grandparents near, secured plenty of coaching. Love was a hope but not considered essential. A strong economic existence was the basis for a good life. It meant having afternoon coffee and pastry breaks; playing cards till two o clock in the morning, smoking cigars, and having a good, clear, foamy glass of beer with a ham sandwich. Walking through the woods for an hour was also a treasured activity. Emphasis was on the simple life. They worked hard, but also cultivated special moments. My state of mind at sixteen was marriage and motherhood. I was dreaming about having a large family.

By the time the war broke out in 1939, my dad had three major businesses going. In the city he was running a nightclub and bowling alley and in the country a hotel. Everyone in the family had to do their part with assigned tasks. Children were told they were to inherit everything, which motivated them to work hard. There was no depression, boredom, nor lack of friends. People had known each other for generations. Life was wholesome.

Taming The Lion

The nightclub in the city was open till four in the morning seven days a week. Every month my father hired a new band and entertainers and my mother stood behind the bar to fill orders for the waitresses and customers. Keeping track of us little girls was not too easy for them. When a car hit my sister we moved to the hotel in the country. My father found a buyer for the city businesses.

The country was ideal for children. The little town of two thousand inhabitants was a resort on a beautiful lake. A boat dock kept five rowboats from drifting off and sprawled onto the lake. Paddle boats and seaweeds were high enough to hide in. Ice-skating in the winter and swimming in the summer kept us happy between chores. The lake framed by a lushly cultivated forest of a variety of trees and the lake had a mysterious island in the middle of it. On Saturdays people swept the sidewalks. Life simply revolved around little gardens, raising a pig or two, geese, ducks, chickens and dogs and cats, very uncomplicated and cherished.

If a child takes life serious that would be a time for decisions how to live life. Mine was to have lots of kids with a good husband for life and living life according to God's teaching. I was attracted to church. I hung around the big organ to help keep it going. Air had to be pumped by standing on boards that went up and down. If I wasn't there, I was watching over the family grave site planting and weeding keeping it looking good. Another favorite place was my old grandpa's garden with strawberries, cherries and everything imaginable to harvest. He had arthritis, lived alone and needed help. Every so often I had to get coal for his stove in a wagon from a distributor at least an hour walk away. The family across from our place had a grocery store run by a mother of two kids. She had an open leg that would not heal. I spent time there to help in the grocery store and with her kids. I still hear my mother calling me across the parking lot to tend to the garden, animals or clean the house.

Gardening and growing a whole variety of fruits and vegetables, I adored. My mother hummed a tune under her breath and I sang along. There were never ending chores with the three-day laundries

Taming The Lion

on scrub boards and big pots for boiling of clothes. Although frozen water pumps defrosted with heated water, table cloths had to be part of the setting for customers. Sundays revolved around handmade ice-cream and dishes up to the ceiling. My father was strict and demanded perfection. Obedience was easy for me. When his or her voice called, there was no hesitation. Teachers and parents were familiar with the rod to maintain order.

On the shores of the forest was a red brick, old Lutheran Church with a high steeple reaching up into the sky. It had large clanging bells that rang through the village on Sundays. At weddings and funerals they reminded people to come together to celebrate or mourn. The church and the 700-year-old tree in town were the big tourist attractions. The church held a carved altar that was famous for it's artist. A jealous man had thrown acid on the artist's eyes and blinded him.

My father had just completed reconstructing the restaurant. He had built a dance floor in the garden and terraces surrounded with glass walls to shelter guests from breezes across the lake. Pansies were lining brick flower boxes. Flagstones framed the large well-kept lawns. Sometimes we had coffee and pastry there ourselves and marveled at father's ingenuity.

World War II had been going on for six months when we received the letter stating: "report for duty in the German Infantry, immediately!" My mother found herself suddenly in charge of the business and her three children. The draft notice reached my dad at age thirty-six. He had not joined any party and had suffered discrimination that continued during the war. He spent five years in the trenches in the infantry and on all fronts. That became a nightmare for my mother. His profession proved to be a God sent. It kept him cooking for soldiers slightly behind the front lines. Separation from his family lasted six years.

The Hitler regime had been in total control for seven years and was very visible and audible. Young children had to hail every schoolteacher and people in authority by throwing their hand in the air at an angle with palm down. Hitler decreed that each child at age six enter the Hitler youth. It was mandatory to come to meetings on Saturdays to sing and march through the streets in uniform. My mother was constantly in trouble with the leaders because she needed us for chores and tried to keep us home. Hitler kept youth separate by gender. The activities revolved around discipline, music and sports.

The hard part was singing patriotic songs for hours holding one's arm up in the air saluting flags. There was much talk in school about the fatherland, patriotism and loyalty. I played the accordion and patriotic marches were the theme of those days, many of them. When the war broke out, all the songs related to the soldiers fighting for the fatherland. People's attitudes were full of enthusiasm and high expectation for the future in spite of everything. Life was not what one would expect in a war because of music. Life went on as usual. My mother's motto was that man gets used to anything.

Hitler had won the people over by giving them what they wanted most. His regime geared into mass-producing housing projects and cars. He made cheap cruises available to the working class. The economy was overflowing with jobs because Hitler's focus was on the working class. He was on speaking tours constantly. His excitement saturated all of Germany. His powerful demeanor demanded respect for authority. People were in fear of him. On the other hand he promised people a secure future.

As the Nazi party developed, they began monitoring people. The German `Partei' had enlisted civilians who were endorsing the organization, placed them in uniforms like the Hitler youth for meetings and identification with the leadership. Otherwise they were in civilian clothes. Neighbors were spying on neighbors. The people, who did not agree and voiced it, disappeared without notice to family members. Not everyone joined the Nazi party, which was to their disadvantage economically and physically. Historical writings state that only five percent of the population was active in Nazi party of the adult population. My mother taught us early not to run in groups and to remain silent if possible. My girlfriend's

Taming The Lion

father found himself in a camp one day. Until his release nobody knew what happened to him. He had a reputation of a self-made, freethinking merchandiser. Nazi's had taken him to a small detention center for molestation purposes. Someone reported his anti Hitler comments. He said they tried to break him down by making him submit to demoralizing acts, including crawling through sewers. He said, he got through by determining not to falter. They finally released him. This incident taught me that the environment could be controlled by self-restraint and was my first contact with willpower.

The regime forbade listening to shortwave radios. Censoring of the media was no secret. Cinema houses presented documentaries of the war. There was not a sign of what was going on behind closed doors. Living in little sleepy villages in northern Germany, it never occurred to people what was going to happen next. People say that Germany is the size of Texas, 267,000 square miles. It is smaller, 181,000 square miles in size. The population is the opposite. In mid nineteen hundreds, Texas had a population of 6,400,000 and Germany has ten times that,. 66,000,000 people live in it. The density caused large losses of human lives during the war. It has many little farm villages and big cities. The cities are mutually exclusive specializing in factories, shipyards, tourist attractions and such.

Adolf Hitler was not originally a German citizen. Christened in the little Roman Catholic parish church in Braunau, Austria, confirmed his name to be Adolf Hitler, born on April 20, 1889. Ironically Buddha's birthday is April 20, and he displays a swastika on his chest in Hong Kong. Biographers wrote that Hitler had an exceedingly happy childhood. As a choirboy and server in the chancel of the Lambach Church, he saw a carving of a swastika for the first time. He was fond of pointing out later that he had serious plans of becoming a priest, and take Holy Orders. His upbringing was at the Benedictine Monastery deeply involved with occult teachings. This came to the surface later in life. He did not smoke and avoided alcoholic drinks and was reportedly a Vegetarian for many years. There is a strong chance that he was a virgin, although the Mormons claim that he had a wife in his early years. I have never heard that anywhere else.

Going back in Hitler's life a bit, Hitler enlisted in World War I. Both sides used gas. On the 13th of October 1918 Hitler found himself gassed and blinded. Pasewalk is a small garrison town 140 miles northeast of Berlin. His blindness was temporary, and his doctors diagnosed the problem as `hysteria'. During his stay at the hospital Hitler claimed to have heard `voices', which he likened to those, heard by Joan of Arc. Those voices told him that he was selected by God to be Germany's messiah. He would save Germany from the claws of international Jewry.

Conditions in Germany had grown progressively worse after the First World War. In later 1918 the German mark was worth nearly 24 cents, but before the end of 1921 it had dropped to 1 1/2 cents. In 1922 the value went to 1/4 cent, and by early 1923, 7,000 marks purchased one U.S. dollar. By midyear a dollar could buy about 150,000 marks, and before the summer was over, one million. It was a dark period of chaos, desperation and for many, actual starvation. In 1920 hunger was widespread.

Hitler's faith in his future was `unshakable'. As an eighteen year old he did not doubt that he would some day possess the money and power necessary to carry out even the most grand of his projects. He was a fervent and incessant reader of both popular and technical books on architecture and art. Hitler's private books were many volumes on nutrition, health and health food, folk medicine, homeopathy, miracle healing, the occult and magic symbols. In 1932 Adolf Hitler became a German citizen. Eva Braun became his mistress after three years of acquaintance. On January 30th, 1933 Reichs Chancellor Paul von Hindenburg appointed Hitler. "If these elections help us to place 60 to 70 of our agitators into the various parliaments, then the state itself will help to equip our fighting machinery and pay for its upkeep. Let no one think that parliamentarianism is our Damascus we come as enemies! We come

Taming The Lion

amongst you as the wolf comes amongst the sheep," Hitler remarked.

Though he had never left the Catholic Church, Hitler discontinued paying church taxes after 1933. After 1933 Goebbels became Hitler's Minister of Propaganda and Enlightenment, perfecting his policy of `the big lie.' He was dynamic and unscrupulous derived from agony of a clubfoot. All civil rights and protections were cast aside. Many of the prisoners were beaten, tortured, or even murdered. He increased from 100,000 to 300,000 the membership of the swaggering, radical and severe storm troopers. The Nazi Party, which had swelled to nearly 3,000,000 (5%) out of 60,000,000 populations soon after Hitler became Chancellor. Hitler used the SS as his private executioners. He descended in person on his old friend Rohm at a Bavarian resort for a SA conference. A sudden and savage bloodbath followed. Rohm had helped put Hitler in power, and murdered other SA leaders and aides. Hitler had taken the law wholly into his own hands. Germany permitted only parties or organizations within the Nazi structure.

Economic crisis of the postwar years marked by mass unemployment. currency inflation strengthened extremist parties and wiped out a large fraction of the middle class. Extreme nationalists adopted terrorist tactics and merged with the National Socialist party. In 1929 another mass unemployment and virtual bankruptcy of Germany brought major gains to communists. The dictator abolished powers of state government and became the focal point of every aspect of German life.

A state of hypnotic communion developed between this leader and his faithful followers. Germany awake! Using magical power and simple imagery, Hitler taught people to believe in themselves. He won the hearts of the German people as the savior of the world on the brink of disaster. He was the embodiment of an Adam-god that spawned the most monstrous careers in history.

Hitler and his inner circle spread fear, but millions flocked to his banners and people's lives meant nothing to them. Adolf was a loud mouth activist, passionate and angry, studying the audience with a manic intensity, speech after speech. He kept changing with the mood of the people. He saw their reactions and adjusted to the public's needs. He gave them what they needed to get their attention: jobs, fun, a reason for existence and social programs.

Keeping the crowd waiting raised the tension and masses switched off thinking processes. In awe they listened to descriptions of goals he set for them as a mighty folk. He formed many personal relationships with people in the crowds. People did not realize this leader's motivation. It was vengeance. His goal was to transfer the vengeance to his audience. It took three years to organize into a tight party that stopped at nothing and attracted thousands. Hitler took full advantage of conditions and they flocked to him. The middle class pinned their hope on him. He wanted to do it alone. He did not accept bribes. He was as an Omnipresent Messiah, engineered with precision. He was on the road full time speaking about the future, tearing down social barriers, arising into a new community of the people. People convinced they could count on him were hundreds and thousands of the middle class and the poor. By 1935 he was promoting family fun and folklore. Souvenirs of Hitler became big business. He promoted eager participation in work and developing ability Work began on the Autobahn. He had posters throughout Germany of young healthy men and women expressing energy dynamics that served to restore national pride quickly..

During rallies display of thousands of flags flaunted a new order. On top of flagpoles was an eagle on a wreath with a swastika in the middle. Hitler had a fascination for Geometry. He celebrated many memorials with a spectacular display of large blocks of people marching honoring death rather than life. He had passion for night ceremonies with mystical rituals and fires. With upraised arms, hailing Hitler and their new flag, people experienced bliss, excitement and happiness listening to him describing their future. For a little while life became good and employment was plentiful. The regime worked hard on their image and developed many events

Taming The Lion

to raise up Hitler's image. They advertised strength through joy, the good life and large families. Community is everything, the individual nothing. The world was under the impression of peace with a modern industrial state leading the world.

Magical, sinister blood banners, hundreds of them, garnered with a large Sun burst topped by swastikas embracing Adolf's thundering voice echoing: "Germany in front of us and Germany behind us and Germany in us!" These blood banners received special treatment from the Fuehrer (Adolf Hitler). He touched every flag physically and performed a ritual to instill the importance of ceremony and idolatry. A passion for architecture, Adolf stood like a god, fulfilling his wildest dreams in constructing monuments to his taste. On his fiftieth birthday, there was a massive military parade. Hitler was a master in the art of deception. He thought of war only and became commander in chief as savior of the world.

Authority based on terror in `The Third Reich' enforced free speech and freedom of assembly. Later authorized house searches without warrant and seizure of property without due process became prevalent. A show of force eliminated opposition. Many former doubters got the point quickly and conformed to Hitler's bold decisions. His only opponents were the Catholic and Lutheran Churches and they were tax-supported institutions. Hitler crushed all opposition in the `Blood Purge' of 1934.

European leaders flocked to him to hear his `will'. Herman Wilhelm Goehring found himself in charge of the air force, the Gestapo (secret police) and the German economy in 1937. Hitler's inner circle had other mystics with their own agenda. The practice of astrology by this group was public knowledge. Kubizek, who observed personal situations told of Adolf's anger: "...The eyes glittered. There was something sinister about them. He stood for hours in front of a mirror practicing his stare. The goal was to melt an opponent with a glare that was straight from the pit. Few opponents left meetings with Hitler unaffected."

Taming The Lion

Adolf Hitler not only told 66 million people he would meet their physical needs but preyed on their biblical illiteracy. His favorite subject was the oppression of Germans by the Jewish bankers. Hitler often compared himself favorably with Jesus and thought himself to be on a `great mission' of freeing Germany from the Jews.

`Wolf' was Hitler's personal namesake and a fascination for him. The name `Adolf' is a modern derivative of the older Germanic name `Athalwolf' correlating to `noble wolf'. The SS, Hitler's private army, called by him affectionately: `My pack of wolves', who would `soon be covered with blood'. In the Scriptures Satan and his cohorts are sometimes defined as wolves.

The police kept a registry of all residents and transients. All people in Germany had to report change of addresses within two weeks. On Nov. 14, 1935, the Nazis issued a definition of how to differentiate a Jew. A mandate went out for all families to trace their genealogy four generations to target Jewish ancestors and report their findings for a detection of tainted blood.

It was Himmler who ordered the famous Hitler horoscope of January 30, 1933, the day on which Hitler came to power. That horoscope made Josef Goebbels resort to astrology during the last two weeks of their lives. In charge of propaganda astrological information suited his purposes to proclaim a positive agenda for Hitler. His office released alleged astrological predictions of German victory. The horoscopes predicted the outbreak of war in 1939 and three years of extreme hardship and privation, culminating in 1948 with the emergence of a Greater German Reich. These predictions were tools to keep people from getting nervous about their future. Occultists know that astrology is a farce.

If Adolf Hitler and his disciples were Christians, as some people think they helped God, Colossians 2:20 could be applied to settle that question once and for all: **"Wherefore if ye be dead with Christ from the rudiments of the world, why, as though living in the world, are ye subject to ordinances,"** Its obvious God did not

Taming The Lion

employ them. The Scriptures Hitler was addressing were Deuteronomy 18:14, where God addresses the Jews: **"For these nations, which thou shalt possess, hearkened unto observers of times, and unto diviners: but as for thee, the LORD thy God hath not suffered thee so to do." "Their sorrows shall be multiplied that hasten after another god: their drink offerings of blood will I not offer, nor take up their names into my lips."** (Psalms 16:4)

Speaking of drink offerings of blood, German's had several dishes that involved pig's blood. One was made of vinegar and blood with large wheat balls, the other was bloodwurst for sandwiches. Had they known Psalms 16:4, they would have refrained from eating blood.

"If thou wilt not observe to do all the words of this law that are written in this book, that thou mayest fear this glorious and fearful name, THE LORD THY GOD;" (Deuteronomy 28:58)

This prophecy applied to Adolf Hitler and his folk who had their own god to worship. "**Moreover all these curses shall come upon thee, and shall pursue thee, and overtake thee, till thou be destroyed; because thou hearkenedst not unto the voice of the LORD thy God, to keep his commandments and his statutes which he commanded thee: And they shall be upon thee for a sign and for a wonder, and upon thy seed for ever. Because thou servedst not the LORD thy God with joyfulness, and with gladness of heart, for the abundance of all things; Therefore shalt thou serve thine enemies which the LORD shall send against thee, in hunger, and in thirst, and in nakedness, and in want of all things: and he shall put a yoke of iron upon thy neck, until he have destroyed thee.**

"The LORD shall bring a nation against thee from far, from the end of the earth, as swift as the eagle flieth; a nation whose tongue thou shalt not understand; A nation of fierce countenance, which shall not regard the person of the old, nor shew favour to the young: And he shall eat the fruit of thy

cattle, and the fruit of thy land, until thou be destroyed: which also shall not leave thee either corn, wine, or oil, or the increase of thy kine, or flocks of thy sheep, until he have destroyed thee. And he shall besiege thee in all thy gates, until thy high and fenced walls come down, wherein thou trustedst, throughout all thy land: and he shall besiege thee in all thy gates throughout all thy land, which the LORD thy God hath given thee." (Deuteronomy 28:45-52)

"Stand now with thine enchantments, and with the multitude of thy sorceries, wherein thou hast laboured from thy youth; if so be thou shalt be able to profit, if so be thou mayest prevail. Thou art wearied in the multitude of thy counsels. Let now the astrologers, the stargazers, the monthly prognosticators, stand up, and save thee from these things that shall come upon thee. Behold, they shall be as stubble; the fire shall burn them; they shall not deliver themselves from the power of the flame: there shall not be a coal to warm at, nor fire to sit before it. Thus shall they be unto thee with whom thou hast laboured, even thy merchants, from thy youth: they shall wander every one to his quarter; none shall save thee." (Isaiah 47:12-15)

The promise to German believers in the Word of God: "Associate yourselves, O ye people, and ye shall be broken in pieces; and give ear, all ye of far countries: gird yourselves, and ye shall be broken in pieces; gird yourselves, and ye shall be broken in pieces. Take counsel together, and it shall come to nought; speak the word, and it shall not stand: for God is with us. For the LORD spake thus to me with a strong hand, and instructed me that I should not walk in the way of this people, saying, Say ye not, A confederacy, to all them to whom this people shall say, A confederacy; neither fear ye their fear, nor be afraid." (Isaiah 8:9-21)

To the remnant of believers in Germany after all this hardship: "For I am persuaded, that neither death, nor life, nor angels, nor principalities, nor powers, nor things present, nor things to come, Nor height, nor depth, nor any other creature, shall be

able to separate us from the love of God, which is in Christ Jesus our Lord" (Romans 8:38-39)

CHAPTER 3

HOW GLOBALISM IS ACHIEVED

The world is becoming one again, a rerun of what is described in Genesis. In fact the European Union used the Tower of Babel as one of its insignias indicating that the leadership knows what they are doing. God did away with that strategy once before because unity is too powerful. Hitler is an example of the power it produces. In Germany's case the unity consisted of only 80 million Germans. The power of a global unity of six billion people run by a small group of elites would be phenomenal. I read a statement yesterday by one of these men that globalism will produce peace because they will all be one. That statement is mentioned in the Bible as the time for the Tribulation to begin like a trap.

In Genesis 11:1-9 we read: **"And the whole earth was of one language, and of one speech. And it came to pass, as they journeyed from the east, that they found a plain in the land of Shinar; and they dwelt there. And they said one to another, Go to, let us make brick, and burn them throughly. And they had brick for stone, and slime had they for morter. And they said, Go to, let us build us a city and a tower, whose top may reach unto heaven; and let us make us a name, lest we be scattered abroad upon the face of the whole earth.**

"And the LORD came down to see the city and the tower, which the children of men builded. And the LORD said, Behold, the people is one, and they have all one language; and this they begin to do: and now nothing will be restrained from them, which they have imagined to do. Go to, let us go down, and there confound their language, that they may not understand one another's speech.

"So the LORD scattered them abroad from thence upon the face of all the earth: and they left off to build the city. Therefore is the name of it called Babel; because the LORD did there

confound the language of all the earth: and from thence did the LORD scatter them abroad upon the face of all the earth."

The name Babel is the root of Babylon. Iraq is where most of the Biblical stories took place and where astrology and the rest occult 'sciences' were developed that are based on imagination. Astrology is a construct that creates an imaginary existence, which becomes reality for those who practice it. Imagining and visualizing has creative powers. People make it happen because they believe what their horoscopes predict. It is an abomination to God and all who practice it deliberately will end up in the lake of fire because they worship another god.

It is a well-known fact today that most leaders are involved in Skull and Bones or Freemasonry, which are crafts. Skull and Bones came out of the Middle Ages when they found Mary's grave with bones laid over her skull instead of where they should have been below the torso. This legend is related to Jesus Christ's supposed marriage to Mary and their children to prove lineage to Jesus Christ. Those who reject that Jesus returned to God believe that He somehow lived after the crucifixion and had a family, which denies that He is God and provided salvation to mankind.

The root of Freemasonry reaches back to Solomon's Temple where astrology was developed. They worship the Sun, another god. That is the reason for the Tower of Babel. They want to get into heaven through the back door without having to bow their knees to Jesus Christ.

The Book of Daniel describes how the world system came to this point. God teaches with stories that we have to understand with the help of the Holy Spirit.

Daniel had a dream and visions of the future in Daniel 7:1-27 **"In the first year of Belshazzar king of Babylon Daniel had a dream and visions of his head upon his bed: then he wrote the dream, and told the sum of the matters. Daniel spake and said, I saw in my vision by night, and, behold, the four winds of the heaven strove upon the great sea. [sea usually represents nations] And** four great beasts came up from the sea, diverse one from another. The first was like a lion [UK], and had eagle's wings [US]: I beheld till the wings thereof were plucked, and it was lifted up from the earth, and made stand upon the feet as a man, and a man's heart was given to it.

"And behold another beast, a second, like to a bear [Russia], and it raised up itself on one side, and it had three ribs in the mouth of it between the teeth of it: and they said thus unto it, Arise, devour much flesh.

"After this I beheld, and lo another, like a leopard [Germany / EU], which had upon the back of it four wings of a fowl; the beast had also four heads; and dominion was given to it.

"After this I saw in the night visions, and behold a fourth beast, dreadful and terrible, and strong exceedingly; and it had great iron teeth: it devoured and brake in pieces, and stamped the residue with the feet of it: and it was diverse from all the beasts that were before it; and it had ten horns. [U.N. created by the U.S. who does their bidding. The ten horns are the ten regions developed by the Club of Rome that are in process now EU, NAU, etc.]

"I considered the horns, and, behold, there came up among them another little horn [the Antichrist], before whom there were three of the first horns plucked up by the roots: and, behold, in this horn were eyes like the eyes of man, and a mouth speaking great things.

"I beheld till the thrones were cast down [Armageddon], and the Ancient of days [Jesus Christ / God] did sit, whose garment was white as snow, and the hair of his head like the pure wool: his throne was like the fiery flame, and his wheels as burning fire. A fiery stream issued and came forth from before him: thousand thousands ministered unto him, and ten thousand times ten thousand stood before him: the judgment was set, and the books were opened. I beheld then because of the voice of the great words which the horn spake: I beheld even till the beast

[Antichrist] was slain, and his body destroyed, and given to the burning flame. As concerning the rest of the beasts, they had their dominion taken away: yet their lives were prolonged for a season and time. "

"I saw in the night visions, and, behold, one like the Son of man came with the clouds of heaven, and came to the Ancient of days, and they brought him near before him. And there was given him dominion, and glory, and a kingdom, [the thousand year Millennium] that all people, nations, and languages, should serve him: his dominion is an everlasting dominion, which shall not pass away, and his kingdom that which shall not be destroyed. .. "

"So he told me, and made me know the interpretation of the things. These great beasts, which are four are four kings, [Russia / Bear, EU / Leopard, England / Lion, Beast with ten horns / United Nations], which shall arise out of the earth. But the saints of the most High shall take the kingdom, and possess the kingdom for ever, even for ever and ever. Then I would know the truth of the fourth beast, which was diverse from all the others, exceeding dreadful, whose teeth were of iron, and his nails of brass; which devoured, brake in pieces, and stamped the residue with his feet; And of the ten horns that were in his head, and of the other which came up, and before whom three fell; even of that horn that had eyes, and a mouth that spake very great things, whose look was more stout than his fellows. I beheld, and the same horn [Antichrist which is ongoing] made war with the saints, and prevailed *against them;* [NWO is doing away with the Gospel]

"Until the Ancient of days [Jesus Christ / God] came, and judgment was given to the saints of the most High [Saints will be judging those who go to the lake of fire]; and the time came that the saints possessed the kingdom.

"Thus he said, The fourth beast shall be the fourth kingdom upon earth, which shall be diverse from all kingdoms, and shall

devour the whole earth [going on today called Globalism], **and shall tread it down, and break it in pieces.**

"And the ten horns out of this kingdom are ten kings [10 regions worldwide are established] **that shall arise: and another shall rise after them** [the Antichrist]; **and he shall be diverse from the first, and he shall subdue three kings. And he shall speak great words against the most High, and shall wear out the saints of the most High, and think to change times and laws: and they shall be given into his hand** [Apostasy due to heretical teachings is prevalent. The churches are overflowing, but the message they are receiving is heresy.] **until a time and times and the dividing of time** [Tribulation] . **But the judgment shall sit, and they** [the saints] **shall take away his dominion, to consume and to destroy it unto the end. And the kingdom and dominion, and the greatness of the kingdom under the whole heaven, shall be given to the people of the saints of the most High, whose kingdom is an everlasting kingdom, and all dominions shall serve and obey him. Hitherto is the end of the matter."**

"Flee out of the midst of Babylon, and deliver every man his soul: be not cut off in her iniquity; for this is the time of the LORD'S vengeance; he will render unto her a recompence. Babylon hath been a golden cup in the LORD'S hand, that made all the earth drunken: the nations have drunken of her wine; therefore the nations are mad." "Nebuchadrezzar the king of Babylon hath devoured me, he hath crushed me, he hath made me an empty vessel, he hath swallowed me up like a dragon, he hath filled his belly with my delicates, he hath cast me out." (Jeremiah 51: 6, 7, 34)

"And he cried mightily with a strong voice, saying, Babylon the great is fallen, is fallen, and is become the habitation of devils, and the hold of every foul spirit, and a cage of every unclean and hateful bird." "Standing afar off for the fear of her torment, saying, Alas, alas, that great city Babylon, that mighty city! for in one hour is thy judgment come." And a mighty angel took up a stone like a great millstone, and cast it into the sea,

saying, Thus with violence shall that great city Babylon be thrown down, and shall be found no more at all". (Revelation 18: 2, 10, 21)

Most Americans are not aware that the U.S. has been in war since Pearl Harbor and are taking over country after country. John McCain who is a presidential hopeful for the next U.S. presidency in 2009, stated that we would have war for another 100 years. He must know. He has been a Senator for years and his ancestors are military.

War and deprivation makes people move to other countries and lose their identity. To lose your identity one has to forget about past traditions and learn the ways of the U.S. or whatever country they move to. To survive in the new country one has to learn what that country is all about and how to fit into jobs. I went to college that was still possible in the 50s. Today with the accelerated cost it is not a way to go anymore. The public library is the next best thing where one can get a free education in just about anything. Internet has become another inexpensive resource.

The U.S. occupies close to 150 countries. Between thousands of missionaries from various cults and denominations and G.I.s, they live amongst the foreigners and socialize. This is how people are gradually transformed into so-called democracies and the American way of life. We all know that we are slaves to shopping for products mass produced by elite corporations. Reason for democracies even though people are told that it is "We the People" running the government, it is the elite who run the world who chose the leaders for whatever purpose they chose.

People vote them in and become responsible for their actions. The rich finally gain power over the whole world. Today in 2008 there are only four countries that have not bowed to the International Monetary Fund / Federal Reserve. They are Venezuela (Chavez), Cuba (the Castros), North Korea, and Iran. All others are members.

Taming The Lion

I visited Germany in 1992 and stayed with relatives. They had television with American produced movies that were done so well in German that they swore they were produced in Germany. They also had a Book of Mormon on the shelf. That is how the people all over the world are becoming a global community. I communicate with Christians in Africa and they know all the evangelists I know. It feels like we are neighbors talking over the fence. They have the same issues we have in the U.S.

Following is a thumbnail description of how I lost my heritage. My home was fifty miles from Hamburg and about three hundred miles from Churchill's head quarters in England. The distance in flight was less than an hour. My family was part of a town of two thousand citizens within a thirty-mile radius of two larger cities. One metropolis was a navy shipyard producing battleships and U-boats and often visited by Adolf. He christened ships personally with Champaign and oratory. We shared that excitement on one occasions. He drew large crowds and created arduous enthusiasm. The other city was a sea of factory chimneys. Geographically our location became an immediate target throughout the war for bombing.

Fully clothed, knowing we had to jump up three to four times a night and make a run for it, we went to bed at night. There was a wine cellar under the restaurant with concrete walls that served to hide us. We grew to detest that musty, damp hole like a tomb. Without alarms we had our ears perked all the time for the hum of planes. Although they displayed English round circles, the planes were American. After Pearl Harbor, they even held American pilots. My future brother-in-law took much pride in sharing that he was one of bombers.

Windows in houses covered with black paper hid people from pilots. They could not see the houses in the dark. People in communities grew very close because it meant survival. The boredom in the shelter often drove us outside to watch the spectacular fireworks in the sky. Anti-aircraft artillery barraged planes with ammunition. Light beams crossed over the glistening planes to point out their whereabouts. Like fireworks one could see the shells head for the planes from all directions. With direct hits, the planes exploded and pieces, bombs and bodies would hurl to the ground. Often pilots released their bombs ahead of their targets to keep from exploding in the air. One pilot corpse fell through a roof unto the kitchen table of a family. Our one big school in town became a military hospital. School classes conducted in various restaurants, meant that we had to travel by foot or bicycle from one class to the next from one end of town to the other. One of my mother's mottoes was: 'man gets used to anything', and we did. War became a way of life. We were thankful for every day we were still alive. It felt like the war was never going to end.

Somewhere in the middle of the war between 1939 and 1945 several horrible nights lay in my memory. One was the night, when the city my grandmother lived in, went up in flames. planes blanketed the whole city that night. The sky looked on fire. We lived eight miles from it. My mother in a frenzy about her mother and brother's family, told me to get our bicycles and start pedaling. All I heard was eerie screams of people running through the burning rubble looking for their loved ones There was no help, no fire engines, since most of the men had gone to war.

We finally reached the street where our relatives lived. We could see a huge crater where a bomb had exploded. Expecting the worst, we made our way to it and to our relief the bomb had hit the apartment house next door. My grandmother's house had a crack from top to bottom but was still standing. We found that the family had walled in under ground in a dirt shelter in their yard. The scared children dug their little fingers into the wooden two by four supports. Thank God for no injuries. We inspected the nightclub on the next street that we had occupied and just recently sold. It had received a direct hit. We became aware of God having a hand on our lives for certain.

Another night was over Hamburg that left deep scars on people's hearts. It was a shock that people could do this to each other. That night the bombers dropped a rain of canisters with a liquid that ignited at a certain temperature. When the canisters hit they exploded, splattering the liquid on people running in the streets, turning them into human torches. They jumped into rivers to get the fires out but many simply burned to death or ended up with horrible burns all over their bodies. Approximately forty seven thousand Germans lost their lives in one night in Hamburg.

While on the subject on another occasion Dresden was carpet-bombed for three days and around three hundred thousand fathers, mothers, sisters, brothers, sons, daughters and babies were buried by debris and killed.

These incidences caused a mass exodus out of the cities. Our hotel became fully occupied permanently. My mother provided a soup kitchen. Refugees stood in line for hours to get a cup of soup.

Threats got worse toward the last part of the war. People and soldiers became exhausted and frustrated. Aircraft began attacking civilian trains, farmers in the fields and children pedaling to classes. The planes suddenly came out of nowhere alone and zoomed down close to the ground and targeted people with their machine guns.

The enemy was closing in on foot. The women and children told to defend the town, pulled trees and debris into the streets to build barricades against tanks. Lacking heat in their homes, some of the braver people dragged the wood at night to their yards for firewood. People wanted to be occupied to stop the killing.

Our location was midpoint between Russian and American occupation. The Russians were heading in our direction from the east and Americans from the west. Horror stories were going around about Russian occupation and even worse about the Polish soldiers. Their soldiers were forcing women to get shots to avoid pregnancy and gang raped them in front of their families, husbands and children. After that they shaved their heads to brand them.

After the war was over, for Germans it was not over. In 1946 From Zeitz - Sudeten S 23 came the following reports that confirmed our fears. A female doctor documented just a few cases picking the worst of people in Czechoslovakian a concentration camp in Olmuetz-Hodolein, after the war was over. It held among many an English citizen, a Jewish woman with her daughter who was very ill, a half Jew, two gypsies who were undressed when captured and made to run through the town stark naked. They had Communists there who refused to accept their doctrine as well as nobles and many children. 17,000 people came through this camp over a year's period to be used for slave labor.

Each barrack was to house 80 people when in fact they put 2800 - 3200 persons in each with men, women and children on the floor without bedding at first. The people brought were taken off the street. Later they got wooden bedsteads with straw sacks, no soap. They worked for ten month in their clothing until what covered them hung in shreds from their backs. Bugs and lice finally warranted disinfections. They sat naked waiting for some clothing which were not available. During the cold winter month 5 kilo coal was divvied out. Their diet consisted of 150 grams of bread, coffee and a potato or soup 500 - 600 calories a day. When people arrived everything they owned was taken away. Glasses were smashed and the people were beaten to oblivion until they submitted. They had to get up at 3:30 A.M.. The drunken overseers had their fun with the tired workers sometimes to 2:00 A.M.

A particular doctor was tortured until he died. First they beat him bloody and then with a hose they pored cold water in his rectum until he died. Stories are just too gruesome. Many died a slow death from dysentery went after their weight was down to 30 kilos. The rooms after a few months were full of sick and dying, to help anyone get well was out of the question said the doctor who reported this. The worst case was a thirteen-year-old girl who had been raped and intestines were hanging out of her. She lived after they operated. The man who operated on her could have lost his life over that.

Secrecy was a must or they were threatened with getting hung. Over a two-day period 68 German elderly were shot and killed because they were useless. A young man wanted to go home to his

Taming The Lion

parents. He had worked for a Czechoslovakian farmer and because of his wish to go home they put him in the camp and beat him till he was unconscious, put him in a dark room till he went mad.

Women were undressed from the waist down and beaten into depression were they committed suicide by hanging themselves or drowning in a reservoir.

On another day 285 women and children, even babies were brought there. Many little ones died because of lack of milk. In the cold season some men stole some coal to heat the place. They were put into a bunker undressed until they got frost bitten and some of their limbs had to be amputated. Without care for the wounds it was unbelievable to witness.

The dead were finally buried in mass graves without names. The doctor said that she didn't feel hatred toward the men who were responsible just so no more hatred would come through her report, but her report is documented and true.

Others came forward with similar reports of how they were captured from their homes and tortured. In front of their kin men women and children, ten by ten, were shot in the middle of the night. The youngest child of this reporter's brother was five years old. The family who was not shot had to dig the graves and bury their kin nude. The woman who reported this said she was shot and stayed under the corpses to save herself from being killed. They beat pregnant women until they lost their babies. Ten women passed away. At one point they didn't get to eat for over a week. She wrote "at a church they made us kiss corpses and lick up blood flowing from their wounds to clean the floor. They burned swastikas into the palms of the hands of German men with candles."

May 20, 1945 we were sent to work and in front of us they hung German children and prisoners by their feet and pored petroleum over them and lit their bodies to burn. There are many more descriptions of horrendous deeds but are too vile to repeat. All I can think of how fortunate my family and I were not to have been living in eastern Germany. We lived 50 kilometers from where the eastern zone began and they took over. Refugees came in the western zones until the wall was built and nobody could leave. Families were separated until President Reagan asked Gorbachev to take down the wall in Berlin during his visit. Germany was divided three ways to get rid of it once and for all.

American soldiers had brochures addressed to all occupying military with the following message: "Deep in the German soul, in their psychological subconscious lie fires of hatred, greed and force ... a true terror threatening world peace. "

All we could do was to pray to God to shelter us from such evil. The first troops through our town were black Americans who behaved honorably. They went out with German women on invitation only. Since there were no blacks in Germany prior to the war, when questioned about their blackness, blacks told the women that they were night fighters. Their job was to collect all weapons from civilians. The weapons collected and placed in front of city hall became a bonfire. The British came next and occupied permanently.

Again we felt God's influence on our lives. No one was sexually molested. I was fifteen at the time. My mother had suffered a complete nervous breakdown and was in bed when they knocked on the door and told us that we would have to vacate our property by a certain time. They wanted to house 36 soldiers in our home and use the business for a distribution center. My mother spoke English and talked them into letting us take our personal furniture out. Our stuff and family members were distributed throughout the neighborhood.

We were on the outside looking in, watching them partying, mutilating the hardwood floors with burning cigarette buds and shooting Beebe's at the chandeliers. They demolished the gardens with their enormous military trucks, dug big holes in the middle of the garden to burn their trash. It became a nightmare for my father when he came back. He came close to loosing his life over that after the war. Morals ceased to exist for many because food became scarcer and scarcer for people who had no connections. The black

Taming The Lion

market had been in existence throughout the war. People were trading food stamps, children, cigarettes, coffee and whatever was desirable. Being in business, we had plenty of everything. We had cigars and cigarettes to trade and could get whatever we needed from farmers and whoever. We grew our own vegetables, fruits and animals and butchered a pig once a year. There was government control on meat. A family could only butcher one animal a year. Eggs preserved in some sort of liquid helped prevent lack of food. A neighbor traded her services for food and sewed our clothes.

Our business had flourished throughout the war although the regime prohibited entertainment. Men who were not in the war came to play cards. My mother had buried the bottles of expensive old wine, her best dishes and belongings she cherished in the back garden. There was a death penalty on that kind of action. Next door to us lived a sophisticated doctor who had a house full of beautiful antiques. It was not long before a moving van pulled up. All their belongings were packed and shipped to England by the victorious soldiers. Just like a bunch of soldiers, these fellows had a dog and he died. Of all places to start digging a grave for the dog they chose my mother's hiding place. Thank God, they stopped just before they got to the bottles. Through this incident, we found out the English soldiers were burying the American rations of Corned Beef and other canned goods they did not care for. At night we dug up the cans and distributed them to the homeless and others who needed food.

Released from an American prison camp, my father came home 1945, loaded with provisions for his family from them. He had become a chef there since he was American. Because my dad spoke English fluently, it was not long after that he negotiated us back into our home. They kept the business occupied to do their distributing.

My mother recuperated rapidly. The endless wait was over. What left an impression on me was their love for each other. My mother wrote to my father daily, which he faithfully answered. Their devotion to each other was unusual. She often recalled how tired she was at times but she wrote nonetheless. Hard times put a lot of emphasis on little things.

The Allied troops marched through Germany without resistance from Germans by the time we were occupied. Citizens tore down barriers to celebrate the occupation who set us free. Everyone knew that Germany had lost and wanted the war to end. To Germans the American troops were saviors. They were received with open arms.

What had been rumors only known by high officials and the SS became audible. Radio broadcasts of the organized mass murder of people in concentration camps including many Germans were broadcast. Stalin's deeds in Russia were publicized. He had driven millions of Germans to Siberia to slave labor camps where they eventually perished. In the meantime the military occupation had discovered the original audiotapes of the holocaust occurrences. The stark reality really set in when they presented them over the radio to the general public. It was the final straw for me. They described that they were using human skin to make lampshades in the prisons and told one gory story after another.

I wanted to leave Germany and never see that country again. This horrible discovery about human beings could only result in an indescribable trauma to a young person of fifteen. It had suicidal effects on me and created fear of mankind, which eventually submerged into the recesses of my mind. Those memories had to become a closed book for all concerned to go on living. The disappointment in patriotic young people who were drilled for years to love their leader was deep. Everybody in town wanted to leave. I don't know to this day what my parents knew. They never discussed it and took everything to their graves with them if they did know anything. It closed doors between parents and their children. I only know that I had no idea until it was broadcasts over the radio after the war.

What made me realize that God had a hand on our family was the church record I found of my great grandmother fourth generation many years later. Her original name on her birth certificate was

Jewish. It was very traumatic for me how close my family came to becoming victims at the camps. The only reason we were protected she had changed her maiden name. She took one letter off and no one could figure out what her heritage was. Every family under Hitler had to do genealogy for four generations to see if there was Jewish blood in the veins. If they were tainted they were picked up.

For the death of the Jews and other deeds, many Nazi leaders and many Germans men, women and children, went to the gallows, condemned to death under the new concept of `war crimes'. For Germans it became a nightmare to live with from then on. It became a dark oppressive cloud over every German to a point where they would not identify themselves as Germans because the holocaust would be part of the conversation without fail. "Why did Germans allow that to happen?" was always the next question. Germans are still paying hundreds of millions to Israel in retribution to this day that is never mentioned, nor is the fact that twenty million Germans perished in WWII. What happened after the war was over was a second holocaust of Germans. They wanted every German dead. I found out in historical accounts that Hitler tried to get the Jews back to Israel before the war but Britain was in charge then of the Palestinian territory and would not permit it.

CHAPTER 4

YE SHALL HAVE TRIBULATION

In the Old Testament God watched over His creation and His focus was on men. He created the universe for His children and was hoping Adam would tend to the earth and make it fruitful. Instead of taking the responsibility, Adam became subject to his woman, who was beguiled by the serpent. The serpent had told her that she could become a god if she disobeyed God's request (see Genesis 3:14). Adam transferred his birthright (his inheritance, his dominion) and authority as God's son to Satan and became subject to Lucifer. God is still in control of this universe and earth with everything in it and on it. He created it keeping every possibility in mind.

The principality of Satan is active from the astral realm, a lower dimension in relation to God (see Ephesians 1:20-23). Satan and his angels left heaven according to Scripture (Luke 10:18). The fallen angels are now demonic spirits. They had been in heaven for the sole purpose of entertaining and serving God and His creation. During Satan's presence in heaven Satan became competitive. He wanted to be equal to God. Since angels were created to help human beings they also have other attributes of which we know little. Fallen angels have the same functions but they help enlarge the sin factor in a person's life that is spiritually destructive. Under their influence persons think they are receiving blessings from God when in reality the advantages come from a different realm. The result is people begin to serve the lower spiritual realm. Instead of serving the Spirit of God, they serve the devil. Directed by Satan whose goal still is to overthrow God, they mean to win even though the contrary is prophesied in the Word of God.

The Holy Spirit is contending for our souls and Satan's goal is to derail that effort at all cost. They are principalities at war with each other. In our physical realm we think the war is probably over numbers of subjects, not so. God is looking for fruit developed by the Holy Spirit in subjects that fit into His kingdom. Human beings cannot produce that fruit without the Holy Spirit. The prime fruit is love toward the `Triune God' and that is the Father, the Son and the Holy Spirit, who are considered to be One God in three persons. The first fruit is unconditional love so focused on God it will transcend everything presented to us. The second fruit is love toward God's creation: including men, women and children and all creation.

Adam put his woman on a pedestal higher than God and by doing that, became subject to demonic spirits instead of the Holy Spirit. Originally God's goal was that He [God] and Adam and would become partners. When God saw that Adam was lonely He made Eve from Adam's rib to be included in that partnership. God planned for man and woman to be coupled with the Holy Spirit and connected to God Himself. One can think of it as a rope of three strands like an umbilical cord connected to God instead of the mother's womb. When this combination does not exist in a marriage, it often does not survive. The survival of a marriage is dependent on unconditional love. Without the Holy Spirit who empowers us, we cannot practice unconditional love. Jesus gathered apostles and told them to go out in pairs. This is also why He told us to fellowship with other Christians. Jesus said: **"For where two or three are gathered together in my name, there am I in the midst of them."** (Matthew 18:20)

Although Adam and Eve disobeyed and God placed a curse over their lives, the potential for their offspring, meaning us, to regain their position under God is still available. It is reachable through faith in Christ Jesus, and knowledge of the truth. Scripture states that the name of Jesus is the WORD OF GOD (Revelation 19:13), which is our only hope in getting back to our Father. The WORD is the blueprint for this creation and teaches how the Holy Spirit's teaching enables us to overcome the demonic forces.

To counteract the prophecy (the Word) and its continuous fulfillment, Satan has set up a counterfeit infrastructure of thousands of organizations. To provide a mechanism for potential Christians who are Satan's focus, many fellowships (churches) have

Taming The Lion

an outward look of Christianity but do not teach Biblical truth. Deception by Satan covers the whole world according to the WORD; only those who have received the Holy Spirit (Spirit of Truth) can understand that Jesus Christ is God in the flesh. God came here personally to teach us how we can overcome death through His blood sacrifice.

The demonic spirits have permission from God to stick it to us every time we sin until we are dead. If we do not know God's plan, we die. Being born again means to live forever. The struggle with sin is comparable to struggling with a dragon. Without God, we loose because Satan has the power to overcome us. This is the reason God has sent Jesus His son to deliver us out of Satan's hand. We cannot do it without Him. The cost of our sin had to be paid in full by the blood of Christ Jesus. There was no other way the payment could be made. It had to be the blood of a man who was unspotted by sin.

Satan tempted Jesus Christ by offering him the whole world if he would bow down and worship Satan. He could not be tempted because he was God. We have the option as well when we receive God's Spirit, the Holy Spirit. Empowered by the Holy Spirit, we can overcome Satan and sin and death. What people don't understand is that the Bible doesn't teach religion. Christ Jesus did not come to condemn anyone. He purchased us and then gave us a choice. We do not have to accept it if we do not want to. If we do wish to become part of our Savior all we have to do is tell Him so and repent of our past. Repenting means to allow the Holy Spirit to guide our life from then on instead of our own spirit to overcome death.

Some people believe they will simply be buried in the ground, which is not the way it is. At death the spirit goes to a holding place until the thousand year Millennium is completed. There will be a resurrection for them and the Great White Throne judgment. Those snared by the devil will be thrown into the Lake of Fire with Satan and the False Prophet for eternity.

Taming The Lion

God teaches the least He wants from us is `yes' or `no'. He is a fair God and the responsibility to make that decision lies with us, not God. When it is `yes', he begins to work with our lives. Sooner or later we begin to discover the miracles He brings about and learn to trust him. He teaches from the Word how to overcome on all fronts of our lives. We learn to win by applying God's Word. This lifestyle works because it is based on absolutes. Every suggestion Jesus gave works because He is the creator. There is patience involved, but knowing that the teaching is true, enables one to have the patience. Incorporating suggestions from Jesus will ultimately bring victory. That knowledge in itself brings the enthusiasm and endurance necessary to carry the project through. Jesus really teaches how to win and I would not live without Him for that reason alone. The blessings built in are too many to be counted.

God lived on earth in the Old Testament under the protection of the Aaronic priesthood. He cannot look upon sin. Baal worship in His Temple made God leave the Aaronic priesthood. Humans have been deteriorating in holiness since Adam, to a point where God wanted to wipe out His whole creation. Because of one man who begged God to give us another chance, God had mercy. He is giving us a second chance. God came to us again in Jesus Christ's human body, who was God's only begotten Son.

Because Adam disobeyed, humans spiritually died. Their eternal connection to God died. God started another family in Christ Jesus. Jesus sent the Holy Spirit to earth after He went back to the Father. The Holy Spirit comes into people's hearts upon invitation only. The Holy Spirit is the Spirit of Truth, who helps us to see the light. He teaches and empowers us into the family of God and how to bring demonic forces under control through knowledge and prayer. The Holy Spirit led Jesus and empowered Him to do miracles. We can also be led by the Holy Spirit to help us maintain our lives daily. It is easy; all we have to do is say `yes' to Him. It makes the difference between operating in light or darkness. He coaches us to win in the long run and to overcome everything.

Taming The Lion

Men and women have a vacuum inside, a longing for love. They seek to fill it with the opposite sex, music, drugs, books, works, television, computers, material success and thousands of preoccupations to make the loneliness go away. That vacuum should be filled with the Holy Spirit. He then by invitation only, moves into this vacuum. Water Baptism by immersion usually follows this event to make the fact public that he or she married Christ Jesus. The life is sealed forever to God. The Holy Spirit in the vacuum (heart) feeds on the Word of God begins to seek after Scripture to fellowship with God and grows fruit for Him. Feeding on the Word gradually gains control over our life.

Application to daily life of the teachings of Christ Jesus is the only defense against Satan. The goal is to overcome death, sickness, evil spirits, poverty, depression and becoming part of the victory Jesus won for us on the cross. In overcoming we begin to realize a desire to get others out from under Satan's oppression and that is all there is to it. It is the most natural process and is life itself. Jesus Christ is God's seed. Man gave himself to Satan and became Satan's seed with the potential of a second chance: of becoming God's seed like Christ Jesus.

Satan's goal is to keep as many out of Heaven as possible. He doesn't function from a victorious level. He is already defeated and still seeks to change his position. He seeks to influence us into violating God and keep the Holy Spirit away from us. The Holy Spirit cannot live in a vile environment no more than God can look upon sin.

Satan tempts us with worldly possessions, prestige, immoralities, or whatever a person finds pleasure in doing. Demonic spirits have access to the body of knowledge of this world. Through that knowledge they can produce the perfect coat, i.e. an organization that fits our need and looks authentic. Our habits are our greatest enemy. Taking control over our body, mastering it and moving it where we want it to be productive, is a prerequisite. To test Satan's power over our lives simply decide to read the Word daily and see what happens. Our body is at war with the spirit and will come up with many excuses why we don't have time to do this now.

"For that which I do I allow not: for what I would, that do I not; but what I hate, that do I. If then I do that which I would not, I consent unto the law that it is good. Now then it is no more I that do it, but sin that dwelleth in me. For I know that in me (that is, in my flesh,) dwelleth no good thing: for to will is present with me; but how to perform that which is good I find not. For the good that I would I do not: but the evil which I would not, that I do. Now if I do that I would not, it is no more I that do it, but sin that dwelleth in me. I find then a law, that, when I would do good, evil is present with me. For I delight in the law of God after the inward man: But I see another law in my members, warring against the law of my mind, and bringing me into captivity to the law of sin which is in my members. O wretched man that I am! who shall deliver me from the body of this death? I thank God through Jesus Christ our Lord. So then with the mind I myself serve the law of God; but with the flesh the law of sin." (Romans 7:15-25)

The reward is stunning for studying the Bible. "There is therefore now no condemnation to them which are in Christ Jesus, who walk not after the flesh, but after the Spirit. For the law of the Spirit of life in Christ Jesus hath made me free from the law of sin and death. For what the law could not do, in that it was weak through the flesh, God sending his own Son in the likeness of sinful flesh, and for sin, condemned sin in the flesh:" (Romans 8:1-3)

Children raised without Christian upbringing in the home have a long difficult road to get Christian roots that are deep enough to reach into God's river. The wells are deep which means that we have to dig by working at it. Scripture is written so we can ultimately grasp it.

"He that believeth on me, as the scripture hath said, out of his belly shall flow rivers of living water." John 7:38 Children inherit wells from their parents. **In my case I had to start from scratch digging a well. With an environment of superstition, rituals, astrology, fortune telling, strict obedience, works, mixed with Luther's Catechism, an explanation of our Lord's Prayer and the Ten Commandments, I was heading into a whirlwind of trouble. As Scripture describes here: "That we henceforth be no more children, tossed to and fro, and carried about with every wind of doctrine, by the sleight of men, and cunning craftiness, whereby they lie in wait to deceive;"** (Ephesians 4:14)

For too many years I was **"Ever learning, and never able to come to the knowledge of the truth."** (2 Timothy 3:7) Like waves breaking against a rock, Satan moves against us in a constant rhythm to wash our faith in God away. If our house is not built on the Rock, Jesus Christ, we end up floating down stream hitting every rock until we are shipwrecked. With a pure heart, hoping to help others to understand Satan's schemes against Christians, I want to warn with urgency there is more to Christianity than just going to church and listening to a few sermons. Satan is a deadly enemy. We need to heed Paul's warning: **"Be sober, be vigilant; because your adversary the devil, as a roaring lion, walketh about, seeking whom he may devour: Whom resist steadfast in the faith, knowing that the same afflictions are accomplished in your brethren that are in the world."** (1 Peter 5:8,9)

Awareness that Jesus Christ was drawing me was always with me. When I sinned I knew it as well. Every decision I made had Christ in the middle of it, but in spite of that my road was extremely unusual for a Christian. Today I fully understand why it had to be and how dependable God was to pull me through it all. I was ready to leave this planet at a young age and would have, if I had my way. Because of God's constant intervention, He sustained me through today. So much was crammed into my life; it feels like I lived three lives.

When I share today, I was shy, blushed at the slightest hint, people don't believe it, nor do they believe that I have been ill with incurable diseases twice and that includes physicians. The cures I also attribute to God. I discovered the Bible is true by His personal teaching through the Holy Spirit. God taught me to trust Him and love Him unconditionally through living life and He released an awareness of His love for me over time. I learned by simply believing that He was walking with me, regardless of how desperate situations looked.

To build faith in God, I took on more than I could chew as a life style early on. I put myself in His hands and worked it out together and found it to be a wonderful adventure. God wants to teach us that with Him we can move mountains and are overcomers. This principle not only works for big ministries or missions, but for every day life. One grows in faith only through opposition. The experiences become larger as we stretch and grow and eventually become other-directed. God's goal is contained in Scripture: **"Master, which is the great commandment in the law? Jesus said unto him, Thou shalt love the Lord thy God with all thy heart, and with all thy soul, and with all thy mind. This is the first and great commandment. And the second is like unto it, Thou shalt love thy neighbour as thyself. On these two commandments hang all the law and the prophets."** (Matthew 22:36-40)

Back to 1947 when I was confronted with leaving home at sixteen I jumped in not considering the consequences. After Germany's occupation by the English army, notifications came to American citizens that they needed to go back to the United States. That included my aunt who was a practicing astrologer from New York. Happy to go home to New York, she began her paperwork and stopped by one day to say goodbye. Suddenly, she said to me: "why don't you come with me?" That thought had never entered my mind. My future was all set in Germany. I had a fellow picked out to marry and was diligently working on a career. I did not feel a need for anything else.

To my surprise this comment intrigued me. Just like that my world turned upside down. I replied: "why not?" I turned to my mother who had talked about New York hundreds of times. She had told us about the five and ten cent stores and the movie houses on every corner. She longed to get back to the life she had known in Buffalo, New York. Unwittingly she agreed.

My mother regretted her consent the next day and wanted to change my mind, but it was too late. Taking her up on her first response, I told her, if she did not let me go, I would run away. Alone, I traveled to the big city and the Consul in Hamburg to get all the paperwork arranged. My parents did not lift a hand to help me. They hoped I would get frustrated and give it all up. Someone in New York needed to pay for the passage since German money became worthless after the war. My grandmother had a brother and family in Brooklyn. A letter went to him and his wife said: no, that I was too young to be coming over and would not be paying back what I owed. One more time, I tried and addressed it to my great-uncle. He broke down and took the risk and sent me a ticket.

The astrologer had sailed for New York. My excitement knew no bounds. I even got a whole new wardrobe. Part of our restaurant leased to a clothing manufacturer was to be confiscated by the soldiers. Rather than letting the soldiers take over that whole inventory of new clothes, they told us to go through everything and take what we wanted. I found a gorgeous camel hair sports coat and a couple of two-piece suits. God was so good. The whole town excited with me about my going to America. Next I got a visitor. A tall blond blue-eyed young man a few years older than myself, whom I barely knew, announced to me that he was planning to go with me. I said: "what? How could you be going to America, when you are not a citizen and have no way of getting a ticket nor a passport?" I laughingly dismissed it as a joke and forgot about it. There had been other young men who had tried to make a connection with me to get an opportunity to come to the United States.

Tearful goodbyes came and went. Beginning to realize what I was letting myself in for, leaving my beloved mother and father was a lot tougher than I had contemplated. Reality set in and I cried for days. Many nights were spent cuddling up on my mother's wonderful soft body. She was two hundred pounds. There was so much to hug. Coming through a war like we had fears of being killed were a constant companion, drew people very close. Someone had to take the place of my mother. Since God promised that he is with us, I placed myself into God's hands and learned to trust him from that point on.

In cattle cars we were shipped from Hamburg to Bremerhaven. Life had not returned to normal yet. Germany was a pile of rubble. The troopship we were assigned to looked enormous compared to the little rowboats on our shore. My stomach was a mass of butterflies. It was January 1947. We were to go on the high sea for two weeks with a stop in England and France. The waves seemed to be as high as mountains and the ship was rolling into one winter storm after another. Trying to stand in line for meals was difficult and dishes rolled down the long tables. There were no pills for seasickness. Everything affected my stomach and I was flat on my back holding on to the bunk. Suddenly someone familiar appeared in the doorway grinning from ear to ear. Stunned and somewhat relieved to see someone I knew, I shouted: "What are you doing here?" He answered: "I told you, I was coming." He asked me if he could get me something out of the kitchen, I said: "I would like some sour herring and black German bread." I don't know how he did it, but he found both. With his help, able to get up, I began to enjoy the ship and the ocean.

My newfound friend confessed that he was a stowaway and was working in the kitchen pretending to be a passenger volunteering his services as a passenger. That worked out for a while until one day they wanted to check all the passports. The name he adopted came over the speakers and my hair stood on end. How was he going to get through this one I thought. His knees were still knocking, when he told me that he had temporarily lifted a passenger's passport who looked like him and passed it on to the examiner who looked at it and accepted it. The passport was put back in the passenger's luggage. It never occurred to me to report him. Often I had

Taming The Lion

experiences when I should have turned people in but it was not in my nature to cause more problems for people than they already had.

God had this case all worked out already without my help. Suddenly there was a major jolt in the ship, it felt like we had rammed into something. How could that happen with the absence of shorelines and nothing but water. The ship had hit an iceberg under water and the damage was on the front of the ship. We prayed all the way to New York on the lowest deck on the ship. The boat hobbled toward the Statue of Liberty. Welcoming tugboats eagerly, they pulled us into the New York Harbor. It suddenly hit me that my friend would again have major problems in getting off the ship. We quickly said goodbye till we meet again in New York.

The Statue of Liberty was a most welcome and magnificent sight. Hopes and expectations were mingled with euphoria of seeing dry land after fourteen days on the ocean. We had seen nothing but water and sky. In freezing cold we pondered the uncertainty of the future. The New York skyline with its one hundred and forty three story Empire State Building swaying in the wind and thousands of cars rushing along on the highways and bridges; I could not believe what I saw. All I was used to was Cobblestone streets with horses pulling wagons three, four times a day.

As I was receiving my luggage on the dock I glanced up at the ship to see if I could see my friend. I wanted to wave goodbye and there he was, pacing back and forth on board. He looked worried and in my mind was also a question mark, how was he going to get off the ship? Due to the war, security was extra tight. My relatives and the astrologer were waiting eagerly. They knew each other from years past. I was expecting to go with the woman I knew from home. She had invited me in Germany to join her. She apologized and stammered: "I can't put you up; I am employed as a housekeeper on an estate." Disappointed and slightly scared I had to accept my great aunt and uncle's offer to come with them.

As usual God had His own plans. With a big smile my aunt hugged me and encouraged me to come home with them to

Taming The Lion

Brooklyn. Thank God, He keeps us as ignorant of our future as possible; I would have never taken another step. In the late nineteen forties, the United States, a republic, had an estimated population of 150 million people. It consisted of 3 million square miles of land (.5 square mile per person), only a little over twice the population of Germany. The difference in territory was extensive. Eighteen times larger than Germany had a considerable effect on one's sense of security.

People in Europe participated in the whole process of existence. Even in the cities they grew much of their own foods. Large areas around the cities reserved for gardening provided their sustenance. People peddled on bicycles to their gardens providing essentials. The climactical difference between Germany and the United States was of magnitude.

One of those typical Brooklyn flats near Flatbush Avenue was waiting for us. My uncle had a big car and off we went through the streets of Manhattan. While they were merrily chatting away at me, I was taking in the hustle and bustle of New York City and wondering how I was going to cope with all this. My English was not doing so well. English in German schools was mandatory, because Hitler had planned to conquer the world. He was right in believing that English would become the world language. He told us to expect to be relocating to some other part of the world; somehow what I had learned was not working.

My enthusiasm had gradually diminished and much still had to happen to get some kind of footing into this new life. I was beginning to suffer homesickness. Any time someone brought up my family, the tears began streaming across my cheeks remembering my mother begging me to reconsider. It felt like I would never be able to be myself again surrounded by strangers from then on. When my aunt asked me what I wanted to do first, I asked her if we could go to a grocery store. Licorice, bananas and oranges were not available at home.

Taming The Lion

There was just enough room for three people in my relative's home, but the atmosphere was heavenly. My aunt was a committed Christian and became the light of my life that later brought me to Christ. The woman filled with love, gentleness, and laughter, loved to bake deep fried cookies and other fancies, soon won my heart. She listened to a female preacher who had canaries twitting behind the gracious voice daily. On Sundays my aunt gathered her friends after visiting a little German Lutheran Church. Like a big family, they ate together and discussed the woes of the world. Her joy was scrubbing floors for a rich woman. Instead of money she received the most wonderful hand-me-downs a person could want. Excitedly, she held up her new dress and reassured me that these clothes were coming straight from God. I had to believe her, she was so convincing. This simple little lady wanting for nothing but making her little family happy and pleasing her God made a bigger impression on me than anyone else over the years.

They had one daughter who was preparing to go on a mission to China for the Baptist Church, which probably added to her delight. Impressed with her plans, I asked if I could go to China too, since I had no roots anywhere at this point. Of course that received a strong 'no'. Her daughter, ten years older, had a college education, which had something to do with going on a mission. Since this will be the only discussion about this family, God was faithful to the whole family throughout their lives. My aunt had a very protected life. When her husband died she moved to California and lived with her daughter until it was almost over. She lived to be very old and she always loved her Savior.

My stay in this home was short lived since I had to go to work right away and pay off my debt of $200. I was eager to send shoes, fabrics and coffee to my family in Germany to cheer them on. My English was not too understandable but with skills in cleaning found work. An authentic Jewish couple from Vienna who had adopted two children, a boy and a crippled little girl, took me in. They treated me like another adopted child rather than a maid. Their apartment on the sixth floor had a baby grand piano in the living

Taming The Lion

room and that is all I needed to feel at home. They took me sightseeing and the children became my English teachers.

Living in, I received $25 a week. On my one day off I practiced riding the subway, shopping and visiting my aunt to make payments on my bill. In the same room with the children, I began having nightmares. The little crippled girl was getting unfair treatment from her brother. In my sleep I saw her on the potty and lightening had struck her body. A powerful scream that curled everyone's hair was the result. The next day with my final paycheck I was looking for another job.

After a couple of month on the second job, I tried to climb through a venetian blind in a high-rise building hunted by two gunmen from a dream. This led to three jobs in six months. My language had improved enough to change into better paying and more familiar work.

Landing a waitress job at famous sophisticated Schraffts at Times Square was a step up. Getting around trim American women and cute black and white uniforms, I shed fifty pounds to look like the rest. Schraffts was part of a famous restaurant chain and they had excellent training and were extremely well organized. Sixty waitresses worked on the floor and in the kitchen. Each girl got three tables to serve and extensive training. The money was good because it included food and uniforms. Thrilled to have that kind of opportunity so soon, I worked hard adjusting to their mode.

It wasn't long before my bill was paid. Interested in learning and developing, I signed up in a modeling school on Fifth Ave New York. No inkling of how prestigious that was, I was totally naive of what I was getting myself into. The administrative personnel of the school signed me up. They thought I was photogenic and could use my face for billboards. Exercising, learning how to walk and putting on make-up was effective? In my innocence of seventeen, I had confidence in people that they were honest hardworking folks like my folks at home. Taking it all in, angels were watching all this and had to do something to intervene in their precious way.

Taming The Lion

My German friend in New York popped up in the German section on 86th Street where he was waiting on tables. He had gotten off the ship the following day with a bunch of drunken sailors, pretending to be a sailor too. There were no customs officers the next day. From there he had visited his uncle in Dover, New Jersey who got scared. Germans had been under pressure and suspicion from the government in the States during the war. His uncle had advised him to turn himself in. Elated, I shared my venture at the Fifth Avenue Modeling School with him and being a few years older and more knowledgeable than I was, he went to the school and told them that he was my brother and that I was under age. He advised them to discharge me from the school, which they did.

My aunt got in touch to tell me that I was subpoenaed to testify in court. It did not take long before I found that my young blond friend from home had turned himself in according to his uncle's advice and during interrogation had told them that he knew me and gave them my address. Barely knowing him in Germany contributed little and they accepted what I said and ordered him to return to Germany. He returned and later tried and succeeded to come back to the United States again and became a U.S. citizen. He kept track of me for a while after I got married and years later my mother found an article that he had written for a magazine about the German war. He had become a stockbroker and had a restaurant in Long Island. Later I realized that we had an opportunity for partnership, but at the time it felt dull to come all the way to the United States to marry someone from back home.

The job at Schraffts had been going well for a few months. My parents had raised me with an attitude that the customer is the highest priority. To my disappointment it did not apply at this restaurant. With sixty waitresses standing in line for their meals and sandwiches, the kitchen rules had the highest priority. We were informed, no exceptions. One of my customers had ordered toast and the cook forgot to put jelly on it. The toast was sitting in front of her getting cold, I ran back into the kitchen to get jelly out of the refrigerator to avoid the line of waitresses. Thinking the manager

71

Taming The Lion

would see my point; I asked to talk to him unwittingly making every mistake in the book and walked out when he backed up the supervisor with his kitchen rules. Again my beautiful job went, only this time I not only lost my job, but my record had a major blemish. Every time someone called Schraffts for a recommendation they told the prospective employer that I had walked out in the middle of a busy lunch.

In the meantime my sister had also applied for her visa to come over from Germany, also a United States citizen. Papers came together quickly and over the ocean she came. By now a whole year had gone by and frustrated that I might be an old maid, I told my sister and my aunt that I needed to get married. I was just 17 mind you. Since I had no luck getting serious relationships under way, I doubled the workload to get enough money to go back to Germany and marry my middle school sweetheart.

My aunt warned me that it was not natural what I was planning to do. She said that I should let God decide when I should fall in love. I insisted that I was in love and wanted to bring him to New York. After all he had given me his ring with his initials. In reality I was missing my parents and needed some pampering. The hotel New Yorker and a hospital kitchen quickly provided what I needed and with an overseas trunk full of gifts for my family, it was just one year later I headed back across the ocean Christmas 1947.

With open arms and a small beautiful bouquet of lilies my school friend welcomed me in Hamburg. My expectations were sky high. We had been writing to each other and he knew why I was coming. Tearfully, he later confessed what he did not have the nerve to tell me in a letter. He said I would have to wait five years, if I wanted to marry him. He wanted to be professionally well on the way before marriage. He had no intention of leaving Germany. My aunt had been right, I was running ahead of God.

My parents were sitting on the couch looking at their picture albums from New York, when I arrived. What a delight to be home with them once again. My mother cooked all the delicious dishes

Taming The Lion

she could think of to entice me to stay home permanently again. Life had not been the same. In those days a person was an absolute celebrity coming from America. Wearing a few good- looking clothes, people thought I should just take everything off and give it to them. They complained about the way I sat, I was too relaxed and my accent from America must be deliberate to show off. In one year I had become an outsider. This visit broke the strings that were still pulling me back.

A dollar was worth twenty-five marks in 1947 compared to .80 Dollars today. My father had taught us to put money in the bank as youngsters and I had fourteen hundred marks that were worth 10% after devaluation. There were other young men interested in marriage because my father was successful but my parents would not consent to anyone. My visit was to last two months. Scheduled to go back to New York early February, time was running out.

With two weeks remaining, my first cousin suddenly arrived. He was the son of my father's older sister. He had spent many vacations bringing girlfriends to our house and we had become good friends over the years. He was ten years older than I and had been going steady with a young woman for three years planning to get married. My grandfather adored him because he had been on the front lines in the SS, Hitler's elite. No idea what had happened in the SS in 1947 and not aware that my own family was moving me into helping him get out of the country. God was watching over me again.

These men had the magic measurements for Hitler's Aryan race and had to have aristocratic genes. He was good-looking and he filled all the requirements. My mother knew that I liked him, I had confided in her that my prince charming would have to look like him. Walking him back to the train station he suddenly popped the question: "Will you marry me?" I said: "that is impossible as closely related as we are?" I wanted a large family.

There was a family in our hometown in which the parents were first cousins. Every one of their children had problems. One of their sons was over twenty years old and still in a baby buggy needing to be shaved daily. I shuddered at the thought. Under the impression that my cousin had many wounds and scars from combat, I had compassion for him. News about him during the war had been about terrible predicaments on the Russian front during the war. He had not been taken prisoner because he did not have a number tattooed on his arm like the rest. He was sick the day it was done. My gift from God was too much charity and that kept me in constant hot water. It wasn't long before I heard my mouth say: "okay already, I'll help you out." He could not find work. In my heart I was counting on my parents. Surely, they would not agree to this. My father could not turn his sister down who had been widowed young by a gambler who had committed suicide. Needless to say I had inherited my dad's generosity, he was like me and couldn't turn his sister down and I lost.

Wedding plans came together quickly. The family members notified and all was ready to go except the bridal gown. A black ballroom dress became my wedding dress that suited the occasion for all. Every guest looked like they were at a funeral. They whispered: "black is bad luck at a wedding." They all knew the truth. Fool that I was, I thought that this man actually might care for me. The guests were people I had loved and trusted, intimate family members from my mother and father's side. They knew that I was being used to get him out of the country. Just recently I found out that the men of the SS were an Order like the Templars, brainwashed to do what they had to do for Hitler. My family had been lied to about his injuries, he had none.

Four days after the wedding I was back on board alone heading for New York. That marriage lasted all of four days. God prevented that tragedy from happening. I was a very difficult project for Heavenly Father, but because of it, I got to know Him well. Now, married, I was sure men would begin to behave with respect and stop making passes. My plan of getting some protection failed. Now men did not have to worry about the bridal gown and ring. Sexual harassment increased. It was a relief to get off the ship in New York.

Taming The Lion

By May 1948, my sister and I landed a job in a large hotel near Reading, Pennsylvania and moved there. We were looking forward to a wonderful summer amid vacationers, sunbathing and golfing in the mountains. The hotel was open only during the summer and most of the help lived there around the clock. All the women lived in one building and the men in another. A new level of education was to take place. Raised in a little town where everybody knew each other, homosexuality was unheard of. I barely knew where babies came from. The young men who worked at the hotel giggled about a book they were reading and made the discovery that the barber was homosexual. Next a woman approached me one night while getting ready for bed. I was offended became aware I did not belong to that group and never would.

We worked three shifts seven days a week. The large trays held a table full of dinners and exhausted after work, the help got together and to dance and play. Very concerned about my sister who was over a year younger, I became her shadow. With the intent of just watching her, we went to a dance on the premises. My goal was to make my new marriage a permanent bond even if it meant going back to Germany. I wanted to live up to my decision to live God's way.

An elderly woman tapped me on the shoulder and said: "you know that young man over there looks so lonely and forlorn, why don't you go and cheer him up and ask him to dance with you?" Being a good little girl I agreed: "I guess there is no harm in that," and waltzed into a calamity that took ten years to come away from. Come to think of it he was in my life from a distance till he died.

Today I realize that God had to use this avenue to keep me from going back to live with a man who had been intensely changed by the Hitler regime and would have presented major problems for a person like myself. On this evening I danced with this man from the hotel, a bellhop, and he would not let me get away. He physically wrestled with me all night. Strong enough to get free, I got away but not for very long. After a few weeks of his pursuits, I told my sister that I wanted to go back to New York and get back home to

Taming The Lion

Germany. I had sent my passport to Washington D.C. for a new permit to go back. It had become obvious that he was stalking me. Better not try to take a train or bus, I thought. He would probably figure that and be there. My sister informed to send my stuff later, I hitchhiked a ride to New York City.

In a one-room kitchenette on the fifth floor on Riverside Drive in New York I felt pretty safe. My sister sent my suitcases and I settled in. A few weeks later, there was a knock on the door. In shock I saw this man standing in the hall asking to come in. He told me that he had no money to go anywhere else, would I please let him in. There was no phone. "How did you find me?" I blurted out. "I hung around your sister until I got your address," he answered. "Now what," I asked him. The only solution I could think of was taking him home to his family in the hope of talking some sense into him. My plan was to go back to Germany to my husband.

His home was in a large colonial house in a little town near Philadelphia. We hitchhiked and he told me that his father was French and his mother Italian and that he had three brothers and a sister. He was the third son. Their family life had been so horrible that he carried a knife in his pocket as a young child to protect his mother. His father would get so mean that he would sometimes break furniture over her back even while pregnant. His mother was a beautiful woman and had married his father, who was twenty years older, at seventeen. Now he was retired from the railroad. Wondering where all the scars in his face came from, they told me that he had made a pass at a married woman and her husband and friends had bound and gagged him and ripped a razor across his face back and forth to teach him.

This young man had been repeatedly beaten with a razor strap and he had left home at fifteen. They were a Catholic family and the father believed in not sparing the rod. Being a mischievous child the young man had been in trouble with his father constantly and ran away, jumped freight trains and finally got too hungry and enlisted at fifteen. He had falsified his birth certificate, placed in the infantry and shipped to the Philippines to participate in live war. One of his

Taming The Lion

favorite stories was about a friend who had a family back home and lost his life right next to him. The young man could never understand why the bullet did not hit him since he was worthless and unmarried. By the time his duty was over, he had a habit of hanging out in bars.

The GI Bill was a real incentive for young people to go to college free and get a home at low interest (4% annually) without down payments. Houses were only around $10,000 then. He had tried to go to a school for Hollywood actors for a while but did not have the confidence in himself. He often bragged about Charles Bronson who had come from the same school and went to Hollywood.

The young man's family was my downfall. They saw me and now I did not only have one on my case but a whole family. They thought I would be able to make him behave. My passport was still in Washington, D.C. and I was planning to pick it up personally and get on a boat. Four o'clock in the morning I finally had him convinced that I had no intention of marrying anybody else. I was going back to Germany.

"It will take at least six weeks to get on a ship, we have no vacancy till then," shouted the voice on the other end. My heart sank to my knees, somehow I knew, I had lost. He would find me, six weeks was too long.

My stuff was stored with a German family in Brooklyn where I had roomed. This family had one son and their hearts desire was to have me for a daughter-in-law. Their son had been dating an Italian girl, to his mother's disappointment. She tried to break that relationship up. The son got so upset with his family that he eventually tried to take gas and kill himself unsuccessfully.

A telegram arrived there from the stalker's brother. "In God's name, hurry back, he is trying to kill himself, won't eat and is completely distraught." The German woman screamed at me, "it's a trick, don't call him!" She had a portrait of me framed behind glass and grabbed it and said: "if you call him, I'll smash this picture into a thousand pieces and we are through." She was serious and the picture hit the floor when I took the phone.

Because I was out of a place to live at that moment, I consented to have the stalker come talk one more time. He came with his big brother to Brooklyn from Philadelphia in an open jeep. The next day I found myself with his mother on one side and this young French/Italian or so I thought, on the other in front of a Methodist pastor, saying "I do," in Trenton, New Jersey. Still under age, the tears flowed. In my heart I knew I had gotten into a fatal situation that would never work, not only was this a major sin against God, `adultery', but what happened was also illegal. We were not even compatible and fought all the time. This was how a fly must feel when it gets caught in a spider-web. The pastor said to him: "I see you are Catholic, hope you realize, in the eyes of the Catholic Church, you are not married at all?" "I know," he replied, "it doesn't matter."

One of the brothers had purchased the family home on the GI bill and all six young people and two daughter-in-laws and parents lived here for the time being. In a little job at a store, people in conversation about the family I was staying with reassured me that both the mother and father were Italian. Italian heritage was no problem to me, but having been lied to was a problem. Now I was dealing with fear of the police expecting them to find out somehow that I was married to two men.

In touch with my family news soon came that my German husband had been denied entry into the United States. This decision was permanent. His girlfriend out of vengeance had reported his affiliation with the SS stormtroopers. My father went to court for me to get an annulment of the marriage.

Like many American boys, my new husband had been working on an old beautiful "Cord" automobile. He had spent every penny on re-chroming parts for some time. Not understanding what that means to a boy until I had sons and watched them, I agreed when he suggested to sell it. He wanted to find an old car and move to

Taming The Lion

California. That day when a fellow put three hundred dollars in his hand, he loaded all the parts on a trailer, he was probably in trauma for a while, but no one knew it. A man had to be tough and could not show emotions. We did not discuss his Cord ever again.

An old Buick took its place. It had spare tires on the front fenders, cost a $100 and off to California we went. I had never been on super highways before and those tractor-trailers scared me. We went on the old route 66, two lane then and most people in those days were driving instead of flying.

The scenic changes were fantastic, especially the Painted Desert. There was something special about the wide-open spaces out in the West. It felt like the sky touched the ground. It was so still. The sunsets were glorious and one could see as far as the eye traveled in the desert much like the ocean. Then the majestic, powerful, quiet mountains that felt like they had always been there were awesome.

The car was old and the tires worn out. We had a few blowouts and usually on top of some hairpin road trying to get around a truck. Riding and sleeping in the car twenty-four hours was not conducive to our emotional condition. In Europe respect is built into the system. I could not get used to people's aggressive behavior. It felt like they could do whatever they wanted with a person. There was no restraint. People addressed each other directly in first person. In Germany it took months of courting before a man or a woman could call each other by first names to maintain an air of respect around people.

Bible principles that I could have applied to help the situation were lacking such as forgiveness, or loving your enemy. We get from day to day by forgiving seventy times seven. Instead I was depressed, sulking and wondering how I could still get away. We had nothing in common. By the time we entered Los Angeles, our $100 was down to just enough to get a little room with gas heat for a week. It was November of 1948. We were in search of some kind of life I thought. Later I found that he was a hobo at heart. He liked going from place to place.

Taming The Lion

We stayed long enough for me to land a little cafeteria job and work a couple of weeks to get money to go on. There was something about me that softened people's heart. I can't remember once getting turned down for anything in those years. There seemed to be an underlying invisible support that I did not really understand since I was out of bounds where the Ten Commandments were concerned. The teaching I was familiar with at the time: God's love only applies if I lived by the rules. God seemed to be there under any circumstances. My husband had no skills and could not land a job. He claimed the reason was his Italian look. He felt discrimination and could not put it behind himself. It never occurred to him that it might be his incomplete schooling. He had left school at fifteen and had no high school diploma. He had joined the army at age fifteen. I believe he saw too much misery and it broke his spirit. He said many times to be careful not to break people's spirit.

Los Angeles was a small town in the early 1950s and Las Vegas just a street with lots of Neon signs on both sides. People hung around in the parks and got on soapboxes turned upside down and told their woes. Many people were out of work because military personnel brought back to the United States needed jobs. The defense industry had come to a halt. Europe and the Soviet Union battered into oblivion made another war unlikely. They occupied Germany from different directions with Russians, Englishmen and Americans to democratize Europe. The Berlin wall divided Germany at the heart. Russians occupied eastern Germany and American and English soldiers occupied western Germany.

My first try to get away only to chicken out, came after a couple of days. On the other side of the world, I knew no one and my husband swore that he loved me and would try to maintain an easier relationship with me. All he had seen in his own family relationships were fights. There was no television in those days and people only had their own families as behavior models. He was under the impression that a man needed to undermine his woman by demeaning her, which is a form of brainwashing. His mother rarely opened her mouth, she just quietly did the cooking for the family

Taming The Lion

and cleaned house. She had never worked outside the home and he insisted that I would not work either. The trouble was, he was not working and we had nothing to eat and no place to sleep. Somehow he could not put the two together that one must earn the money to have sustenance.

In Chicago, icy winds, snow and an old car to sleep in, I tried another escape and again I returned with my head hanging figuring I better wait till we were back in Pennsylvania. I remember the fight we had. I had gotten a waitress job in a restaurant that was on the second floor. It poured rain that night. As I waited on tables and looked out the window he was standing in the rain watching me the whole eight hours. Not knowing what to expect when I came out of the place, I soon found out. He remembered each customer and wanted to know what I had talked about. I could not believe my ears.

My husband's family had moved from Youngstown, Ohio to Philadelphia suburbs and his grandmother still lived in Cleveland. By now it was snowing and we were so broke and hungry. His grandmother was not too happy to have us since she was old with a small income. Upset still with my father-in-law who had stolen her daughter at a tender age of seventeen, she was still angry. She let it be known what she thought of him.

A job advertised in downtown Cleveland, one hundred and five blocks from their house was available. Though I had become a beggar by now, something held me back from asking for a nickel for a bus ride. Walking the hundred and five blocks was the other alternative. It was so cold that I had to stop in little stores to warm up and continue. The job was mine. They put me to work right away, fed me and gave me money to get home.

Big chunks of tires had fallen off the car from the freezing weather. The day came for packing and grandma was glad. In shaking hands she pressed a list of everything we had consumed into her grandson's hand with the hope we would send the money later. I realized then why I had not asked her for a nickel. What she

Taming The Lion

did not know, his favorite motto was: "why have two people worry about a bill, let them worry about it." We did not go back to Philadelphia but went to Brooklyn. We were both miserable. We had traded keepsakes and our personal possessions for gas. He had a beautiful cigarette case someone had given him and people took what we offered because they felt sorry for us. I had my accordion and a suitcase full of embroidered linen, which I considered my hope chest, in the pawnshop more than out. Somehow I always managed to get them back.

We talked an old lady into putting us up in a little flat on the second floor. She pointed to the floor and apologized and promised us a rug. She was so happy to have us. In my heart I knew the woman would not get her rent and my heart broke for these people every time we skipped out.

My dad had put so much emphasis on honesty. Our actions were against my grain. My husband left to hunt for a job and my heart did a somersault. Now was my chance to leave. The door locked behind, I got my suitcases together and put my coat on that had a large fox fur collar, opened the window and climbed down the fire escape, suitcases and all. People were gathering down on the street wondering what I was doing. They did not see a fire. Ignoring them, I quickly moved away.

I had found a job with a family where I could live in. It worked for a week and my head got in touch with my heart and I began to realize that I had been wishing for a family. Ties to my husband were beginning to develop in spite of problems and hope had developed that a child would probably shape everything up.

He was very upset. He thought I had tried to commit suicide. They had to break into the room and the curtains were flying around the open window, but there was no body on the ground. This time I was repenting and promising that I would stop the nonsense and try to do better. He was ready to call it quits. When the rug came, it was linoleum and we still laugh about that. We moved back home to his Mom and Dad for a while.

Taming The Lion

My husband's older brother had attended a private Catholic school and became successful because of it but later left the Catholics. He became involved with Dianetics in the early 1950s now called Scientology. He had severe effects from the processes and became hospitalized for a while. He never discussed it with me. History repeats itself and I touched base with Scientology again many years later.

No one believes me today but my father-in-law read the Bible in front of me. He was in the sixties when we met and reprimanded me for washing clothes on Sundays. He wanted me to abide by the commandments.

Because of the GI Bill, that provided low interest and no down payment, housing projects sprang up nationwide and jobs in construction became plentiful. Three sons out of this family had served in the armed forces, and later the fourth son also joined the air force. My husband started roofing homes and out of that he founded a construction company. His deck was stacked to succeed, this type of construction was new and people were buying homes like hotcakes. God had put an older Jewish man in his circle to advise him how to handle this opportunity. "Stay in low income project homes priced around $10,000 and mass produce," he told him. I managed to get $3000 from my sister and repainted and papered the family home from top to bottom to sell it at a good price and received $3000 from his oldest brother. With that seed money and the GI Bill, we persevered to get a construction loan from a bank.

To my dismay and everyone else's, he started to build a dream home with expensive stonewalls and bay windows and a lot of fancy built-ins. He ran out of money much sooner than expected and some lucky person ended up with the house for half price when auctioned. The subcontractors foreclosed on us and we declared bankruptcy. We stored our furniture with my in-laws since the court didn't want them. To our amazement we could not get them back later.

Taming The Lion

It took a couple of years to get with child. My womb was like a child's and that happened to many young German women during the war. The natural development of reproductive organs was interrupted from the trauma of war. It made young females temporarily incapable of conceiving. The doctor prescribed hormones. Finally, our first son arrived.

We lived in a little annex on the second floor of a home, one room, kitchen and a shared bathroom. It had an oil heater in the living room. It quit working shortly after the baby arrived. We had to remove the smoke stack. It rained and flooded the place. Baby and I lived in the kitchen. Life was a continuous string of calamities.

Probably every woman thinks she is the only one who has had a child with the first baby. It is such an overwhelming event. I felt like a queen when they laid my tiny new son in my arms. He was so perfect. Every fingernail so beautifully formed and it felt magnificent to have and to hold a bran new little individual all to myself. Someone to wrap your life around, someone that no one could take away and someone to love and take care of. Motherhood was for me a thrill. I wanted to start on another one right away, it felt so right. Fortunately, I was home with my baby around the clock. My personal life was complete. I crocheted little sweaters and embroidered articles for our sweet little baby boy.

Baptism became an issue right away. Our landlord was a practicing Catholic family and they wanted to be godparents. Because my place was under my husband, I wanted to become Catholic so we could start going to church. We did not get to first base since we had not married in a Catholic Church. They told me that I would never be fully acceptable. In my heart I knew there was something wrong with that statement. Already knowing then that somehow I could become 100% under Christ but how that was possible was to be a secret for forty-five more years because of the direction I was drifting into.

Taming The Lion

That Christ had died for me I understood but did not comprehend what that really meant. Martin Luther had addressed the issue we were struggling with. He recognized marriages if they had been recorded legally and sanctioned them regardless of denomination. Man made rules was causing major internal conflicts that never did get resolved. My husband had no interest in going to church and I had no connection with the church due to my status at the expense of my children's spiritual development. I did the next best thing and read scriptural stories to them. To appease me and make me think that he had an interest, my husband bought religious trinkets for me, which kept me hoping that he would consider coming to church some day.

To go back a bit for a backdrop of what is to follow: during the World War II, Democrat Franklin D. Roosevelt was in power in the United States. His presidential career began in 1932. He took on severe social, economic and political problems. The whole world was in a depression. He started the Social Security Program revolutionizing economic stability and social welfare. Reelected for three more terms, in his fourth term his reform was progressing steadily. He developed a full-blown 'good neighbor' policy and sought first to bulwark its insular security by the Neutrality Act.

The United States strove to stay out of the war in Europe, but after the fall of France in 1940, it drew closer to Great Britain with the issuance of the Atlantic Charter. The Charter is not what drew the U.S. into the conflict. The Japanese attack on Pearl Harbor on December 7, 1941 did. The United States is not allowed to declare war unless it is attacked. It is a known fact that President Roosevelt knew before the attack that it was going to happen and allowed it to happen so he could get into the global conflict to stop Hitler's aggressions. The United States declared war. They became involved in a long hard global conflict.

Many young men went into armed services. President Roosevelt, Winston Churchill and Joseph Stalin were the three Great War leaders. In 1948 President Roosevelt was a key figure in creating the United Nations, a peacekeeping organization. Japanese surrendered in 1945. The war ended ushering in the era of the atomic bomb. Many controls had to be carried out at tremendous financial cost to the people. This caused new developments within the labor class. The next President set up a National Labor Relations Board. President Harry Truman, a moderate liberal, came into office to protect the small man. The next threat was Communism.

Our little family was feeling the effect of the stress the country was experiencing. We were out of work for ten years except a few construction jobs. There was no help from unemployment because he had no employment history and could not get anyone to give him a way of apprenticing to get skills. Social Services had no food stamps or any other help to offer. Because of this nationwide dilemma, my relationship with my husband continued to deteriorate.

The baby had the opposite effect from what I expected. My husband was looking for love and emotional nourishment and I was still harboring resentment of not getting back my life. I had no spiritual understanding of how to overcome that or even deal with it. My parents were still overseas and could not help with advice. My in-laws had their own problems so did other members in the family who had married. II was not a reader and had no idea how to help myself. There were three young newly married couples in the family trying to make it and struggling to survive.

With only radio programming, Christianity was not represented in the media as it is today. Money was very scarce. I got $15 a week for groceries and incidentals. There was no money for clothing for the baby. God again stepped in again letting me know He was aware of our problems. We got in the car one day and a box containing baby clothes from 1 to 4 years old was sitting on the seat. I never did find out who did it. My sister kept me in clothes. We had moved to a bigger apartment and every month I had to tell the merciful landlord that we just did not have the rent. Our young son was three. Depression was with me, and drinking and hanging out with the boys was with him.

Taming The Lion

Christmas in another little apartment in another year became quite a memory. Waxing the hallway, I was getting ready to celebrate and the tree sat in the living room decorated and lit up. He came home drunk in the middle of the day, terribly upset that I had decorated the tree. He grabbed the bottom of the stem and brought it into horizontal position and threw it through the room down the hall at me. The balls flew and splintered into little pieces and candy slid under the furniture. It became a memory never to be forgotten. Wax from the can landed on the ceiling and walls. We had no money to replace anything and Christmas celebration ended in a puddle of tears.

Disappointments were a daily routine. My controlling my own emotions by being this perfect little wife and mother irritated him. He could not fulfill his end of the bargain. Violent outburst without reason became the norm. The power of the mind remembered from an incident in Germany, began to play into my thoughts. My mind was remembering what happens when goals are set. They call it willpower. Thinking to myself I thought if I think myself sick, I would eventually die and get out of this whole situation. My husband had sexually and verbally abused me since we had met and we were bound up in constant failure experiences for seven years straight. How to help him was totally out of reach and pointing out that something had to change was not helping the issues. Now it was not only for my sake but his son's sake.

My son was three years old when I suddenly began suffering with rheumatic fever. The family doctor had no idea what was wrong with me and told me to stay in bed. The problem started in my foot and began moving through every joint. I had a fever for months and they finally put me into a Catholic hospital. We had no hospitalization. I was in agony with pain. Left for two weeks without a visit from my husband nor the family, the hospital administrators informed me to leave because of the unpaid bill. My in-laws ignored everything. Their family doctor came to see me. The family had told him that they were not planning to take me back. He told them that they had no choice about that. They had a legal responsibility to take me back. The hospital personnel were planning to put me in the street.

God again came to me in the form of a beautiful big bouquet of flowers. A pastor brought it to me. He visited people who had no visitors. So moved was I, that the flowers were never forgotten. Back at my in-laws home, I was in a room on the second floor still bedridden. Full of fever, arms strapped to boards to prevent excruciating pain from movements, God had given me what I had desired. My weight was down to eighty pounds from a hundred and thirty-five pounds, I lay there day after day. My husband came home from work and refused to come up to see me to say hello. My heart broke into millions of pieces. Totally helpless at this point, mercy came from God. This was a most painful lesson from God never to take life for granted again, but to cherish it under any circumstances.

In secular literature, the general concept of God may be said to be that of an infinite being, often related to as a personality, who is supremely good, who created the world, who knows all and can do all, who is all-knowing. In most Christian's understanding He lived on earth in flesh as Jesus Christ. The biblical emphasis is that He is a triune God. God revealed Himself personally to Israel. There are several famous demonstrations of the existence of God. The argument from the first cause maintains that since in the world every effect has its cause behind it, the first effect in the world must have had its cause; in itself both cause and affect i.e. God.

The Cosmological argument maintains that since the world and all that is in it seem to have no necessary or absolute existence, an independent existence (God) must be implied for the world as the explanation of its relations. The theological argument maintains that, since from a comprehensive view of nature and the world everything seems to exist according to a certain great plan, a planner (God) must be postulated. The ontological argument maintains that since the human conception of God is the highest conception humanly possible must have existence as one attribute, God must exist. In my case I was experiencing His love.

Taming The Lion

In spite of everything since I had left Europe in January of 1947, we had begun paperwork to have the family come back to the United States as soon as my sister and I got a footing in this country. They had lived in Buffalo for seven years, so we knew they could maintain. They knew the language and my father had expertise in the restaurant business that applied anywhere. It had been six years since I had seen them.

After I left Germany, my father still in Germany had built a new Rathskeller on the lake, dug the foundation, laid bricks, roofed it and finished it inside with a fireplace and all by himself. During that construction German money was suddenly devaluated which caused major problems. It was an aftermath of WWII. No sooner did they get a loan going, the refugees came in from Eastern Germany to get away from Communism. The occupying government, in this case English occupation, ordered that every business be given an extra tax to pay to support the refugees. That was the straw that broke the camel's back. My father transferred the place to a refugee allowing a second mortgage for a down payment, which was never paid and eventually lost everything. The Ratskeller later burned to the ground. There is not a trace of my father ever having lived there today.

My family became refugees themselves and moved to southern Germany into the American zone to get jobs. After waiting seven years they suddenly received notification that permission to enter the United States had been granted. When they arrived in New York, my father was age fifty, mother forty-six and two children still living with them. They had fifty dollars between them and their clothes on their backs and suitcases. My sister was still working the hotel near Reading, Pennsylvania and had found a mobile home for them for $50 a month. It wasn't very long before they came to visit me. They were aghast when they saw the condition I was in and packed me into their vehicle and took me home with them I had been in bed three months.

My mother cooked wonderful soups and lots of fresh vegetables and I responded to my mother's love like a baby to mother's breast.

Taming The Lion

My father found work right away. My mother had no use for my husband which was understandable. The only advice they had given me was not to marry an Italian because Hitler had brainwashed Germans to remain pure.

Prejudice was not part of my make up and I could not identify with my mother's thinking. My husband started sending long stemmed roses and expensive rhinestone jewelry. My mother warned me not to fall for that and she would talk me out of the jewelry. Then he dared to come visit and created an upset with me, to show them how much control he had over me.

The temperature in the mobile home was over a hundred degrees that did not help and I went into heart failure. They called a country doctor, a very unusual doctor. He brought his own medications, mixed some of it up and gave it to me to make me sweat and told me point blank that he wanted to see me in his office in two weeks. Looking at him like he was crazy and with a weak voice I replied: "there is no way I'll see you in two weeks. I have been in bed for three months." He said: "we'll see," and shut his suitcase and left. Sure enough in two weeks I showed up in his office on my own power and was on my way back to health.

Back to my old weight and happy around my family, my husband came for a visit once again. To avoid another fight I told him to come take a walk with me in the near by woods. Instead of telling him my parent's wish for us to get a divorce, I made love to him. A few weeks later, my mother checked me out and asked me: "you want beer for breakfast?" I said: "yes!" Not a drinker, she knew right then that I was pregnant. In my heart I wanted what God wanted: a father and a mother for my son and to gain that status back, I had allowed him to make love to me again.

Now with my family in the country, hopes were high that my husband's behavior would improve and my family would help support us emotionally for the children's sake at least. The doctor was delighted. He said: "now don't let any doctor talk you out of this baby, you will make it through the pregnancy fine."

Taming The Lion

My young son had been with my in-laws through this odd deal. He was delighted to have his family back together. My sister was alternating between Reading in the summer and Miami Beach in the winter. She had made excellent money and had real estate investments in West Palm Beach. She told us we could rent her new house and even negotiated a job in construction for my husband. We moved to West Palm Beach.

Sure enough in my fourth month the doctor in Florida stuck me in the hospital for a blood culture. The sedimentation in the blood was so high that he worried I would not make it through delivery. I had a little German Bible my cousin in Brooklyn had given me. I took that with me to the hospital.

Four doctors determined to make me have an abortion, told me that I should never get pregnant again, that my heart was too damaged. I held that Bible in my hand and said: "you are not taking this baby, God has a reason for this." The baby stayed, my health improved with the pregnancy rapidly. The ocean was wonderful therapy. In those days one could still go to the beach freely and enjoy the sun without interruptions. We had no money and no furniture, slept on bran new hardwood floor on blankets but we had a roof. The relationship went well for a while. The separation had made us work a little harder and we were looking forward to the new addition to the family.

Two weeks before my second son was due I went into labor barely making it to the hospital and he was delivered. Another eight and a half pound perfect healthy little boy was in my arms. Again the doctor never did get his money because there was none. No diapers for the baby and an empty refrigerator, my sister put some food into it and gave us $50 for baby things.

In those days hospital stay was a whole week for maternity cases that was a big help for women. The girl next to me in the hospital room whose husband was a garbage collector became my friend. They had bought some swampland, put some horses on it and had built and furnished a house from the collections with the dump

Taming The Lion

truck. They picked through the trash for utensils, furniture, washing machine and lumber and lived in it. They had a bunch of children. We visited after the hospital to compare notes concerning our babies and to my horror my young son sat under the table ate a bottle full of pills without a label. We rushed him to the hospital to get his stomach pumped and all went well.

There was still no regular income and soon we were out of my sister's house and again no place to go with my two children. We had to find another place. This house we rented was boarded up for months, like so many homes of people who came to Florida for the winter. Electricity was off and we had no money to get it turned on. My father had bought me an old Ford. My family had taken a job in Baltimore, Maryland. An old school building with a high wall around it had been developed into a German Club where people came to dance and eat. Business was wonderful. My dad prepared all the old fashioned German dishes.

My husband had a job interview at the Hotel Pennsylvania in West Palm Beach. Frustrated because his shirt could not be ironed, no electricity, we drove to the hotel. One word led to another in the car and suddenly he hauled off full force and backhanded me across the face. My nose hurt for days. The one and only promise I had made to myself was that a man was never going to beat me suddenly took over. Our clothes packed, I went to my friend to borrow $10 and started driving to Baltimore with my two sons. A job and babysitter was found the next day. Working for my parents on weekends I was paying for a change. A couple of months later working the cash register at the club I lost our third child and was hospitalized again.

My dad again had to move on and took a job in upstate New York. A large resort hotel was waiting for us. The hotel was only open in the summer. My father never told me that he had lost that job in Baltimore over the children and myself. A letter was in his files after he passed away, written by one of the board members of the German club. They had asked for his resignation because his family had moved in with him. My parents had a small apartment

Taming The Lion

on the top floor of this old school building. The activity was not interfering with anyone because no one else lived there.

Little did we realize that God's protective hand was at work again. A few months later the man who had taken the place of my father was found by the furnace cut up in pieces. Someone had broken in and chopped him up. The place was eerie: dark, damp, old, cold with immense broad stone steps leading to the upper floors. I was happy to leave there.

The new place was a country club type hotel in the upstate New York hills. They had all kinds of rooms for guests, a bar, dining rooms and an extra large kitchen. People came there to vacation and play golf. We were planning to run it as a family operation; even my sister from Miami was planning to join us with her new husband. My boys landed in the playpen all day and I was on from six am to two A.M. doing the office, the advertising and the bar.

Everyone was on overload with too much to cover and getting more upset by the day and suddenly a family fight broke out. My youngest sister tired of scrubbing floors started running me down and my mother did nothing to stop it. Some tips I had made were the issue; I had put them into a bank account. That had upset her. Quite concerned about my two sons cooped up in the playpen all day caused me to be torn between my children and my family.

It did not take much to realize that it was a no win situation again and was not going to work. The children could not be expected to be tied down in a play pen like that all day. Although I planned to end the marriage, time was not up. We had separated three month ago. Announcing I was going back to my husband, my mother went hysterical. She begged me for the last time to reconsider. Gently I told her that it would not work out over the long haul and that I needed to leave. The issue was about fairness. My sister had started the fight and my mother had supported my sister's complaint. Feeling cornered and helpless, I felt to run was the only alternative open to me.

Taming The Lion

There was a real effort to cover all bases. My mother finally as a last resort said I would never be allowed to set foot in their home again, if I insisted on leaving. Quickly, I packed up my belongings called my husband in West Palm Beach to get me. Once out of the hotel, I was without a penny to my name and they locked the door behind me and went to the second floor and opened the window. They did not want to be tempted to let me back in. The tips were in a bank account and the bank was closed till Monday and this was Friday. How I got through that weekend, with screaming children, I don't remember. Diapers were washed in the river. We had the car but no food. My husband came without a nickel to his name. On Monday we got the money and went back to West Palm Beach.

Enough to pay a month rent in advance, we moved into a motel in Lake Worth. In the summer renters were hard to get. Again we tried hard to get along and make it all work out. We were four of us. My first son was five by now and my second son a year old. Home with them, we spent all our time together. My husband began talking about hitting it big one of these days.

CHAPTER 5

DON'T FOLLOW PEOPLE'S GODS

So we have discussed the environment we as human beings find ourselves born into. Astrology, secret and mysterious as it is, was a real drawing card for me. We want to know what tomorrow brings. It is taught as a science and the fact that the Moon controls ebb and flow of the sea, why wouldn't it have an influence on our lives as well? It made sense.

The reasoning was: if the Moon influences our lives then the rest of the planets must influence us as well. Brick by brick Satan built his slick way of constructing a life that was completely fictitious next to the life that was supposedly led by God. Instead of believing oneself to be a child of God, one accepts the fact that one is a child controlled by one's geographic moment of birth.

Whatever constellation is active at that moment of birth, has assigned to it a great number of characteristics. Without questioning we take them on and actually become the person described in the horoscope believing it to be our reality. By measuring movement in degrees by the planets and their relationships to each other's distance, the astrologer predicts events with such certainty that we believe that to be true. What we are then in fact doing is setting goals and goals have a way of becoming reality because we believe in them. Without realizing we become our own gods. We pick a mate by the same method and now have the ability to choose when and what kind of a child we are going to bring into this life. It is quickly obvious that the astrologer rather than God controls a person living this kind of life.

When I arrived in New York in 1948, astrology was illegal. In Germany the penalty was even higher for practicing witchcraft. Royals, as well as Hitler were practicing astrology.

Taming The Lion

Since Hitler lost the war, that should have been a clue that astrology is a hoax.

The Bible is a prophecy of conditions on this planet from its birth to death. It touches every facet of our life and answers every question while in existence. It should have been the road map for both parties involved at this point. But I was ignorant of the truth. Teachers of the Gospel want to keep the attention on themselves, they only teach partial truth. They make people dependent on them. They don't teach that we should study the Bible personally.

I got involved in a system developed by Egyptians and Greek philosophers who observed nature and the hosts of heaven (the planetary system). They figured out the natural laws and use this knowledge against God to this day. Persons want to become gods themselves. They teach human divinity which only allows for divine people. It excludes God, the Father, the Son and the Holy Ghost. They revere an imaginary temple in the sky in the likeness of Solomon's Temple and a counterfeit notion of the death and resurrection. The teaching is perverted truth laced with demonic lies, intended to gear people into thinking they have plenty of time, life after life to make a commitment to God, that can achieve eternal life without God. They taught that through evolution all mankind is going to become a god. It keeps men and women completely off guard. Today's books on death experiences are an example of the counterfeit.

Like an animal who had been in the desert without water for years and found a well, I drank and I drank believing like Eve that every sentence was true, not understanding that Lucifer was speaking to Eve, who was of course lying about becoming gods equivalent to Jehovah God. What Lucifer was talking about was gods who belong to Lucifer's kingdom. The Bible describes our hearts as gardens where seeds are planted. God and Lucifer are both gardeners competing to seed our garden. My garden had God's seed in it, but now I allowed Lucifer to plant his lies with the result of a delusion according to God's Word. **"And with all deceivableness of unrighteousness in them that perish; because they received not**

the love of the truth, that they might be saved. And for this cause God shall send them strong delusion, that they should believe a lie:" (2 Thessalonians 2:10-11) Since Scripture principles are the key to improvements in our lives, Satan has to use them also to change people's lives. The tragedy is that Satan gets the credit and people loose their salvation. We then also believe that we don't have the option of getting saved because the delusion prevents us from understanding the truth. We can't comprehend what Jesus Christ did for us because we prefer to believe the lie.

The truth is veiled from the investigator because all man made systems are unbiblical. Jesus Christ takes on an unbiblical character. Even when we say He is God in flesh, we really don't accept it, because man is incapacitated. We have to realize that we are at God's mercy unequivocally and we cannot stand to be out of control. Occult teachings put us in control of our lives for a while; it is really only a mind alteration. We only undergo the change; people in our environment are not affected by it and stay the same. In making the change in ourselves we begin putting the whole burden of getting through upon our own shoulders really compounding the burden of life. That is why Jesus advised us: **"For my yoke is easy and my burden is light**." (Matthew 11:30)

In occult teachings Jesus is a most highly developed divine human person and they teach that man can develop this divinity himself. That concept allows Lucifer to teach that every one can become a god. It is one's choice. This lie runs around every teaching I ran through. Occult teachings feed into human control over life by controlling the mind. They believe God is love and teach if you love everyone you are god, because God is love. It is as far removed from God as the East is from West. God is Love all right but we cannot comprehend it to the fullest extent because He is omnipresent, all knowing and all-powerful. His love makes events come together that we can only imagine in the smallest detail. The timing is the point of recognition. By the timing one can tell the Holy Spirit is involved. The Holy Spirit will go to any length to bring something about. We do not comprehend the work of the Holy

Taming The Lion

Spirit in most cases because we don't believe and don't watch Him in action. We cannot love the way He does. To believe I could do it was causing all my problems and they deepened in application of the wrong teachings. Jesus brought down to our level, created the opportunity for man to be in His likeness.

In Freemasonry men are evolving into divinity by benevolent acts. That is the reason Freemasons support hospitals and other social organizations. God does not acknowledge such giving for selfish gain of a man's own divinity to make himself equal to God. In Mormonism, Jesus was not divine, but a spirit brother of Lucifer and of all mankind's spirits in the pre-existence, again putting a person on the same level with God. Search through the teaching objectively and the truth will rise. Life on earth is a cause and effect system and God created the social system in the Old Testament personally and most of the principles are still in effect, even the judicial system was originally developed from the Old Testament. Following biblical principles makes life work. To study it, is to study the mind of God and to learn how to live in His grace and reap His love daily.

In occult teachings God's principles are applied for self- serving purposes and they work. Paul wrote in 2 Corinthians 10:5: **"Casting down imaginations, and every high thing that exalteth itself against the knowledge of God, and bringing into captivity every thought to the obedience of Christ."** Satan turns it around and uses the imaginations and exalteth himself against the knowledge of God, and bringing into captivity every thought to the goal instead of Christ. Of course it works, only they call it today the power of positive thinking. On the surface it looked innocent, especially if a person did not know Scripture but God calls this perversion of scripture. It works because it is a Bible principle backward.

Man has built empires on this one Scripture and application of these teachings changed my life too. I became actively engaged in setting goals for my future. Instead of allowing someone else to control me, I took the controls. Doing this principle in obedience to Jesus Christ brings a person into the narrow path. It means repenting and allowing Him full access to one's life by becoming involved with Him through the Bible. In the opposite direction it can be as effective in getting one's every material desire fulfilled, because we become what we believe.

There is a tendency to forget that Satan was close to God and has access to knowledge of spiritual laws. He deliberately perverts anything to do with the Gospel and we don't realize where it is coming from. The opportunity to move into a self- serving system becomes a tremendous temptation for a person who is not serving God. That the teachings apply to life became clear quickly. The Rosicrucian teachings involve soul mates. To attain divinity involved love and another human being willing to get involved. Now we have doubled membership. Naturally the first goal becomes finding a new partner but not consciously. My mind would not allow such a thought to surface because I was committed to God. The goal submerges behind the veil of consciousness.

Two personalities begin to develop; the Christian and the Baal worshiper. This state of existence is also called double-mindedness. Not understanding the Gospel, I came to the conclusion that God had not worked out my problems because my education was inadequate. Convinced that He was giving me this added information accessible to few people to help me get out of my problems. Without my understanding it fully, my goals began to change. The goal of keeping my marriage together was changed by Lucifer himself.

My upbringing had instilled in me to have the other person in a higher position than myself, to be serving rather then self-serving. To just sit and let my imagination go to work was unfair to the other person, I reasoned. It lacked the sweat of the brow by which the godly man was supposed to earn his living. Teachings that gave me an unfair advantage, I knew in my heart were wrong.

Occultists, who are more than intellectuals, try to attain to the divinity of Christ in their own strength and end up invoking spirits to get it done. The basis of occult teaching is evolution in some

Taming The Lion

form. Mormonism, an offspring of Freemasonry, teaches that their god was a spirit, came into human form and became god. They can't tell who the first god was when asked. Their god has at least one wife, so he can reproduce new spirits, who undertake the same cycle of evolution. The foundation of Mormonism is evolution and is not biblical. God was, is and always will be God. There are no other gods. In Hermetic teachings life began with a divine spark of positive (male) and negative (female) polarity and they split and evolved toward perfection at which point they meet again and become god. They evolve by soul transfer through mineral, vegetable, animal, man (woman) and the next existence similar to a glorified life that walks through walls and never sleeps.

The soul according to their belief picks up information necessary for the next stage through an evolutionary progression through these stages of life. It all sounds very logical but is not what God teaches. According to the Bible, we did not exist in the spirit or soul before we arrived on earth. Our soul is imparted with the first breath. Physical life begins with conception in the female. The soul is the first breath of Life.

A sermon recently confirmed what I have come to believe: one has to be a little irrational to understand God. To rationalize God cannot be done because we cannot comprehend Him. **"But when Jesus heard it, he answered him, saying, Fear not: believe only, and she shall be made whole."** (Luke 8:50) Just believing the gospel is all we need to do. In studying the Old Testament it becomes obvious that God watches His creation. He only wanted Israelites. Judaism is a belief in an omnipotent transcendent God, the Creator, who chose Moses in the time of Abraham, to be the father of Israel. Because of this, the Jews have kept their racial integrity with religious sanctions. They regard their God first a God of Israel, but since the destruction of the temple where God dwelled in a peculiar manner, things have changed. The ancient Aaronic priesthood was abandoned. Judaism was sustained by a hope that a prince, the Messiah, will arise in Israel, and make their God worshiped by the entire world. Not only did the Jews allow Baal

Taming The Lion

worship in the temple that ultimately led to its destruction, but they rejected Jesus Christ as the Messiah whom God had promised. God allowed Gentiles, by adoption, access to Himself after the Jews rejected Him. Gentiles are any person who is not a Jew.

Much of the anti Semitism grows out of scriptural content of the Old Testament and jealousy, because the Jews are an extraordinary group of people intellectually, economically, spiritually and socially. They have survived a tremendous amount of emotional trauma due to their roots and continue to stand out from the rest of the world having a powerful influence on the lives of all people in the world. All attention is on Israel.

As stated in the Book: Religious Movements in Contemporary America, by Irving I. Zaretsky and Mark P. Leone, some occultists will say they are religious, others see themselves as scientists and yet others as philosophers. The two features that consistently mark the occultist are a) his interest in the more immediate forms of the charismatic manifestations and b) the repugnance [dislike], both moral and intellectual, which he feels toward the personal God-Heaven-Hell theodicy of the established churches. For instance Mormonism does not believe in hell, there is only outer darkness and the Telestial Heaven still affords opportunity to evolve that is similar to this existence and not a threat.

Occultists believe that all mankind will eventually make it to godhood by repeating the experience until the neophyte (beginner, initiate) gets it and moves into the next level of performance. Based on the theory that the whole universe is one being and all are evolving toward perfection. About the first trait, it may be only one aspect of the charismatic that intrigues the occultist: Faith healing, or communications with the dead [Mormonism] and he is apt to feel that such experiences have some validity. About the occultist's rejection of the established Christian theodicy, it must first be noted that this does not imply a rejection of Christian morality. Martin Marty found, in his survey of contemporary Occultist publications, that a sort of `generalized' Christian morality is assumed among the readership and no need is felt to spell out such matters (Marty 1970:

Taming The Lion

228). Articulations of this morality have not been lacking; however, especially in the nineteenth century Charles Braden found in his investigation of both Theosophy and Spiritualism, as did Geoffrey Nelson in his more recent study of Spiritualism, that both doctrines explicitly accept the moral teachings of Jesus (Braden 1951, 245).

The issue is not 'moral teachings of Jesus' but the Doctrine of Atonement. What is rejected is specifically the Doctrine of Atonement [Mormonism] and the notion that the unrepentant are damned to eternal punishment. Dohrman found among his 'Mankind United' informants who were like most occultists of that day, from predominantly Protestant backgrounds, and had an inability to swallow `hell and damnation' preachments of the churches (Dohrman 1958. 104).

The punitive side of God is equally lacking in Christian Science, Unity, and the New Thought movement in general. It is not just the picture of a spiritually inadequate man faced with a merciless and demanding God that seems to account for the occultists distaste but he complains too of what he perceives as the hypocrisy and insincerity of the average church-goer. Thus under the Orthodox Christian scheme, not only is any immediate experience with the transcendent order apt to be unpleasant, but nobody seems to take the chance very serious anyway.

The occult world offers an alternative for those who, usually by dint of some uncanny experience in their own lives or their need for a more immediate and direct religious consolation, cannot encase themselves in `contentment with the finite'. On the other hand they reconcile themselves to a concept of the infinite that seems a) remote and b) potentially hostile.

But exactly what is it that these people embrace in turning to the occult? It produces materialism. Is the occultist's anathema [In Mormonism, Word-Faith movement] obedience to the doctrine tied to material success and physical health is a sign of being the apple of God's eye? The tradition of magic has its hand on a sliding scale of knowledge and practice that has mysticism at one end and the straightforward manipulation of events in the physical world at the other. The magic arts have a tendency to be scientific knowledge or on the other hand lean toward trickery. Humans are drawn by the supernatural and know that life is temporary. They wish to have some concrete evidence there is an after life.

In my case, the point of contact with the occult teachings was not a goal. Spiritual drift due to passive behavior was more like it. Circumstances and continuous failure gave me a desire to control my circumstances. It had not occurred to me that the Gospel provides all the answers. In Europe the Bible was not taught as a lifestyle except for the ten commandments which are really not applied to born again believers because they cause death, Born again believers are in a higher life style which encompasses the ten commandments but not as a goal but we should rather engage in love as a goal.

Today the occult concepts are called 'New Age' even though they are still the same old same old ancient concepts. Lucifer wears the dress of religion to cover up and ensnare. Hitler was an advocate of the power of positive thinking, discipline, survival of the fittest and an awareness of a superman potential. He had prepared the groundwork for Lucifer's next step. Extremely fortunate that all communications were through the mail, I was not in a group setting. The harvest may have been worse than it was.

Eastern religions saturated the West in the 1950s and all the fads have now taken root in society. They were just budding and receiving much notoriety. America is riddled with these organizations. They are quietly growing now by keeping a lower profile. The Hermetic teachings warned never to undergo hypnosis or any kind of psychological manipulation through psychotherapies, transcendental meditation or other mind altering exercises and drugs. Something inside me was holding me in a certain place while going through this. My constant concern was about keeping my basic Christian belief in tact. Loving Jesus Christ and discovering God's intervention had made my relationship personal during moments of great despair. No one else could take that spot, certainly not Satan, not money and not man. God was the only one who was really caring, all knowing and omnipresent. Too close to death too many times kept me from taking my existence lightly ever again. When they suggested astral projection,I said `no'. They did describe the dangers of it.

When Hollywood presented Shirley McClain's film `Out On A Limb', she and her friend went to a very remote lake in India for safety purposes. It was irresponsible that they did not explain that. In trying to understand the occult teachings, I was walking a tight rope. Their motto was `knowledge is power' and it set me on a course to get an education. It moved me into developing my talents and becoming actively engaged in living my life. The real danger of occult teachings is the gradual development of sensitivity to the psychic realm. Experiences began to occur that can't be explained nor deliberately demonstrated or proven. Thinking that it does not have an effect, if I don't want it to have an effect, is a fallacy. This extra awareness has unexpected ramifications and Satan comes sooner or later to collect. Many end up having to become Satan's advocates.

The first lesson taught was to take responsibility for my actions and stop blaming others for my failures. There was nothing wrong with that. It was true I was waiting for someone else to provide a life for me. It is a habit we all develop while we grow up and is only natural. Parents think every thought for us and decide everything and suddenly they disappear. No one takes over and tells us what to do next, or how to be different or even what went wrong. A vacuum begins to exist when we leave home. We were brought up to obey someone and whoever slips into that spot gets the lead. Attitudes and habits needed a lot of attention and changing took discipline no different than what the Bible demands.

It changed my physical circumstances but spiritually I was going in the hole. This system was teaching me to overcome in my own strength somehow and watch what happened. God said in 1 John 5:4-5 **"For whatsoever is born of God overcometh the world: and this is the victory that overcometh the world, even our faith.**

Taming The Lion

Who is he that overcometh the world, but he that believeth that Jesus is the Son of God?"

This `New Age' Church, I had signed up with, had secret lessons not available without passing written examinations. In the 1950s astrology was forbidden in the United States that is hard to believe now. The deterioration that has taken place in the last forty years is phenomenal. One big question mark in my mind is: what happened to Universal Welfare (now global welfare) and Love? The opposite is reaped from these teachings. It made a lot of sense when they taught that God put every human being on an automatic map (horoscope) for life so He could quit worrying about it. No two people could be born in exactly the same spot, longitude and latitude made sense. The trouble was after spending days of calculating all the positions of the planets and aspects, houses and so on, and trying to delineate a chart, I found it was impossible to merge all the different elements involved into one event.

It was not something to be worked out scientifically. A computer could not even solve the problem. Based on plus and minus, information cannot be blended. If I predicted anything correctly it was purely accidental because it was a guessing game, similar to a physician, who tries to come to a conclusion about a dozen symptoms. He is guessing some of the time.

Mathematically inclined, I was attracted to the challenge of exercising my mind with complicated calculations and astronomy. There was so much to learn. The prospect of finding out what was ahead was hard to resist, but I soon found out by making some major errors that it was a hoax. Astrology is a lifestyle of classifying people by sign and brings hideous prejudices into play. Taking `what sign people are born under' into decisions colors information in a layer of lies. It is living in a system that is non-existent. An astrologer who can predict has to be psychic, channeling or guessing to make accurate forecasts. There is no practical system that works. The effect of astrology is auto suggestion. One plays with a person's mind telling them that this and this is going to happen. They believe it and make it happen. It sets up someone else's goals in a person's mind. What became very clear to me, it is playing God with people's lives.

Thank God, I had no desire to become a psychic and did not spend time trying. Astrology taught as a science, makes it acceptable to people. It is not acceptable to God. They also taught the Universal Welfare with `Love' as the highest vibration that conquers all. It is another perverted Scripture. The Bible does not teach that we should become one with the whole world and embrace (love) it. God wants us to come out of the world. Don't participate in it if you can help it. To apply it in that respect creates major problems for a Christian when practiced. In a universal sense it takes down all barriers between all and everything. It takes away Scriptural standards about homosexuality, sorcery, rape, murder and all the rest. To love all encompasses all.

God is not saying that at all in His two basic commandments: **"Jesus said unto him, Thou shalt love the Lord thy God with all thy heart, and with all thy soul, and with all thy mind. This is the first and great commandment. And the second is like unto it, Thou shalt love thy neighbour as thyself. On these two commandments hang all the law and the prophets."** (Matthew 22:37-40) He states seek the kingdom of Heaven first and then love your neighbor under the guidance of the Holy Spirit. Note: heart, soul and mind are three distinct parts of persons. The heart is the seat of the Holy Spirit. Without Him in our hearts, we cannot love God. The soul is also inside the body separate from the heart. It is what is susceptible to Satan and should remain encased in the body until death. The mind is the seat of choice of what is going to enter the person's life and it's eternal destiny.

The occult kind of love is unconditional love without expectation of a return and is impossible without the Holy Spirit's help. Human beings might believe they can do it, but when analyzed objectively there is always a self serving motive and consequences of applying these concepts without Holy Spirit intervention can be devastating. Occult beliefs teach to give first and you will get back what you give multiplied. I did not find that to be true in all practicality. To make that a reality principalities have to get involved. Loving means always walking the extra mile and the minute a return is expected, that is where a person is most vulnerable and will end up hurting. Practicing scripture principles will get the results expected because the Holy Spirit gets involved. Developing talents will reap its benefits because it is Scriptural.

Years later, Scripture brought to my attention its accuracy, while the information I was experiencing and plowing through from occult sources was unreliable and caused major grief. The Bible had the following to say about it and I came to it after the fact. It was on the mark: **"Therefore hear now this, thou that art given to pleasures, that dwellest carelessly, that sayest in thine heart, I am, and none else beside me; I shall not sit as a widow, neither shall I know the loss of children: But these two things shall come to thee in a moment in one day, the loss of children, and widowhood: they shall come upon thee in their perfection for the multitude of thy sorceries, and for the great abundance of thine enchantments.**

"Therefore hear now this, thou that art given to pleasures, that dwellest carelessly, that sayest in thine heart, I am, and none else beside me; I shall not sit as a widow, neither shall I know the loss of children: But these two things shall come to thee in a moment in one day, the loss of children, and widowhood: they shall come upon thee in their perfection for the multitude of thy sorceries, and for the great abundance of thine enchantments. For thou hast trusted in thy wickedness: thou hast said, None seeth me. Thy wisdom and thy knowledge, it hath perverted thee; and thou hast said in thine heart, I am, and none else beside me.

"Therefore shall evil come upon thee; thou shalt not know from whence it riseth: and mischief shall fall upon thee; thou shalt not be able to put it off: and desolation shall come upon thee suddenly, which thou shalt not know. Stand now with thine enchantments, and with the multitude of thy sorceries, wherein thou hast laboured from thy youth; if so be thou shalt be able to

profit, if so be thou mayest prevail. Thou art wearied in the multitude of thy counsels. Let now the astrologers,the stargazers,the monthly prognosticators, stand up, and save thee from these things that shall come upon thee." (Isaiah 47:8-13)

This scripture applied to my future. I learned through these experiences that the Bible applies to our lives and protects us and makes the life that God promises available here on earth. Each of us is a unique creation, invented and planned by Him personally and the more we cooperate, the more pleasing to Him we become to Him. He has an eternal plan of love for us that is limitless.

In conclusion about occult teachings, they are the man made religions that accommodate human existences with whatever they wish to do. It reminds me of Luke 4:5-8: **"And the devil, taking him up into an high mountain, shewed unto him all the kingdoms of the world in a moment of time. And the devil said unto him, All this power will I give thee, and the glory of them: for that is delivered unto me; and to whomsoever I will I give it. If thou therefore wilt worship me, all shall be thine. And Jesus answered and said unto him, Get thee behind me, Satan: for it is written, Thou shalt worship the Lord thy God, and him only shalt thou serve."**

"I counsel thee to buy of me gold tried in the fire, that thou mayest be rich; and white raiment, that thou mayest be clothed, and that the shame of thy nakedness do not appear; and anoint thine eyes with eyesalve, that thou mayest see. As many as I love, I rebuke and chasten: be zealous therefore, and repent." (Revelation 3:18-19)

Although occult teachings state that the soul cannot be destroyed, when the Bible expresses a different opinion: **"For what shall it profit a man, if he shall gain the whole world, and lose his own soul?"** (Mark 8:36)

The King James Version states: 'lose his own soul'. In occultism the unit (soul) thrives to reach perfection by evolution and works. It finally reaches godhood. Note that God has nothing to do with even

Taming The Lion

creating the individual, according to that teaching. The ego is the driving force moving toward its goal. Webster's Dictionary describes the Ego philosophically as the self, variously conceived as an absolute spiritual substance on which experience is superimposed, the series of acts and mental introspectively recognized in psychoanalysis as that part of the psyche.

The big bang theory is mathematically impossible considering all the accidental happenings that would have to happen simultaneously for each species and within species. Christian scientists have found explanations for Dinosaurs and carbon dating. Robert Charles Darwin who was partly responsible for bringing evolution into the mainstream of all people, bitterly regretted misleading so many people with evolution. He converted to Christianity in the last weeks of his life.

Taking occult teachings concept after concept, Scripture will disprove it. Applying occult teachings to life ends in defeat over time and Scripture stands as a Light. The Holy Spirit cannot be defeated because He is the Spirit of truth. God encouraged trying and testing His Word. It will stand.

With this educational program life went on. Again it was not long before we had to move on. This time with a few dollars down payment we managed to buy a $360 mobile home. It was thirty-six feet long, inside the size of a large room divided into three parts. The wood inside had maintained its natural beauty under high gloss. I cleaned and waxed it, made little curtains with white pompoms and recovered the furniture. The payments were only thirty-six dollars a month and lot rent twenty dollars and life was working again. We made friends with some people in the park and were partying together. One night they decided to have a Martini party in another trailer, I thought I would die the next day. The man must have put straight liquor into the drinks. On my hands and knees all day the next day I was trying to take care of my two sons.

My husband was selling waterless aluminum cookware to farmers. We prepared a whole meal in it to show the product and

Taming The Lion

people gathered to sample the meals. We hoped to sell the pots for $300 a set. One day my husband traded my Ford (my dad's gift to me) for a new Buick without a word to me. He came home with it and announced that we were moving. I said: "where to?" "Denver, Colorado," he said, " I heard people are getting rich in Colorado finding Uranium!"

My husband identified with stray animals, dogs and cats, and periodically brought one home. This time it was a little black mongrel mutt. We planned to take him along in the mobile home. The motion in the trailer had put the dog into such confusion that he tore everything up. The curtains ripped from their rods, clothing torn out of drawers and trash was thrown from end to the other. As if that was not enough, my husband saw an injured, mangled looking cat and put it in the trunk. It got so scared; it had a bowel movement all over the car.

He had never pulled a trailer that size and did not realize the brakes would get hot. We were moving down a hill and suddenly realized that we had no brakes. The hill ended downtown, we went right through town without brakes, no one got hurt. Scripture states that children have guardian angels. We kept them busy.

We made it to Denver, found a reasonable park, and the park owner directed us to a lot next to a mobile home about our size. That little black mutt was still with us. To allow him some space, I loosely tied him to a tree and without fail the dog got all tangled up and howled and yelped. The park attendant insisted that the dog had to go after tackling him from Florida. It was as though the dog had heard the woman. He snuck away before we could take him to the Dumb Friends League. We looked for him for days, never did find him.

The woman who lived next to us with her little family of husband and two daughters was to broaden my road into the whole New Age agenda. She was a writer working on a book about reincarnation and frequenting the Public Library. She was writing about several generations and needed to know their way of life to make the

Taming The Lion

background of each incarnation authentic. She got me acquainted with Edgar Cayce and his psychic phenomena in healing, the book: Feminine Mystique, Philosopher Ralph Waldo Emerson, and Religious Experience by William James, Yogananda and other Eastern Religions. The year was 1957. She had no interest in my subject matter although it was the same type of material. Today it is all called 'New Age'. Later I found out that she was interested but did not share that with me.

North America, because it was virgin land, uncultivated, drew people who were pioneers wanting to settle on the land somewhere. The people had no historical culture to learn from. Once the ground breaking was done, people began to immigrate from all over the world, bringing with them their philosophies. Eastern states saturated with Freemasons from France, Germany and England were rooted into the Rosicrucian history. California became a haven for Oriental transcendental meditation, reincarnation, various types of Buddhisms and many other 'isms'. In Colorado it all came together.

This was my first exposure to a library and free at that. I came home with armfuls of books and began a broad education of all the various concepts, presumably religions that promised improvements of life's wretched condition. Metaphysics was one and many mind sciences and philosophies. My desire grew to search for the truth. Growing up in Europe Biblical teachings were very basic and related to the Ten Commandments more than anything. Grace was taught but receiving the Holy Spirit baptism was not part of my education. Infant baptism is what saved according to Lutherans whose teachings were similar to the Catholic Church. I had given my heart to God at fourteen when I was confirmed in the Lutheran Church, but the seed was dormant. I did truly want to live a life that was pleasing to God.

Sorting out information I read by lining it up with God's commandments: The entire law is summed up in this commandment: **"For all the law is fulfilled in one word, even in this; Thou shalt love thy neighbour as thyself."** (Galatians 5:14)

Taming The Lion

Somehow, they all presented an unfair advantage over people. My spiritual foundation was the root of my problematic marriage. My husband and I were taking unfair advantage of people's generosities and it was eating me up alive. Taught to work for my keep. I continued to be unhappy.

Mary Baker Eddy's Christian Science and Science of the Mind were part of this curriculum. Years later evangelist Benny Hinn described her three day catatonic state as a state supposedly induced by the Holy Spirit. Webster's Dictionary describes it as a disorder marked by catalepsy. It is a condition of suspended animation and loss of voluntary motion in which the limbs remain in whatever position they are placed. It is a form of seizure. Later in studies of Abnormal Psychology, I read there are people in mental institutions who are in these catatonic states and the doctors have no cure.

The book `Feminine Mystique' turned out to be the beginning of the Women's Liberation movement. Today they are called Feminists. Many women of today forgo the natural role of womanhood. They dedicate themselves to careers and move up the professional ladders, even in `male only' oriented employment. The men did not slow it down because it allowed them an affluent life style. Children had to pay the price. They exchanged their mothers for fathers, who cooked, cleaned and took jobs less demanding. Families began to disintegrate. Women became bundles of frustration trying to cope with a life that was too demanding. Swept into that whole plot, wanting to do it all. I had been going in that direction for a time since my husband refused to take on any kind of responsibility.

It all sounded like it would be the perfect answer but I make that kind of thinking responsible for a complete physical breakdown. Women were told that they were expected to take on all the responsibilities of the household, including men's jobs. This movement pushed men into the background. Men became confused about their roles. They found themselves babysitting, while the mothers went to college to develop careers. To me, the `Women's Liberation Movement' was more like `Women's Loss of Dignity' in her home, I was trying to be in three places at once. The movement was definitely an attack on the family and was responsible for many divorces and children without one or the other parent.

Then there was Gibran and his book: `The Prophet' and his final distorted drawing of Christ portrayed defeat. He did not find the real answers. The more I read the more I realized that men were all looking for answers but their final product was not satisfying the hunger for something to fill the constant void in life. That inner realization there was a perfect answer somewhere began to ring louder and I knew if I would keep on digging I would finally find the truth.

My neighbor thought she had found the truth in Reincarnation. She spent fifteen years working on her book, collecting, cataloging and writing. Her book was too large to publish and she stopped writing after publishers turned down her masterpiece. Soon after she was widowed, she maintained alone in her little mobile home watching television.

The reason I am bringing this neighbor into the story is the influence people have around us. How remarkable that the warning in Deuteronomy applies to our lives: **"Thou shalt fear the LORD thy God, and serve him, and shalt swear by his name. Ye shall not go after other gods, of the gods of the people which are round about you; (For the LORD thy God is a jealous God among you) lest the anger of the LORD thy God be kindled against thee, and destroy thee from off the face of the earth. Ye shall not tempt the LORD your God, as ye tempted him in Massah. Ye shall diligently keep the commandments of the LORD your God, and his testimonies, and his statutes, which he hath commanded thee. And thou shalt do that which is right and good in the sight of the LORD: that it may be well with thee, and that thou mayest go in and possess the good land which the LORD sware unto thy fathers, To cast out all thine enemies from before thee, as the LORD hath spoken.** (Deuteronomy 6:13-19)

Taming The Lion

We communicated every Christmas for thirty-six years after she moved away from Denver. Our relationship suddenly polarized. It disintegrated, when I laid my life down to serve my Lord with all of myself. I began sharing that I had finally found the truth and felt a strong desire to witness to her about the `Pearl of Great Price'. I asked her how she felt about reincarnation. We had not discussed those areas for years. To my surprise she answered that she still believed reincarnation. There had been no change in her thinking since I had known her.

Sharing the gospel with her and at first she was holding onto the relationship, she pretended that she was also a Christian but that crumbled quickly. The Bible verses are a two edged sword. The Scriptures cut through to the heart. Hiding out behind a facade is impossible. Every correspondence took another layer off. I wanted to bring her to Jesus Christ and assure her redemption through Him. That process is like wrestling with a dragon and here are pertinent parts of the letter before the final good bye on her part from early 1994.

Her last letter read: " Awfully distressing to read in your letter, right at first glimpse, that you're considering "divorcing" me! [I was giving her the option to slow down the communication to give herself some space, because truth is a hard-hitting process] However, I'm so practiced at, so good at, by now, falling back on faith and trust in the perfect outworking, that I just shifted that gear in my head and heart and forged ahead, knowing that surely our long and tender relationship was going to survive this bit of rockiness [she had been presented with Scripture] and emerge even better and stronger on the far side. It's distressing to sense that you have lost trust in me, in what I write you, in the sincerity of my intent. I truly, truly, most truly do enjoy your letters. And yes, I do mean and stand behind the things I write to you; why would I dissemble [put on a false appearance] with you? I am not a feather head who blathers at the keyboard. I take my beliefs very seriously, as you do and I give you leave and permission to do, not `requiring'

Taming The Lion

a single thing of you in order that I may continue to keep loving and cherishing you.

The references were to a `procrustean bed', meaning an arbitrary standard to which exact conformity is forced. Example: "...so he demands that she should fit in this Procrustean bed of his expectations." I wouldn't do that to you. If you wrote and told me you had joined the Flat Earth Society, or had become a Skinhead making pilgrimages to Hayden Lake, or had become a raging feminist about to take part in a march on the nation's capitol, I would probably think: well, it surely isn't my cup of tea, but God go with her and I'd stick by you. This is what unconditional love is all about. Unconditional love, as you know, never says I love you, provided you meet my requirements.

Plato said Socrates said, "God grant that my adversary be articulate that we might arrive at the Truth faster." In saying so, he was implying that he knew from the git-go that neither he nor his adversary has a corner on Truth, therefore, between the two of them, most probably they would -- if they chatted long enough -- both be enlightened and arrive at the heart of the matter. I think that's really neat, philosophically speaking.

My sister wrote me awhile back, "...you can't believe a single thing the media tells you. I replied, "I think it's like the public library. You read just a single book, or a couple of books, and yes, you really do risk being misled, if that's your only exposure. But you read darned near every book in that library, and you bring your own discernment and judgment to bear, you weigh and consider all aspects, and have a pretty good chance of coming up with solid information. So that's what I do: I hearken to all degrees from the political/religious spectrum, weigh and consider, and arrive at a conclusion that serves me very well." ..That program of self-education has really been on a fast track...with no instructor, no professor, no teacher to assign me tasks, I simply did what came naturally, and that was to search out the truth in whatever avenue my inclinations led me. My own reference library, topics covering a surprising number of fields, plus all of the well-indexed and filed clippings from periodicals, make me almost totally self-sufficient insofar as information and research goes.

But there, you see, my aim is to follow truth (of whatever) wherever it might lead me. I think to do that is to grow, to maintain a well-balanced life. If my premise is, at the outset that thus and thus is truth, therefore I will shut out all information that does not fit in with my preconceptions, golly Moses, would I be missing out on a whole lot of knowledge. My education would end up terribly lopsided and there would be entire areas of experience in which I'd be poorly informed. My innate feeling, my instinct, is that we are put on earth to develop ourselves as fully as is humanly possible, like a plant is. I think the Heavenly Gardener in the Sky sent us all here to thrive and grow to our maximum ability, according to our nature. If it's our destiny to be a conifer, then branch out and try to be the best shaped and fullest, most lushly branched conifer you can possibly be. If you're a fantail carp in a Japanese pool, try and grow the handsomest derrière your energies can come up with.

You can see, can't you, that my proclivities lead me more to philosophy than to religiosity. But then that is my nature, isn't it? We all aren't destined to be conifers, only some of us. The point, though, I believe, is that whatever you are born to be, you must try to branch out and be the biggest, the fullest, the very, very best you can be.

I.. had an.. Illumination, very different from your experience, and at the time I most certainly did not know that events had names, that what happened to me was classified as an `Illumination'. .. We were.. dirt poor. I was then just your average stupid Bakersfield,.. Oakie-type housewife with no particular aim in life, no particular fixed standards to guide me, but neither was I a problem to my husband and children or to the civil authorities. .. My husband had to stop to buy spark plugs.. I waited where I was. And all at once, for no reason that I had ever been able to figure out, the entire world fell away and.. Reality totally vanished. I was transported into some miraculous realm, something, somewhere I later could not remember for the life of me, but I was immersed in such beauty, such an experience, such rapture, such wonderment, that I honestly thought I would not survive it. I don't know how long it lasted,.. but when I returned to my senses .. all I could think of was: I have got to get home quick and write down a description of what happened! I have experienced heaven! I was wordless, not wanting to disrupt the trance that still lingered to some extent.

At home I ran for a pencil and paper and all I could write down.. was: We are all one! None of us are separate from one another! We are all one being!

I was corresponding then with my artist friend .. alongside a whole colony of intellectuals, .. writers and artists. I asked her.. what is this thing that has happened to me? .. The consensus was that I had experienced an Illumination ... It was recommended that I go to the public library and check out Bucke's 'Cosmic Consciousness' and Raynor Johnson's 'Imprisoned Splendor'. Both books confirmed.. what had happened had also happened to hundreds if not thousands or millions of others. .. I was so in love with my Creator from that moment on. .. I carried the conviction that the reason it had happened to me was as a reward for having taken that very first step in a brand-new direction, by buying that book (Bartlett's Quotations), .. wanting to learn all I could from it. I had at last set my feet on the right path, the path that was meant for me. .. I was actually rewarded .. it must be okay with my God that I invest in books!

So.. there is no way I could ever view my fellow man or woman as separate and apart from my own self, whatever his/her creed or color or belief. When you get the word from 'On High', as you very well must know, from then on that is what you live by, isn't it? .. oh yes, my beloved friend, I do embrace all faiths, all earnest seekers of truth do, however misguided I might think they are at any given moment. They are all following their own inner light, just as I am following mine, I must not interfere with that seeking unless they just plain pin me up against a wall and demand to know my opinion...

Taming The Lion

I hope I don't dismay you if I confess that I love it that the Dalai Lama and the Catholics and the Buddhists and the Christian Scientists and whatever else comes down the path (except for those ill-intentioned and money-grubbing and overtly evil cults) are all coming together in the ecumenical sense, compromising with one another, smoothing out the rough edges that might clash, finding common cause, allowing each other breathing room, not trying to force the other into some procrustean bed. No matter where in this current world you turn your attention, e.g., Israelis/Palestinians; Nat'l Organization of Women/pro-lifers; homophobes/Act Up flagrant gay groups ... it's the radicals, the extremists at the far ends of the spectrum that are causing all of the dissension, .. the terrorism, the bombings, adding to the hatreds that threaten to consume us all.

If all the uncompromising extremists of every stripe were suddenly to be removed from the earth, whether religious or political, my, what a beautiful and harmonious place it would be. We are all one, all merely cells in the body of God, as I see it. I sense that is how we please that Great Gardener in the Sky. .. Lets go on with the dance for as many days as God still does allow us.."

A few more points from a prior letter deserve mentioning from the `New Age' point of view of this lady, " I just can't buy that `pronouncements of the Pope are infallible, that he is in one way or another the direct descendant of Peter, the apostle. Beware of the man of one book... (speaking of Jack Van Impe) yes, Jack, the world around us surely does appear to be going to hell in a hand basket, and I am as aggrieved as you are at our current immersion in Sodom & Gomorrah and wish we'd finally bottom-out and commence our restoration, our renaissance. .. It reminds me of Gregory the Great, [who occupied the papal throne from the year 590 to 604] who said "the bliss of the saved in heaven would be incomplete unless they would gaze across the abyss and behold the sinners tormented in hellfire." (Back to Jack Van Impe and the man of one book) Jack, you have memorized almost every darned word of it, but you're still a man of only one book. I have a problem with that.

Taming The Lion

So I have been forevermore left with a healthy respect for astrology.. practiced by some people and their healthy motives. But just by nature I have this built-in aversion to wanting to be influenced by something outside myself, be it channelers or astrology or whatever. Preferring instead to listen to that still small voice within, letting it be my guide. There was a Christian mystic who said that even if a thousand angels appeared before him and insisted that [whatever] was so, he would not necessarily believe it. But if there was this certain kind of sunrise in his soul, then he would believe it. I always have relied on that same sunrise, what others maybe call the small still voice within.... take good care, always.."

In summary her bottom-line was `liberty' in `New Age', being as free as a bird, at what expense: eternal life with God. God's opinion is: **"These are wells without water, clouds that are carried with a tempest; to whom the mist of darkness is reserved for ever. For when they speak great swelling words of vanity, they allure through the lusts of the flesh, through much wantonness, those that were clean escaped from them who live in error. While they promise them liberty, they themselves are the servants of corruption: for of whom a man is overcome, of the same is he brought in bondage.** (2 Peter 2:17-19)

Adam and Eve elected to find truth the hard way, without the Holy Spirit, it is impossible. According to Scripture all else is delusion. My reply to that: society that talks about being one body a lot but they don't practice it. They have no tolerance for what they don't agree with. This lady bore it out by bidding me farewell; she could not handle what I had to say, when in fact she was advocating total tolerance.

God sets us completely free. **"For, brethren, ye have been called unto liberty; only use not liberty for an occasion to the flesh, but by love serve one another. For all the law is fulfilled in one word, even in this; Thou shalt love thy neighbour as thyself. But if ye bite and devour one another, take heed that ye be not consumed one of another."** (Galatians 5:13-15)

Taming The Lion

Not knowing Scriptures and scrutinizing Christians is dangerous, because many are still deluded, not born again and professing that they are. To base one's opinion on these people relative to God is an incredible trap set by our opposition. Many give up on God because they see ungodly behavior among ministers and Christians. It is dangerous not to concentrate on one's own behavior and not understanding the gospel.

God is the only one who allows anything and everything to happen with only one exception and that is blaspheming the Holy Spirit. He allows it and forgives it in total on the spot. People will receive what they choose: either regeneration or death and eternal torment. There will not be any excuse. It will be our own choice that condemns us if we make the wrong choice. We are speaking of eternal life. Really think about it, is it worth the risk over a notion from someone or an experience from somewhere that was not part of God's desire for us or He would have said so?

In answer to her complaint that I may be trying to convert her.. preachers teach that we make it happen, I don't think so. I conclude that every redemption is between God, the Father, the Son, the Holy Spirit and the person redeemed. The name of the person addressed with the gospel has to be in the Book of Life (which by the way has every individual's name in it) and they either respond to it or not. All we can do is point to the Bible, there it is and if they have no desire to understand the road they are on, they cannot comprehend the Bible. The Holy Spirit has to be present to open the Scriptures to a person. People can quote Scriptures and live in them that is not necessarily proof of a Holy Spirit resident in an individual. They think that they are the saviors of others as taught by cults. They want their members to become another Jesus. Jesus was God Himself. All we can attain here is redemption; the rest is up to God and his plan.

About the `procrustean bed', Christianity is misunderstood. Robots are far from what God has in mind. Every believer is traveling toward God and is in a slightly different position in his sanctification then the next believer. Christian's assumption that they are all knowing, is incorrect. What advice applies to one, does not apply to another. God has individual goals for each of us. The better we understand it through reading His Word, the better we can run with it. God is hoping that we fall in love with Him and develop a strong relationship with Him. The Holy Spirit grieves when we turn Him down. He is the Spirit of truth.

The Old Testament bears out that God allows us to stray hoping that we'll open the door somewhere along the line and let Him in as this Scripture bears out: **"Likewise, I say unto you, there is joy in the presence of the angels of God over one sinner that repenteth. And he said, A certain man had two sons: And the younger of them said to his father, Father, give me the portion of goods that falleth to me. And he divided unto them his living. And not many days after the younger son gathered all together, and took his journey into a far country, and there wasted his substance with riotous living. And when he had spent all, there arose a mighty famine in that land; and he began to be in want."**

"And he went and joined himself to a citizen of that country; and he sent him into his fields to feed swine. And he would fain have filled his belly with the husks that the swine did eat: and no man gave unto him. And when he came to himself, he said, How many hired servants of my father's have bread enough and to spare, and I perish with hunger! I will arise and go to my father, and will say unto him, Father, I have sinned against heaven, and before thee, And am no more worthy to be called thy son: make me as one of thy hired servants. And he arose, and came to his father. But when he was yet a great way off, his father saw him, and had compassion, and ran, and fell on his neck, and kissed him. And the son said unto him, Father, I have sinned against heaven, and in thy sight, and am no more worthy to be called thy son. But the father said to his servants, Bring forth the best robe, and put it on him; and put a ring on his hand, and shoes on his feet: And bring hither the fatted calf, and kill it; and let us eat, and be merry: For this my son was

dead, and is alive again; he was lost, and is found. And they began to be merry." (Luke 15:10-24)

Greek philosophers were blamed for corrupting Christian beliefs. Many people are now an extension of these philosophers. They represent man trying to do it his way because he wants to have something to do with it. We cannot grow without an opposing force. We are to learn with God's help to overcome this world. We are choosing in this life where we want to live for eternity. Once we have made that decision, choose Christ Jesus to become our Lord and Savior and ask Him for forgiveness, we begin the process of sanctification. Tried and tested are we: **"All the commandments which I command thee this day shall ye observe to do, that ye may live, and multiply, and go in and possess the land which the LORD sware unto your fathers. And thou shalt remember all the way which the LORD thy God led thee these forty years in the wilderness, to humble thee, and to prove thee, to know what was in thine heart, whether thou wouldest keep his commandments, or no. And he humbled thee, and suffered thee to hunger, and fed thee with manna, which thou knewest not, neither did thy fathers know; that he might make thee know that man doth not live by bread only, but by every word that proceedeth out of the mouth of the LORD doth man live. Thy raiment waxed not old upon thee, neither did thy foot swell, these forty years. Thou shalt also consider in thine heart, that, as a man chasteneth his son, so the LORD thy God chasteneth thee."**

"Therefore thou shalt keep the commandments of the LORD thy God, to walk in his ways, and to fear him. For the LORD thy God bringeth thee into a good land, a land of brooks of water, of fountains and depths that spring out of valleys and hills; A land of wheat, and barley, and vines, and fig trees, and pomegranates; a land of oil olive, and honey; A land wherein thou shalt eat bread without scarceness, thou shalt not lack any thing in it; a land whose stones are iron, and out of whose hills thou mayest dig brass. When thou hast eaten and art full, then

thou shalt bless the LORD thy God for the good land which he hath given thee. Beware that thou forget not the LORD thy God, in not keeping his commandments, and his judgments, and his statutes, which I command thee this day: Lest when thou hast eaten and art full, and hast built goodly houses, and dwelt therein; And when thy herds and thy flocks multiply, and thy silver and thy gold is multiplied, and all that thou hast is multiplied;"

"Then thine heart be lifted up, and thou forget the LORD thy God, which brought thee forth out of the land of Egypt, from the house of bondage; Who led thee through that great and terrible wilderness, wherein were fiery serpents, and scorpions, and drought, where there was no water; who brought thee forth water out of the rock of flint; Who fed thee in the wilderness with manna, which thy fathers knew not, that he might humble thee, and that he might prove thee, to do thee good at thy latter end; And thou say in thine heart, My power and the might of mine hand hath gotten me this wealth. But thou shalt remember the LORD thy God: for it is he that giveth thee power to get wealth, that he may establish his covenant which he sware unto thy fathers, as it is this day." ()Deuteronomy 8:1-18)

Scripturally God makes himself responsible for everything that is occurring here on earth. We can slow the opposition down considerably by understanding the Gospel. Jesus Christ met the same penalty not for His sin but ours. Scripture study was a real eye opener for me; I had no notion what was in the Bible although I listened to many sermons. God is not at all what some preachers make Him out to be. God says work out your salvation in fear and trembling. Man is overwhelmed by the sinful world because society is infiltrated with lies causing much confusion.

Even if one frowns on a person of one book, the Bible is the most important book on this earth. Hitler tried to overturn the Bible by wanting to start his new World Order that included exterminating designated people. God's plan also included these designated people to fulfill His prophecy. Hitler was unsuccessful. We have now again

Taming The Lion

a New World Order that is to be `user friendly'. This one is all-inclusive under the pretext of peace. The goal behind this one is only larger, more encompassing than that of Hitler. He could not get it done with his elite. It was not powerful enough. By combining the whole world politically, economically and spiritually, it is thought that the prophecy of the Scriptures can be overthrown. When beneath this agenda, civilization is still trying to rid itself of the Christ by neutralizing authentic Christianity.

Scriptures forecast a merging of religions with government. Pope Paul II has a following of approaching a billion Catholics. Evangelic organizations are lobbying Pope Paul II to raise their image into the Pope's light. Merging all religions will create power over all nations individually to make peace because many members within their nations are part of the religious world community. A new religious, politically correct World Order of the rich and poor is on the horizon. The Holy Spirit will have to leave to make room for this powerful beast to come into its own. Five hundred television channels will make a World leader accessible to everyone. God wants the Gospel available to all and Antichrist wants to be seen worldwide when he proclaims himself to be the new ruler of all nations.

When the question of truth comes up, what is it? That depends on what kind of truth one is looking for. Is it about this present existence or our reason for existence? Mormons proudly announce that they know where they came from, why they are here and where they are going. That was what I was grappling with throughout my life. There had to be more to it, than just existing for the sake of existing. Finding the truth to that question kept me digging for answers. I had fallen for Satan's lie in the garden of Eden: **"And the serpent said unto the woman, Ye shall not surely die: For God doth know that in the day ye eat thereof, then your eyes shall be opened, and ye shall be as gods, knowing good and evil."** (Genesis 3:4-5)

Since Satan does everything backward, the truth of this Scripture was "'You will surely die,' the serpent [should have] said to the

Taming The Lion

woman. `For God knows that when you eat of it [the tree of good and evil] you will be made blind, and will [not be like God], knowing good and evil." No one had ever mentioned that to me. I believed Satan was telling the truth. God showed me that He expects us personally to participate in this struggle to understand truth. He gave us a brain and placed the Holy Spirit of truth into our hearts to help us figure the Bible out. Before He fully participated, I had to acknowledge Him as part of the all-knowing Godhead and take myself out of the drivers seat. We cannot depend on other persons to teach us.

About creation there is only one truth and that is the Word. The question is really, how much do we want to know? Do we really want to know the whole story from beginning to end. I for one needed to know. I made a full circle in 61 years right back to square one and realized I could have saved myself a lot of money, time and heartache if I had just stuck with that one book and done more with my life than I have. In my opinion God set us up because we didn't listen in the first place. We end up back at His doorstep only for Him to tell us: `I told you so!' My mother used to say, `if you don't want to hear it, you have to feel it.'

During my final working days, a Feminist approached me to join her group. She showed me a book that related to the movement she had joined. The cover of the book portrayed a cross with a fist in it. She had discovered watching me at work that I cared about the customer I was serving. She found that unacceptable. She admitted to being a Satan worshiper. I asked her: what attracted her into Satan worship, she said power over people. She said: "you are on dangerous ground." I said: "not so, God is in control of this universe, not Satan." I asked her: "who is your god?" She replied: "I am one with all." I said: "and then what? You really have no existence, do you? When you become one with the whole universe, you are really at the mercy of good and evil forces and that could have disastrous consequences." I told her in Christ, we know who our leader is. He exemplified his leadership by laying down His own life for us. Becoming one with a glob is dangerous. Cosmic

Taming The Lion

Consciousness is a consciousness of this planet, an oversoul of collected knowledge used to get an advantage over human beings in addition to benefiting mankind. As a participator a person could easily become the disadvantaged. Without standards of good and evil, there is nothing to prevent a person from becoming a victim. In God's kingdom, victimization is impossible because there is no death. Why not run with an eternal winner.

In 90 AD a letter from the Apostle John to the children of God stated the following: **"But ye have an unction from the Holy One, and ye know all things. I have not written unto you because ye know not the truth, but because ye know it, and that no lie is of the truth. Who is a liar but he that denieth that Jesus is the Christ? He is Antichrist, that denieth the Father and the Son. Whosoever denieth the Son, the same hath not the Father: (but) he that acknowledgeth the Son hath the Father also. Let that therefore abide in you, which ye have heard from the beginning. If that which ye have heard from the beginning shall remain in you, ye also shall continue in the Son, and in the Father. And this is the promise that he hath promised us, even eternal life. These things have I written unto you concerning them that seduce you. But the anointing which ye have received of him abideth in you, and ye need not that any man teach you: but as the same anointing teacheth you of all things, and is truth, and is no lie, and even as it hath taught you, ye shall abide in him."** (1 John 2:20-27) At some point in the future after the thousand year millennium this world as we know it is destroyed and replaced with a Celestial existence of perfect harmony. Christ is about submission, not extremism. Jesus is described as the lamb, a healer and the teacher. He humbled himself to the washing of his disciple's feet. If that is extremism that needs elimination, I must be having a problem with language. The biggest problem we have in trying to identify Christianity: we look for Christ in people and wonder why we cannot find Him. Jesus stated that His kingdom is not of this world. The world cannot recognize Christ; only the Holy Spirit can perceive the spiritual. That is why Jesus was crucified. Christ said on the cross: **"...Father, forgive them; for they know not what**

they do. And they parted his raiment, and cast lots." (Luke 23:34)

Getting rid of what New Agers call extremists (Christians), will maintain all those practicing Satan worshipers behind closed doors. The Holy Spirit located in the hearts of extremists [Christians], will disappear with them. The Holy Spirit restrains evil from total expression. I for one, would not want to remain on earth when He is removed. In the flesh we cannot live with God, in the soul we cannot live with God, there has to be a spirit birth in us. As Jesus was a Holy Spirit fathered first-born son of God, so do we have to be Holy Spirit born. Without that new life we cannot be part of God. To be in God, we have to be in Jesus. To be in Jesus, we have to be in the Holy Spirit and the Holy Spirit has to be in us. We all became flawed through Adam's transgression and need redemption. All that is asked of us is the following: tell God that we are sorry for being so blind and ask His forgiveness and believe that Jesus was God in the flesh who died for our sins, resurrected and went back to heaven to prepare a place for us. We become justified [receive rightness (righteousness)] through Christ Jesus. The Holy Spirit takes care of the rest. He becomes our intimate teacher.

CHAPTER 6

IN YOU I TRUST, O MY GOD

It was two o'clock in the morning; someone was banging on the mobile home door. "Open the door," we heard, "let us in!" We got out of bed and opened the door. Next they yelled: "we are here to repossess the mobile home, now!" We had two children, two and six, and not believing what I heard, I asked: "what do you mean right now?" The sheriff anxious to get it done, answered: "We followed you from West Palm Beach (2000 miles), and you are not getting away again. I came personally, to make sure of that!" We finally got him to sympathize to at least give us a day or two to try to get the money, just $360 and pay it. We had no friends who could help, so we had to relinquish the trailer and find an apartment. My husband was working for a freight line company in sales but only making commission that was not enough to cover expenses.

We found a German lady downtown in one of the old overhauled apartment houses. She was generous. We had no money as usual. She made a little basement apartment available for us. So grateful and so tired of begging, I insisted on getting a job as a waitress. In getting acquainted with other people, I found that other women were having marital problems as well. It was a human condition. One day at the restaurant a horrible incident happened. A waitress who had six children found herself widowed. Her husband had mixed rat poison in his beer and died. "Why?" I asked: "you have such a wonderful family." In shock herself, she confessed: "my husband decided that I would be better off without him because we could not make it financially. He took out a $30,000 insurance policy and waited till the time of the suicide clause had passed. When he knew the insurance carrier would pay, he killed himself to get $30,000 to his wife for the children. Of all the human tragedies I had heard about, that one stuck with me over the years, I had a hard time dealing with that. It would not have happened if they had God in their lives.

128

Taming The Lion

A police officer stopped me one night after work, "you need to get a Colorado license plate," he said with a big smile. "I have been watching you." It wasn't long before the rent was overdue again and it wasn't long before we had to move again. It was close to Christmas of 1957. We found a little motel room for $15 a week. By now it had been ten years of this kind of life. My oldest son was now in first grade. He was upset with us, we were fighting all the time. He was hanging signs up in the one room we all occupied together with the words: "please stop fighting!" My husband had little interest in the boys. He went out a lot to keep himself from thinking about our condition. When he got involved with the boys, he was teaching them skills like boxing. He loved to watch boxing matches and promised to pay them a dollar for each bloody nose. That upset me. We were in constant turmoil about everything.

A job was available in a little fast food chain open 24 hours a day. Babysitters were out of the question since there was no money. With the first hundred dollars I bought an old `Nash' automobile shaped like a beetle. I spent more time in the public library with self help books. I began to realize that one could control one's environment. One could make people ineffective by not tuning in on the verbal abuse. In my conversations with God, I determined that we could probably make my marriage work out over time, if I took a permanent job. In total submission to my situation, I stopped fighting it. My husband began staying away for two and three days at a time, trying to make it hopeless for me to work because someone needed to tend to the children. Determined with all this newfound knowledge that I could manage, I kept hoping to fulfill my dream of one happy marriage. I wanted my family to stay in tact. My mother and father managed to stay married till they died giving them fifty years together. They provided a wonderful example to all their children. They had rough spots but kept working it out.

In my heart I believe God couldn't put up with it anymore. He had watched me suffer with this person for ten years and called a halt to it. My life was about to take a 180-degree turn. Christmas

Taming The Lion

was coming up and I could not sit by without anything for the boys again. In getting acquainted with co-workers, I got to know a young man who was working his way through college. He worked nights to pay for college tuition. I think his high chef's hat might have triggered something in my mind. My dad was a chef during the early years of my life. George was his name kept asking me if I had a sister. He was looking to get married. Our eyes met often working together and little by little a romance began to grow that way. I found myself thinking about him more than I wished to and of course everyone else around us began to notice that something was happening between us. He was having physical symptoms from frustration of not being able to date me and I was beginning to have more problems at home.

We were only one month apart in age, twenty-eight. He was shy and kept his distance since a wedding band decorated my finger. A person does not have to be in physical contact or even near a person to have love happen. Christmas came and went. A big box with a lot of little toys and gadgets went over big with the boys.

Coworkers were coming to us, telling us about the stars in our eyes. "What are you going to do, you two are in love?" We would look at each other and giggle and keep working. We had not discussed this with each other even. My husband must have noted the joy I was feeling in my heart because we got into a most awful fight. He threatened to leave. Quietly, I said that would be okay with me. He looked at me in shock and began pleading for time. He said: " give me six months and I'll shape up, we'll get the house you always wanted and if we do separate, you get the children." I don't know what made me think that he would stick to his word, because he had never done that before.

Living on hope had become a way of life. From experience I knew he would not behave, but I believed that I would have the boys in the end because he did not show much interest in them. After this episode, I asked George, to take me home. A confession of what had transpired was appropriate now. He agreed and I shared that I had fallen in love with him, that I was not interested in an

Taming The Lion

affair, but that I was interested in marriage to him. Love or devotion to another was outlined in the book I was reading as the most potent energy that contained within it healing of all hurts, material blessings and general happiness. In my estimation if love were present from both partners compatibility would take care of itself. To my delight, his interest had also developed and the people around us had been correct about both of us.

From a practical point of view, after five years of college, George only had one year left to get his degree in engineering. The college he was attending was the most prestigious in Colorado. How could I miss but have a worthwhile life with him and my two sons. As steadfast as he was, I had no doubt that my future with George would be quite an improvement.

There were of course hurdles to overcome. He told me it would be hard to convince his mother that I was the right girl for him, because she had problems over every girl that had an interest. "I'll take care of that," I promised. His mother surprised when I invited her to her favorite restaurant, agreed to come to the American Legion Hall. We met and clicked almost immediately. It was strange. Now I know why: she participated in Eastern Star, a Masonic organization and was the wife of a member in the Order of Elks. Their children had participated in Masonic youth organizations: DeMoleys and Daughters of Job, of which I was kept uninformed for thirty- four years. Studying literature about this area was apparently causing a meeting of the minds. We felt comfortable with each other. I found out that George had stopped going to school and she was anxious about that. I told her that I would devote myself to get him back to college. That was what she wanted to hear.

I want to state here while I'm on the subject of ancestry such as parents, grandparents, etc. involved in Freemasonry, they bring generational curses into play on families along with their spiritual effects. People with ancestors in Masonic organizations or cults are spiritually drawn by these same organizations because their rituals involve oaths and so called prayers that are uttered over their family's future lines. Satan and his fallen angels have influence over our lives for Satan's gain just as God has influence over our lives when we submit to Him.

During this allotted six months extension of time to work out our problems, my husband collected evidence against me for future court proceedings. He had lied to me but pretended to go through the motions. Instead of really giving it another try, he set up a scheme so that I would be forced to move with him when the time came. It was long before the six months were up on a Friday, he told me he was going up into the mountains to throw himself off a cliff.

As naive as I was, I believed him. I was horrified. My body went numb that whole weekend. Terribly worried and unable to determine where he went, I had to resign myself to just wait for Monday. It came and he came home. He said he had to leave town, since the police would be looking for him. In unbelief I said: "why?" He said; "I cashed a whole series of bad checks; fifty of them and went to Las Vegas to gamble to get us a house. Please help me pack and let's leave together as always." We had $28 between us. "You can have half", I told him. He began pleading for our oldest boy. He said that he would go completely down the drain if he had nothing to live for. He promised to go home to his family and start over. There was no way I could make that decision. Turning to my seven-year-old son, I asked him: "do you want to stay with me or go with your dad?" In my heart I was hoping and relying on being chosen by him. To my deep disappointment, he chose his dad. Emotionally, I was cut in half. Helping them pack their clothes, I drove them to the train station. To go all the way to the train with them and wave goodbye was impossible. Half of me was walking away from me.

The police came the next day wanting to find him. In those days leaving the state put people out of their jurisdiction. He had returned to his parents in Philadelphia and could not come back to Denver because he was wanted. The stage was finally set for me to get this matter settled without his interference. The decision to divorce was made and I started dating to get to know my future.

Taming The Lion

Of course I wanted custody of both boys but the lawyer I used informed me that an oral agreement was as good as a written contract and that it would be considered a legal contract. I had agreed to let my oldest son go with his dad. The lawyer could not change it.

Devastated having to be without my oldest son and slightly scared about getting into another relationship after ten years of hurt and pain, I needed time out and comfort from my own family. My parents had disowned me over my husband. They wanted me to divorce him since they could not handle how he treated me. I was anxious to get my relationship back with my parents.

To rush into a new life blindly was not as easy as I thought. My friend was sad and thought sure this was probably the end of our relationship. That old Nash was on its last leg. My young three year old climbed into the car with me. After ten years of marriage we had only a few household items, such as vacuum cleaner my husband had received as a gift instead of money, a set of that waterless cookware that he had tried to sell, a scrub brush and bucket, a broom and my husband's tools: a hammer, saw and chisel. My sister's clothes, my accordion and the famous suitcase with embroidered hope chest articles neatly stashed in the trunk. We began our seven-day tour. We were to drive 2400 miles. The axle cracking underneath the beetle and the clogged radiator kept speed to a turtle pace. Even at forty miles an hour, it overheated continuously. Every time a truck zoomed by I had to get off the road on the two-lane highway. My son and I were consuming pop continuously to replace the sweat. Not expecting my mother and father to take me in made a difference when I arrived and all went well. Apologies did not come forth from them and I did not care. To be back with mom and dad was all that mattered.

My whole family had moved to Miami. My parents had a restaurant on Miami Beach. In constant touch with George, I could not separate from him emotionally. My mother kept reassuring me that he did not love me, or he would have followed me to Florida. Reassuring her that he did love me and that the very reason I loved him was his respect for me. He allowed me the space I needed to make up my own mind. The lawyer in Colorado was trying to negotiate the divorce. He had been trying to get papers served to my husband. My husband told the sheriff that this man the sheriff was looking for, did not live there. The sheriff did not know what to do next. Without serving the notification of the divorce hearing there could not be a hearing in Colorado.

My mother again begged and pleaded not to go near my husband that it would cost me. She said, "don't take your boy near him." Again I had to follow my heart. Disobedience is costly. Had I read the Bible and been obedient to it, I would have saved myself a whole lot of more grief to come. The Bible would have warned me with this verse: **"Honour thy father and thy mother, as the LORD thy God hath commanded thee; that thy days may be prolonged, and that it may go well with thee, in the land which the LORD thy God giveth thee."** (Deuteronomy 5:16)

As a child I had an extra dose of charity and enjoyed doing chores for people. My mother had a tendency to gear into that charity to serve her purposes, because they were always in business seven days a week around the clock' there were many things to do. Because of my tendencies I had to keep distant from my family. She wanted me to dedicate my life to her. She had been through a lot and I had compassion for her and loved her dearly.

In my case, she had problems with her grandchildren, my children, being half Italian. Germans became very prejudiced through the Hitler regime. The Fatherland was everything and the Aryan race was everything. Mixing blood with other countries was an abomination to the whole family and is still going on with German relatives that are alive. I was an outcast because I had intermarried. My family had not offered to help care for my son. I felt I had no choice but to take him with me and meet the situation head on. Somehow I still trusted my husband to stick to our agreement. It is impossible to understand other people's minds and hearts. There had to be something of myself in this man, I reasoned.

Taming The Lion

My youngest sister was involved with a man she wanted to marry and he would not respond properly to it. It did not take much to persuade her to come along with me to Colorado. From Miami to Philadelphia is about twelve hundred miles. We were within 75 miles from our destination, when the Nash came to an abrupt stop. There was nothing I could do to move it. The transmission froze. "It will take at least three days to rebuild it and will cost $75," the mechanic blurted out. Used to problems I unpacked our stuff and called my husband's brother's wife to see if she could come and get us. She did more than that; she offered to give us a room. We accepted gratefully not realizing that they wanted to have control over us while we stayed there. They also allowed us to use their car. We went to the sheriff's office to announce that he could now get his papers served by our identifying my husband.

My two sons flew into each other's arms when they got back together. It was obvious they missed each other as much as I had missed my oldest son. My life had revolved around my two children and part of me had gone out of me when I lost my child. To get it resolved was next to impossible. My son had high hopes, that we would all be together again, but goodbyes came only too quickly. It was time to get back to the car. My sister-in-law suddenly withdrew the car. She informed me that she could not get me back to the car that my husband would accommodate us. Some miles down the road on the highway, my husband suddenly started a fight of such magnitude, that I asked him to stop the car, so we could get out. My heart began beating too fast telling me to do something. My sister and I took our suitcases out of the car. When I went to take my son into my arms, my husband grabbed him and raced off. My son was screaming in his arms.

My sister and I sat on the highway with our suitcases and found out soon that we were trespassing according to the police. Hysterical and on my knees I began talking to God: "don't ever give me children again, if this is what you are going to do with them and me." I knew then and there, that I had lost everything I cherished. Intensely brokenhearted I repeated over and over: "he lied to me, he lied to me!" He had broken his gentleman's agreement. A vague memory of the Book of Job from the Bible began to unravel right in front of me. **"I cry unto thee, and thou dost not hear me: I stand up, and thou regardest me not."** (Job 30:20)

In spite of what I felt at that moment, I knew God was the only one I could count on. There had never been anyone else. For a mother to have her children torn from her bosom after laying down her life twice also brought Jesus to mind when He was in the garden of Gethsemane pleading with His Father: **"Saying, Father, if thou be willing, remove this cup from me: nevertheless not my will, but thine, be done."** (Luke 22:42)

God was teaching and He uses the rod when he has to. I learned first hand who my Father in Heaven was. He did not cut corners. Then He kept bearing down on me with: **"Dearly beloved, avenge not yourselves, but rather give place unto wrath: for it is written, Vengeance is mine; I will repay, saith the Lord."** (Romans 12:19) If I had not listened to that one, the price could have been even higher.

My head was reassuring me that I would come back to retrieve the children somewhere along the line. God was in control of my life, not my husband. He had never taken up his responsibility as a husband and father. God was dealing with him as well as myself. He wanted to make a son of God out him, even now.

A police officer came almost immediately. Timing has been a way to identify God's involvement. "Can't you read?" hollered the officer. "No pedestrians allowed!" Tearfully I told him what had happened and he said: " I can't help you ladies, he kidnapped his own child, neither of you have custody. You will have to work that out through the court." With my father's help the bill for the repaired transmission was paid. George in Denver helped with fifty dollars to get us back to Denver. We were not going to leave without an effort to try to retrieve the children. First we drove to the school and talked to the administrative clerk. She had strict orders not to relinquish my son to his mother under any circumstances.

Taming The Lion

Next we went to my in-laws where the boys lived with their dad. My husband was at work. My three and a half year old son was there. He was busy investigating his new environment. His last comment, I'll never forget: "Mommy, come to pick me up!" His little mind could not comprehend what was happening. When I didn't return his mind blocked me out of his memory.

God was teaching me to walk His walk regardless of what I thought. His will had the highest priority in my heart and that kept us from complete destruction. At that point I already knew God well enough to depend on Him even for my children's safety. Pleading with my mother and father-in-law to have mercy on the children did not achieve anything. They knew the truth. My father-in-law had a little paring knife on the drain board and looked at it, stating that his son threatened him. It would be his life against mine, if I tried to take my son out of that kitchen. My father-in-law was not a big man and in his sixties and my sister, a strong German girl asked me: "shall I take him?" "No!" I said: "God will deal with this in His own way." My father-in-law died in his sleep two years later.

My mother-in-law told us to wait till her son would come back from work. "Surely, he will do what is right," were her last words. "You will have total responsibility of the boys without reimbursement," I told her and begged to no avail. They were very poor. My father-in-law had a small railroad pension.

My husband came and sat down at the table, after he retrieved a briefcase from his room. It looked as if filled with all kinds of documents, at least four inches thick. He pulled out papers that he had lifted out of my purse while we were still together. He called his lawyer right in front of me to verify his rights. Transient, between living quarters, I was from another state and could not prove a home for the children. He had the upper hand even legally. There was no doubt now in my mind that he would not honor his own oath after what had just happened. He had taken acting lessons and this drama was probably his best performance. He might have been talking to no one on the other end and had the briefcase stuffed with newspapers to frighten me. He stated after he hung up that he planned to take me to court and that the children would be present in court listening to his stories about me. He said it would be his word against mine. In his plan to lie about me, he planned to tell the court that I was a drunk like himself, indoctrinating his sons with wrong teaching and infidelity. For that moment defeat was imminent. Nothing was written down about our past, I could not prove anything about my husband.

Not only did God expect me to turn the other cheek, but also to love my enemy and forgive him. Diligently, I kept these biblical principles in front of me and began walking this painful walk. For a year straight, I cried daily. God honored every bit of my effort to continue to please Him. In trying to live the gospel in some respect, I was failing miserably in another area because of lack of knowledge. My relationship with God became very real to me during these painful years to come.

Planning to stay in Philadelphia to get a lawyer was quickly interrupted. God had put someone with me, to keep me from being as foolish as I had been. She emphatically stated: "you promised to take me to Denver? Lets go!" With my head hanging, in tears, I had to put the whole matter into God's hands. There was no other option that I could see. We climbed into that old Nash and headed west. We were crying over spilled milk together. Keeping my mind on constructive thoughts to prevent depression, I had a habit of reading and picked up a magazine. God knows our habits and works through them. He knows what we read and whom we listen to. There was an article in it about Solomon and the two mothers who came to him. One mother had suffocated her baby during her sleep and had decided to steal the other mother's baby and claimed it to be hers. She put her dead baby in the other's arms. The mothers knew their babies and knew what had happened but could not prove it. King Solomon said: "get a knife, and cut the living baby in half, give each mother half." The real mother had the knife in her hand and handed it to the other mother, because she could not do it. King Solomon gave the baby back to its real mother. Case closed. The writer of the article stated that whoever loves the most gives up.

Taming The Lion

God was teaching me through my experiences, how to become a godly person in spite of everything. Light began to break through that God was dealing with me personally.

That was really the beginning of looking at life from a different perspective. Events were analyzed from then on. My car had broken down within seventy-five miles of my husband out of five thousand five hundred miles round trip travel. It was uncanny. It became obvious that someone other than myself had set the stage. Before I had wondered about strange coincidences, but this one I could not put aside as a coincidence. Convinced there was intervention and continuing with tangible undeniable evidence, there was no way I could miss it and not become a believer. God wanted to encourage my undertaking of really applying Scripture teachings to my life. He wanted to show me that the Bible is true.

The final decision was to let God handle this problem in His own way and I placed both of my sons into God's hands. It proved to be the only decision possible from what I found out later. People in general persecuted me for allowing my husband to get away with everything and assumed that I was running out on my children. In my heart I hung unto allowing the Word to run my life regardless of what it looked like to others. God confirmed that many years later. He brought a mother into my life who had six children. Faced with the same dilemma, she had followed her human instincts and went to court. Her family had become a disaster from going through one custody suit after another. Both parents had lost their resources paying lawyers to get custody. They had no peace. Their problems went unresolved, affecting all their lives.

I was reaping what the Bible teaches. Had I studied the Scriptures before I got involved with astrology and the occult teachings I would have known what the reward was for such behavior: **"But these two things shall come to thee in a moment in one day, the loss of children, and widowhood: they shall come upon thee in their perfection for the multitude of thy sorceries, and for the great abundance of thine enchantments"**. (Isaiah 47:9)

Taming The Lion

I had lost the children, because I had been into forbidden fruit. Dabbling in Satan's territory had caused the changes that I was entering into. Satan teaches: if you are willing to pay the price, you can have anything you want. The magnitude of the cost is not revealed until it is too late. The horoscopes did not reveal these events, reason being horoscopes are only usable for psychics who channel information.

My husband told his friends that I had died. One of his female friends found one of my letters and wrote to me a twenty- five-page letter. I found out just a few years ago that he secretly married this lady without telling the boys. He did not move in with her because he had free housing at his parents. The marriage lasted less than a year.

Keeping track of my family was not easy. It took intervention from God to keep in touch. God was faithful throughout all the years. My husband built our house. He sent me pictures of the boys and himself in front of this new house, enticing me to return to Pennsylvania. After the death of his father, he had to move on and sell the house. He never moved into it.

Somehow information through a phone call at packing time or a letter of their whereabouts kept me connected to them. He moved to California with the boys and every time they moved, God provided an avenue for me to stay in touch. He was teaching me to trust Him completely during those years. He made it possible to bear the separation although there was no physical contact for fourteen years with my children. My husband did not trust me because he could not trust himself. To go through this experience is harder than having a child die. A mother's heart is with her children and their wellbeing.

The three men lived together and relied on each other. My husband began to work in construction and provided for them for twelve years. He sent me an audiotape of their conversations about their experiences and pictures of their camping trips and flights to visit family. In spite of everything I lived with the hope that somewhere along time he would have a heart and bring them back to me. He knew how much I loved those boys.

For me a job at the airport was next, so I would be right there when they arrived. Also watching the highway thinking one day they would come walking down the highway became a preoccupation.

One of the benefits working for airlines was free travel after a year. The day of the free ticket did not come until 1968, ten years later. I had reservations to fly to my children and suddenly fell terribly ill. Completely crippled from head to toe over night, the ticket became obsolete. Again God intervened because the timing was off. My day came four years later, when I got a call from my divorced husband. "Do you want me to send the boys out to Colorado?" the words traveled to my unbelieving ear. "What did you say?" He repeated the question. "Of course!" I screamed back in delight. "When are they coming?" I laughed. He replied, "I'll let you know as soon as I get their tickets."

My heart was dancing. Plans for all the sightseeing we would do in one week flooded my mind. Wonder what they look like in person, I thought. Excited I peered through the crowd rushing through the gate at the airport. There they are. I knew it, yes, there they are. The connection was still there, as if time had stood still. My heart held no doubt when I first laid eyes on them after many years that they were in fact my sons. They had grown to be six foot four inches tall. A refrigerator full of food and a large bowl of fruit was our communication. We went to a department store, one of the boys needed shoes and I said: "help yourself and get what you need." They did and stayed within reason. Next we went sightseeing to Colorado Springs, the Air Force Academy and all the other spots to look at. The week did not last long enough for all I had planned. My heart stood still again at the thought of giving them up again. It became clear that I could not have sent the children back and forth over the years. God had the right idea. Heavyhearted I brought them to the airport, promising myself from that day forward to visit them annually no matter what.

Taming The Lion

This was 1972, fourteen years later, it wasn't about my heart but about my telling my sons that they needed to move out of their dad's house because by now their dad had seven children living with him. He had married a young woman, twenty years younger with three daughters and a son. My husband had been unreasonably jealous as a young man and my sons were now grown men and both very handsome. German and Italian genes make a great combination for children.

My sons felt a responsibility toward their father and were not planning to move out. I was to pass on the news that their father was expecting them to move out. At the airport I told them the good news and their lives began to take different directions. Every year now began the difficult task of mending our relationship and visiting with each other. It was a long hard struggle over time because a lot of damage had been done. For my husband to keep control of the situation he unrelentingly painted me as a witch that they would not wish to be with. Little by little the mountain separating us became smaller and smaller and we have embraced each other ever so gradually. They each married and began their own families with their own set of problems that taught them how to understand what had happened to them as children. Somehow I had to prove to them that I was not the runaway mother I had been made out to be and that I loved them with all my heart.

God had been my pilot and together we walked a tightrope. It worked. My divorced husband had another son and his third marriage ended in a bitter divorce. They had sold their house and made ten-fold return on the house, which was a great deal of money. He had never taken control over himself, his alcoholism and general behavior. The marriage disintegrated again not without extreme emotional damage to a few more people. His third wife was Jewish and took him to court for child support. She did not allow him to see his youngest son for over ten years, confirming the Scriptures: **"Be not deceived; God is not mocked: for whatsoever a man soweth, that shall he also reap. For he that soweth to his flesh shall of the flesh reap corruption; but he that soweth to the Spirit shall**

of the Spirit reap life everlasting. And let us not be weary in well doing: for in due season we shall reap, if we faint not. As we have therefore opportunity, let us do good unto all men, especially unto them who are of the household of faith." (Galatians 6:7-10)

He has no contact with his youngest son at this time I wrote this. His son later had a child out of wedlock and needed money. He did seek out his dad but it is always about money and that did not last very long. They have no contact anymore.

To help my son understand what happened when he was abducted and to witness to him that God is ultimately in control, motivated me to tell this story. A loving Father in Heaven is waiting in the wings for us to show those that are willing to try life His way to prove to us that He is truly with us watching us and helping us grow into His sons and daughters forever. Anyone who chooses Him will begin to see Him set the stage to teach the principles of the Gospel one by one. We find that no person on earth has that kind of love for us. His Gospel principles work every time.

CHAPTER 7

YOU REFINED US LIKE SILVER

As we entered Colorado, my sister asked me: "how do the cars get up one mile? I heard Denver is a mile high?" Laughing I reassured her, not to worry, they place the cars on a scaffold on ropes and pull them up. Little did she realize that her life was about to change as well. George in Denver was waiting. He never in his wildest dreams thought that our lives together would become a reality.

"Divorce granted," shouted the judge as the mallet came down on the podium. The lawyer proceeded to tell me that I had custody of my second child. To get him extradited, I would have to go to court in Pennsylvania. My husband did not attend the hearing nor did he contest what the lawyer had presented. In fact years later he wanted proof of this divorce. He thought I had made up a story.

Amazed that my life was really going to change, the tears flowed again. The struggle was over finally. My little wedding was set for two weeks later, one day after Christmas and we were to move to Miami. It was in my heart to go the highest mountain and spend my wedding night as close to God as I could. It snowed so hard that night that we headed south instead. The celebration was with my husband's neighbors, two sisters, both single and George's mom and dad. We exchanged vows in a Baptist church accompanied by my 'reincarnation author' friend and her husband.

The little old Nash tied to his Buick we began our journey to Miami. George had never been out of Colorado. He was raised by doting women and enjoying comforts of long nights in bed. "Is it always going to be like this," moaned my new husband as hot water headed for his face when he removed the radiator cap. The radiator had overheated from pulling an extra load. The excitement of being bride and groom obviously didn't last very long.

Taming The Lion

On a second time around, reality about marriage had set in and before the contract signing, certain rules had to be established. While growing up, for some strange reason my prince charming had to be a poor man. It was the rebel in me who did not wish to fit into the mold my parents were creating for me. My mother came from people who were not afraid to work and help out. My grandmother was fun to be with. She and her friends liked to sit and play cards. The men smoked cigars and all enjoyed glasses of hot wine and telling jokes. They simply had fun being together. She was widowed during the First World War and took her husband's place much like my mother had done through the war. My father's people were aristocrats. I found royalty way back in the line and it made a difference. His people were aloof, critical and hard to know. My mother did not realize that one can only get `class' genetically. She worked hard to overcome her status and did not really change. The children have a little of both, divided a little differently in each child. My mother wanted us to marry aristocrats. None of us did because we moved to the United States. Even if I had remained in Germany, there was no attraction to that level.

There is a lesson in this. Desires should not be engaged in haphazardly. My first husband had an unusual sex drive, which led me to wish for a man who had as little as possible. My first husband would not work well under others and never held a steady job for long while I was with him. Out of these unmet needs evolved the future man. God has a tendency to give us what we ask for if it is conducive to our spiritual growth. There was a quality in this man that was essential to bring to pass what was to happen next. What I realized over time was my independence. God had to spend a lifetime on me to break that independence. For me it was stressful to be subject to authority. Needing to be in the lead, I was comfortable with people who were willing to be in a lesser role. This tendency developed from being a girl in a household where only boys were wanted. My father wanted sons and my mother came up with four females and finally the last one was a boy.

Taming The Lion

My new husband had grown up as the oldest in an all girls home and loved to cook and bake and tend to the household. We worked out well together, but it was as far from what I had in mind as the Sun is from the Moon. God puts obstacles in our path to make us grow. This man allowed me freedom in anything I wanted to do. Not realizing what he had in mind, I walked into uncharted waters again without the slightest notion of what I was getting myself into. After one major failure, the goal became willingness to pay even a greater price to make it work. The one and only rule I set was that I would work without interference. He was making $50 a week when we met and for him that needed to reach. He wasn't planning on being more productive.

Florida's economy with mostly low paying jobs presented a challenge for ordinary people. People from Colorado have a hard time adjusting to hot, sultry weather. My new husband soon decided that Florida was not for him and complained until we were back in Denver. Working together made a big difference. With a $300 dollar down payment we assumed a home loan and began fixing up a little house.

My husband's incomplete education became the next issue, which lasted till he was too old to try again. Plans to go to college began to gel for me. My new partner had never agreed to go back to college and after three times of trying to pick up where he had left off, he decided to let it go for good. I gave up on it too and concentrated on becoming who I needed to become. For me there was no way around taking the lead position looking at the future over time. It just was not working to be the little wife waiting for someone else to gear into what needed to happen. He laid his fifty dollars on the table and that had to cover. It did not matter to him what I thought. It was going to have to do. We never argued but discussed the future calmly and if the conversation got heated, he simply went to bed. Used to constant fighting this method was not so easy to adjust to. Sometimes I got so frustrated, I parked somewhere to just scream it all out. He liked to sleep twelve hours a day. Eating too much was the other favorite.

Taming The Lion

Kitchen chores became our communication system. We always did that part of the day together, cook and wash dishes. It removed the pressure of having to perform a certain way. We did not realize until many years later that our conversation revolved around spiritual subjects. He had no interests but was steadfast with a job. Over time he got involved with yard work and watching sports on television.

Taking our jobs serious as little as they were, made all the difference in the world. God has a sense of humor I realized. He puts extreme opposites together hoping it will bring growth to both parties. Scripture states that we reap what we sow. Rejecting my first husband's sexual advances was reaping rejection now when I was hoping for just the opposite. I had to be doing the bidding with little success. He preferred to sleep. It became obvious quickly that changing partners was not about leaving problems. It was about exchanging one problem for another.

God teaches through our environment and He wants to be number one on our priority list. He is not going to give us circumstances that endanger that priority. He is a jealous God. Being a very dedicated person he had to keep me from getting around people who would take advantage of that. Developing characteristics that are pleasing to God are for example unconditional love. How can we learn that without subject matter? Developing talents is another high priority on God's list of dos and don'ts. He was turning me loose to discover who I was. We have no idea until we explore and get involved. Times were still good through the sixties. Opportunity for a low cost college education was then a possibility. An abundance of energy had been part of my heritage and God had a whole lot planned for me.

"Out of a hundred IQ tests your scores landed on the bottom of the pile," the counselor pointed out. "I would not even try to go to college in this university. You would never make it. These young people you would be competing with come fresh out college prep courses and know the subject matter. You have no background in any of it and would be competing with such kids. Not only that, you

Taming The Lion

are too old," he emphasized, hoping I would leave. I timidly asked him: "what courses would it take for me to get in?" "Remedial courses in English and algebra," he stated. Thanking him for his time, I left and went straight to admissions and signed up for remedial courses. To everyone's surprise, they offered me a class for honor students the following semester for doing so well. By spring of 1960 I enrolled in a full load of college courses at the University of Colorado with a major in psychology. God was about to teach me endurance and what man's sciences were about. If I had known what I was attempting to do, I would have never set foot in that college.

In my case He developed fruits of the Spirit in my daily challenges. My faith in God gave me the courage to walk this walk. The tuition and books came out of my own earnings. There was one hurdle after another and walking the extra mile became habitual. There was no other way to get there. He stretched my patience anyway He could, but I learned to keep walking regardless of what it looked like on the outside. Inside I knew He would not let me down. My goal was completely irrational and derived from wanting to help people who had problems. Little did I know then what was behind all that. I wanted a profession that was supposed to have answers. Clinical psychology was the long-range goal that meant Medical School. Setting a high goal gets the energies to a higher level. The mind has to adjust to long-term discipline. It kept me from getting more involved with the occult. Ultimately God had other plans for me but wanted me to experience the sciences that man had invented. Psychology was the perfect subject for me because it proved that psychologists had no answers to help people improve their lives. The only applications that had anything to offer were lobotomies and shock treatments. These kinds of cases were usually found in institutions.

Newly married, a family needed to happen again. My first husband had said: "you can make a new family, I can't." My schedule became pretty hectic. Working, college and babies along with a husband took a lot of juggling. Underlying all this, I had a

Taming The Lion

burning desire to become part of the American mainstream. Somehow people could always detect my accent and the conversation would go to the holocaust. The question came sooner or later: "how could the Germans allow that to happen?" People refused to believe that the German public did not know what Hitler was doing in neighboring countries deep in the woods without the consent of the people. Germans lived in fear of the Nazi Party because they did not shrink from picking up their own neighbors to camps.

Wanting to loose my accent, I reasoned if I were to saturate myself with the American educational system, I would get rid of it. I was hoping my heritage would disappear. Instead I found out what is going on under the surface in the United States. One of the most cherished attributes for someone like me who was raised in a totalitarian government is freedom of speech. I soon found out that is not really the case.

The college professors were molding their eager students as they came through the classes into what they wanted to see in leaders of the country. It is not noticeable until someone comes to class with a different background. In a class "English Composition" for instance the teacher went so far as to select my paper and ridiculed my religious connotations in front of the entire class. He bluntly stated, words implying religious notions would not be permissible in class nor in society. The other area that became clear was the weeding process. Thirty percent of the class members found themselves encouraged to leave in the beginning of each semester. One had to learn to realize that much of it was bluff. Continuing classes regardless of what it looked like helped counteract this weeding process. It meant taking a class twice sometimes to get to the finish line.

In the habit of running independently, I selected curriculum that suited my interests. People had no access to discourage me. My parents thought I was crazy. They were business people and didn't have much use for higher education. I found out later that Hitler had disdain for higher education as well. It must have rubbed off on the general public. Colleges had denied him access to higher education. My parents felt intimidated as I grew in academic understanding. In Germany higher education was for the rich and sophisticated. From a middle class point of view, education was ridiculed as being unproductive.

In the senior year of psychology classes, a teacher sat on top of his desk in front of the class and asked us students what we thought we were going to do with a degree in psychology. He flippantly related what the future held for most of us. "For the clinical psychology curriculum they pick fourteen student from a nationwide pool, who have a four point grade average. Aspiring students had to have had achievements such as football stardom in high school. They had to have parents on the board of medical schools to help the votes to be a `yes' for the candidate." That left me out on all counts. Disappointment was running high as it was, the textbooks really could not produce evidence of curing patients. Even the psychological testing was often productive of error. There was no reason for the existence if psychologists could not promise improvement. Freud was the only psychoanalyst who produced successes, but a patient had to practically live with him and spend a lifetime in therapy. Lots of research was going on, but no product. Disillusioned, I lost interest in psychology but too close to graduating to change major. I decided to finish my education in psychology and graduated in 1973 with BA.

The teacher had been correct. There was nothing one could do with such a degree regarding jobs in counseling. It demanded a Master's degree. By now I had spent 14 years to get to this point. Forty-three years old and I was still unproductive professionally. I was bookkeeping now. Between college courses, I had managed to take a correspondence course in bookkeeping to get some marketable skills. A year later I had completed a year interning in Elementary Education hoping to find work as a schoolteacher. With a BS I spent two years substituting as a teacher. A permanent teaching position was out of reach because there were two thousand applications on the rack at the personnel office.

Taming The Lion

Again I returned to college to take business courses in accounting and management, went through the Certified Public Accountant's test a few times. An interview for a job as a technician in a government agency turned up. It was the lowest level of jobs available. This development for a professional job took from 1959 to 1976.

The State of Colorado hires personnel from a central personnel agency that provides all state agencies with thoroughly tested and investigated employees. They maintain lists of people who have tested for positions. When a request is placed they hire from the open lists of qualified candidates. The lists are usually open for 12 months. Today most agencies have been privatized and the process has changed. Agency heads can hire their friends and relatives if they want to. Salaries have been cut to bare minimum. Three employees took my job at a third of what I was earning.

A temporary position found through an ad became available. On the questionnaire I filled in blanks that applied to any time of day, anywhere and temporary, if not full time. Giving them total access gave me an opening. The test scores have to be good enough to get into the top three spots on the list. I landed in number twenty-five spot. Competing with state employees who had knowledge of government subject matter made for stiff competition. It felt hopeless. This job was under the Department of Corrections that then included mental hospitals. It was not a desirable place to work for most people. The job was temporary which took more candidates out. Nineteenth on the list now, they hired me as a temporary. Temporaries did not have to be in the top three. That was the first hurdle. I began working in the accounting section of an agency as a technician without hope of getting hired permanently. My predecessor was on maternity leave.

Just about the time the six months were over, the girl on leave notified personnel that her husband transferred to another city and she planned to join him. Her position opened. God was honoring my efforts finally. The second hurdle taken care of, there were two more to go. Then instead of hiring me permanently they kept putting the

151

paperwork off. The list closed which meant technically that they could not hire me. My heart told me to go in to talk to the personnel director in our agency. I sat there and told him about the war and other particulars about myself not really thinking about influencing him but just sharing.

A couple of days later I found out that the personnel manager had gone downtown to the State Personnel Department and had the list reopened so he could hire me. We still did not have a green light; I was number nine on the list and needed to be at least number three. They started working on the applications. They could not just cut people. Five candidates had found other jobs that brought me into fourth position. Personnel started interviewing and one person did not show up for the interview that put me into position to be hired. Out of that narrow margin came a sixteen-year career that led me to high positions and the knowledge that we can count on God keeping His promises.

The first two years I worked with people who had group homes for mentally disabled. The director of the agency was institutionalizing people who could be integrated and live directly with people simulating a family environment. The state agency bought a large home, put a married couple into it and placed a group of disabled children with monthly payments per child for food and utilities. Impressed and inspired with the elaborate system they had in place, an opportunity arose for me to develop a whole new level of existence of assisted living. Some people had ability to live in apartments and hold jobs and support themselves with periodic visits from social workers. I traveled and really enjoyed working there. My education in psychology proved to be very appropriate after all.

Life did not settle down professionally for very long. Opportunity came for promotions and I had the education to qualify for many positions. I moved over to the Executive Director's office and managed his accounting section for a year and then downtown to the Department of Labor as a full-fledged professional accountant. Hired as a cash accountant in the Department of Labor and

Taming The Lion

Employment, I found myself in charge of moneys coming in from 80,000 business accounts that were paying taxes for unemployment and thousands of payments going out to the unemployed. Not only did they have these employer accounts but a hundred other sources and investments. The government data processing system and internal systems became new challenges. Because of constant audits, they kept a complete bookkeeping system by hand. Learning was endless and had to be a pleasant experience to want to put up with it. Being in touch directly with the Federal Treasury in Washington D.C. was prestigious. Everything was calculated and done according to specifications. Obedience to rules was extremely important to maintain one's job.

State auditors and Federal auditors parked in our office for months to comb all the detail looking for problems. More college courses became necessary to cope with internal computer problems. By the end of that year they added responsibility for seven employees to my position and I had my hands full. God was holding my hand through this maze of activities. On my own I could have never begun to do what my German supervisor expected me to do. Walking from desk to desk became running. Amazed at what was in me, there was no end to it. Trusting my Father in Heaven to sustain me made it work out by faith daily.

My German supervisor had come to this country as a war bride. Our relationship was never close contrary to what I had hoped for. Employees around me were also expecting it and they would have had a reason to persecute her and me. She did not have an American education and had problems with most employees. Her method of keeping people in line was by creating an atmosphere of fear. When the workload is stressful understanding from others was a high priority but was non-existent.

To demonstrate the stress in another section a beautiful young mother of several children from sheer exhaustion fastened a hose to her automobile exhaust pipe and killed herself. Governmental offices are like giant machines, cold and ruthless. One has to be extremely careful to survive and not be swept up, chewed up and spit out. It happened to some employees in one form or another. Like war, it also becomes an excuse for low morals.

People in management were usually on power trips wanting to build their own political circles, handpicking their employees and expecting favors. My goal was to live the way God wanted me to live, with integrity that meant no politicking. It worked but it was not easy. It required working harder than others because the supervisors tried to put the pressure on to make me move on. They wanted to hire their friends. One had to have an attitude of letting them steal one 's shirt and give them one's coat to survive. They looked for problems to write up, so the slate had to be cleaner than anyone else's.

In 1981 President Reagan took office. His budget cuts caused a layoff of employees. It was done by seniority and I was last on the totem pole in that office. My professional life again was out of control. Many went on unemployment. If there were no jobs with same job titles open in other sections, the state had no obligation to provide jobs. Again an accountant on maternity leave provided my opportunity to move to another insurance carrier, this time Workman's Compensation. While addressing President Reagan, his legislation had long-term effects on my life. He changed the Social Security benefits for government employees. It didn't matter if one had worked in the private sector and paid insurance premiums to Social Security with matching funds from their employers for many years as in my case. I worked for 20 years in the private sector when I retired my Social Security was eliminated. My widow's part when my husband passed away was not paid. Social Security is an insurance paid in by employees. It is not a free benefit from the government as they make us believe.

A new test was announced. I landed in a group of black employees. My supervisor was a young black woman who was running the accounting office as an Accountant III and I was in for a treat being white and German. God had a new round for wishing to teach me how to deal with prejudice. Because my black supervisor was smart, good looking and church going, I admired her, but to my

Taming The Lion

dismay she rejected the fact that I was not prejudice. I was white and in her mind I had to be prejudiced and she acted accordingly.

Raised in Germany without black people, I could not detect prejudice against blacks in my heart and felt comfortable around them until this period in my life. The first black I had met was on the ship to the United States. God's teachings never fail and apply to every level of life that comes up. She insisted that it had to be lurking in me somewhere. Determined to bring it to the surface by creating situations that would make a normal person jump out of their skin, she wanted to see if prejudice would not jump out of me sooner or later.

Remembering one incident especially when we were in a room together going over her evaluation of me. She bluntly stated to me, that no one liked me in the office. Surprised at that statement because I was under the impression that I had many wonderful acquaintances, I urged her to bring them in. "Let's see if they agree with you to confirm your statement. If they do I might believe it to be true," I urged. She quickly changed the subject. Every word I spoke was on the scale for five years, because the wrong word could have been my demise. It was a most uncomfortable situation but I hung in till it was over.

My job was hand posting the General Ledger and formulating financial statements monthly for the director. We had $500,000,000.00 coming in annually from 44,000 employers for workman's compensation and investments and the same amount distributed. The money coming in was invested in stocks, bonds and the treasury to earn interest. They had two totally different data processing systems and hand records of everything. Reconciling the three systems was part of my assignment. Their slush fund was $200,000.00 an allowance that auditors granted for errors. When I balanced to the penny, they did not accept it although everything was documented. They insisted that I had to be dishonest without checking the documentation that backed up what I had done. It is interesting to be doing life the way God sees it. I was spoiling their fun with the slush fund.

Taming The Lion

Hoping to upgrade one more notch, I was working hard to prove I was worth it. Seven years in the same level had been a long haul. Many prayers went to God unanswered. My upgrades in pay were invested for retirement. In government 10% of the pay stays in their public retirement fund. In addition to that they now pay Social Security and Medicare, which is rarely retrievable. Most public employees loose their Social Security benefits completely.

Five years were up and my supervisor took a vacation during which time all annual financial statements are usually submitted to the Executive State Agency. I had done it before so I thought I would proceed to do it while she was gone and surprise her. When she came back and found out what I had done, she was furious. She had been three months behind over the years and it proved to the State agency that it could be done on time. Suddenly all the accumulated agony I had experienced over the prejudice blew up inside me like a pressure cooker. I felt abused and misunderstood. My intentions had been to lessen some of her burdens.

Not aware that I had been networking with other sections and supervisors, two jobs became available the moment I asked for the opportunity. A friendly smile and a good reputation made the difference. When the personnel officer put my black supervisor in a room with me to see if we could not straighten out our differences, I remained silent hoping she would have regrets and apologize. She did not allow that to happen. The problems were never discussed; I just wanted to move on. I knew there would not be anything gained by forcing issues. She came and shook hands at my retirement party that was to me a sign of acknowledgment.

This time I chose roadwork. Auditing was a man's job and it was my next choice. My goal was personal maturity as well as a permanent annuity to contribute something back to society during my final years. Through this job, my relationship with God grew very secure. Now dealing with people's financial records and personal checkbooks, often threatening their very existence, I really needed God's help. Driving throughout Colorado daily put me into somewhat of a jail cell with a tape recorder, radio and phone.

Taming The Lion

Not in the habit of wasting precious time, I realized that I had a way of giving myself a biblical education. Reading and taping Scriptures on Sunday after church, gave me tapes of the Old and New Testament. In my own voice, I played them to myself during the week. Then for variety I listened to Christian teachers, music and prayers. Every day driving from business to business to examine their books most of the time in private homes was unnerving. Fear of going in was a monster at first. Never knowing what was going to happen behind closed doors and being female did not help.

Scripture study was a wonderful tool to affirm daily that my life was in God's hands. This type of work is high stress and there is never a dull moment. It was another whole life. Often I had opportunity to talk about our Lord Jesus in the privacy of people's homes but also became aware that it provided the policyholder with a weapon that could be used against me. An unspoken rule existed that religion had no place at the workplace.

When the job deals with other people's purse strings, agreement about the billing was rare. Insurance is unproductive and something paid last if at all. Workmen's Compensation is mandatory and engendered many battles with policyholders and employees who got injured on the job. Driving in city traffic all day every day was not conducive to peace inside a person. Supervisors were constantly at odds with decisions that us auditors made at businesses on the road and writing up audits till one and two in the morning left no time for anything else.

Boldness was never part of my makeup but God wanted that to be part of this person. God became my closest friend during the next six years after training. The job was the hardest I had ever had. It took a year of training. To classify businesses by the danger of their activity brought much controversy. The price hung on that decision and they had hundreds of classifications.

This stretch was about putting myself aside. A person of many talents, I liked to sew, paint and name it, I wanted to try it. It was not easily brought down. It had to go and I knew it. My personal life disintegrated right in front of me except church on Sundays. I worked with a group of dedicated men. They had families and everything depended on their jobs and they submitted. Each had a religion of some sort to deal with this kind of work. All too often we had to put the final straw that broke the camel's back on people and they lost their business. My respect for American employers grew and I was grateful for this new understanding.

Employees have little understanding of what the burdens of employers are and what they give to keep people working. Many times employers went without pay to keep people in money to take care of their families. People who employ others in small businesses usually have a need to provide a living for people. It gave me another understanding of God's provision for us. He placed these desires into a certain number of people to provide for us. What amazed me more than anything was the discovery that the people's lives were all hanging by a shred financially, yet in most cases they kept things going. That became the daily miracle. It was as if an unseen hand held life in place for people. God is active everywhere. This underlying love in people for each other keeps life moving on day by day.

Sometimes someone did capitulate like one lady. She threw her hands in the air and said: "I'll go scrub floors before I'll come forth with one more piece of red tape." And she meant it. She did close down a beautiful printing business. Thinking one of these days the governor would get involved and do something, but instead they began privatizing the agency. Government was throwing their hands up too. They had fifty million dollars outstanding in uncollectible insurance premiums. They held meetings on how to collect it.

One day all of us employees received notice that we had to either become private employees or begin looking for other jobs. They were privatizing. The governor threw the problems to the employers and said, "you do it!" They chose employers and their employees and a former state employee as director of the new Board of Directors. Screening processes of prospective employees by state personnel were dropped. None of these people had the foggiest notion of what the insurance business was all about. They took the top layer of supervision and the director out to pasture and began new machinery.

Monetary upgrades for higher performance were slower because politicking helps and it was off limits in character building. Prayers seemed to go unanswered. Performing at a higher level moved my `standard performance' to a higher level. Being female did not help. Three years before I reached the final upgrade, Auditor III, I had a dream.

According to Scriptures, God sometimes communicates through dreams. On an elevator, wanting to go the third floor, I found it was under construction. It just did not go up. It kept me hanging in and after three more years the opportunity came. I had been eligible for ten years. It meant taking on an extra two hours of driving. I knew God would help me make it through.

Young unmarried college educated women had taken the supervisory jobs, making half of what I was making was upsetting to them. That was really at the bottom of it. These women began redesigning the system. They spent untold hours in meetings. The new healthcare strategy such as preferred medical providers came out of this design. They even attached medical teams to their unit and people had to get used to using prescribed care by designated providers (doctors). Anyone who did not comply in the system was excluded. One could not hire employees without workman's compensation. Grace periods for payments became a week and if the money was not in they lost their coverage and their opportunity for business. An added problem became penalties and interest to delinquent accounts. It was mandatory to have coverage. The unions now bemoan a drastic cut in benefits.

A prestigious glass high-rise with spacious offices, all new office furniture and health club on the main floor was next. The workforce almost doubled within a few years but wages and benefits were cut to less than half for new hires. Every employee was on their own wage scale and raises were up to management and kept secret.

A friend of an employee was hired as a programmer. He developed a new computer program that went from fifteen screens of available information to thirty-four hundred screens. They were collecting unusually detailed information about employers, which meant that much more work for auditors. They had to collect this information to feed the computers. The programmer developing this computer program got lost in his own system and had a nervous breakdown half way through completion of the program. Someone else had to pick up the pieces. When the day of the big switch came, the program did not add correctly and the way they wrote the program, it had to be dismantled layer by layer to get to the problem. Employees spent many weekends on their own time at the office doing hand records to keep track of payments coming and going.

The public has no idea what goes on behind the scenes. God was so wonderful; my boss suddenly informed me that they were not going to give me assignments anymore, four years before I was ready to retire. Because God had prompted me to save my increases and invest them, I now had the money to buy the remaining four years to get full retirement. The timing could not have been more perfect. To add that computer break down to the burnout I was experiencing could have put me over the brink psychologically.

The last transaction for me after I had retired was a court case. A man killed on the job had left his family penniless. The employer had the burden of covering the loss and had no money. The employer's policy lapsed within a few days of due date, because privatization had many new rules and the grace period had been practically eliminated. The death occurred just days later. The hearing never took place because they had no case. The policy ceased to exist just a few days before the accident. Putting the federal health care on top of the benefit package already in place is going to add a tremendous, possibly insurmountable burden on employers.

Taming The Lion

The retirement party came and went, and all was well, so much for social and financial success. Getting through it all on God's terms was not an easy ride, but I am grateful to Him for making it all possible. My spiritual education written in Romans 5:3-5 **"And not only so, but we glory in tribulations also: knowing that tribulation worketh patience; And patience, experience; and experience, hope: And hope maketh not ashamed; because the love of God is shed abroad in our hearts by the Holy Ghost which is given unto us."**

This Scripture does not only apply to our salvation but also to our daily lives. It is a spiritual principle that works. God is faithful, He states: **"I know thy works, and thy labour, and thy patience, and how thou canst not bear them which are evil: and thou hast tried them which say they are apostles, and are not, and hast found them liars:"** (Revelation 2:2)

We have the opportunity to build character anywhere we are. God's goal for us is such that: **"According as his divine power hath given unto us all things that pertain unto life and godliness, through the knowledge of him that hath called us to glory and virtue: Whereby are given unto us exceeding great and precious promises: that by these ye might be partakers of the divine nature, having escaped the corruption that is in the world through lust. And beside this, giving all diligence, add to your faith virtue; and to virtue knowledge; And to knowledge temperance; and to temperance patience; and to patience godliness; And to godliness brotherly kindness; and to brotherly kindness charity."** (2 Peter 1:3-7)

Taming The Lion

CHAPTER 8

BLAST OF THE TERRIBLE ONE

As to not to confuse the issue, this chapter played out during the early days of my marriage to George and represents the spiritual part of me. Because humans function on more than one level it is impossible to integrate it when addressing one level of life that is as full of action as the previous chapter. As human beings we wear several hats. We have at least a public life and a private life and many also participate in organizations, such as churches, clubs, sports or Lodges of various kinds.

Past twenty-eight years old, going back to the struggle for material success, two more babies and a night job to pay for books and tuition, took staying power only God can provide. The only time I used babysitters was during finals (college tests) and usually some critical occurrence would come up for the baby-sitter to complicate matters. Nine years later still maneuvering toward the finish line, I was getting three hours of sleep a day for eight months straight.

In the teachings of `The Power of Positive Thinking' they advocate that our energies are also unlimited and sleep is a matter of habit and can often be curtailed. In fact in the spirit realm there is no sleep. This kind of thinking is a temptation straight out of the pit. The result was sudden loss of health over night.

A young Japanese woman and I went to a steam bath in March and the next day I was down with rheumatoid arthritis covering my entire body. It was an all out acute attack. My world came crashing down around me once more. The airplane tickets in my pocket to see my two sons in California expired. I could not move to get to the airport. The useless tickets were as useless as my body. My job went and senior classes in college had to be canceled. Weeks of bed rest turned into months and that in tremendous pain.

Taming The Lion

The house we lived in was new and perfect for us. We had purchased it with three hundred dollars down and $135 a month and everything had worked out so far. We even had furniture. Good at recovering old furniture and sewing clothes we saved and managed financially. My husband and I installed a four hundred foot wooden, white fence around the property. A luscious green lawn from seeds had been quite a challenge. I had no desire to let go of this property.

During sicknesses a Christian often finds him- or herself in an unusual spiritual high. At the hospital I was inspired to witness to people that Jesus had given His life for our eternal life with Him. In turn people around me kept insisting that I would be in a wheelchair for the rest of my life that I had an incurable disease and would not walk again.

Somehow I managed to get myself over to the window and watched people walking and taking it all for granted and here was my body all infected and swollen. In rheumatoid arthritis the lining between joints disappears. Bone on bone causes inflammation. Water collects to keep the bones from injury. It is very similar to rheumatic fever. It travels from joint to joint and in my case the spine got involved. I could not lay, not sit and not walk. The pain was excruciating and there was fever that would not come down. The doctor wanted to put me on Cortisone immediately to get rid of the agony. God is so good. Not only did he get literature to me about the side effects, but he put me in touch with a neighbor who was on Cortisone with a broken hip. She had developed side effects and was dying from the side effects. I had a doctor who was shy. He allowed me to decide about my own body. When he begged me to take Cortisone, I said: "no, I'll take the pain as long as I can and then we'll discuss it again."

The fever was uncontrollable and I finally consented to three days of treatment. It broke the disease. It still took two years of work: praying, dieting, changing climate, mother's love and patience to get it completely controlled. I was taking so many aspirins for pain that I was having nosebleeds every ten minutes. Now symptoms are so minor that my present doctor rejects the notion that I ever had it. The symptoms remind me to get enough sleep, eat right and not take my body for granted.

With television, Christian sermons became a way of life on Sundays. Exciting preachers, musical groups and movies like the "The Greatest Story Ever Told" and other fabulous biblical films became part of the American scene. Billy Graham, Rex Humbard from Ohio, Pastor Blair from Denver were preaching invitations to come forward and receive Christ.

The political scene was in turmoil. Robert Kennedy had come through Denver in 1968 and was assassinated while giving a speech. His brother John F. Kennedy, our President at the time, was shot splattering his brain all over, shortly before that day. Americans were in shock and mourning. Famous Charismatic Kathryn Kuhlman held a crusade in Currigan Hall in Denver. She had a healing ministry and people came from all over and stood in line for hours to attend her meetings. There were always a whole lot of people who had to go home for lack of space.

Lucky to get in, I was standing in the last row of the auditorium. I could not believe my eyes when I saw her on stage looking like an angel in a slim white satin dress with big, puffy sleeves. Singing `He touched me' with Dino on the piano, I was moved to the very core of my being. In touch with my heart where the Holy Spirit resides for the first time, I was overwhelmed with His Holiness. I just dissolved into tears of humility and awe before God for such a beautiful moment. It was a gift that I never could duplicate again in other crusades.

She came on a later date to Calvary Temple and preached till two in the morning getting completely carried away with the Holy Spirit's work of touching people. Media was not allowed in her meetings. She loved the Holy Spirit, spoke of Him as someone she knew and had a relationship with. She demanded respect from the audience for His Majesty. It made a difference. From my own experience I found that one could not manipulate the touch of

Taming The Lion

Holiness. The minute one had an expectation of repeating this awesome moment disappointment was the result.

Doubt crept in that a person in today's society could actually have such pureness as to become a vessel for Jesus Christ. The childlike attitude that can receive gifts from the Holy Spirit had become an analytical adult. In my heart I believe the Holy Spirit decides when and whom to give His gifts. One touch from Him lasts throughout a lifetime. Kathryn Kuhlman was on the road most of the time. She had no hours, she spoke of the Holy Spirit and Jesus Christ's ministry till late in the night in a personal way and enjoyed people, children especially. She finally collapsed before she reached seventy and died while receiving heart surgery. It was a sad day.

Satan was planting his seeds into her radio programs. Unwittingly she taught that God has a body. The Bible states that He shows body parts but that He is a Spirit. Instead of teaching that God is a triune God in three personages she didn't include that. I assumed from her teachings that God has a body, which had dire consequences later.

Thinking that I was getting a biblical education, I neglected to study the Bible myself in depth instead of just reading it, during these years. That neglect turned into a grave error. The preachers only concerned with having people come forward and receive Christ, stuck to sermons that had that effect. What they neglected was warning people about astrology, metaphysics, Christian Science, yoga, psychology and all the other little anti Christian movements that were creeping through America causing problems for Christians.

There was no emphasis on personal Bible study. Preachers took for granted that people knew the basics such as Mary's immaculate conception. That the Holy Spirit was the father when Jesus was conceived was unknown to me till many years later. Even though it should have been understood long ago for some reason we don't think about the words we hear and question them as to what is really meant. The 'Virgin' Mary is mentioned over and over and preachers assume that people know and understand the basics but we just hear the words. The conception needs to be taught specifically.

If I had understood that, I would have realized that we can't compare ourselves to Jesus Christ. He is 100% God and 100% human. The occult belief that Jesus was just a divine human being would not have gotten to first base had I understood that. In occult teachings Jesus was divine and a spiritually highly developed man whom we can imitate by doing good deeds. That I had to be born again and become a new creature, spiritually alive in Christ remained veiled till late in life. 'Born again' means death and resurrection in this life. We do not die physically but our old life has to be put to death. We do not have the Holy Spirit in our hearts until this actually happens and it is an event that is discernible. There was a change in my life.

Scripture proof is this verse: "**At that time Jesus answered and said, 'I thank thee, O Father, Lord of heaven and earth, because thou hast hid these things from the wise and prudent, and hast revealed them unto babes.'**" (Matthew 11:25) Jesus said that we can't understand the hidden parts of the Gospel until we are born again and become as little children ready to receive the truth **"Although they claimed to be wise, they became fools."** (Romans 1:22) These lessons were true and painful to learn.

Altar calls, dedication and re-dedications, convinced me that all was well spiritually when it was quite the contrary. Integrating Bible principles into one's life bring the good life but they don't insure security from Satan's diabolic desire to take us to hell with him. That awareness took many attacks to understand.

Absorbed with the world and what it had to offer, I wanted success, prestige and self-esteem. Operating under the power of positive thinking, Robert Schuler's course in Possibility Thinking; M. Williams' channeled 'Believing in Miracles'; Bristol's Magic of Believing and Maltz's Psychocybernetics, I had created a bubble of positive energy that carried me wherever I wanted to go. They didn't teach that God's universe based on natural laws can't be violated without consequences. To maintain equilibrium we have to have both kinds of experiences to maintain a natural balance. Disturb that balance and life becomes unnatural with built in consequences. This collection of positive energy carries with it a collection of negative energy that becomes effective periodically with serious consequences. God did not create us to use spiritual forces, but to be children in the hands of a loving God. Since Adam, most of humanity has not accepted that role and it is reaping the result. The world is turning into Sodom and Gomorrah.. .

Immorality is raging and humanity is disintegrating with determination. Sharing my experiences is a confession of sin and its harvest. It is the result of dabbling with unknown forces. God is a disciplinarian and carries a big stick when we have a desire to come to heaven and live with Him forever. Building self-esteem, loving oneself, learning how to be selfish, has exactly the opposite effect of what God is looking for. He sends us through life hoping we will recognize that we are total spiritual failures. Only at that instance when we recognize our sinful nature, will He come to our rescue and impute His righteousness to us, so we can receive eternal life in Heaven.. Without that imputation we are dead in sin and will spend eternity in hell, wishing we had had more sense. The futility is that most of us are going to loose it over a technicality: `lack of knowledge'. God gave it freely to all, but most are not going to take advantage of the gift because they are too proud and too busy to read the Bible themselves. When someone tries to explain it, they think how can that person know something I don't already know.

The childlike attitude gets us into constant hot water, but without it, we do not have a chance of understanding what God is trying to get across to us. Jesus attracted tremendous opposite forces. They wanted Him to leave the area. People realized that all the sick would be heading His way to get fixed. That is why His ministry had to be short and why His life was hidden to the public as a growing child. My training was about learning to respect the power of the enemy. It cannot be taken lightly. The reason Jesus told us to love our enemy is to get through life as a Christian. We cannot have a long life outside His teachings.

When I got sick, my husband laid down right beside me with tightening of the chest. He was sure he was having heart attacks. We were not church members anywhere and could not call on prayers of a Christian body. I had tried to go to my neighbor's church. When she did not show up to meet me, I did not have the nerve to go in by myself. Church fell through the cracks over and over. We remained married to televangelists and attended their crusades.

On the mend gradually, able to sit in a chair, I could hear the slushy noise of fluids on my joints. My mother visited and seized the moment to move me back to Florida under her wing. I had one more year left to graduate, lived in a new wonderful home with a full view of the mountains and had no intentions of moving. Again God was moving me in opposition to my will through my mother and husband. My husband was offered a job in Florida. He set my life aside and took the job. Our furniture and the house were up for sale just like that. They all drove off to Florida and left me behind with my children to pack up a whole household, I could not believe what they were doing.

Resting every ten minutes, crawling on all fours around the house, weak from being down for five months, I managed to pack up books, dishes and all the rest. The house sold to the first family who came to look it over. A farmer from Kansas with six children began piling their furniture in before I was out.

On angel's wings we made it to Florida by car, my back still inflamed. To my dismay after adding up what needed to be paid against what we received, we had a zero balance. Our rude awakening of just occupying a space temporarily here on earth helped adjust our attitudes about our future.

Florida was going through some dramatic changes in 1969. Not only were the Cubans coming into Miami by the droves due to Fidel Castro, but also blacks were busting up white neighborhoods.

Taming The Lion

The Floridian climate did help to speed up recovery. Burying feet in the hot sand and laying in tub warm, ocean water with the sun bathing my entire body made healing progress at a faster pace. Still limping, I began job hunting, walking the streets for six weeks every day applying and interviewing. My sister allowed us to stay with them until we found a house. My husband had been making pretty good and had saved for a down payment on a house.

House hunting was unique. We found most beautiful homes abandoned for sale, whole neighborhoods full. It was eerie. One could tell there was something wrong. We inquired at a Realtor and he told us that it would be dangerous to try to live there. We kept looking. The way it was done, one black family bought a home in a neighborhood possibly through a white negotiator so the white people did not realize the family that was to move would be black. After moving in, they started trouble in the neighborhood to make the rest of the white families move out.

We finally found a home. With six locks on the back door, I don't know why I thought it was safe. In Florida, builders like to drain the ground by digging lakes that reach down to the ocean under the coral. The extra sand gives higher ground on which to place a home. The torrential rains cause water to build quickly. Our backyard bordered on such a lake. Ducks waddled through the lush green grass and we even had a banana tree. Those lakes can't be used for swimming because ocean fish like sharks can swim under the coral and accidentally land in a lake.

Half a dozen job offers came in and I picked one of the large hospitals to work at. They needed someone in accounts payable. Our office was in back over a repair shop, very close quarters. I found myself working with two homosexual men, two Cubans who had money in Cuba and a supervisor who had married a rich woman and was having an affair with an employee. My tendencies were always to meet people where they were emotionally, treat them with respect and mind my own business. My mother had taught every time I tattled on my sister: **"And why beholdest thou the mote**

that is in thy brother's eye, but considerest not the beam that is in thine own eye? *(*Matthew 7:3)

It was easy for me to identify with immigrants since I had come from another country, but homosexuality was a different story. It had no effect on me one way or another. I tried to ignore it. Homosexuals usually have a special attitude, friendly and hospitable, over compensating to cover up their immorality. Living with them day to day was not an issue.

Dealing with invoices for supplies purchased for the hospital, I noticed large shipments of jewelry. To make sure these were hospital billings, I asked my supervisor and he said: "oh, don't worry about that, we buy the jewelry for gifts for people who donate large amounts to build the new hospital wing." Then one night, I had to work overtime and I noticed my supervisor had also stayed late. I thought, that's strange, he never stays over. It suddenly hit me that he had plans that related to my body. Sure enough, suddenly he was next to me wanting to take my clothes off. In shock, I said: "you must be kidding?" and ran out. I came back to work the next day and acted like nothing had happened, hoping he would respond properly and not try anything else. He was grateful that I did not press charges and left me alone after that.

Spiritually, we are in the following condition: **"And the LORD shall scatter you among the nations, and ye shall be left few in number among the heathen, whither the LORD shall lead you. And there ye shall serve gods, the work of men's hands, wood and stone, which neither see, nor hear, nor eat, nor smell. But if from thence thou shalt seek the LORD thy God, thou shalt find him, if thou seek him with all thy heart and with all thy soul.**

"When thou art in tribulation, and all these things are come upon thee, even in the latter days, if thou turn to the LORD thy God, and shalt be obedient unto his voice; (For the LORD thy God is a merciful God;) he will not forsake thee, neither destroy thee, nor forget the covenant of thy fathers which he sware unto them. For ask now of the days that are past, which were before

thee, since the day that God created man upon the earth, and ask from the one side of heaven unto the other, whether there hath been any such thing as this great thing is, or hath been heard like it?

"Did ever people hear the voice of God speaking out of the midst of the fire, as thou hast heard, and live? Or hath God assayed to go and take him a nation from the midst of another nation, by temptations, by signs, and by wonders, and by war, and by a mighty hand, and by a stretched out arm, and by great terrors, according to all that the LORD your God did for you in Egypt before your eyes? Unto thee it was shewed, that thou mightest know that the LORD he is God; there is none else beside him. Out of heaven he made thee to hear his voice, that he might instruct thee: and upon earth he shewed thee his great fire; and thou heardest his words out of the midst of the fire.

"And because he loved thy fathers, therefore he chose their seed after them, and brought thee out in his sight with his mighty power out of Egypt; To drive out nations from before thee greater and mightier than thou art, to bring thee in, to give thee their land for an inheritance, as it is this day. Know therefore this day, and consider it in thine heart, that the LORD he is God in heaven above, and upon the earth beneath: there is none else.

"Thou shalt keep therefore his statutes, and his commandments, which I command thee this day, that it may go well with thee, and with thy children after thee, and that thou mayest prolong thy days upon the earth, which the LORD thy God giveth thee, for ever." (Deuteronomy 4:27-40)

Addressed to the Israelites, these verses also apply to our lives today. When we accept Jesus Christ as our Lord, we become the children of God just as Israelis were in the Old Testament.

Some Cubans are well known for practicing black arts. One day walking through the data processing section with my Cuban friend, she tripped me to get the attention of the man who was running data processing. She was pointing me out to him. Studying any subject matter gives awareness in that area. Study of the occult gives awareness of psychic levels of activities not perceivable to physical senses. Humans are by nature shielded from that experience because physically we cannot control the spirit realm.

It is too threatening when we experience it. An awareness of an electrical field around this man began to develop and meeting him in the hall electrical impulses hit me from top to bottom. They felt like fiery darts scripture talks about. Another Cuban was hired. As we got to know each other and he wanted to show me what kind of psychic power he had at his disposal. He said: "watch this: I'm going to tell that lady to turn the radio down telepathically and she will do it." She turned the radio to the station he had told her by telepathy. This phenomenon often happens between husband and wife, one will be thinking of something and find the other partner doing it.

The payroll job became vacant and I got the job over the new young man who wanted it as well. The office had such close quarters that it was easy for people to get real close to one another. Scripture warns people about touching people. This new young Cuban came real close to me and I suddenly felt like a lightening bolt had hit me, but no lightening going on. I became disoriented.

I knew that something had happened to me that I had no control over and that I was in trouble. My objective mind was rational, but awareness that I was injured somehow in my electrical body worried me. Through these experiences I learned that an electrical field surrounds our bodies. While driving I became aware of electrical impulses from other drivers when they wanted to pass. In the physical reality we feel discomfort when someone gets anxious behind us and let him pass to get rid of that feeling. The only explanation I had, my awareness (soul) was hanging out of my body. With this kind of damage on the functional level, I had no idea how to deal with it, nor could I go to anyone to get fixed. That night we planned to go bowling. My husband was with me and I could not concentrate on bowling. Scared I began relating to my husband what had happened. There were no words to explain the problem.

The whole picture was not available till months later. In the hope of finishing my education while in Miami, I had enrolled at the University of Miami in several courses including an art class. My sister is an artist and had been teaching me to paint with acrylics. She entered my first painting and won a ribbon and sold it.

I had invited myself to participate in an art show with her at suburban shopping center. We were planning to meet there and spend the day showing paintings for sale. My two boys were with me. Their ages were seven and nine years old. My sister was already at the show busy setting up her paintings. As I got out of the car, she pointed to a man and said: "oh look who is coming!" She mentioned his name. It was her old flame. I had helped her move out of that relationship by inviting her to come to Denver with me twelve years ago.

My sister had met her husband in Denver. She was happily married and had two little daughters. Of course it looked like her old flame and her were still communicating. When I laid eyes on that man, I suddenly became aware of a demonic manifestation. Like a black cloud, it began following me around. Quickly, I jumped back into my car and drove away from there as fast as I could, hoping to make whatever it was following me, go away. That anxiety would not leave and I was suddenly in total fear.

In the spirit world, there are no walls. There is no place to hide and no protection. It even appeared to have an effect on the car. In a mental state where I could get locked up, I noticed a river and was suddenly experiencing scriptural words in my mind. I stopped the car and ran down to the river bank and the words became clear as the water in the river: it was the 23rd Psalm of David **"The LORD is my shepherd; I shall not want. He maketh me to lie down in green pastures: he leadeth me beside the still waters. He restoreth my soul: he leadeth me in the paths of righteousness for his name's sake. Yea, though I walk through the valley of the**

shadow of death, I will fear no evil: for thou art with me; thy rod and thy staff they comfort me. Thou preparest a table before me in the presence of mine enemies: thou anointest my head with oil; my cup runneth over. Surely goodness and mercy shall follow me all the days of my life: and I will dwell in the house of the LORD for ever. *"*

Another car stopped, a lady came running: "are you all right?" Knowing that she might take me to the nearest doctor, I reassured her that everything was okay. I walked back to the car and realized that I had left my children there with my sister and needed to pick them up. I told my sister that I wanted to go home and left. My husband was working on a road construction job and I had no idea where that might be.

My son had to take over. " I have to get to your dad and you are going to have to get us there." To my amazement, my son somehow piloted me to him. I don't know to this day how that happened. My husband came home with us and tried to calm me down and it helped a lot to have him close. My sister came to find out what happened in the evening. Unable to talk to anyone, I stayed in the bathroom till she left splashing cold water on my face to get myself off what was going on with my mind. It was impossible to explain what was going on.

That night my little family came with me to a motel. In the nightstand I found a red Gideon Bible and opened it to the 35th Psalm where David talked to God about all his enemies in pursuit of him and I could see myself in that chapter. The Bible so far had been like reading Greek. It was like reading the New York Times fresh out of another country, not understanding the language. Now suddenly the Bible related to me. Hoping my mind would stabilize we went home the next morning.

In continuing my college courses at the University of Miami I had been taking an art course. I had a drawing of motion sitting against the wall. It was just scribble. My husband's eyes rested on that picture in disbelieve. The thought hit me that he must think I have lost it. That could only mean going to a doctor and sure enough he began talking about seeing one. Quietly, I got my purse and told him, I was going to the grocery store and pick up a few groceries. I was amazed, he let me leave. Thinking to myself, no one is going to put me away, I got in the car and started driving north. The black cloud was there again full force. Every person was potentially a threat in this condition and even animals. Today in 1994 someone might have at least analyzed it. People did not openly discuss this type of phenomena in 1970.

In another Psalm of David 35:1-9 **"Plead my cause, O LORD, with them that strive with me: fight against them that fight against me. Take hold of shield and buckler, and stand up for mine help. Draw out also the spear, and stop the way against them that persecute me: say unto my soul, I am thy salvation. Let them be confounded and put to shame that seek after my soul: let them be turned back and brought to confusion that devise my hurt.**

"Let them be as chaff before the wind: and let the angel of the LORD chase them. Let their way be dark and slippery: and let the angel of the LORD persecute them. For without cause have they hid for me their net in a pit, which without cause they have digged for my soul. Let destruction come upon him at unawares; and let his net that he hath hid catch himself: into that very destruction let him fall. And my soul shall be joyful in the LORD: it shall rejoice in his salvation. "

There is a price to everything in life. Satan wanted to collect. I would not voluntarily give in to him so he tried to take over by putting me into a series of spiritual terrorism. On a spiritual level, I tried to get help from the occult church, I had long since rejected those teachings. My curiosity wanted to check out what would happen. All it produced was skeletons. Not able to enlist help anywhere else, I kept my mind focused on `Our Lord's Prayer' and cried to Him for help. That was the only Scripture, I knew by heart. The Bible confirmed **"LORD, in trouble have they visited thee,**

Taming The Lion

they poured out a prayer when thy chastening was upon them."
*(*Isaiah 26:16)

By the third night without sleep, thoroughly exhausted, I pulled the car into a field. In the dark of the night I laid still praying, I heard a rushing sound like a waterfall, can't really describe the sound exactly. Watching my life going through my mind from childhood on like a filmstrip, I was experiencing a death experience. Considering myself to be a `good person' in spite of everything going wrong continuously, the words `vanity, all vanity' floated through my mind. Vanity was in direct contrast of what I believed about myself. More communication was coming, "I am going to use you and am taking you to the cross." Shocked, thinking I might become a martyr, for lack of understanding, I said: "why me?" A cloud shaped like a hand appeared over my whole body that filled me with a tremendous joy and comfort that was beyond description.

Overcome with a certainty that I was safe forever it took the fear away in an instant. An overflowing desire to shout the good news from the rooftops that we really had this wonderful hope of eternal life. Next there was a vision of all the people in darkness hand in hand and up in the sky was a brightly lit area behind a veil. People appeared to be moving behind the vail in the light. My estimate was that I was witnessing the spiritual condition of man.

Researching the experience later I discovered these verses. "**For, behold, the darkness shall cover the earth, and gross darkness the people: but the LORD shall arise upon thee, and his glory shall be seen upon thee.**" (Isaiah 60:2) This experience never left me. It caused me to look at my life with that prophecy in mind. It took years to understand what had happened in the car. "**The people that walked in darkness have seen a great light: they that dwell in the land of the shadow of death, upon them hath the light shined..**" (Isaiah 9:2)

Because, I had desperately called on God for help, He had mercy on my soul and filled me with the Holy Spirit. "**Ask, and it shall be given you; seek, and ye shall find; knock, and it shall be opened**

176

unto you: For every one that asketh receiveth; and he that seeketh findeth; and to him that knocketh it shall be opened. Or what man is there of you, whom if his son ask bread, will he give him a stone? *(*Matthew 7:7-9). An absolute assuredness that I was now off limits to terrorism filled my soul released all fear of that ever happening again. A desire to serve Jesus Christ also filled my soul, and becoming part of a Christian Body as well. That experience was so powerful that it has remained with me in that form as a constant comfort and has kept me committed to Christ waiting for the day that He would use me directly somehow.

Searching for a phone to tell my husband not to worry, that everything was taken care of, I continued to drive north to Denver and remained on my own for a while to make sure I was not in some kind of hallucination. I walked through the University of Colorado study areas to try and recapture the excitement of the college experience but found myself unmotivated without my family. My youngest son kept popping into my mind. He was close to seven years old and must have been thinking about me. **"Expect me to be home in a couple of days, I'm starting out tonight,"** I told my husband and he was relieved.

Somehow I knew that nobody would believe me, and they didn't. I could not share this experience. My whole family thought it was all nonsense, that I probably had had a nervous breakdown. **"But the natural man receiveth not the things of the Spirit of God: for they are foolishness unto him: neither can he know them, because they are spiritually discerned.** *"* (1 Corinthians 2:14)

My husband listened to everything and humored me along. He was just glad I was back home safe and back to normal. He had gone to a Baptist Church with the boys during this trauma and was probably praying as hard for me as I was.

At the hospital, an extra large check was waiting for me with a pink slip. The Cuban took my job. Some years later, my mother sent newspaper clippings out of the Miami Herald. The director of that hospital was a Jew, had left the United States to hide out in

Taming The Lion

Switzerland. The Miami police had uncovered a group of people including my supervisor and the director of the hospital, involved in confiscating large shipments of jewelry from the hospital. The director transferred the jewelry to his jewelry store to sell it at full price and collected the money. There were payoffs to the people involved who made it possible. This newspaper article answered some of the questions I had, but not all.

The director had left the country when the news broke and sometime later he tried to sneak back to the United States and got caught at the airport. **"Dearly beloved, avenge not yourselves, but rather give place unto wrath: for it is written, Vengeance is mine; I will repay, saith the Lord."** (Romans 12:19)

Searching Scriptures and putting pieces together took years. Just recently, I discovered that the hand I saw, not a physical hand but a cloud, could have been a manifestation of the Holy Spirit. The Holy Spirit is described in the Bible as leading people with cloud manifestations in the Old Testament. .

"He spread a cloud for a covering.." (Psalms 105:39) **"And it came to pass at the seventh time, that he said, Behold, there ariseth a little cloud out of the sea, like a man's hand.."** (1 Kings 18:44) **"In the daytime also he led them with a cloud.."** *(*Psalms 78:14) **" "Shew thy marvellous lovingkindness, O thou that savest by thy right hand them which put their trust in thee from those that rise up against them.** *"* *(*Psalms 17:7)

Regarding the veil which separates us from the light I found these verses: **"But their minds were blinded: for until this day remaineth the same vail untaken away in the reading of the old testament; which vail is done away in Christ. But even unto this day, when Moses is read, the vail is upon their heart. Nevertheless when it shall turn to the Lord, the vail shall be taken away.**" (2 Corinthians 3:14-16)

It is also described in Isaiah 25:4...7 **"For thou hast been a strength to the poor, a strength to the needy in his distress, a refuge from the storm, a shadow from the heat, when the blast**

Taming The Lion

of the terrible ones is as a storm against the wall. Thou shalt bring down the noise of strangers, as the heat in a dry place; even the heat with the shadow of a cloud: the branch of the terrible ones shall be brought low. .. And he will destroy in this mountain the face of the covering cast over all people, and the vail that is spread over all nations."

I had long talks with my sister about this man who showed up at the shopping center, warning her that there would be consequences if she did not behave and that I wouldn't be able to stop them. She kept insisting that this former boyfriend just appeared out of nowhere. It was difficult to accept since we were in a little suburb shopping center.

She told me that one of her children was having problems with a large dog. She had two daughters around the same age as mine. I still had all the occult books and she wanted me to give them to her to burn everything.

Her daughter was suddenly killed in a collision between a tractor-trailer and a car. Her and the family's grief were immeasurable. The two girls had been going to Sunday school and elementary school at a Baptist Church in Miami. The day before her little girl left this life to be with Jesus, she had a conversation with her mother about Jesus. She asked her mother: "are you saved?" Her mother reassured her that she had received Jesus Christ. My sister eventually confessed that she was simply going through the motions for social purposes.

My niece had also complained about her head hurting the day before she died. Her injury was where she was hurting. She hit the pavement head first and died an instant death. Her father was driving a tractor with a flat bed carrying a bulldozer. The brakes sat in water and gave way. Her dad hit a car, killing the driver as he went through a red light without brakes. No seat belt on his young daughters and the impact threw one of them through the window.

The funeral was beautiful. She was just about to turn seven. She had the most beautiful innocent victorious look in her face, I could

Taming The Lion

not be sad. Through her death six people came to accept Jesus Christ. My father and mother were in their sixties and had never been to church that I know of. There was a font up high in the wall of the church behind a large window so the whole congregation could watch.

My father, an old staunch Kraut, a slogan used for Germans, put on a white gown and was baptized. My mother followed suit because she loved him. The mother of this child became dedicated to Jesus Christ through this death and adopted a little girl to fill that spot.

In August of 1982, I spent time with my dying mother at a hospital in Miami for a week. She had a woman attending her at the hospital who remained with people going through this final stage of dying. My sisters had told me: "don't be shocked. You will find mother's personality gone. It feels like she is not there anymore." How right they were. It felt like the entity in her was leaping out at me in a rage. I stayed with my mother for a whole week. I slept on two chairs in the hospital room with her and my mother came back to her body.

Whatever it was in her could not stay in the same room with me. The woman came by periodically waiting for me to leave. I thought she might be able to explain what had happened to me in regard to the incident with the Cuban. She said to me that the Cubans had done a number on me. Whatever that meant I don't know. A pastor had tried to see my mother before I came to visit and this woman would not let him near my mother. My mother with her own presence quietly slipped away a few days later surrounded by her family at home.

Satan was not giving up yet. One certainty I have, demonic spirits were never able to occupy, but they try to deceive every opportunity they get. Satan had a whole new agenda lined up for me around the bend.

Convinced if I shared what happened in my 1960 Thunderbird in a field in the middle of Florida, people would have thought I was mad. There was no way to describe the initial experiences that had caused the situation in conversation. To share my experience with the Holy Bible and the Holy Spirit, I began painting what I had experienced. Bible study should have been next instead.

Painting full time occupied my time for the next twelve months. In the first painting oddly enough, I chose a pyramid, not realizing its implications, because it represents one of the indestructible seven wonders. I believed that God must have been behind that wonder somehow since it still stands after thousands of years and nobody has figured out how they could have built it so many years ago. My pyramid had Jesus Christ with Adam and Eve inside His body intertwined in the top representing the Light of Christ, the cross and His love for us.

In our purses we carry another pyramid on the one-dollar bill that is a well-known satanic symbol used by many businesses as well to gain success with Satan's help. At that time I had no understanding of the power of symbolism. The occult teachings did not belabor the pyramid. They had much to say about the star of David. Egyptians leave the cap of the pyramid separated as it is on the dollar bill where the cap is occupied by the all-seeing eye. The all-seeing eye represents Satan not God. Pyramids are tombs. The reason Egyptians leave the top open is so that their souls can leave after the body is mummified. They hope to be resurrected at some point as well.

In my pyramid I was hoping to paint a circle of clouds with the dark side down toward the people to show the darkness. With photographs of clouds to look at and copy, I began painting the cloud formation. To my surprise and unplanned the cloud turned into a large sleeping serpent in wait of its prey. It did not bite its tail like it does in satanic literature but showed a narrow opening between the head and the tail that led to the cross above. "**Because strait is the gate, and narrow is the way, which leadeth unto life, and few there be that find it.**" (Matthew 7:14)

Taming The Lion

Below the cloud on the dark side were many people with their backs toward Jesus slaving at attaining material possessions. Every person was unique. The crumbling pyramid was more significant than I thought. Pharaoh in Egypt enslaved Jews to build the pyramids.

God made no bones about his intentions and we need to heed what He has to say. We need to take our minds off gaining material possessions and spend time discovering our Redeemer God in our lives. Here are His plans to those who do not read His Word.

"And I saw an angel come down from heaven, having the key of the bottomless pit and a great chain in his hand. And he laid hold on the dragon, that old serpent, which is the Devil, and Satan, and bound him a thousand years, And cast him into the bottomless pit, and shut him up, and set a seal upon him, that he should deceive the nations no more, till the thousand years should be fulfilled: and after that he must be loosed a little season. And I saw thrones, and they sat upon them, and judgment was given unto them: and I saw the souls of them that were beheaded for the witness of Jesus, and for the word of God, and which had not worshiped the beast, neither his image, neither had received his mark upon their foreheads, or in their hands; and they lived and reigned with Christ a thousand years. "

"But the rest of the dead lived not again until the thousand years were finished. This is the first resurrection. Blessed and holy is he that hath part in the first resurrection: on such the second death hath no power, but they shall be priests of God and of Christ, and shall reign with him a thousand years. And when the thousand years are expired, Satan shall be loosed out of his prison, And shall go out to deceive the nations which are in the four quarters of the earth, Gog and Magog, to gather them together to battle: the number of whom is as the sand of the sea." (Revelation 20:1-8)

Taming The Lion

"And the devil that deceived them was cast into the lake of fire and brimstone, where the beast and the false prophet are, and shall be tormented day and night for ever and ever. Revelation 20:10 "And death and hell were cast into the lake of fire. This is the second death. And whosoever was not found written in the book of life was cast into the lake of fire." (Revelation 20:14-15)

The painting took six month of eight hours a day. What followed was a whole series of other spirituals depicting Jesus from the back. Even if I could not share my experience with the people I loved, something had to happen to give vent to what was in me. My sister had taught me how to stretch a canvas and outline a picture and start painting with acrylic paints.

Moved by an impression or memory of particular scriptural subject matter, I painted it and after completion there was the Scripture that described the painting. My husband became the model because I have no ability to draw from memory. Everything came from other physical objects. There is no physical description of Jesus in the Scriptures, except that he had a beard and it says that no one has seen the face of God. Artists, who try to capture the face of Christ, have a tendency to paint their own faces. The second coming was part of the collection.

To share the message, I became part of the art world for the next seven years in Miami and Denver. At the opening of the Denver Art Museum in late 1971, one of my paintings was chosen from all over Colorado out of 1700 entries. The Critic Alfred Frankenstein selected one of my spiritual paintings, my favorite Christ painting. He chose 200 works by Colorado artists for the First Colorado Biennial Exhibit presented December 18, 1971 through January 30, 1972.

Scripture placed on the frame confirmed the action in the painting. In art shows in shopping malls, the group of paintings had the effect of a feeding station. People gathered around them and read every scripture on them. A novice at the business of art and no

Taming The Lion

schooling in it, I had no idea what it meant to be selected to show at the Art Museum. Later I found out from other artists, what an honor it was. Many had tried for years to enter a show like that and getting in on a first try was unheard of. In my heart I knew it was not me who had gotten me into the show but the Holy Spirit.

In Miami while painting, the neighborhood suddenly turned into a disaster. There was a Seven Eleven on the corner. Coming home one evening, passing the store, it was swarming with police with their rifles waiting for people to leave the store. They were in position to shoot or be killed.

A few days later the field covered with bushes across the street from us was set on fire deliberately. Praying that it would not spread across to our place, I was grateful when firefighters came quickly to extinguish it. A few days later, I came home from the store and a man the size of my husband laid on the ground on our lawn getting kicked and beaten. At least ten black young men were around him. They took turns placing and turning their heels in his face. Petrified that it was my husband, I stood there in shock and screamed.

There was nothing I could do as a woman. When they saw me they let go of the man and ran. "I did not do anything, what did they want? I don't understand," the victim cried. "Can I take you home?" I replied. It was clear to me, they were planning to bust our neighborhood. Next a little four year old was merrily riding his tricycle along the sidewalk. A group of blacks took the little boy, tricycle and all, ran through my backyard and threw him and his tricycle into the thirty-foot deep lake. Luckily a man saw that happen and jumped in to rescue the boy. My children could not be left alone for any reason after that. Another move was again in the wind.

Taming The Lion

CHAPTER 9

IN SHEEP'S CLOTHING

Six month of painting had gone by, when there was a knock on the door. Two missionaries stood there smiling in black suits with their bicycles. My usual attitude was not to talk to any people at the door. Another week or two later they came back. "Sorry, but I can't talk to you," I stated. When they showed up the third time, I changed my approach and invited them in, hoping to talk them into forgetting about us. It occurred to me to ask them why they kept coming back. "We pray over neighborhoods and your house was impressed on us," was the missionary's answer. They presented their Mormon testimony and my family, husband and two children were convinced that we had missed a good thing throughout our past lives, by not being Mormons. The missionaries physically picked us up on Sunday after the six weeks of instruction introducing us to the Church of Jesus Christ and of Latter-day Saints.

God was about to show us what cults were all about. Not realizing that these missionaries were lying to us, we found later that their church was anything but the church of Jesus Christ. Being European, I had no idea who the Mormons were. I had not done my homework and studied the Bible myself therefore had no way of telling that they were lying to me. I depended on the fact that Christians were not supposed to lie. God gives us a long rope and even greases the banister when we wish to slide down to the bottom. Inviting these missionaries in was against the rules according to the Word of God from the start and cost us 20 years in a cult, many, many dollars and many, many hours serving them for zero in return all the way around. God did not count that as serving Him even though I thought I was serving Him.

An article fluttered in my memory that had described their puritan attitudes. Mormonism was not traditional like the Lutheran Church, but completely American. That was a drawing card for me, still seeking to break the German image. In trying to join traditional

Taming The Lion

Churches in America, something had always interfered. I tried the Baptists but the loud clapping and excited singing and preaching did not to line up with German churches. In German churches you never talked loud. One could hear a pin drop. The cathedral ceilings so high there would have been an echo had there been any noise. It was a place of utter peace and silence. Altar calls were unheard of and Holy Communion was only for the privileged away from the group and not very often. That is how I identified with a church and my impression of holiness was peace in the sanctuary.

Mormon missionaries talk to each member of a family privately in another room and ask a lot of personal questions. I asked the missionary, "do you permit sinners in your Church?" He said: "of course!" My next question was: "can I reach perfection?" The missionary answered with a "yes" and that was all I needed to know. The last yes turned out to be the biggest lie of them all. Mormons never get there because their theology is solely based on works and it so arranged that they never make it and it is their own fault. They use works to control the sheep. My ignorance in biblical understanding was incredible. What I should have asked: " do you believe in the Trinity? Was Jesus Christ God in the flesh, born of a Virgin and conceived of the Holy Spirit, raised up on the cross to give His blood to cleanse us from all our sins? Did he die on the cross and was He resurrected after three days in the same flesh and bones?" They would have probably said, "yes" on all counts not even realizing that they would have had to lie because that is not what Mormons believe. The missionaries are taught everything that could come up and to agree in trying to get people to join. They actually believe whatever is in the four standard works. They have been taught to turn their brain off. Those books contradict each other but cover all that could come up. They use the King James Version Bible as one of those four books and they learn to recite it. When Mormon children begin high school they start doing seminaries before school for four years to keep them from losing their testimony that Mormonism is the only true church. They study the KJV and memorize verses. They are being prepared for eternal marriages, which includes going on missions for two years and

Taming The Lion

college run by Mormons. .To get married for eternity requires celibacy till marriage. Add the Word of Wisdom to this morality that includes no smoking, no alcohol, no caffeine, no drugs it truly impressed me and did keep my children out of problematic areas. Mormon girls go so far as to turn men down for marriage if they did not go on a mission. From that point of view it was hard for me to believe that they were not Christians.

The missionaries carry the KJV Bible in addition to the Book of Mormon and claim to be subject to it like Christians. Scripture was the facade in the occult Brotherhood of Light as well as in Mormonism. In 1994 I had occasion to be invited when Mormons tried to convert Christians to Mormonism The missionaries are so sophisticated they had me convinced they were born again Christians and insisted that Mormons speak in tongues. Again that turned out to be a lie. Joseph Smith Jr. spoke in tongues and at one point he said that he didn't know whether he was communicating with God or Satan and forbade the church to speak in tongues. I never heard a Mormon speak in tongues once.

"I will instruct thee and teach thee in the way which thou shalt go: I will guide thee with mine eye. Be ye not as the horse, or as the mule, which have no understanding: whose mouth must be held in with bit and bridle, lest they come near unto thee. Many sorrows shall be to the wicked: but he that trusteth in the LORD, mercy shall compass him about. Be glad in the LORD, and rejoice, ye righteous: and shout for joy, all ye that are upright in heart." (Psalms 32:8-11)

What Christians don't realize Scripture promises personal instruction regardless of place or time from the Holy Spirit. God uses the whole creation to teach. He can use any experience.

After my personal experience of being sealed, ideally baptism was very appropriate and attendance in a fundamentally sound Christian Church should have followed. My baptism had happened at three and confirmation at fourteen. John the Baptist was baptizing adults who were repentant. According to Matthews, people were re-

187

baptized to receive Christ fully aware of their sinful natures and the need of a spiritually new nature that only the Holy Spirit can create. Not totally realizing that, I was a sitting duck for Satan to move in on me again. Essential at this point was Scripture study. Instead I left it to God thinking that He would move me into the right Church. From my own experiences I should have known that God leaves our lives up to us. He works directly through our experiences. The information sitting in our brain is not taken away until we leave this life. The only counter action we can engage in is personal daily Scripture study. It is the way to get discernment of the truth. Not until filled to overflow with pure Scripture is Satan stopped. He despises the Gospel. Otherwise there is always another number he can play on us to deceive us. Believe me he has thousands of methods.

Mormonism has a similar concept as the occult soul mates and that was very familiar to me. I chuckled when I heard about their eternal marriage because it fit what I had learned in the occult teachings. There is Scripture in the Bible that alludes to a mystery of God. Mormonism is for the vane. The theology sets people apart as the special select few in the only true church to whom that mystery was going to be revealed.

Men were drawn to Mormonism originally because they could have unlimited women to impregnate practicing polygamy and after they are dead they would receive their own planet from an unlimited amount of planetary systems.

The Mormon teaching also based on evolution is parallel to occult teaching with different twists. Their belief that we were created spirits (souls) first and evolved through various stages, which is more, like a ladder to heaven. Mormon theology teaches that God wanted someone to save this planet and asked for volunteers. Jesus and Lucifer, who were spirit brothers subject to a council of gods, both came forward. In the Pearl of Great Price, one of their standard works, is revered as part of their Bible: Abraham 3:3 **"And the Lord said unto me: These are the governing ones; and the name of the great one is Kolob (star), because it is near**

unto me, for I am the Lord thy God: I have set this one to govern all those which belong to the same order as that upon which thou standest."Abraham3:22,23: **"Now the Lord had shown unto me, Abraham, the intelligences that were organized before the world was; and among these there were many of the noble and great ones; and God saw these souls that they were good, and he stood in the midst of them, and he said: These I will make my rulers; for he stood among those that were spirits, and he saw that they were good; and said unto me: Abraham, thou art one of them; thou was chosen before thou wast born."**

Satan's recommendation was to force people to worship God and save them all and Jesus wanted to give people a choice. God chose Jesus. If God chose Jesus then Jesus' name should have been Satan because that is what this Jesus represented. All will be saved, believers and non-believers, due to baptism for the dead. There is no hell in Mormonism. Because dead people cannot refuse baptism or endowments, there is no free will about it.

I know many who do not wish to go to heaven because they simply do not believe God exists.

In LDS theology, God chose Jesus and Satan got mad. All spirits were asked to take sides; one third chose Satan and left heaven with him, never to be incarnated in a human body. What is very significant in this theology all people are equal to Jesus and Satan in the spirit world since humans were spirits before their birth into bodies. Another most significant concept in Mormonism is that humans have already chosen Jesus in the spirit world. That is how they explain that all will be saved. The fact that Jesus had not gone to the cross doesn't matter. The choice between Jesus and Satan had already been made in the spirit realm. Those who did not get baptized while alive get it done by proxy after they die. These Jesus spirits came to earth and no matter what sins they committed, repentance therefore is irrelevant. For some strange reason they teach repentance at baptism at eight years of age when children are considered innocent of sin or for new members before they become members of the Church, probably to make it look like Christianity.

Taming The Lion

If all humanity is already going to heaven, what reason is there for repentance? None.

Mormons believe that only spirits who chose Jesus in heaven are here on earth in bodies. Brigham Young taught that Adam is really their god. Through Adam all people are automatically saved because Adam was baptized by immersion and received the Holy Spirit Baptism making him the first born Son of God. What's wrong with that supposition? Jesus had not given the Holy Spirit until 4033 later after He was crucified and resurrected. Since the inception of the Mormon Church, members are working on baptizing every living and deceased person (by proxy) so they can receive the Melchizedec priesthood to give all the opportunity to become eligible to live in the Celestial Heaven with God and receive a planet like Adam.

To satisfy that all human beings chose Jesus in the spirit world, they have to make all human beings eligible through baptism. Their belief excludes the Holy Spirit birth necessary for eternal life with God. The word `reborn' is never used in Mormonism.

"Jesus answered and said unto him, Verily, verily, I say unto thee, Except a man be born again, he cannot see the kingdom of God. Nicodemus saith unto him, How can a man be born when he is old? can he enter the second time into his mother's womb, and be born? Jesus answered, Verily, verily, I say unto thee, Except a man be born of water and of the Spirit, he cannot enter into the kingdom of God. That which is born of the flesh is flesh; and that which is born of the Spirit is spirit. Marvel not that I said unto thee, Ye must be born again. The wind bloweth where it listeth, and thou hearest the sound thereof, but canst not tell whence it cometh, and whither it goeth: so is every one that is born of the Spirit. Nicodemus answered and said unto him, How can these things be? (John 3:3-9)

The Bible teaches that God created Adam and Eve in flesh bodies as one husband and wife who bore children. They gave Lucifer their authority, which caused their spiritual death first to be followed by physical death. In Mormonism Adam and Eve believed that Satan was telling the truth when he tempted Eve into eating the forbidden fruit, the apple of the tree of life. They believe that they will be gods. "**And the serpent said unto the woman, Ye shall not surely die: For God doth know that in the day ye eat thereof, then your eyes shall be opened, and ye shall be as gods, knowing good and evil.**" (Genesis 3:4)

Mormons don't believe God when He stated that Satan is the author of lies. Mormons belief spirits are waiting to receive bodies so they will have the opportunity to become gods. Their gods cannot become gods unless they have flesh bodies first. In their theology God has a body of flesh like Jesus Christ. They even have pictures of both standing by each other.

Mormons will be comfortable with the New Age teaching that we are all one. Because all human beings have bodies means that all Satan worshipers, criminals and anti Christians are really Christians because all humans chose Jesus before they came to earth to get their bodies.

In a session with Mormon missionaries recently an Elder came along to help a prospective member to join Mormonism. Called into the situation, I questioned the Elder about his inability to be objective. He made an interesting statement: "I turned my brain off and let them do the thinking for me, when I joined Mormonism." Since I lived in Mormonism for twenty years, I can agree that most Mormons have done that. Really considering their concepts with some scrutiny brings to the surface that they are not even logical. Us humans are so gullible.

In California invited to a celebration of my son's baptism at the bishop's home, my daughter-in-law asked the Mormon bishop's wife: "why do you have so many children (she had ten)?" The bishop's wife replied that she believed that she had probably promised the spirits `bodies' (they cannot become gods without bodies) and wanted to be sure that she had not forgotten some spirit. My daughter-in-law laughed and said to me later: "they are cracked!" Offended, I did not respond but years later found out she was right in certain respects. Mormons are not cracked but taught a lie and it affects every day of their lives in everything they think and do. God is not a love bear but a disciplinarian Who is to be feared. God sent Mormons a strong delusion that they should believe a lie and will be damned if they don't renounce it and submit to the Holy Spirit.

"And then shall that Wicked be revealed, whom the Lord shall consume with the spirit of his mouth, and shall destroy with the brightness of his coming: Even him, whose coming is after the working of Satan with all power and signs and lying wonders, And with all deceivableness of unrighteousness in them that perish; because they received not the love of the truth, that they might be saved. And for this cause God shall send them strong delusion, that they should believe a lie: That they all might be damned who believed not the truth, but had pleasure in unrighteousness". (2 Thessalonians 2:8-12)

To me Mormonism was a hard experience in spite of the self-discipline I practiced on a daily basis. To try to sell other people on joining Mormonism was not in my heart. The responsibility of someone's failure in a church did not appeal to me. Thank God, I don't have that on my conscience now.

My ex-Catholic daughter-in-law got curious about me. She wanted to know what made me tick and talked my son into joining with her. My son had a severe accident soon after their baptism. He fell through a skylight covered with black plastic during construction of a home. Concrete just pored and covered with plywood was protective, but bones shattered in his right leg and wrist. The blessing was that his back and neck remained in tact. After six months of convalescing in casts, he gradually came back to a normal life. My daughter-in-law associated the fall with the Mormon Church and called it Satan's church. They left soon after that. Some intervention can be painful. Again God allowed this fall to intervene.

Taming The Lion

It was easy to switch over to Mormonism from previous occult readings. In trying to convince us to join, they elaborated that they were the only true Church and described the problems Joseph Smith had as a youngster looking for a church. Every Christian deals with that issue because they are looking for true Christianity in action. Men and women fall short of the outward appearance that Jesus exemplified. Mormons' Celestial Heaven (where God resides) depends on their good works and they peddle hard to make it in their own strength. Christians designated as hypocrites the minute they don't measure up are oblivious of this Scripture: "**But we are all as an unclean thing, and all our righteousnesses are as filthy rags; and we all do fade as a leaf; and our iniquities, like the wind, have taken us away.**" (Isaiah 64:6)

This area is one of Satan's favorite hot buttons and the reason I landed in Mormonism. Mormons look like an example of Jesus. Their lives revolve around assignments from the Church. It makes them feel secure that they have something to do with their journey to heaven. It represents having control over one's destiny.

One young pipe-fitter had six children. During a deep freeze, weather-wise, many pipes broke and he fixed them free. He had a lot of other assignments because he was so willing. Concerned with his well-being I asked him one day: "why are you working so hard?" He said: "I don't want to scrub floors in heaven." He confessed one day that his testimony of Mormonism is very fragile and how he tries to avoid us. He is worried I'm going to blow down his house of cards. It explained why generational Mormons don't integrate with converts. It would be difficult to tell someone like him, that you are serving the wrong god. Sometimes I wonder where Mormons shop. They avoid the stores that inactive members frequent to make sure they don't get approached.

Not knowing which Lutheran Church [there are four different types of Lutherans] I needed to join and the black cloud I had experienced in the vision were described in Joseph Smith's prayer and vision and they were also connecting points. These similarities hooked up like magnets. "Which Church is right?" God had told

Taming The Lion

Joseph Smith Jr. that they were all wrong, that he should start a new one. That was logical but not biblical. "The name of the church: The Church of Jesus Christ and of Latter-day Saints confirms that it is the Church of Jesus Christ," insisted the missionary. "There is not a church in the world that carries His name." That proved to be another lie since I found others later that included the name of Jesus.

In the early 1970's the missionary's presentation was their welfare system. Again, ten years of poverty set me up for this strategy. Today they don't concentrate on those areas because it brought too many people with financial problems who needed help. They told us that they would pay our rent if we ran into problems. One could get employment through their employment service and buy cheaper foods through their exceptional purchases in quantity. One could get second hand clothes from collection centers and preserve foods in their canneries. Fruits and vegetables grown on their land purchased for membership to use was another incentive. After the poverty I had gone through, this was manna from heaven. We never used their offers because God provided for our needs to be met from our own incomes. Had I known the truth about this Church, I would most definitely have turned down anything connected with it. Satan comes with a perfect coat for a person to wear. **"My people are destroyed for lack of knowledge: because thou hast rejected knowledge, I will also reject thee, that thou shalt be no priest to me: seeing thou hast forgotten the law of thy God, I will also forget thy children."** (Hosea 4:6)

Tithing would be next to impossible, I told the missionaries, we were living on $104 a week for a family of four. I was not working. "Oh don't worry about that, we often give people money so they can tithe." Their belief is that one's life improves by tithing and to make it improve to a point where a person can tithe, they will pay tithing for a person. How much of that was really going on I don't know. We never used the church for that purpose. There were a few cases when women were in desperate straits and nothing was coming forth from the Church with the excuse that they had not participated

194

in the temple ordinances, indicating that help was only for the elite Mormons.

Dressed in white, three of my family immersed in their baptismal font received the baptism in the name of the Father, the Son and the Holy Ghost. After the baptism we became members of the Church by confirmation and a vote from the membership. Baptism is mandatory to get into the only true church. They teach that new members have be cleaned up with the baptism. The confirmation is done by a group of Elders, Melchizedec priesthood holders, by laying on of hands on new members' heads. One supposedly received the Holy Spirit. The Holy Spirit is also known to be the Spirit of truth. Mormonism is proven to be a cult, built on lies and not of Christ Jesus. It represents another Jesus; the laying on of hands cannot represent the transfer of the Holy Spirit. It is written in John 16:13 **"Howbeit when he, the Spirit of truth, is come, he will guide you into all truth: for he shall not speak of himself; but whatsoever he shall hear, that shall he speak: and he will shew you things to come.***"*

If the following verses in John 1:33,34 **"And I knew him not: but he that sent me to baptize with water, the same said unto me, Upon whom thou shalt see the Spirit descending, and remaining on him, the same is he which baptizeth with the Holy Ghost. And I saw, and bare record that this is the Son of God.***"* are true, how can Mormons be baptized with the Holy Ghost, since their Jesus is a different Jesus. In their doctrine their Jesus is a spirit brother of Satan and all human spirits of the living and pre-existing? Without the Holy Ghost baptism there is no eternal life in heaven.

Mormon Melchizedec priests are temple Mormons that means they are participating in a form of Freemasonry not Christianity. How can they be a vessel for the Holy Spirit? God addresses this question in Scripture as well. Jesus portrayed as the vine and born again Christians as the branches through which the Holy Spirit bears fruit, leaves no doubt.

Taming The Lion

I'm convinced that Mormons have help from the spirit realm in more than one way. Like the missionary said they pray over the neighborhood and are guided to prospects. They seem to know where the newly converted Christians are. Newborn Christians are so grateful to God that their sins have been forgiven, they wish to serve the church in some way as their worship. Converts get all the work done. Only about 25 – 30% of Mormons attend church and are otherwise actively involved. I was in charge of reporting activity in Sunday School.

Members are free to use the membership list for solicitations to keep productivity and earnings within the Mormon family. Within the first year in the church, Mormons approached us to join the Amway hierarchy in Miami. To accommodate them, I invited all my relatives. My family became disgruntled when they found out that I wanted them to participate in Amway. The Amway group got so insistent, that we decided to move, which really upset my family.

Amway wasn't the only reason another move became necessary. My health was back and I was looking forward to completing my education in Denver. We sold the house to a white person who turned out to be a front for a black person. Shortly after, all the neighbors had their homes on the market. People next door were old, they had their life in their beautiful garden. The harassers pelted their house with rocks and my neighbors got the point. We realized a few thousand dollars this time, loaded all our stuff into U-Haul trailers and headed back to Denver. I made a rule from then on: no more moving. We found a house across from where we had lived before and kept close to my parents by visiting every year.

Our records transferred to Denver, we began attending the LDS church every week and became involved in all the activities. After seven years of coordinating the Junior Sunday School and lots of substituting for `no show' teachers, they phased out Jr. Sunday School internationally. That enabled me to attend some gospel doctrine classes. They study the Old Testament for a whole year and then the New Testament. Scripture taught out of context does not take hold in the heart of a person. The teachers only use verses that fit into Mormonism. They had Scripture for everything: the garments, the name change, the plural marriages in the Old Testament, the priesthoods, baptisms for the dead, the three heavens and whatever came up it was Scriptural. Most of their doctrine was never discussed and did not receive attention until after we left. Their standard works contain all the doctrines but they keep people too busy to study. Even missionaries don't know what they really believe.

Never did I see one Mormon disagree when voting in the twenty years I attended. Emphasis in Mormonism is to get all minds into unity worldwide. They frown on disagreement and punish that behavior by demoralizing members in question in some form publicly. New members are inundated with jobs to prove their worthiness. A Mormon has to participate to get the work done. Every member gets assignments. They are supposedly straight from God so there is no choice about it. They teach members that it is about obedience and growing by doing. It is part of their sacrifice to God. With the positions they apply rewards and punishments and build self-esteem. They tell members that leaders fast and pray over positions. When a position becomes vacant, they claim that God personally tells them who should fill that position. One feels very special selected by God personally. Every offer is accepted at first.

If one does not turn one's brain off, certain procedures become obvious quickly. They have an inner circle like any worldly organization that get the choice jobs. Flattered that they had confidence in my ability to serve, I accepted four positions. Assignments are also used to teach conduct and understanding of what Mormon leaders expect from their members. It turns into a never-ending continuum. They have a method of letting people know that they have deficiencies and have a long way to go to make the grade. Just when one thinks one has it all down pat, there is another corner to turn. Women taught by word of mouth, are too busy with chores to attend classes. At least four families which usually turns into six, assigned to each woman to visit once a month to insure that all is well. These visits cause people to get to know each other intimately. Allowing a visit is considered a sacrificial offer to God.

Often people were not too happy to have their time taken up with strangers in their home. Visits were done in pairs causing problems of scheduling. I had continual problems dealing with everything because of my own schedules at school and work. The men get the same kind of assignment and this explains why many Mormon children feel abandoned. Their parents are constantly running errands for the Church. Church becomes the focus of their lives and something is going on every day especially when the temple visits are added. The reason for all this activity is control. Mormons don't have time for television, sports and nightclubs. They have to learn to get along with each other. They are together a lot. They get to know near every detail about each member.

Genealogy is a major issue. Landing in the library right away as an assistant, I spent hours cutting out obituaries for their collection of information. Genealogy became an additional major expense. Researching in Europe, sometimes the only alternative was to hire someone there to unlock a dead end. Also paying for each birth, marriage and death certificate overseas with postage ran into hundreds of dollars. Some bureaus of vital statistics took advantage of researchers and charged hundreds of dollars for documents. The LDS Church wanted accurate records that made these procedures necessary. Researching my family line, I put together 3000 names for temple work. Each name found, researched and fitted properly into the family order, took many hours of dedication. These names submitted to temples the world over, keep Mormons busy coming to temples to do rituals for the dead. They tell people: "isn't it wonderful that you are the savior of all your relatives? Just think how well you will be received as their savior when you get to heaven. They will thank you for setting them free." Jesus has nothing to do with neither the temple nor its work.

The opportunity to get baptized by proxy had an effect on family members who were not members. They put off becoming part of the Body of Christ till after death.

Taming The Lion

Mormonism is a social system within a social system. It fills every need for a person from birth to death. A baby blessed soon after birth, is made to feel that it is being cared for throughout life and eternity. When aged they still receive visits, meals and help with chores in sickness till the corpse goes to a funeral home, untouched by unauthorized hands and buried in priesthood garments.

The tragedy is, it is a masterpiece of a counterfeit Jesus. An example of the grip this church gets on an individual was the passing of George. We had cut all ties to the church 11 years prior to his death. The funeral home called me and wanted to know if they should put priesthood garments on his corpse. The man who was attending to George's body was a Mormon. In shock I told the caller, "absolutely not".

It is difficult to relinquish the brotherhood of this Church because it is real and comforting. The relationship with God has to be personal and have the highest priority before a person can move out of Mormonism. God warns that we need to love Him with all our hearts and minds. This warning is not for His sake but for ours. We cannot get out of the hands of Satan without that kind of commitment. To me the whole Bible was written for that purpose. We cannot have victory without practicing what God teaches. He is not a respecter of persons. We have to care enough about ourselves and take His advice. He cannot do it for us. That is the tragedy of it all.

Adam gave dominion to Satan. God is not on planet earth except by the Holy Spirit and the teachings of the Scriptures. Without cooperation from us God does not bring us out of darkness. We have to ask for His help. God wants all of us but many have rejected Him and the emphasis of the Gospel is on the fulfillment of the prophecy as the Bible presents it.

To me the Mormon coverage of every facet in the physical was very reassuring. If only there was the opportunity to get into God's hands, it would have been wonderful. For Mormons to get into

Taming The Lion

God's hands they would have to tear down the temples and throw Joseph Smith's revelations out to correct the church. Freemasonry has been proven to be Baal worship and is an abomination to God. Books by former 33rd degree Freemasons revealed that they are subject to Satan in Freemasonry.

Mormonism is a form of Freemasonry practiced only in the temples shrouded in secrecy. Participators are under a death threat if they reveal what goes on in the temples. They teach the same rituals, identical hand grips, and good works. There is lots of opportunity to do works for a Christian, only God cannot receive it because works negate what Jesus Christ has already done. "**O foolish Galatians, who hath bewitched you, that ye should not obey the truth, before whose eyes Jesus Christ hath been evidently set forth, crucified among you? This only would I learn of you, Received ye the Spirit by the works of the law, or by the hearing of faith? Are ye so foolish? having begun in the Spirit, are ye now made perfect by the flesh? Have ye suffered so many things in vain? if it be yet in vain. He therefore that ministereth to you the Spirit, and worketh miracles among you, doeth he it by the works of the law, or by the hearing of faith? Even as Abraham believed God, and it was accounted to him for righteousness. Know ye therefore that they which are of faith, the same are the children of Abraham.**" (Galatians 3:1-7)

Mormons are redoing the Old Testament even though Jesus has fulfilled it and ended it. Old and New is not a continuation. They teach that the Church of Jesus Christ fell into apostasy after Jesus died. Although God used the Levitical priesthood to set up His Glory here on earth Himself as written in the Old Testament with the Aaronic priesthood, Mormons tell their members they are from the tribes of Ephraim or Manasseh and are practicing the Aaronic priesthood. All Mormon men take on the Aaronic priesthood to begin with.

Anyone who fulfills their requirements and becomes eligible for the temples can become a Melchizedec priest. There are many thousands of them. All men who have gone through the Temples are

Melchizedec priests which includes missionaries. They have over fifty temples that do ordinances daily from early morning to late at night.

The original biblical Aaronic priesthood practiced within Aaron's family line, is by direct genetic connection. God abolished it when Jesus received the eternal priesthood of Melchizedec. This priesthood is not transferable to anyone else, nor is there any connection to the Aaron priesthood. Mormons are in direct violation of the WORD OF GOD.

"In the beginning was the Word, and the Word was with God, and the Word was God. The same was in the beginning with God. He made all things; and without him was not any thing made that was made. In him was life; and the life was the light of men." "And the Word was made flesh, and dwelt among us, (and we beheld his glory, the glory as of the only begotten of the Father,) full of grace and truth." (John 1:1-4, 14) **" And he was clothed with a vesture dipped in blood: and his name is called The Word of God.**" (Revelation 19:13)

"And Melchizedek king of Salem brought forth bread and wine: and he was the priest of the most high God." (Genesis 14:18) **"The LORD hath sworn, and will not repent, Thou art a priest for ever after the order of Melchizedek."** (Psalms 110:4)

The seventh chapter of Hebrews shows why the Levitical priesthood was done away with. It describes why Jesus Christ is the only one eligible to receive the Melchizedec priesthood. To assume that all men are eligible is blasphemy.

Hebrews 7:1-28 **"For this Melchizedec, king of Salem, priest of the most high God, who met Abraham returning from the slaughter of the kings, and blessed him; To whom also Abraham gave a tenth part of all; first being by interpretation King of righteousness, and after that also King of Salem, which is, King of peace; Without father, without mother, without descent, having neither beginning of days, nor end of life; but made like unto the Son of God; abideth a priest continually**.

Taming The Lion

"Now consider how great this man was, unto whom even the patriarch Abraham gave the tenth of the spoils. And verily they that are of the sons of Levi, who receive the office of the priesthood, have a commandment to take tithes of the people according to the law, that is, of their brethren, though they come out of the loins of Abraham: But he whose descent is not counted from them received tithes of Abraham, and blessed him that had the promises.

"And without all contradiction the less is blessed of the better. And here men that die receive tithes; but there he receiveth them, of whom it is witnessed that he liveth. And as I may so say, Levi also, who receiveth tithes, payed tithes in Abraham. For he was yet in the loins of his father, when Melchizedec met him. If therefore perfection were by the Levitical priesthood, (for under it the people received the law,) what further need was there that another priest should rise after the order of Melchizedec, and not be called after the order of Aaron? For the priesthood being changed, there is made of necessity a change also of the law. "

"For he of whom these things are spoken pertaineth to another tribe, of which no man gave attendance at the altar. For it is evident that our Lord sprang out of Juda; of which tribe Moses spake nothing concerning priesthood. And it is yet far more evident: for that after the similitude of Melchizedec there ariseth another priest, Who is made, not after the law of a carnal commandment, but after the power of an endless life. For he testifieth, Thou art a priest for ever after the order of Melchizedec."

"For there is verily a disannulling of the commandment going before for the weakness and unprofitableness thereof. For the law made nothing perfect, but the bringing in of a better hope did; by the which we draw nigh unto God. And inasmuch as not without an oath he was made priest: (For those priests were made without an oath; but this with an oath by him that said unto him, The Lord sware and will not repent, Thou art a priest

for ever after the order of Melchizedec: By so much was Jesus made a surety of a better testament."

"And they truly were many priests, because they were not suffered to continue by reason of death: But this man, because he continueth ever, hath an unchangeable priesthood. Wherefore he is able also to save them to the uttermost that come unto God by him, seeing he ever liveth to make intercession for them. For such an high priest became us, who is holy, harmless, undefiled, separate from sinners, and made higher than the heavens; Who needeth not daily, as those high priests, to offer up sacrifice, first for his own sins, and then for the people's: for this he did once, when he offered up himself. For the law maketh men high priests which have infirmity; but the word of the oath, which was since the law, maketh the Son, who is consecrated for evermore."

Every Mormon boy grows through the stages of priesthood. How flattering to introduce your son as a priest, twelve years old. My children informed me from the start that they were not planning to go on a mission. The songs were teaching in the junior classes what the leaders of the church expected of them later in life. Told to start saving money for their mission early on, many young men and women began putting their allowances up for later.

Most of the lessons were about Joseph Smith and his vision in the woods, and conduct. I rarely went to the women's meetings because they were offensive about my job. They wanted me to quit and spend all my time at church. I had spent ten years in the streets without jobs and had tried to be home in this marriage with the same results. They want men to work and women to stay home and have children, regardless of consequences in old age. Being dependent on the LDS church keeps the members in their ranks. Many try to leave only to come back to the fold because they have become dependent on their social system.

Their expectations were not fulfilled in my husband; they did not put him in a position for years, not until I approached a member who worked with me. A bishop advised me to get a divorce if I wanted temple marriage. There was uneasiness in my heart all the time. Something was wrong and I could not put my finger on it. When we think of Satan worship, we think of blood sacrifices. Reassuring myself that they would understand the truth one of these days, I kept rationalizing into continuing from month to month and year to year. The members were college educated and in my reasoning mind would not be deliberately serving Satan. The problem was, they were blind to the truth.

My spirit was grieving in me, especially during bread and water sacrament that was supposed to be Holy Communion. In my mind transgressions by members were kept insignificant tied to individuals, because the church of Jesus Christ had to be flawless.

Being a bishop was just a title. They had no formal education in ministry. The leadership consisted of people off the street who had joined. Any member in good standing could become a bishop; in fact the church leadership expected it. The only paid jobs people had were clean up jobs.

My husband did not comply with tithing and attending meetings and that created much pressure on my marriage. A woman has to adjust mentally to one of many wives as Mormon doctrine still teaches. The LDS church does not practice polygamy but it is mandatory in a spiritual sense. That is why fundamental Mormons break away and practice it illegally. They can't change the Book of Mormon because it is the new religion given to Joseph Smith Jr. and their unchanging word of god.

Wives are also dependent on their husbands to get into heaven. If he does not call her name and allow her into heaven, she cannot get in. A man and woman get a new name in the Temple that is necessary to get saved. The husband knows her new name, but she does not know his. It causes strange relationships because the men have their minds on plural marriages as a future prospect. That aspect takes emphasis off their wives. The sealing of husband and wife for eternity gives a sense of security but is often abused. It is difficult to become unsealed (spiritually divorced). Godhood depends on this relationship and focus moves to the spirit existence. In my case I began thinking about what it would be like to be a god. It did not take long before I knew that I wanted no part of it. To be a god must be nothing but grief.

The temple veiled in secrecy, became a stumbling block for me. Jesus did not believe in hiding information. He represents the Spirit of Truth. Hiding information does not give a person a free choice. To be expected to participate blindly in something did not seem to be Christian.

In occult teachings, they spread everything in front of pupils. They thoroughly explained the dangers of certain activities. The responsibility moved to the participant by making him or her sign a contract. LDS members who have participated in the temple take an oath and put their lives on the line, should they discuss rituals, even with family members. Death threats make discussion about the temple impossible.

James 5:12 warns that we should not engage in any oaths: "**But above all things, my brethren, swear not, neither by heaven, neither by the earth, neither by any other oath: but let your yea be yea; and your nay, nay; lest ye fall into condemnation.**"

Satan knows that secrecy draws us like a bird draws a cat. Curiosity was my weakness.

When Scripture does not agree with Mormonism, they parrot that the Bible is not interpreted correctly. In their King James Version is a dictionary and a reinterpretation by Joseph Smith Jr. Their standard works include the Book of Mormon, Pearl of Great Price and Doctrine and Covenants and the Holy Bible. They do not correspond doctrinally. People commented to me that the Bible forbids adding to the Scriptures. LDS answer to that is that they were only adding other books without changing the Bible. If a person attended a class and questioned anything the teacher made it such a negative experience that it would not happen again.

Taming The Lion

My children got tired of the competition. Every member in the church, invited to do family presentations on Sunday, participates. Later I found that it is usually reserved for generational Mormons. Converts are rarely asked. In twenty years they never asked me to speak, though I diligently served. Today I'm grateful that I was spared. There is no preaching in church. Members share their experiences. This sharing enhances unity. Listening to off tune violin concerts was part of one's sacrifice to God.

Bishops are administrators. Now and then they coach people to have more than a travelogue or they read a letter from the prophet of the LDS Church in Salt Lake City. Boredom even got to the leadership. People did not take their responsibilities very serious. The whole curriculum comes out of Salt Lake City. Bible study independently or in groups outside of their prescribed curriculum is discouraged.

After a year of good behavior that includes living the word of wisdom (no coffee, no cigarettes and no liquor), tithing and coming to all the meetings, visiting assigned families, one becomes eligible for a Patriarchal blessing. My patriarch was home alone at appointment time and a stranger to me. He took me to a bedroom in his home. Not knowing what to expect, I was a bit unnerved. He sat me down on a little table with a tape recorder and laid hands on my head and began speaking rapidly about what appeared to be intimate information at the time. Looking it over later, it could have applied to any Mormon.

The result was another lesson about expected behavior from a member in good standing, if they wanted to be in the first resurrection (as if Mormons have anything to do with the first resurrection). The millennium according to Mormonism is for genealogical purposes. The patriarch told me that I was of the tribe of Ephraim and that was technically incorrect according to my genealogy. God has something to say about people who assume a Jewish identity when they are not Jews: "**I know thy works, and tribulation, and poverty, (but thou art rich) and I know the**

blasphemy of them which say they are Jews, and are not, but are the synagogue of Satan. *(*Revelation 2:9)

They would like people to believe that they are channeling this information from God. In my case it was about genealogy. God's Word states: **"Neither give heed to fables and endless genealogies, which minister questions, rather than godly edifying which is in faith: so do." 1 Timothy 1:4 To confirm: "But avoid foolish questions, and genealogies, and contentions, and strivings about the law; for they are unprofitable and vain."** (Titus 3:9)

LDS genealogy records in Salt Lake City contain millions of names sorted by the membership through their personal genealogy. The goal is to establish every person who lived on record within a family and connecting all families back to Adam. The missionaries all over the world have been photographing records in churches, government records of vital statistics, censuses and whatever records of people available such as military, ship and immigration records. The geographical sources indexed by country and province is recorded on films. The films rented directly from the Salt Lake genealogical library by mail are viewed on machines.

Today the records are available `online'. Microfiche is another widely used medium to research. Ironically few members get involved with their family history. Non-members patronize the LDS Genealogical Libraries. Now CD disks with millions of names are advertised from Utah costing over a thousand dollars each (1994). Millions of dollars are spent on these records that have nothing to do with the New Testament. Millions of hours spent by members serving this area, relative to God go unrecognized by Him. Joseph Smith's ultimate goal was to tie back into the Aaronic priesthood to make it legitimate.

Genealogy was an interesting journey that I enjoyed. It explained my genetic makeup. My own ancestry established in their records, dates back to the 1200 and the earliest name was Kersten later changed to Carstens. The earliest paternal great...grandfather was a judge, called into city government to straighten controversies over moneys collected from citizens for building cathedrals in Luebeck, Germany. He moved there and became involved in the political world of this international seaport. The men in my line became bishops of Catholic cathedrals for four generations. They later became Lutherans when Martin Luther reformed Catholicism. Luther lived close to this city.

Freemasonry practiced in conjunction with Catholicism, is still very visible in the cathedrals. An astrological clock, the size of a large wall, still sits by the entrance pointing to paganism. This research became a whole life in itself and very time consuming. Satan's strategy is to keep us busy, like a Ram to be sacrificed but caught in a thorny bramble bush.

Mormons claim that their dead ancestors help them in their search for documents all over the world. It often appeared that way when there was a break through. If they were correct and there was help, it would have been from demonic spirits, since angels would not be interested in baptisms for the dead. The souls of the dead who did not go to paradise are sent to Hades for holding purposes until judgment day. In my heart, I contemplated that it had to be a Genealogical Society using the church membership to sort everything out.

A person could put off their baptism and sealings and have a relative do it by proxy. Relatives of Mormons can be sure that they are baptized and endowed by proxy into the 'body' of the LDS Church after they die. They even added Martin Luther to their collection in the 19 hundreds as well as Adolf Hitler. The deception has the same effect as reincarnation. A person can accept Jesus Christ in a future life if they keep coming back to live other lives until they have overcome their Karma.

In truth these religions are lies. If we are not already committed to Jesus Christ, we only get one opportunity to become part of the Body of Christ, that is NOW! We may be dead tomorrow.

The latest devised method that guarantees the temple work is the extraction program. It does not require a relative to enter a name for temple work. People volunteer to extract random names and submit them to Salt Lake City LDS Genealogical Society. All names will become part of their records, and will be baptized and endowed over time.

Mormonism does not accept a biblical hell. Their hell is an existence much like we experience or better. There are contradictions to that, because they threaten temple Mormons with outer darkness, if they don't hang unto the iron rod (Book of Mormon) and stay on course. These concepts had the tendency dilute the threat of the eternal lake of fire. I found out later that I had a hard time accepting hell from a loving God.

Hell is very much part of the teachings of Jesus Christ Himself, he mentioned it between 20 and 30 times during His ministry. LDS teachings are contradictory, ignoring the Bible whenever it is inconvenient, yet they peddle Mormonism as a Bible based religion.

The temple was on the shelf in my mind for years because my husband would not obey the rules. He knew he was not cutting it and the temple would bring even more responsibilities he did not want to meet. We had many, many demoralizing episodes over the temple. It put our marriage in bad straights for years. I had long given up on going. This dilemma motivates people to seek other partners and the church supports that. Then some thirteen years after we had joined, a Mormon decided to change that situation. Thinking back, I now believe this brother kept tab on our family for years and was probably assigned to us permanently without our knowing it. He often appeared when least expected and I trusted him as a friend.

One day this Elder brought another missionary. They converted my husband to the Temple in no time. Next we headed for Salt Lake City, although my husband had not met requirements to get a temple recommendation and they gave it to him anyway which became another problem to me. The Elder and his wife chaperoned us and showed us all the procedures. After thirteen years of waiting, we were finally to marry in the temple for time and eternity. Although

Taming The Lion

Scripture states clearly in Luke 20:35 **"But they which shall be accounted worthy to obtain that world, and the resurrection from the dead, neither marry, nor are given in marriage:"**

Mormons claim that is why they do it now. They ignore the Word of God: **"There is neither Jew nor Greek, slave nor free, male nor female, for you are all one in Christ Jesus**." (Galatians 3:28) To confirm that: **"How great is the love the Father has lavished on us, that we should be called children of God! And that is what we are! The reason the world does not know us is that it did not know him. Dear friends, now we are children of God, and what we will be has not yet been made known. But we know that when he appears, we shall be like him, for we shall see him as he is."** (1 John 3:1,2)

We did not have an inkling of what we were going to experience. There was a temple preparation class and all they discussed was the clothing we would have to buy but no other details. They said that it would be a learning experience just like going to a university. Much talked about is spiritual warfare when one undertakes going to the temple. The weather was snow and fog and the roads icy through the Rocky Mountains from Colorado to Utah. On the floor of our Van, afraid to watch the road, I could hear the men saying: "Can you see the road?" The fog was so thick. " No I can't, what are we going to do?" We had to be in the temple in Salt Lake City by 4:00 AM for the washing and anointing. They had to keep going.

Planning to rent a wedding gown at the temple, my imagination was trying to visualize what was about to happen. I was so excited thinking I was going to walk down the aisle with my man in a wedding gown and finally get married for eternity. What a let down when they separated the men from the women, even the newlyweds. Ushered through the various stages of instructions on how to handle the underwear we were about to put on for the rest of our lives, we intently listened. After the washing and anointing of our bodies wearing a covering at all times, we received blessings. Finally led to the room where the rituals were to be performed, the men seated themselves on one side of the room and the women on the other.

Taming The Lion

Two good books that describe temple rituals are: `What's Going On In There', by Chuck Sackett and `Secret Ceremonies', by Deborah Laake.

When I laid eyes on my husband in his temple clothing, I almost burst into loud laughter, he looked so funny in the priesthood garment. In a whisper they informed me that loud laughter was not permitted. Soon I was to find out that one had to sit like a zombie not knowing where to look or how to hold one's face for long stretches, some simply went to sleep. A light went on inside my head when the rituals began, I was doing Freemasonry. The occult Brotherhood of Light lessons came up in my memory. After I disconnected from Mormonism, I repurchased the book: `Ancient Masonry', by C.C. Zain {Hermetician Order - derivative of Rosicrucianism) The Brotherhood of Light} could not believe my eyes when I came to the page of the `five points of fellowship' which is the final token written word for word. The ritual calls for a blessing (would mean cursing, with the sign of the nail, a satanic grip) of one's children, grandchildren and all future generations.

The brethren have no idea what they are doing by the veil because they don't know the truth. A Mormon Elder stands behind the veil and a female or male member in front and they connect, foot to foot, knee to knee reaching through the slits in the veil doing certain hand grips and conversation. Before the veil rituals we had to commit our talents, time, our tithe, chastity and obedience to our husbands and the Church. I found myself committing everything I owned (assets) to the Church if the President in Salt Lake City decided to enforce the `Law of Consecration'. We had to swear that we would hand everything over. This is what they call the `endowment'. I could not believe my ears. When I ran my hand along my throat and stomach swearing to secrecy, it did not occur to me that I would allow them to cut my throat and open my bowels if I talked about the temple rituals. They did not explain anything before we arrived. If they did explain it, no one would go through the temple that I know of. Not till after I disconnected from the LDS

Taming The Lion

Church and began putting the pieces together, did I know what had happened in the temple ceremony.

Stunned I looked at all the people in the room with us, the doctor, the engineer, the CPA, the dentist and men and women that I had gone to church with us for thirteen years. They can't all be dumb or they would not be here. "Would anyone in their right mind jeopardize their eternal life with Christ?" I reasoned. There were no evil bloody sacrifices going on. Everyone was in white priesthood clothing with green fig leaf aprons. It did not feel threatening. How could I make a fool of my brothers and sisters and walk out? These thoughts were racing through my mind. An endowment ceremony that includes the rituals lasts close to two hours and since we came from Denver to Salt Lake City my Mormon friends wanted to stay and go through all the sessions throughout the day. This meant we had to participate several more sessions two hours each. That day was the most hideous day of my life.

The word endowment is a bequest according to Webster's Dictionary. Mormons say that a person receives an endowment. They don't explain what an endowment is. In looking at `endow': `to furnish with an income (like a hospital)', endowment: `the part of an institution's income derived from donations'. Why would they be endowing the dead? Their possessions are dead to the church. I was fuming when I got home and thought about how we had been tricked, but time was not up yet for us.

Their motto that they are building Zion, covers the wound. Little did I know what Zionism is. "The temples and the church as a whole package will be handed to Jesus at his return to earth," members insisted. Years later I discovered public records that just a few men incorporated in the presidency of the church own the assets (estimated value according to the stock market was $30 billion in 1992, not the church membership itself. Already too indoctrinated, I blindly kept walking. In my heart restlessness about the secrecy kept nagging at me. Jesus did not do anything in secret. It did not make sense.

Taming The Lion

Mentioning something about the temple to a brother made him shriek back in fear that I might make him disobey. He would not discuss it. Reassuring myself that Mormons were trustworthy since they acted like Christians, I kept making excuses for them and kept coming every Sunday. Everything in me was working against going to church but they talked about this spiritual warfare a lot and I wasn't going to let Satan win.

It made me realize how Adolf Hitler got away with keeping the concentration camps under wraps. His SS Stormtroopers submitted to indoctrinations modeled after the Orders of Knights. They had to take oaths or be killed. What pains me so now, millions of people world wide are submitting to these rituals daily in more than 50 temples and most of them do not know what they are submitting to. To explain what God had to say about this and why I was in this condition and could not move out on my own volition when I should have is this Scripture: "**And with all deceivableness of unrighteousness in them that perish; because they received not the love of the truth, that they might be saved. And for this cause God shall send them strong delusion, that they should believe a lie:**" (2 Thessalonians 2:10-11)

Shortly before the rituals were changed in 1990, they found pockets in Utah where satanic rituals with sacrifices were being performed because members were witches. People were having flash backs from previous Satan worshiping experiences. The new rituals hide the hideousness of their evil origin even more.

The prayer circle with the arms of the brethren in a square pointing up is identical to invoking demonic spirits. God hates every shred of what goes on in Mormon temples, although the membership teaches that God walks around there. It is so sacred that one has to remove all outward clothing down to shoes and stockings and replace them with a temple wardrobe. When the Denver temple opened for viewing to the public, all carpeting was removed and replaced afterwards. According to reports it had to be cleansed for God.

213

Taming The Lion

"**And they forsook the LORD, and served Baal and Ashtaroth.**" (Judges 2:13)

"**And he reared up an altar for Baal in the house of Baal, which he had built in Samaria.**" (Kings 16:32)

"**And Jehu said, Proclaim a solemn assembly for Baal. And they proclaimed it**" (2 Kings 10:20)

"**But what saith the answer of God unto him? I have reserved to myself seven thousand men, who have not bowed the knee to the image of Baal.**" (Romans 11:4)

"**I will also stretch out mine hand upon Judah, and upon all the inhabitants of Jerusalem; and I will cut off the remnant of Baal from this place, and the name of the Chemarims with the priests;**" (Zephaniah 1:4)

"**And them that are turned back from the LORD; and those that have not sought the LORD, nor inquired for him.**" (Zephaniah 1:6) "**Then all the people went to the house of Baal, and brake it down, and brake his altars and his images in pieces, and slew Mattan the priest of Baal before the altars**" (2 Chronicles 23:17) "**And it shall come to pass, if they will diligently learn the ways of my people, to swear by my name, The LORD liveth; as they taught my people to swear by Baal; then shall they be built in the midst of my people..**" (Jeremiah 12:16)

At this point, I knew I had been lied to. Often people were bemoaning that no financial statements ever came forth. Large sums of expenditures talked about regarding renovations and new buildings, kept the peace. For years members were assessed extra amounts for new buildings and utilities. Tithing and offerings were mandatory plus time and talents if one wanted to participate. There were at least two wards in each building with not more than six hundred members in each ward. If a member separated from friends because of redistricting, tough, they made no exceptions. One had to attend where one was assigned.

Taming The Lion

All rules are built around obedience. Activity during home visits had a format that was to be followed. To teach anything that did not come from Salt Lake City was against the rules. I tried to teach a class `Our Lord's Prayer', not used in Mormonism, I lost my teaching position never to be called again as a teacher although I had a degree in teaching and without explanation. What it amounted to: one mistake and you are out is certainly not what God advocates.

Mothers start early to get their children into accepting that they were going to follow with the whole program of missions, college on an LDS campus and temple marriages. One young fellow in Sunday School stood up one Sunday and confessed that his mother was playing tapes on how to be a good Mormon at night in his bed. He told the group that he was going to put a plastic bag over his head if she did not stop it, hoping someone would tell her. That family moved to another town.

Participation and having to go in front of the whole congregation and share their testimony was something my children never could do, they were too shy. The children and adults where expected to say certain sentences in their testimony that would run the same information by people's ears hundreds of times. They had to say that they believed that the Church is the only true Church, and that the president (by name) is a prophet and that Jesus is the Christ. Little three year old children did not know the difference and were told to say it, made me cringe every time. I got up a few times in the twenty years because something would come over me to make me shoot out of my seat and literally stumble up to the pulpit. It was suggested at times not to get up unless prompted by an inner surge. My heart would pound as if it were going to jump out of me. The episode turned into a demoralizing experience of apologizing for my family's disinterest and my failure to produce fruit for the church.

My two sons told at home that God wanted them to choose Him out of love for Him and that He promised liberty, not bondage, saved my whole family in the end. When they got out of high school my two sons both left the church. Thank God, they had a mind that was not turned off. My popularity down totally after that, they did not make any attempts to get them activated again until just before I left. That really struck a cord because there is a lot of emphasis in Christ's teaching about the lost sheep.

In trying to cultivate a friend, I agreed to drive a female member to the temple periodically and go through the Denver temple with her. She said to me during a session: "Did you know, you are expected to concentrate on the dead person's spirit when you are endowed for them by proxy, to let them know that they have been endowed and baptized by proxy?" That was news to me. At that time I did not know that Necromancy is also an abomination to God. Later I heard people talk about their spirit visitations, after I left the church.

Just before we disconnected from the church, my husband and I were sealed to our dead parents and the same chaperons were there who had witnessed our eternal marriage. The Elder asked me afterward if I saw my father standing next to me. He said he saw him, I should have asked him: "what did he look like?" He probably would have described him to a `t', I read that spirits know the person they are imitating and can be pretty convincing. At around twenty years old, a close friend of mine passed away with Leukemia. An apparition of him appeared to me in his mother's house right after the funeral. He had gone to sixty pounds when sick but appeared in full healthy stature looking beautiful.

This was not conjured since it was long before involvement in any books. Mormons convinced they have visitations of dead relatives, look for it when they do ordinances. Demons are trying to convince us that the Bible is not true. The Bible teaches that the dead go to a holding place until judgment. They do not float around in the spirit world. Since the Bible is truth, we have to accept that. Satan and his demons are liars. They only have access to some very convincing information.

Young Mormons on missions, worldwide, live with their own sex for two years and opposite sex is forbidden fruit. That gets them ready for the opposite sex on campus at college. There they select their partners while participating in their college curriculum. With their temple wedding behind them and their educations completed they receive jobs on campus and go wherever the best deal comes up. Many don't return home. The progression is ideal from a worldly point of view and most Mormons who are born into the Church opt for this golden ring. They can't loose in relation to the world, but sadly enough stand little chance for eternal life with Jesus Christ. The more successful they are, the smaller the chance of getting them out of Mormonism. The Apostle Peter warns in his writings: **"Be sober, be vigilant; because your adversary the devil, as a roaring lion, walketh about, seeking whom he may devour:"** (1 Peter 5:8)

Happiness and love are a low priority. If Mormons sidestep, they usually shipwreck. It is very difficult for a young Mormon to maintain independently should they marry outside the church. Their environment programmed and protected skews their personalities. Life is dependent on partnership and life becomes a threat when that goal is not met. I watched some devastating examples for the people involved and don't recommend getting involved with Mormons without a commitment. It will create continuous stress. The members work hard to impose their way of life on converts and converts never change their status. The members are told to remember there is a difference between a lifetime member and a convert. With the help of magazine articles and behind closed doors they are obedient to the Church above all. My complete failure was heaven-sent and turned out to be a magnificent blessing. I don't have anyone stuck in Mormonism.

Because shunned, it became very difficult for me to attend. Every Sunday, I came up with an excuse why I had better things to do but I made myself go. Still praying to the same God, I had always prayed to and believing in the same Jesus Christ, I had always believed in, I analyzed everything with the Bible in mind. My hope was that one of these days they would get it. The line between offerings to God and works was blurred. Mormons always come up with the right answers because they know all the questions raised about Mormonism. I did not know until I was out, that they were not accepting grace and they would probably deny it, if faced with it.

A cross on a necklace around one's neck had to go. The comments from people were always the same: "would you wear a gun around your neck?" There are no crosses anywhere to be found. Angels and candlelights were forbidden. One of our home teachers confessed that he had tried to leave Mormonism but only lasted six months because of all the confusion that is going on in Christianity today. I wish I could talk to him today and relate what I have learned since.

There is an amazing similarity between the Order of the Templars and Mormonism. The emphasis in Mormonism, as in the New World Order, that is bringing all nationalities under one roof as a brotherhood and practicing peace, was also the main thrust in the Templar Orders. LDS Magazines filled with stories from people of all over the world, serve as a conditioner to global thinking. The Templars voted their peers into office that is also a Mormon practice. All members wore specific mantels to show who they were, another Mormon practice in the temples. Mormon underwear has Masonic symbols embroidered over each breast, the navel and one knee. They are all white same as the Templars. Mormons buried in their priesthood clothing are as those worn during temple rituals same as Templar's practice. Mormons establish all their dead relatives on record and perform their ordinances by proxy. The Templars were giving donations to absolve their dead relatives and themselves. Before entering Mormonism certain vows and interrogations that have to do with entering the temples, have to be performed before permission is granted, is also a Templar procedure.

Another parallel between the Order of the Templars and Mormon temple rituals are that endowed persons have to swear to uphold chastity, obedience, loyalty, secrecy and offer their talents, time and belongings as a sacrifice to the church for time and eternity. They also kneel and pray together, learn secret hand-grips and new names to identify themselves to their brothers in time of emergency. They call each other brothers and sisters and allow whole families into this life style. Mormons are also independent of any other organizations and a law unto themselves but told to submit to government statutes if possible. They come from all walks of life and are a self-contained social system within society and respected for their moral values.

Templars kept the units at fifty people with a leader and hierarchy that is broken down into knights and serving brothers, where Mormonism has 600 persons in a congregation, divided when it gets beyond the 600 members. Within the 600 are the Quorum of seventy (Elders), Melchizedek priests comparable to knights. The Templars started out committed to serve Jesus Christ indicated by their identification as Templar Christi and over time their goal became wealth that ended in destruction. Joseph Smith Jr. is thought to have had direct access to God, Jesus, Peter, James and John, and the Church's success is attributed to this encounter and additional revelations. The only new revelation Joseph came up with was the planet Kolob where God lives and he described the people living on the Moon. Little did Joseph realize that the United States' astronauts would actually have access to the Moon's surface to disprove that revelation.

All I can say we have an awesome God, He backs His children to the hilt. His precious Son gave us only two commandments: "**Jesus said unto him, Thou shalt love the Lord thy God with all thy heart, and with all thy soul, and with all thy mind. This is the first and great commandment. And the second is like unto it, Thou shalt love thy neighbour as thyself.On these two commandments hang all the law and the prophets.**" (Matthew 22:37-40)

"**Then saith Jesus unto him, Get thee hence, Satan: for it is written, Thou shalt worship the Lord thy God, and him only shalt thou serve. Then the devil leaveth him, and, behold, angels came and ministered unto him**". (Matthew 4:10,11)

Taming The Lion

"**For, brethren, ye have been called unto liberty; only use not liberty for an occasion to the flesh, but by love serve one another. For all the law is fulfilled in one word, even in this; Thou shalt love thy neighbour as thyself** " (Galatians 5:13,14)

CHAPTER 10

TEST THE SPIRITS

The big question is always, "how did you get out of Mormonism after twenty years of serving?" The answer is not that simple. Two people who were important to me tried to do something. My sister, a Baptist, handed me a little missionary book from Moody Press that I ignored because she was little sister. The Christian aunt from Brooklyn who was the example of the Light in my life shining ever so simply just screamed at me many years later, "you are in Satan's church." It had an effect, because I respected her judgment, but she couldn't tell me what the problem was and I was looking for proof. Mormons had the outward appearance of pure Christians and it kept me convinced that they had to be Christians.

Every comment made to a Mormon contrary to their church has an extremely unsettling effect. It stays with the person like a worm in their soul eating away at this belief to break it down. It becomes a magnet to pull in more information that begins the long climb out of the pit. The biggest problem for Mormons is that the leadership teaches them that people are going to try to get them out. Every time someone tries that, it makes the church teachings even truer. A different approach is necessary.

One of my strongholds for the church was their consistency. Mormons rarely change teachings to keep people under the impression that everything is straight from God, who is the same yesterday, today and forever. God states: "Be as wise as a serpent," when the opportunity arises, strike suddenly and with as much ammunition as possible, not poison but truth.

There are only a few opportunities in a Mormon's life because their altered minds cause delusion. Just before I became a temple Mormon, in 1980, I hired a female accountant who turned out to be a former Mormon. Raised in a Mormon family, she confided to me later that her father had molested her. She turned her back on

221

Taming The Lion

Mormonism because of it. Sharing with her, I confessed that my need for the gospel was not met at the Mormon church and she suggested listening to Ken Copeland's sermons on Sundays. This occurred twelve years before I left, that is how similar Mormonism appears to be to the Word Faith Movement, taught as Christianity.

Taking her advice, I took to his `down to earth talk' like ducks take to water. Copeland talked a lot about "doing" the Word to gain of health, wealth, a happy life and general blessings. It is a by-product of following the commandments, but it prevents us from the recognition of our need for a personal relationship with God. People in Mormonism equate their good life with God's blessing and that is not what the Gospel is essentially about. God does not want love that expects to get. God wants us to get beyond that. God is teaching unconditional love toward God. The most important commandment is to love God with all our hearts and minds, no addendum `**and you will receive all the blessings'**. He also tells that His kingdom is not of this world and we will be brothers in the inheritance that Jesus has received. This is the reason the disciples ran when they found out there was not going to be a high position for them. The only reason the disciples geared into their ministry after Jesus shed His blood for them was the Holy Spirit. They were baptized in the Holy Spirit and they gave their lives to God and received the fire to teach the Gospel. Mormons do it through indoctrination, respect for their parents and the promise of certain success delivered through participation in the church.

John the Baptist is a good example. Jesus knew he was in jail waiting to be beheaded. Jesus did not make one move toward John. He expected him to endure to the end. Mormons teach endure to the end clinging to the iron rod, the Book of Mormon which teaches that Jesus is going to arrive in the United States to take charge of the only true church, their church. Scripture teaches not to rely on physical evidence, just believe the Gospel under any circumstances.

Our belief is in trouble when it is based on material blessings when they don't come. Christ exemplified `no' blessings for himself, not even a place to sleep at times. He was totally subject to people's charity. God's miracles were for sinners to convince them that Jesus Christ was God. Jesus received His reward after He got the job done (in other words after He died). He is our example and He expects us to take up that same cross. God provides but not in the style we are accustomed to. In Mormon doctrines, the discrepancies were not obvious, that must sound strange to people who know Mormonism is a cult. Mormons don't know that. .

Ken Copeland got an important principle through to me: the imputed righteousness, something I had never heard of.

All Jews were told to be circumcised 8 days after birth, which set them apart as Israel, God's family. All others were considered Gentiles [heathens] who could not become part of the family. Because Israel abandoned God in the Old Testament for Pagan gods, God abandoned them as well. Rather than destroying the whole creation He sent His only begotten Son to the Jews once more to get them to listen and come back to God, but they again rejected God and were indirectly responsible for putting Jesus on the cross to bleed and die.

What Jews were not aware of was the fact that Jesus was the redeemer, their Messiah who came to redeem them from punishment for their sins. There was no way they could have missed the fact that Jesus was God due to all the miracles He performed and the sermons He shared. Jesus resurrected after three days and remained 40 days with his disciples to prove His resurrection. After that He returned to the Father in Heaven and released the Holy Spirit to gather those who believed that Jesus was the Christ. Every believer received the imputation of His righteousness for future application when they confront their judge, God in Heaven.

Because God cursed all creation it could not redeem itself. That is why Isaiah called us to be as filthy rags. We would have remained as filthy rags forever had it not been for Jesus Christ and His sacrifice. God had mercy on us once and for all time forever. This mercy was not only directed to Jews but to all mankind. All sins were forgiven when Jesus gave Himself in obedience to God to bleed and die on the cross.

Jews do not have to be circumcised anymore but can become part of the Body of Christ by imputation of His righteousness. No more sacrifices of animals or tithe are necessary to get into God's graces. Instead God's grace abounds through His only begotten Son Who obeyed to become the unspotted lamb to be sacrificed for our sins once and forever.

In New Testament teaching all believers are circumcised on the heart rather than the penis as described in Romans 4:11 "**And he received the sign of circumcision, a seal of the righteousness of the faith which he had yet being uncircumcised: that he might be the father of all them that believe, though they be not circumcised; that righteousness might be imputed unto them also:** "

In Romans 4:22 this circumcision is called imputation, which is equivalent to receiving a credit in your account as a gift. A good example is when one is broke and someone puts money in one's account for future use. Our own righteousness is not sufficient to cover our sinful nature in God's eyes. We receive a deposit of the righteousness of Christ Jesus because He did not sin and was the only One Who could cover our sins. He purchased us with His blood. Romans 4:22 "**And therefore it was imputed to him for righteousness**". James 2:23 bears out that Abraham received the same imputation for simply believing God and proving it by obeying Him when Abraham was ready to sacrifice his son Isaac. Abraham was not a Jew but a Gentile and father of the Jews. "**And the scripture was fulfilled which saith, Abraham believed God, and it was imputed unto him for righteousness: and he was called the Friend of God.** " (James 2:23)

Adam and Eve were created to have eternal life and authority over the whole creation. They disobeyed; God cursed them and consequently all of humanity was to die spiritually and physically in their sins. I think it was 14 generations when God decided the

Taming The Lion

depravity was so bad that He would destroy all but one family and start over. "**And God said unto Noah, The end of all flesh is come before me; for the earth is filled with violence through them; and, behold, I will destroy them with the earth.**" (Genesis 6:13)

Out of Noah's line God discovered Abraham who believed God and obeyed. Out of Abraham came God's family Israel out of which was born Jesus Christ whose Father was the Holy Spirit and whose mother was the Virgin Mary.

This proves that Mormonism is on the wrong track. Only through Christ's perfect sacrifice, can we be set free from sin not by works of Mormonism The secret is that there is only one way we can receive the Holy Spirit as our teacher by realizing that we are completely helpless in sin due to God's curse and by asking God for forgiveness and mercy and repent (discontinue our sinfulness) we will receive Christ Jesus as our Redeemer and He will baptize us with the Holy Ghost..

God at that point forgives our sins and imputes the righteousness of Jesus Christ into our hearts, changes our stony heart into a soft heart and we become children of God.

The Holy Spirit changes us into new creatures acceptable to become the Bride of Christ to be raptured / resurrected in the first resurrection to reign with Him in the thousand year Millennium.

"**And the great dragon was cast out, that old serpent, called the Devil, and Satan, which deceiveth the whole world: he was cast out into the earth, and his angels were cast out with him.**" (Revelation 12:9) "**Wherefore, as by one man sin entered into the world, and death by sin; and so death passed upon all men, for that all have sinned:**" (Romans 5:12) "**But not as the offense, so also is the free gift. For if through the offense of one many be dead, much more the grace of God, and the gift by grace, which is by one man, Jesus Christ, hath abounded unto many . '** (Romans 5:15) "**Rejoicing in hope; patient in tribulation; continuing instant in prayer;.**" (Romans 12:12) "**And be not conformed to this world: but be ye transformed by the renewing**

of your mind, that ye may prove what is that good, and acceptable, and perfect, will of God. *(*Romans 12:2)

I discovered listening to Copeland's concept of being an associate of God similar to the Mormons he put mankind on equal terms, which lined up with Mormonism and is corrupt teaching. He also described God's hand the size of human hands, indicating the God has a body. On one of his videos Ken Copeland and his daughter wore Masonic symbols. His daughter had an Eastern Star emblem on her top. On another he used the compass and square, the emblem stitched into all Mormon priesthood garments worn under their clothing. Copeland makes no bones about the fact that he believes that we are all one brotherhood. It explains why there was no conflict between the two doctrines: Word of Faith and Mormonism. In the twelve years I listened to his sermons. There was no conflict while I was a Mormon.

In the late 1980s, an inactive Mormon lady handed me a book to read which had stunned her. She wanted my response. I read it and found myself so dumbfounded and embarrassed, that I quietly handed the book back without comment. The name of the book was `The Mormon Enigma of Emma Hale Smith', by Linda Newell and Valeen Tippetts Avery. It was available in LDS bookstores. It has a comprehensive bibliography and the fact that the LDS church sells it must mean its good information. Later researching anti Mormon literature, I found the accounts of the book confirmed.

That book was the beginning of the breakdown. I had no idea that Joseph Smith Jr. was a polygamist before I read the book. The biography of Emma and Joseph was a painful blow below the belt to me. The story describes the founders of the Church of Jesus Christ of Latter-day Saints and their private lives. Discipline, one of Mormon's virtues, keeps them from discussing areas that could cause problems. In all those years, no one had shared that information with me. They had beautiful pictures of Joseph everywhere in a fine blue uniform. It was easy to think of him as a prophet. Thinking back, my gullibility proved to be extraordinary.

Taming The Lion

The authors described a man who was completely contrary to what I would call saintly.

Embarrassment kept me from talking about it. He effectively built a religion to legitimatize his lifestyle regardless of how many scriptural rules he had to break. Uncaring of anyone who got on this bandwagon, he betrayed many parents. Their beautiful young daughters were duped with propositions of becoming goddesses on their own planet, if they agreed to marry Joseph Smith Jr. and have sex with him.

His wife fought Joseph's flings when she realized what he was up to. He promised to behave and continued his activity behind her back. She had to manage everything while he sat upstairs rewriting the Bible, and writing the other three standard works for Mormonism. She gave birth to eleven children. She adopted other children and cared for many people in their home, a hotel, to accommodate his plans. Some of her children died from exposure.

To paint a picture of the environment of witchcraft that surrounded Joseph and Emma in the early 1800's, really begins with immigration of Europeans in the 1700's. When America, as we know it, was born, it was patterned according to a Constitution written by men who loved their newly found freedom and wanted to preserve it at any cost. Among these men were quite a number of Freemasons desiring to insure practice of unchristian as well as Christian beliefs, indefinitely. The symbolism on our dollar bills and government documents are proof of a predominance of Freemasonry. They even built cities like Washington, D.C., with that symbolism in mind. The obelisk in Washington is modeled after the Egyptian obelisk also evident at Saint Peters at the Vatican in Rome.

Researching early Mormonism, I found a book, now out of print: `Early Mormonism and the Magic World View', by D. Michael Quinn. Mr. Quinn, was recently excommunicated. He did an extensive study into Mormonism, which the church holds in disdain. The fact that he remained in Mormonism after his findings indicates that he agreed with Mormonism knowing that Joseph was into witchcraft. The leadership prohibits this kind of activity by members, because they do not admit to Baal worship. The book, extremely well documented, because he traveled internationally to research, is still available in the Denver Public Library in the historical section. It is out of print. The author described what was going on socially in the community. On page 193 he writes: "In addition to sharing the folk beliefs common to all Pennsylvania Germans, Peter Whitmer Sr. (father of one of Joseph Smith's three witnesses) for more than a decade also lived in close proximity to the Ephrata commune and Rosicrucianism fostering alchemy, astrology, treasure divining, and ceremonial magic. He had originally lived in Lancaster County, Pa. Cocalico Township on the river where Ephrata mystics were performing baptisms for the dead only six miles away in 1790." What is interesting here, my mother-in-law (a member of Eastern Star) and her father, a Freemason came to Colorado from Lancaster County, Pennsylvania.

Ten Palmyra residents wrote a letter describing New York Mormons `The whole gang of these deluded mortals, except for a few hypocrites, are profound believers in witchcraft, ghosts and goblins', Painesville Telegraph, 22 March 1931." Page 194: "the three witnesses were involved in folk magic." page 195: a discussion of the brown seer stone, part of the landscape of folk beliefs. Page 180: "Priesthood practices of Ephrata Commune August 1740 leader of the commune consecrated brother Onesimus (Israel Eckerling) practiced laying on of hands and admitted to the ancient Order of Melchizedek by having a degree conferred on them in ancient form." Page 165: "John Beaumont wrote in 1705 that the Indians "talk with the devil, who answer them in certain stones." (1705, 294) Indians were accustomed to scrying and using `wizard sticks'. Lutherans, comparable to Martin, opposed contemporary magic practices in 1810

Luther chased practitioners out of the church in Germany. Substituting the synonymous `occult' for `hid' (including `hidden' and `secret') and `sorcery' for `works of darkness'." Page 158: "Contemporary Encyclopedias thus equated the Jewish Cabala with

Taming The Lion

Egyptian mystic hieroglyphics. Nephi's opening words in the Book of Mormon did the same, aligning the cabalistic reference `learning of the Jews' with language of the Egyptians... equivalent to `the wisdom of the Aegyptians', where magick was no small share (The Magic of Kirani 1685, Pref 12)" page 159: "Gold plates included mysteries of the works of darkness (Moses 8:9, Alma 37:21). One of the works of an Rosicrucian stated that the number one `engraven on Brasse.. bringeth a spirit' (J. Heyden 1662 c,11)."

"Moroni was the name for a swarthy man, `Maron' was one of the Holy names for conjuration according to a widely circulated magic manuscript, the `Key of Solomon' (Mathers 1888, 28)." Oliver Goldsmith's 1774 History of the Earth (part of J. Smith's Library) explained that Moron was the name of a venomous salamander. Moroni, a name of magic invocation... Scot's 1665 Discovery reported "But if astral spirits as fairies [sic], Nymphs, and ghosts of men, to be called upon, the circle must be made with chalk, without triangles ... directly under the undeciphered inscription is the large Jupiter symbol {talisman Joseph Smith was wearing at time of death, confirming that he had not converted to Christ Jesus} from astrology... stated that one of the spirits "governeth those things which are ascribed to Jupiter... to cast open treasures; reconcileth the spirits of the air, that they give true answers. (1665, 179, emphasis in original 1783, 278)" Page 130: "Sentinel, 12 May 1824, 11 Dec 1829:

Oliver B. Huntington's 1836 patriarchal (prophetic) blessing, probably by Joseph Smith Sr. predicted: `Thou shalt have power with God even to translate thyself to heaven and preach to the inhabitants of the Moon or planets if it shall be expedient.'" Page 59: "Astrology gives much attention to questions concerning marriage, and there appears to be a pattern of astrological - numerical correlations in the marriage dates of Joseph Smith Sr. and Jr.. Joseph's polygamy multiplied the opportunity for astrological correspondence. Historical evidence provides exact or probable dates for eighteen of Smith's marriages, and all of these wedding dates have astrological correlations showing awareness of magic and the occult." Page 175: "Three glories: Celestial, Terrestrial and Telestial correspond to Swedenborg's theology of three heavens (similarity to Angelology)." Page xiii

"One traditional distinction is that religion is supplicative (an appeal by God's servants) and magic coercive in intent, or as anthropologist Lucy Mair writes, "the difference between religion and magic... might be epitomized as the difference between communicating with beings (God) and manipulating forces" (1972, 229). Joseph Smith's family was using Maltese Crosses for ceremonial magic, used by Hitler extensively as well as the Pope (when visiting Denver 1993, his clothing was decorated with these crosses).

There is literature claiming that another author wrote the war stories between the Indians and whites in ancient times, which became Israelites in the Americas in the Book of Mormon. The stories were found later. Many investigations have been conducted since Joseph founded the church to expose how it all really came together.

People flocked to Joseph and Emma from all over. Joseph busily taught other men the polygamist principles to reinforce his own stand and many men supported his position of unlimited women under the guise of religion. A mob actually tarred and feathered Joseph one night. Joseph and his group had major funding problems and opened their own bank to print money that ended in bankruptcy. He even tried his old treasure hunting trips got revelations about buried treasure for his enterprise in another city that they followed out only to come back empty handed. He developed a newspaper to gain a following and people who wanted to bring Joseph down began publishing anti Mormon literature.

Joseph took matters in his own hands and with his male followers mobbed this publisher, demolished their printing equipment that proved to become the catalyst to his end. He had been in and out of court and became a fugitive from the law. He finally capitulated with his brother and went to jail. When the mob broke into the jail he tried to shoot his way out, jumped out of the window and fell to his death. They also shot his brother. How Mormons came up with a martyr is still beyond my comprehension.

The `Word of Wisdom' is a tough rule to live with for converts. It forbids smoking, drinking caffeine and wine on occasion. I had given up cigarettes ten years before I joined, but coffee was a real issue. Europeans adore coffee and a glass of wine with dinner. On family occasions it meant trauma. My family, parents and siblings, thought I was crazy giving up the few little luxuries that we had. It was an issue at every family event, to a point that we shunned family events to avoid these confrontations.

It is mandatory to follow the `Word of Wisdom'. Belief that it is from God makes it possible to bear the deprivation. When I read the following account my `testimony' about liquor and coffee became an issue from then on. Lies began to creep in. Following is a thumbnail account of Emma and Joseph Smith: "Often when the prophet entered the room to give the school instructions, he would find himself in a cloud of tobacco smoke. Temperance societies worked to abolish the use of alcohol, tobacco and the eating of too much meat. Thus, Emma faced almost daily with having to clean so filthy a floor as was left by the men chewing tobacco, she spoke to Joseph about the matter. She said it would be a good thing if a revelation could be had declaring the use of tobacco a sin and commanding its suppression."

"Joseph made the issue the subject of prayer, and the `Word of Wisdom' was the result. Joseph's revelation came showing forth the order and the will of God in the temple of salvation of all saints in the last days. It advised against the use of strong drinks or tobacco and would someday mark the Mormons quite distinctly in their religious habits."

What I realized was that they were developing a plan for their own convenience. It was not from God. Following are a few more excerpts from the book itself. "On February 24, 1834, a newly organized high counsel of governing body within the church

Taming The Lion

selected Joseph as Commander-in-Chief of the armies of Israel. The purpose of the army was their redemption of Zion. They were planning to go to Missouri to redeem Mormon lands, spiritual life, loyalty, political power, and church organization. Joseph accompanied by a big bulldog was the best equipped. They left Kirkland May 1, 1834. He carried a pair of brass-barreled horse pistols with silver mountings, a fine sword, and a rifle and traveled under the alias of Squire Cook. The Missourian Intelligencer reported that 600 Mormons armed with every kind of instrument of destruction from scalping knives to doubled-barreled rifles marched toward Missouri. Citizens across western Missouri began arming themselves.

Cholera scoured the world from 1832 to 1834. Joseph, like many others, regarded disease and deformity as punishment meted out by an angry God and Joseph said to try to heal the victims by the laying on of hands, but the disease seized him. Fourteen members of the camp fell victim to the plague. Joseph disbanded the camp. Each man received $1.14 and was to make his own way home to Kirkland.

To add to the confusion a certain Michael Chandler arrived with a traveling exhibit of four Egyptian mummies together with some roles of papyrus covered with hieroglyphic figures. He had heard that Joseph Smith could translate unknown languages. Emma went to a high council meeting with Joseph. The matter of business was the trial of a couple charged with whipping their daughter unreasonably. Lucy Smith began to testify about matters that Joseph believed had long ago been settled by the church, and he objected to his mother's comments. William Smith rose and charged Joseph with invalidating her testimony. Joseph told William, he was out of order and asked him to sit down. Enraged, William said he would not sit down and Joseph knocked him down. Joseph threatened to walk out of the meeting. The parents were finally reprimanded for raising a daughter that required the whip at fifteen.

Emma had to earn their income by running a hotel. Joseph's life was experiencing constant disruptions because of his seductive behavior with women. Mormons believe that Joseph asked the Lord why plural wives were acceptable in a day of Abraham, Isaac, and Jacob, but not in his day, in spite of the fact that the Bible is explicit about marriage. "**A bishop**{in this case Joseph Smith Jr.} **then must be blameless, the husband of one wife, vigilant, sober, of good behaviour, given to hospitality, apt to teach;**" (1 Timothy 3:2)

Thirty to fifty years later several of Joseph's contemporaries stated that he had received a revelation approving plural marriage in 1831. In 1882 Hyrum Smith's son, Joseph F. Smith, dated a revelation approving plural marriage in 1831 and added, "the Lord showed him those women... and at that time some of these women were names given to him, to become his wives when the time should come that this principle would be established. Apparently Joseph introduced the subject through revelation received near Jackson County, Missouri in 1831 stating, "for it is my will, that in time, you should take unto you wives of Lamanites and Nephites (Indians) that their posterity may become white, delights them, and just, for even now their females are more virtuous than the gentiles."

The copy of the revelation is in the handwriting of William Phelps, who adds "I asked Brother Joseph, privately, how we, that were mentioned in the revelation could take wives of the natives as we were all married men?" He replied instantly, "in the same manner that Abraham took Hagar and Keturah: that Jacob took Rachel, Bilhah and Zilbah: by revelation. The saints of the Lord are always directed by revelation." Mary Elizabeth Rollins claimed that Joseph had a private conversation with her in 1831; she was then twelve years old. She said "Joseph told me about his great vision concerning me. He said I was the first woman God commanded him to take as a plural wife...to make the Mormon's position on marriage very clear, W. W. Phelps had introduced an "Article on Marriage" at a general assembly of the church on August 17, 1835. The assembly voted unanimously to print it in the Doctrine and Covenants, where it remained in all editions until 1876 when LDS Church officials removed it. "Inasmuch as this Church of Christ has been reproached with the crime of fornication, and polygamy; we declare that we believe, that one man should have one wife; and one woman but one husband, except in case of death, when either is at liberty to marry again."

Plural marriage has never been removed from their Doctrine and Covenants. Mormons are excommunicated now for wanting to practice the original doctrine because they believe it was a revelation from God. William E. McLellin believed "the presidency to a great extend were absolved in temporal things." He wrote in 1872 that the "presidency and leading men," about fifteen couples, hired expensive carriages and drove to Cleveland. Some became intoxicated and "smashed things up generally" before coming home the next day still under the influence. Joseph was charged with fraud. Emma, now thirty-three, packed her wagon, knowing whatever she left behind would become common plunder. She made a place for Julia, six, and Joseph, five, and eighteen- month-old Frederick among the scanty provisions. Emma left Kirtland as she had arrived; pregnant, and in the dead of winter. Zion in Missouri lay eight hundred miles away. On June 2, 1838, Emma gave birth to another son. Joseph left two days after the birth.

Lieutenant General, Joseph Smith Jr. (1840), wore a blue coat, gold-colored epaulets, high black boots, and a sweeping hat topped with ostrich feathers. He carried an impressive sword. Only John C. Bennett outshone him, resplendent in gold braid, buttons, and tassels. Emma and the wives of "other distinguished officers accompanied their companions on parades."

Joseph planned two large buildings for Nauvoo: a temple and a hotel. He wanted the Nauvoo Temple to be the most splendid building on the Mississippi but his polygamy problems kept dogging him. "Any man who will teach and practice the doctrine of spiritual wifery will go to hell, I don't care if it is my brother Joseph." Twentieth-century historians disagree on the number of marriages Joseph took part in. Andrew Jensen documented twenty-seven, from statements and affidavits of the women themselves or from witnesses to the marriages. Fawn Brodie later added other sources to total forty-eight. Joseph fathered children by at least four of his plural wives. He told some of these men to keep plural marriages a secret from their first wives. Joseph argued that it was a test of faith, and the more wives Brigham took, the greater would be his glory in heaven.

"No, it was an angel of God," Joseph reassured her. "The angel came to me three times between the year 1834 and 1842 and said I was to obey that principle or he would slay me." Mary Elizabeth said Joseph told her that the last time the angel had come with a drawn sword and threatened his life. He offered salvation to Mary Elizabeth if she would accept his proposal. Brigham Young officiated at her marriage to Joseph. New revelation was now the basis for their religion, and Joseph insisted that the revelations that he received from God were absolute and he expected them to be obeyed.

Although many revelations appeared to come forth spontaneously, others came piecemeal, building 'line upon line, precept upon precept.' Many revelations of the latter kind culminated in the Mormon Temple ordinances, including baptism for the dead, an extension of the concept that baptism is necessary and, therefore, should be available by proxy to the dead. Other temple ordinances were washings and anointings, celestial marriage (or sealing for eternity), the endowment, and a higher ordinance sometimes referred to as the 'second anointing.' The second anointing was news to me, another secret kept from temple Mormons who think they have arrived in Celestial Heaven. The second anointing is kept for the privileged few only and guarantees godhood. Similar to Jehovah's Witnesses where only the 144,000 are chosen for that privilege, the rest are not eligible to meet God face to face. Keeping privileges away from those in bondage keeps them giving up rights to attain the high position.

The thief on the cross next to Jesus had compassion for Jesus and asked to be remembered in heaven. "

Jesus answered him, **"And Jesus said unto him, Verily I say unto thee, To day shalt thou be with me in paradise"**. (Luke

23:43) In other Scriptures reference to Paradise is made. "*And* **I knew such a man, (whether in the body, or out of the body, I cannot tell: God knoweth;) How that he was caught up into paradise, and heard unspeakable words, which it is not lawful for a man to utter.*"* (*2* Corinthians 12:3,4) This final Scripture confirms that Paradise is with God: "**He that hath an ear, let him hear what the Spirit saith unto the churches; To him that overcometh will I give to eat of the tree of life, which is in the midst of the paradise of God..**" (Revelation 2:7)

Keeping some from reaching the presence of God through the veil is heresy. With Jesus' sacrifice the veil was rent in two to give us direct access to God. "**Jesus, when he had cried again with a loud voice, yielded up the ghost. And, behold, the veil of the temple was rent in twain from the top to the bottom; and the earth did quake, and the rocks rent;** (Matthew 27:50,51)

The following Jamieson-Fausset-Brown Commentary further explains what these verses represent:" 51. And, behold, the veil of the temple was rent in twain from the top to the bottom-- This was the thick and gorgeously wrought veil which was hung between the "holy place" and the "holiest of all," [describing the Levitical Aaronic priesthood] shutting out all access to the presence of God as manifested "from above the mercy seat and from between the cherubim"--"the Holy Ghost this signifying, that the way into the holiest of all was not yet made manifest" (Heb 9:8). Into this holiest of all none might enter, not even the high priest, save once a year, on the great day of atonement, and then only with the blood of atonement in his hands, which he sprinkled "upon and before the mercy seat seven times" (Le 16:14) -- to signify that access for sinners to a holy God is only through atoning blood. But as they had only the blood of bulls and of goats, which could not take away sins (Heb 10:4), during all the long ages that preceded the death of Christ the thick veil remained; the blood of bulls and of goats continued to be shed and sprinkled; and once a year access to God through an atoning sacrifice was vouchsafed-- in a picture, or rather, was dramatically represented, in those symbolical actions-- nothing more.

HERE IS WHY ONLY JESUS CAN RECEIVE THE MELCHISEDEK PRIESTHOOD **"But now, the one atoning Sacrifice being provided in the precious blood of Christ, access to this holy God could no longer be denied; and so the moment the Victim expired on the altar, that thick veil which for so many ages had been the dread symbol of separation between God and guilty men was, without a hand touching it, mysteriously "rent in twain from top to bottom"--"the Holy Ghost this signifying, that the way into the holiest of all was NOW made manifest!" How emphatic the statement, from top to bottom; as if to say, Come boldly now to the Throne of Grace; the veil is clean gone; the mercy seat stands open to the gaze of sinners, and the way to it is sprinkled with the blood of Him--"who through the eternal Spirit hath offered Himself without spot to God!" Before, it was death to go in, now it is death to stay out. See more on this glorious subject on"** (Hebrews 10:19-22).

Next the Apostle Paul, the teacher assigned to Gentiles / MORMONS confirmed Mathew 27:51 **"And not as Moses, which put a vail over his face, that the children of Israel could not steadfastly look to the end of that which is abolished: But their minds were blinded: for until this day remaineth the same vail untaken away in the reading of the old testament; which vail is done away in Christ. But even unto this day, when Moses is read, the vail is upon their heart. Nevertheless when it shall turn to the Lord, the vail shall be taken away. Now the Lord is that Spirit: and where the Spirit of the Lord is, there is liberty. But we all, with open face beholding as in a glass the glory of the Lord, are changed into the same image from glory to glory, even as by the Spirit of the Lord."** (2 Corinthians 3:13-18)

March 15, 1842, Joseph began an association with Masonry. The Illinois Grand Master Mason presided over the installation of a Masonic Lodge in Nauvoo and inducted Joseph 'on sight.' "I was with the Masonic Lodge and rose to the sublime degree," Joseph Smith Jr. related. Just over six weeks later, on May 4, he began the endowment ceremony, an ordinance of religious instruction committing the recipient to God and the church. Some scholars have suggested that Joseph drew heavily from Freemasonry for the endowment while others argue that he recognized ancient temple rites in the Masonic order and restored them to a more perfect form. Heber C. Kimball wrote that Parley P. Pratt related, "There was near two hundred who had been made Masons (here)...All of the twelve apostles have become members. Except Orson Pratt...there is a similarity of .. Hood in Masonry. Brother Joseph ses Masonry was taken from priesthood, but has become degenerated." Joseph's communications to the women contained references to Masonry. He spoke of being good Masons, ancient orders, keys, tokens, examination, order of the priesthood, degrees, secrets, candidates, lodges, signs, and rules, in preparation for an endowment for both men and women. In describing her early endowment, Lucy M. Smith, married to Joseph's cousin, George A., revealed the intermingling of Masonry with it. Endowments were given in Emma's house and in the Masonic Lodge room, but eventually were done in the temple. Building the temple took priority over all work projects.

The women named their own organization the Female Relief Society of Nauvoo. Emma and Joseph together outlined the purposes of the society `to provoke the brethren to good works.' Joseph advised, "The society should grow by degrees, according to the ancient Priesthood. Concerning speaking in tongues, Joseph cautioned, "If any have a matter to reveal, let it be in your own tongue. Do not indulge too much in the gift of tongues... I lay this down for a rule that if anything is taught by this gift of tongues, it is not to be received for doctrine." Where abortions were concerned: "..Unhampered by any moral or theological framework, Bennett approached women with his own rationale: where there was no accuser, there was no sin. Pregnancy would be taken care of with an abortion. When refused, Bennett stated he came with Joseph's approval.

Taming The Lion

Mormons discovered the delights of river boating during the months of 1843. Joseph bought the Maid of Iowa from its captain, Dan Jones. Emma and Joseph boarded the boat for floating parties up and down the river with a hundred guests. all were dressed in their best finery. At some point Joseph Smith accused Emma of poisoning him. Joseph had frequent short illnesses, and his manner had begun to change. He now lost his temper more frequently, and his actions were abrupt. He `kicked (Josiah Butterfield) out of his house...and into the street' on March 28. He lost his temper again with a tax collector and `followed him a few steps and struck him two or three times.' After the incident Joseph went home and tried to work, but felt too sick. On September 28, 1843 Emma received the highest ordinance of the church, that of the second anointing. This ordinance also called `the fullness of the priesthood.' Joseph became sick at dinner.. His self-diagnosis was that he had every symptom of poisoning.

Twenty-two years later Brigham Young described a `secret council,' probably the November 5, meeting, at which he said Joseph accused Emma of the poisoning and `called upon her to deny it if she could...He told her that she was a child of hell, and literally the most wicked woman on this earth, that there was not one more wicked than she. He told her where she got the poison, and how she put it in a cup of coffee... His wife Emma had become the ruling spirit, and money had become her god.'

"We now know who Joseph's successor will be; it is little Joseph, I have just seen him ordained by his father," said Newel Whitney. He poured the oil on his head, and he was set apart to be his father's successor in office, holding all the powers his father held. For he shall be my successor to the Presidency of the High Priesthood: a Seer, and a Revelation and Prophet, unto the Church which appointment belonged to him by blessing and by right.

In the midst of the turmoil with the Relief Society, Emma watched Joseph launch a new effort by declaring himself a candidate for President of the United States in the 1844 election. Word of Emma and Joseph's domestic difficulties spread to outside sources... Emma left on a steamboat for St. Louis on April 19, 1844.. Emma entered the main room of the Mansion House on April 24. A bar, complete with counter, shelves, and glasses for serving liquor, stood in the room. Porter Rockwell reigned supreme over it. "Joseph, what is the meaning of that bar in this house?" Joseph countered that all hotels had their bars. The arrangement was only temporary. "As for me," she continued, "I will take my children and go across to the old house and stay there, for I will not have them raised up under such conditions.

A hundred loyal men had left Nauvoo for the East to campaign for Joseph's presidency. He defied his opponents: "I have more to boast of than any man … I am the only man that has ever been able to keep a whole church together since the days of Adam." He indicates here that he is beyond and greater than Jesus Christ. Comparing himself to "Paul, John, Peter and Jesus," he asserted, "I boast that no man ever did a work as I... the Latter-day Saints never ran away from me yet.

On June 12, Joseph and seventeen others were arrested on charges stemming from the destruction of the press and were acquitted by Judge Daniel H. Wells. On the evening of June 22, Emma, now four months pregnant saw to the needs of her family and household. The mob kept coming and wanted him in jail. Joseph accused of running when the heat was on by church members, asked his older brother: "What shall we do?" Joseph stood silent for a few minutes, and then looked at his older brother. "If you go back I will go with you, but we shall be butchered." Joseph stated, "that it was to be that he should lay down his life as a martyr. He took off his garments with the Masonic symbols that he wore for protection.

Joseph told members of the household, "I go as a lamb to the slaughter, but if my death will atone for any faults I have committed during my lifetime I am willing to die," said Joseph. It was obvious here that he did not believe in the atonement of Jesus Christ. He wanted to atone for his own sins, because he believed he was the new savior. He believed that Christ did not get the job done because the church went into apostasy, in spite of Romans 5:11 **"And not only so, but we also joy in God through our Lord Jesus Christ, by whom we have now received the atonement."**

The next day a messenger delivered a letter to Emma from Joseph. "Myself and Hyrum have been again arrested for treason because we called out the Nauvoo Legion," he wrote, "but when the truth comes out we have nothing to fear. We all feel calm and composed." The first writ thirteen days earlier had been for destruction of the press, but Joseph explained in his June 22, letter to the Governor that the Nauvoo court had already acquitted him. The governor sidestepped legal entanglements by making treason the grounds for this second arrest.

Joseph and Hyrum grabbed for hidden guns, then the four bolted the door and held it. Unable to gain entry, the mob fired through the wood. A ball hit Hyrum on the left side of his nose, shattering bone and flesh and knocking him backward to the floor. "I am a dead man!" he cried as another bullet entered his head from under his chin. Joseph opened the door a crack and fired until the gun chamber clicked empty. Bullets from outside the window sprayed the room. Taylor fell against the windowsill. Joseph leaped for the window as a mob burst through the door, pinning Richards behind it. Two bullets penetrated Joseph's back as a third entered his chest. With a cry of "O Lord, My God!" he lurched through the window, hung on the sill for a moment, then plummeted to the ground below. Joseph landed by an old well.

Above the well and inverted elongated pentagram is displayed as a memorial [pentagrams represents the goat's head of Satan]. Lucy Smith (Joseph and Hyrum's mother) entered then, sank back, and cried, "My God, my God, why hast thou forsaken this family!" She positioned herself between her dead sons, resting a hand on each body. An estimated ten thousand mourners came "to look upon the noble, lifeless forms..." Apparently Lucy Smith worried about Joseph's estate, telling Emma that Joseph's "creditors will come forward and use up all the property there is." When Joseph had applied for bankruptcy in 1842 he listed his debts at $73,066.38 (more than $500,000 in today's dollars).

As Brigham spoke, many in the audience believed they witnessed a miracle took place. One said, "I saw in.. Brigham Young the tall, straight, and portly form of the Prophet Joseph Smith clothed in a sheen of light covering him to his feet and I heard the real and perfect voice of the Prophet." The incident satisfied many people in the church that the "mantle of Joseph was on Brigham."

Emma argued, "it was secret things which... cost Joseph and Hyrum their lives, and it will cost you and the twelve your lives." With her (eleventh) pregnancy approaching term, she decided to move her family back into the old Homestead house the week of November 4, to gain some measure of privacy. At nine o'clock on the morning of November 17, 1844, four months past her fortieth birthday, Emma gave birth to a son. About this time newspapers published stories that several Mormon leaders had been ejected from the church and Emma Smith was soon to be among them.

Emma remarried after Joseph's death and left the Mormons and founded the Reorganized Church of Latter-day Saints. Her son Joseph never did receive the honors that Joseph Smith had promised him. He was to be the new president of the LDS Church.

Taming The Lion

CHAPTER 11

OUR STRUGGLE AGAINST EVIL

Through my government job, I found myself involved in an `est' training seminar, now called `The Forum'. The seminars developed by Werner Erhard, emerged out of a myriad of studies including Scientology. Scientology is the foundation of est. Erhard took the process one step further in developing 'est' seminars.

Werner's road was parallel to mine with the exception of Mormon and Christian aspirations. He turned his back on God and I was looking for truth. He ended in Scientology and had an encounter that he never discussed with anyone of public knowledge. Werner's profile is important because it also reveals what happens when people defy God and deliberately walk into the opposite direction.

As in Mormonism, no explanation of what a person is about to enter, is in itself excluding choice or free will that God granted us. People who had participated either could not remember what had happened to them or they were sworn to secrecy. My supervisor got involved and persuaded her underlings and coworkers, and many of the people in the department signed up. She had moved to Denver from California, very educated and admired for her ability to climb right to the top of the ladder. She sent me flowers on my birthday in the office and that was unheard of from a supervisor. Some ingredients during the temple sessions reminded me a little of the 'est' training.

People locked into large rooms in a motel from early morning till four o'clock in the morning on the first night in my case. Usually sixteen to twenty hours each day (two weekends) without opportunity to go to the bathroom as usual, eat, take pills, smoke or fulfill the general body functions. The emphasis of the seminar was to shock one's routine by not allowing it to function naturally. Confined with a group of approximately three hundred people, it was to give a person the opportunity to discover bad habits and make one's life work.

To give a little background, these `est' encounters began in 1971 through 1984 but are still conducted under different names. They have been somewhat modified. An estimated 700,000 people participated in a period of over thirteen years. `est' attracted lots of criticism for their authoritarian form of indoctrination and produced hundreds of obsessively eager acolytes talking others into their seminars. The acolytes were unpaid and willing to talk people into becoming new trainees.

'est' participants paid what used to be $250 each and now at least $625 for a seminar for two weekends locked up in a motel. The theme was based on the notion that life wasn't working. Most had a problem that needed to be overcome. One girl was afraid to have children, after the training she got pregnant. Another person was afraid to get married wanted fixing and sometimes it brought desired changes and sometimes not. Not knowing what was involved, it got my curiosity and I trusted this woman to be my friend. Her description about what to expect sounded almost too simple and certainly not anything threatening. The theme talked about indicated: persons needed to get rid of extra baggage and become transformed. Forbes Magazine in September 1991 reported that 'The 'est' Corporation' owed $14 million to the IRS that the corporation racked up $76 million in gross profit between 1975 and 1981. Werner Erhard's where abouts became a mystery for a few years until last year his own daughters exposed him. He sold the corporation to his trainers. An article in August 1975 in Psychology Today, by Mark Brewer, describes some of the procedures. What is interesting, the people who attend these sessions are intellectuals, educated people, and famous Hollywood personalities and from the middle class in general. He described it as a pop-psych trip [exceptionally misrepresented]. The motto was `When you know you are a mechanical anus, you've `got it'.

Information in the Department head's office was available after it was over. They knew of this problem. It was a mental hospital

Taming The Lion

where we worked. They neglected to warn their employees. The agency was a political football and they were careful to stay on the sidelines. They did not want anything to leak to the press. That did protect me from loosing my job.

Once again I came to the conclusion that God intervened because I did not go through the whole training realizing what was going on, I refused to be scared by their scare tactics. I stayed in the training for two days, one weekend and left town because I knew they would not let me get away with it. How right I was. They tried to catch up with me. I knew too much about what they were doing and they did not want it exposed.

Working on a degree in Psychology, I had some understanding from that education and my occult background filled in the rest. First they put people into a hysterical state of mind where their souls literally jump out of their bodies and then hypnotized them and inserted their sales pitch without people's knowledge.. To get the whole process done took two weekends. The candidate had no clue what was stored in their minds. It wasn't very long before each person would find out what they were stuck with.

Using ocean waves covering up distorted the words is a subliminal procedure to get past the built in censure. The article I got a hold of afterwards stated that prominent lawyers, doctors and psychologists endorsed the training. Werner Erhard claims that he had tried for years to develop techniques to motivate people into selling products. Finally had an illumination in his car and got the answer. Strange that he could not describe this experience.

Called training but not teaching anything, were the words coming out of the trainer's mouth. According to Werner, "what it does is give people the space to learn from themselves." Because there is a psychological change maybe even a spirit change, many friendships and marriages disintegrate afterward with people who have not undergone the training. They cease to agree with the body of people they belong to and move into the body of people created by Erhard's method to promote his product: `the 'est' training.' It reminds me of what is going on with most people today. To have a relationships with others one has to die to one's own ideas and be in complete agreement with the other party or they cannot handle the relationship. Whoever is most aggressive will set the tone. Cults are like that as well. All have to agree or are made to think alike. When one marriage partner leaves Mormonism they become 'unequally yoked' as the Bible calls it, which produces spiritual warfare between the two. Mormon leaders try to break up the marriage to keep the committed one in the cult. My husband and I were unable to have a civil conversation until we were both out of Mormonism.

The writer of the article describes the following: "What trainees come out with is the understanding that their minds are perfect machines or robots. They have become trained human beings, and they love it. They also come out feeling a sort of ecstasy." That ecstasy comes from being part of a group of individuals, who have been taken to zero and reprogrammed with affirmations about themselves with a desire to work for the organization. Who knows what else happened from the spirit realm. My experience was not ecstasy but disgust that people would stoop that low for the dollar. The processed get an overzealous desire to tell others about the training, but not about content, and the excitement on how wonderful it is quickly convinces others to put their money there.

Only a small group of paid staff supported by an army of volunteers, who give up to forty hours a week at times. They have a zombie like attention to duty. Their unfailing adulation of Werner Erhard [then, the rich and famous], makes them become branches of Werner, much like Mormon missionaries become branches of the LDS Church and the Hitler Youth and SS Storm troopers, branches of Hitler.

The principle, this technique is based on, is biblical. "**I (Jesus Christ) am the vine, ye are the branches: He that abideth in me, and I in him, the same bringeth forth much fruit: for without me ye can do nothing. John 15:5 For if the firstfruit be holy, the lump is also holy: and if the root be holy, so are the branches.**" (Romans 11:16) This leads back to the two spirits, the Holy Spirit and the spirit of this world. One or the other is the root of the tree, we are the branches for the leader we identify with. **"And I will punish the world for their evil, and the wicked for their iniquity; and I will cause the arrogancy of the proud to cease, and will lay low the haughtiness of the terrible.** *"* (Isaiah 13:11) **"Thou shalt bring down the noise of strangers, as the heat in a dry place; [even] the heat with the shadow of a cloud: the branch of the terrible ones shall be brought low."** (Isaiah 25:5) There are many false prophets is the reason `ones' is plural.

The Training described as ghoulish and unexplainable, has a reputation of a brave new application of classic techniques in indoctrination and mental conditioning worthy of Pavlov himself. [That is a misrepresentation from beginning to end. The technique is ancient]. The representatives boast about it giving a strong sense of personal worth. The recruits arranged in three groups of rigid order, sit in chairs for more than sixteen-hour days. The trainers harangue and cajole the recruits [much like the military] into believing that their lives were not working [using vulgar, filthy words and bad language, demoralizing recruits by calling them vile names]. They described [planting suggestions in recruit's heads] the anxiety they were going to experience shortly. Next they described what the trainees were going to endure through the coming hours. "...Your mind is so confused with beliefs. that you are incapable of experiencing life.." Therefore, yelled Tony, "we're gonna throw away your whole belief system. We're gonna tear you down and put you back together"...while Tony bombarded them hour after hour, the recruits shook, became confused and finally, in a great majority of cases, dislodged the old ideas and behavior patterns.

When I asked Werner the difference between est and mass mind control, he brushed my query aside as not being a 'representational question'. Even some members of the est Advisory Board, whose duty it is to evaluate the techniques and results of the est training, are not much clearer about what's going on.

Taming The Lion

Tony's assault on belief continued. Endlessly he seemed to recognize hands, dull-faced assistants hustled down the aisles with mikes to trainees who wanted to share their stories.

Tony assured them all, confusion was the first step toward 'natural knowing,' the very pinnacle of est-think. ..Six hours of deprivation felt like seven years of locusts, and when aching backs, filling bladders, and desperately wandering minds finally neared the point of open rebellion, Tony showed the `est's curative process. He told them to go inward, [while] he sipped.. tea. He gave direction to create space in their bodies.. Reminiscent of some.. mass hypnotist.. affirmations. the big truth process.

The writer goes on: [The next day] "..250 of us, lying on the floor, writhing and gesticulating, amid a din of whimpers, sobs, wrenching and ..groaning." The writer refers to William Sargant, a British psychiatrist, who studied and wrote in `Battle for the Mind' (1957), about the described abreaction as `a timeworn physiological trick that has been used, for better or worse. Generations of preachers and demagogues use it to soften up their listeners' minds and help them take on desired patterns of belief and behavior'. The writer closed his article by stating that the recently federally funded 'est' training of school children is a step in the direction of making people happy and efficient and such training is the wave of the future."

Another article in the same issue of Psychology Today, by Richard P. Marsh `I am the cause of my world', "a San Francisco State professor took 'est' training twice, and felt a surge of life." This surge of life is momentary.

Compare these comments with Jesus' advice about eternal life, "**And the Father himself, which hath sent me, hath borne witness of me. Ye have neither heard his voice at any time, nor seen his shape. And ye have not his word abiding in you: for whom he hath sent, him ye believe not. Search the scriptures; for in them ye think ye have eternal life: and they are they which testify of me. And ye will not come to me, that ye might have life." (John**

Taming The Lion

5:37-40) "For whosoever will save his life shall lose it: but whosoever will lose his life for my sake, the same shall save it " (Luke 9:24)

Mr. Marsh states further: "In describing what goes on behind the locked doors among the approximately 300 participators during a session, keeping people squirming painfully in their seats for endless hours while (the trainer) expresses his love for the crowd by using vulgar and abusive language to wake them up to the possibility of a more abundant life."

The mechanics are very similar to the Mormon Temple rituals. The boredom during est is what creates a tremendous problem. `Getting it' is the goal. In Mormonism, `Getting the rituals down pat, the actions, the words and the grips' is the goal.

The author goes on to say: "I recently took the est training for a second time as a fringe member of an invited group of 250 leaders in psychiatry, education, law,science,aviation and the human potential movement. The training is in some respects painful and exhausting. bathroom, food, and sleep breaks are minimal. Smoking and drugs are forbidden...Nearly all invited participants endured the four grueling days required. I can only speak for myself," the writer goes on, "I `got' that I would rather be right than alive. In order to be right, I very ingeniously make other people wrong. This tactic preserves my righteousness, but the price is no less than my own life...I `got' that my mind is a pile of multi sensory snapshots, recording my moment-by-moment experiences. This picture album that is my mind has a single purpose: to insure its own survival. I `got' that I am the cause of my own world and not the effect and am therefore responsible for it... I was tired because I was under pressure. The long hours and the tough ground rules had taken their toll... I consider nonsense the charge made by some critics that the est training is a form of brainwashing.

Precisely the reverse is true. Brainwashing attempts to confuse by sudden reversals of logic, to frighten and humiliate a captive subject in order to break his will and insinuate forcibly into his mind the

Taming The Lion

belief system of his captor. The est training is coherent and non-contradictory; it is respectful of the individual at all times, being based on a set of agreements about procedures freely entered into by all concerned; as a point of doctrine, it asserts the foolishness of all belief systems." The writer calls it, "De-hypnosis perhaps...but whatever 'est' is.... ??" This writer apparently forgot what happened which is indicated by the statements he made. The statements were on the other end of the spectrum.

Right after I got back from California, a week after the traumatic experience with 'est', a letter went out to my mother. It was dated November 4, 1978.

"Dear Mom and Dad, I had a terrible training in that `est' seminar I told you about over the phone. It was like meeting Satan in person, horrible. They got us into the training under false pretenses. Talking to eight people before the training and receiving reassuring comments that it would be a healthy encounter, I felt save. These were people I worked with day in and day out. Not one told me what was going on in the seminar. Everything looked legitimate, what a shock when they locked the door behind us and positioned guards by the door.

A group of three hundred, which included myself, subjected to extreme physical discomfort and verbal abuse, was torture for me from 8 AM to 4 AM the next day. That same morning, we were to come back at 10 AM and stay till 11 PM that night. Starving till 11 PM, we sat in a straight back chair. We spent the first 6 hours following rules. People had smuggled all sorts of `helps' in and began confessing. Then they processed us with hypnotism, brainwashing, meditation and how to leave your body. Feeling like they must have in the concentration camps getting ready for the gas chamber. They broke people's personalities down to zero. The trainer told us to throw out everything we believed and accept everything they had to say. They said if we stopped in the middle of this training it would be like stepping off a roller coaster up in the air at its highest point. We would crash mentally.

Taming The Lion

So scared during one of their processes, I became unconscious, got diarrhea and came close to vomiting. Hysteria with screaming, shakes, and breaking out in cold sweat was next. People all over the room were passing out and throwing up. Can you imagine this is going on today in America in 1978? By the time dinner break came at 11 PM, I fled out to the car, it was pouring raining, I was sobbing in the car, nauseated and trembling all over. When the training was over I was completely disoriented and got lost trying to get home at 4:00 AM. Without any rest, I went back the next day. They had rearranged the whole room, everything in perfect order with sort of a podium the whole length of the room. The process called `danger' followed, mind you 300 people in this process.

They had a row of wardens sitting in the back of the room. They looked like wardens, never moved a muscle in their faces. Each row had to line up on the podium and look at the audience and the trainer was screaming: "look at these people: they are supposed to be loving you, they are unconscious robots. "They looked awful and their faces full of fear and dread." My heart beat like it was going to jump out of me. People were screaming passing out, throwing up, crying, laughing hysterically, they had lost their personality. These were prominent people like a Scientist from the Colorado University, a Psychiatrist, business people, and the wealthy with diamonds, even a movie star from Hollywood and her boyfriend. Dope addicts, pushers, alcoholics and the like identified themselves. One girl confessed she had tried suicide twice with overdosing. Women who had aborted babies and on and on, they were there to get rid of their guilt feelings. They were confessing all over the place.

The trainer pointed at a man and screamed again: "look at this Psychiatrist," who stood there crying like a baby. "Look at his twisted body and you go to him and pay $ 25 for his advice." There were even young teenagers, 12 years old and people 70 years old. You would not believe it. It was the job of wardens to stare each of us down. They appeared dead in their eyes and faces to a point where I wanted to slap them across the face to wake them up. Young girls stood there and sobbed. I never experienced anything so horrible. People had come from all over, Kansas, Texas, Nebraska and many from Salt Lake City (Mormons). Two young girls who were Mormons got up and talked their way out on the first day. They got scared right away. Analyzing everything in spite of strict orders not to, they kept reassuring everybody that the training would not work for people who did that.

To me it appeared as if some of the people were possessed with demons after the processes. I could see one hanging over me during a process. Praying to get to the truth of what this was all about, I came to the conclusion that Satan is gathering himself an army. The whole atmosphere was evil. When the people got through with the whole training they dedicated their lives to this organization without pay.

The people I worked with spent 20 hours a week there guarding, giving out name tags, running the microphones and what not for free. They came out proclaiming that the experience was worth thousands of dollars. They suddenly belonged to this large group, all loving each other because they had become the same through this process. Trouble is after they are processed, they can't get along with the rest of the world and they talk all their friends and family into undergoing the process. Werner Erhard processed his own mother and the whole family to get along with them according to a biography about him.

Refusing to complete the training, I called my supervisor and gave two weeks notice. Many of the people processed worked with me and they were working on everybody, even the head of the department. I was scared. The director did not let me quit for fear that I would report the whole episode. He told me to call back when I returned from California, so we could work things out. Telling no one including my husband, where I was heading, I left. They would try to find me, was on my heart. The `est' people knew right away what happened and called my supervisor and others called the house trying to find out where I had gone. I drove two and a half days and was without sleep for a week. Unable to eat, that stuff went around and around in my head. The more I thought about it the more frightened I became. Twice I got lost traveling and came close to suicide. The belief that I would go to hell kept me from it. But my biblical anchor had suffered a critical blow.

Finally, I landed at my hide out. It stabilized me and I shared with them what had happened to me. It gave me an opportunity to share the importance of Jesus Christ who had empowered me to leave without fearing their threats of a mental crash. Somewhere tucked in the corner of my heart I knew Jesus Christ would carry me through the whole episode, he had done it so many times before, your loving daughter."

I went home and called the office and went back to work. The head of the department gave orders for people to stop harassing me. By some strange coincidence they had found these articles I mentioned and began investigating and found that 50% of their personnel was under the influence of that organization. They were shocked. This was the department of Institutions, which included a Mental Hospital. They kept the whole situation and their predicament under wraps, because the Department of Institutions was a political football. They could not afford a scandal. My supervisor had a heart attack at 38 years old and later died, not too many months after this happened. He could not stop smoking three packs a day. He was so up tight about loosing his job, that he came back to work two weeks after open-heart surgery.

The administrators of `est' called me to come to their office and confess what I had experienced. "No way," I told them. They said I was going to get my $300 back since I had not completed the experience. Begging people to listen, I told everyone I knew to keep them from going but curiosity got the best of some of them. I witnessed for Christ but they did not hear me. What they could not understand was that I was the only one who came out of there with that kind of conviction. That is why I did not expose it myself. No one would have believed it and I would not have had a leg to stand on in court. In 1992, I decided to write about this and researched books dealing with this subject. They were in the library. The information I found confirms what I experienced. One, a biography, characterizes Werner Erhard by his own admission.

Two ladies, who kept on harassing me, lost their jobs. It wasn't long before an opportunity came for another job away from this agency. One of their processed young men whom I had befriended, kept approaching me for many months but in vain. It is sixteen years later and I sit here and wonder how many people had major spiritual damage.

David in the Old Testament was aware of the warfare against his soul. **"Let them be ashamed and confounded together that seek after my soul to destroy it; let them be driven backward and put to shame that wish me evil."** (Psalms 40:14) **"But those that seek my soul, to destroy it, shall go into the lower parts of the earth.*"*** *(*Psalms 63:9) Jesus Christ warned in Matthew 10:28 not to fear the devil but to fear God Who can destroy both soul and body in hell: **"And fear not them which kill the body, but are not able to kill the soul: but rather fear him which is able to destroy both soul and body in hell.*"***

From the Book `The Transformation of a Man Werner Erhard, the Founder of est', comes an insight into the character of him. Though by descent half Jewish, he did not receive a Jewish upbringing He went regularly to Episcopal Sunday School. The belief that Christ was the savior was with him all the way. "I was an altar boy there for eight years. Not much later I first began to learn something of Eastern religious thought. This was not originally out of desire for spiritual attainment.

It was only later, in studying spiritual disciplines that I heard about spiritual attainment. Incidentally, there is no such thing as attainment when it comes to being spiritual," said Werner Erhard," according to the author. Werner was right, according to Romans 7:15-21: **"For that which I do I allow not: for what I would, that do I not; but what I hate, that do I. If then I do that which I would not, I consent unto the law that it is good. Now then it is no more I that do it, but sin that dwelleth in me. For I know that**

Taming The Lion

in me (that is, in my flesh,) dwelleth no good thing: for to will is present with me; but how to perform that which is good I find not. For the good that I would I do not: but the evil which I would not, that I do. Now if I do that I would not, it is no more I that do it, but sin that dwelleth in me. I find then a law, that, when I would do good, evil is present with me."

Werner further stated: "I remember how I first got into Yoga. I was eleven or twelve. I did all the exercises and practices. I did this on my own. There was nobody with whom I could discuss it. I was trying to walk without expending energy. I got one leg to float along without effort. It wasn't just physical disciplines that I went into. I also had conversations about God with myself. I wondered whether there really was a God and what it all meant what I was taught to believe. I wondered why God made it so bad? Why did he make war and famine? I also asked whether I was really responsible. I don't think I put it that way then. I would have said: "Can you get away with breaking the rules? Why do you have to keep the rules?"

Werner told me, the author continues: "I had begun to detach myself from my surroundings, from my family, my friends and my teachers. What was going on within, removed me from the world around me. I became very lonely. I was becoming aware of my intelligence. My family could not really respond to my intelligence. They were uneasy. I was by now dissecting everything that I encountered. I was interested in the problems of human existence, human relationships, love, sex, the purpose of it all, values, ethics and integrity. I could not discuss such things with my family, school friends or teachers. It was all right to write about such things, but not to talk about them. That was forbidden intimacy.

After some considerable personal problems and to sort things out, he went to the beach by himself and lay still in the sun for a long time. "It was quiet, in the sense that few people were around making noise. Yet I was surrounded by, immersed in sound: the sound of the waves and the rhythmic beating of the surf, the jangling sounds of the boardwalk. I just lay there, doing nothing, being bathed in that sound and that white noise. As I lay there I began to have the most extraordinary experience. I just detached from everything. I hate to call it an out-of-body experience, but I transcended myself as a personality there. With my eyes closed, I could see what was happening there on the beach, how others were moving, how I myself was lying there. And then I could see everything and everywhere. I experienced a oneness with the universe. I lost the kind of consciousness that locates one in a place. I became the universe!"

Werner got married and began to experience major hell, and admitted marriage was not for him. He began reading and searching. As a car salesman, changed his name to hide his Jewishness and began extra marital affairs. "This part of my life was a long disaster. I messed up everything I touched." In 1959 he moved his wife and three children to Hatboro, Pennsylvania to carry on his affair somewhere else. His wife said later that she was pregnant with number four when he asked for a divorce. "The fact is, until people are transformed, until they transcend their minds, they are simply puppets, perhaps anguished, hurting, strongly feeling puppets, but one is nonetheless limited to a fixed repertoire of responses. And that is what karma is all about," Werner stated philosophically. Pat filed for divorce.

"You could tell by looking at him that he was living a double life at this time," Werner's Aunt Kitty Clauson told me about it. In the glove compartment Pat (his wife) found false identity papers, Social Security cards and drivers' licenses, and a checkbook for both Werner and June, his new partner.

Werner proceeded to find a typically American answer, in the books of Napoleon Hill and Maxwell Maltz on positive thinking and self-image psychology. Hill was the author of `Think and Grow Rich'; Maltz, the author of `Psycho-Cybernetics'. Maltz and Hill exude optimism and the go-getter energy, fellowship, and boosterism of the Rotary Club. What Werner actually found was a sort of religion. He also came across the human potential movement through the study and application of motivational techniques. From

Taming The Lion

there he was to go a step further to what he now self mockingly calls the `business of transformation'.

Make detailed statements of goals, specify what one is prepared to pay in order to reach them, and color them with desire and imagination. One must visualize oneself `on the road to success,' take definite steps toward those goals and then see oneself as having attained them. [Visualization is described in the Scriptures as imagery]

What came to mind as I'm reading this was Oral Roberts. He stated this very same application to a stadium full of aspiring preachers. Here is what the Bible has to say about that. To God these kinds of formulas are an abomination.

"Then said he unto me, Son of man, hast thou seen what the ancients of the house of Israel do in the dark, every man in the chambers of his imagery? for they say, The LORD seeth us not; the LORD hath forsaken the earth. He said also unto me, Turn thee yet again, and thou shalt see greater abominations that they do. *(*Ezekiel 8:12,13)

The Hindus call Kundalini: the transmutation of the sex drive. A genius is one who, by the sublimation of sex, has increased his mental vibrations to the point where he can communicate with sources of knowledge not ordinarily available.

He was already familiar with hypnosis and experimented by auto hypnosis on himself and others who grew out of Yoga. Hypnosis is potentially very dangerous. Hypnosis characterized by an altered state of consciousness, a trance state, is induced either by oneself alone or with the aid of another person. Franz Anton Mesmer discovered it, a Viennese physician who did a spectacular healing that he called animal magnetism, akin to electrical magnetism.

Hypnosis is often described as a `special form of trance developed in Western civilization', many states reached through hypnosis resemble those reached through meditation and Yogic practices. The ritual and paraphernalia and the setting are, to be

Taming The Lion

sure, different: the so-called `induction' or relaxation procedures vary [Werner used the beach with the noise of ocean waves]; so, too, the Oriental will use a Sanskrit word for his mantra (the sound associated with trance induction).

One may expect a unified theory of altered states of consciousness to emerge. Confronted is the whole matter of `suggestion.' Western hypnosis is frequently reduced to manipulative suggestion. Thus, the hypnotist might give his subject a posthypnotic suggestion to perform a particular action after leaving the trance state and not to remember consciously that he had been given such instructions. Unscrupulous persons might gain control over others. Werner believed that people are already, normally, in trance and thus it is easy to hypnotize people with a single word or action.

"The point is to be dehypnotized," Werner emphasized, "to go beyond the mind is what I call the Self," which is what Eastern disciplines believe. Werner began investigating motivation and human development. He began encounter and sensitivity groups and his curiosity touched base with a whole list of psychologists, beginning with Maslow's selfactualizing. He got interested in the discipline of telling truth absolutely. He noticed that people including himself almost never tell the truth. He had a `peak experience' and had a profound sense of Self. "It was only later, as I worked through Zen and Scientology, that I began to understand the matter better," Werner said.

He calls it `Getting to the top of the pile of bodies' he began to get skeptical of reality. There was a shift in values, things that had been important: success and satisfaction ceased to be important suddenly. He touched base with Zen by Alan Watts an Episcopal clergyman who renounced his priesthood and became an advocate of Oriental religions. Disciplines taught more about the Self also called Being, Essence, or Buddha nature. Not until Scientology did I get a clear distinction between Mind and Self.

Taming The Lion

Werner also nonchalantly probed areas that would have been forbidden ground to most academic investigators and even off limits to Alan Watts, whose practice of Zen never strayed far from the respectable. Werner probed the bizarre, eccentric, exotic, and utterly disreputable new movements, Subud and Martial Arts and religions that were growing in California, and ransacked them for notions and practices of value to him in his own quest. Werner later participated in latihan itself, which is a form of meditation aiming at `inner stillness' and opening of the mind to meaning and `divine energies' [There is only counterfeit divine energy without Christ Jesus].

"I had no idea what Scientology was," Werner told me, wrote the author. "But I did what came along and agreed to have the Scientology communication course presented to our organization. The course was arduous. There was no brain work in it, just exercises that at first appeared to have no relationship to life. There also was a two-person, two-hour, eyeball-to-eyeball confrontation. I did the exercises. I saw their point, and I saw how to apply them. The course was brilliant."

"Werner encouraged his whole staff to take the Scientology communication course. Werner went through five Scientology levels, and received a total of about seventy hours of auditing. Werner encountered that the mind was the root of all the trouble. He states that he was able to get back to his `memories' of past lives."

Reincarnation does not exist according to Jesus' declaration: **"Jesus answered and said unto him, Verily, verily, I say unto thee, Except a man be born again, he cannot see the kingdom of God. Nicodemus saith unto him, How can a man be born when he is old? can he enter the second time into his mother's womb, and be born? Jesus answered, Verily, verily, I say unto thee, Except a man be born of water and of the Spirit, he cannot enter into the kingdom of God. That which is born of the flesh is flesh; and that which is born of the Spirit is spirit.** *"* (John 3:3-6)

Werner was getting in touch with something, but it was not past lives since we are only born once to die. **"For I was alive without**

the law once: but when the commandment came, sin revived, and I died. And the commandment, which was ordained to life, I found to be unto death.." (Romans 7:9,10) "**And as it is appointed unto men once to die, but after this the judgment:** " (Hebrews 9:27)

To continue Werner's recollection: "After my experience with Scientology, I saw what it means to see the Mind as a machine." said Erhard. Hubbard is a variant more usually associated with Eastern philosophy, particularly with Buddhism. For Hubbard, the most important thing in the universe is a god like creative force called the `thetan', itself the creator and definer of universes. The thetan does not exist in space and time, and has no mass or energy. It is the true Self of the individual, his soul, or `essence', and is immortal. The world of matter, energy, space, and time [abbreviated] the MEST universe, as Hubbard calls it. Buddhists call it illusion. It is created by the thetans, and has no independent existence. The thetan is a `MEST production unit.'

MEST is the material counterfeit to Hebrews 11:1 "**Now faith is the substance of things hoped for, the evidence of things not seen** ".

Man as we know him exists in a fallen state. He has forgotten his essential, immortal Self. He has entrapped himself in the MEST universe. He even believes himself to be wholly MEST. No worse fate could have befallen him. For the MEST universe is a universe of force and slavery, where honesty, justice, reason, and integrity are impossible, a universe wholly at war with the thetan essence, which is `naturally good', honest, and just full of integrity.

[It is not possible to equate Thetan with the Holy Spirit, because the lower spiritual realm without Christ Jesus is demonic. Therefore, it cannot be `naturally good'. "**I thank God through Jesus Christ our Lord. So then with the mind I myself serve the law of God; but with the flesh the law of sin** ". (Romans 7:25) We can only be empowered through the Holy Spirit to overcome sin. That fact Werner did not acknowledge. Werner was looking to find

Taming The Lion

this freedom in Eastern religions such as Zen-like Buddhism and Scientology.]

According to Werner Erhard, the way to happiness is to win freedom from this entrapment by the world of mass, energy, space, and time, to regain thetan freedom and creativity. So far, little in Scientology differs from Buddhism and other Oriental philosophies that search for escape from the `wheel' of birth and death. There are also similarities with Gnostic and Christian attempts to free the spirit from the flesh.

Every time the individual encounters a new experience reminding him in any way of an earlier trauma, the reactive mind goes into operation and the person goes unconscious, automatically acting as he did earlier [until] he no longer has space in which to create; he "goes solid." He is hemmed in by traumatic memories, and by all the agreements that he made with other persons and with the MEST universe. He comes to think that he is MEST body, and forgets his non-MEST origins.

The goal of Scientology is to retrieve the individual from his agreement with the MEST universe [thus his commitment to God if that is an agreement he strives for]. To reduce the apparently infinite power of the MEST universe over him to zero and to increase the apparent zero of his own personal universe to infinity.. [To reduce his commitment to Christ Jesus to zero and increase the zero?? Gobble de guck!

Next Mind Dynamics.. a mind-expansion program features extraordinary demonstrations and intensive training in memory feats, in enhancement of psychic powers, ESP, precognition, and psychic diagnosis and healing, techniques drawing on hypnosis and autohypnosis, and on autogenic therapy, in addition to techniques. They were also cultivated by `natural psychic' Edgar Cayce, and by Jose' Silva, founder of Silva Mind Control. ..a number of colorful effects drawing from Rosicrucianism, Theosophy, and other disciplines. Clairvoyance, extrasensory perception, and healing have always been reported with the hypnotic trance. Alexander Everett, the Englishman who founded Mind Dynamics. Alexander told me, 'Searching for methods to reach the inner spiritual state was the aim. I still didn't find a way to reach the spiritual level effectively.'

Werner got involved with the Edgar Cayce group. "It was the same thing that I had encountered with Madame Blavatsky with Rosicrucianism. She did not know how to teach you to get there either. I learned in Theosophy the power of imagination and visualization, he said." Now he was ready to create his own reality.

Somewhere between Corte Madera and the Golden Gate Bridge, the man in the car on the freeway was transformed: the individual who emerged from the Mustang in San Francisco a half hour later was a different kind of being. Werner had an extraordinary experience, and found what he had been searching for, in one discipline after another, for nearly eight years. Werner could have saved himself much time and money by just looking in the Scriptures, everything he talks about is written. He claims money was no object. He could have had eternal life with God. Werner never did explain what happened. Erhard had no words to explain what happened in the car, but the effect was an altered life. He began identifying himself as the space, the creator, the source of all stuff. "I became Self. Experience," Werner said, "is simply evidence that I am here. It is not who I am. I am I am."

[Werner is saying, he is god. **"Thou shalt have no other gods before me***." (*Exodus 20:3) " **For though there be that are called gods, whether in heaven or in earth, (as there be gods many, and lords many,) But to us there is but one God, the Father, of whom are all things, and we in him; and one Lord Jesus Christ, by whom are all things, and we by him..**" (1 Corinthians 8:5,6)]

It is as if the Self is the projector, and everything else is the movie. Before the transformation, I could only recognize myself by seeing the movie. Now I saw that I am prior to or transcendent to all that.

Taming The Lion

[What he is saying here is that he has realized that he is a branch, a projector, in other words a medium, through which the force of creativity flows from the spirit world.]

Werner admitted: "I had reached the end. It was all over for Werner Erhard." One is now complete according to Erhard.

[Completion comes through a commitment to Christ Jesus and the Baptism of the Holy Spirit. If the Holy Spirit is not occupying that vacuum, we try to fill it with substitutes and the longing does not get satisfied.]

It makes no sense to be committed to anything: beliefs, ideologies and traditions. The problem is to propel one from Mind to Self [the counterfeit I am]. How is the transition from one state to the other what Werner calls transformation to be achieved?

Werner Erhard is correct, 'no discipline or route leads to the Self' as he admitted earlier. People usually submit to someone to have a life of substance and they become the controller. There is really no Self in a believer, the Holy Spirit lives in a believer and gradually takes control leading to the death of the self, which is the case when the person submits to the demonic spirit entities. He stated that he found out he was a projector through which the movie was being played.

"Now we have received, not the spirit of the world, but the spirit which is of God; that we might know the things that are freely given to us of God. " (1 Corinthians 2:12) This verse states there are two spirits, the spirit of the world and the Spirit who is of God. Werner is talking about contacting the spirit of the world because he rejected the spirit given to us of God earlier. **"Wherein in time past ye walked according to the course of this world, according to the prince of the power of the air, the spirit that now worketh in the children of disobedience: '** (Ephesians 2:2)

"Hereby know ye the Spirit of God: Every spirit that confesseth that Jesus Christ is come in the flesh is of God: And every spirit that confesseth not that Jesus Christ is come in the

flesh is not of God: and this is that spirit of Antichrist, whereof ye have heard that it should come; and even now already is it in the world. Ye are of God, little children, and have overcome them: because greater is he that is in you, than he that is in the world. They are of the world: therefore speak they of the world, and the world heareth them. *"* (1 John 4:2-5)

The `est' training that Werner Erhard developed, provides a format in which siege is mounted on the Mind. It aims to press one beyond one's point of view. Teaching no new belief, it aims to break up the existing `wiring of the Mind,' and thereby to trap the Mind, to allow one to take hold of one's own Mind and then to blow the Mind. The training and its style is irreverent and intrusive. Thus, a transformed individual is unlikely to become a `true believer'.

Looking at what the previous sentence said, these kinds of seminars could easily apply to: **"For what shall it profit a man, if he shall gain the whole world, and lose his own soul?"** (Mark 8:36) Our minds are precious and need guarding, because they belong to God and He advises each of us: **"And be renewed in the spirit of your mind; And that ye put on the new man, which after God is created in righteousness and true holiness."** (Ephesians 4:23,24)

The training aims to enable transformation to occur, not to convey information. The training is about sixty hours in length. The choice is absolute: the cost of righteousness.. one transcends Mind and gives up the `hunger and thirst after righteousness'. This is what Jesus had to say to oppose and warn about the result of the training. Guilt and hunger and thirst for righteousness will be eliminated: " Who points out our flaws and hungers for righteousness none other than the Holy Spirit in us. He is removed with this process.

"Blessed are they which do hunger and thirst after righteousness: for they shall be filled. *"* (Matthew 5:6). That will most likely not be possible when the desire for it is gone because we have to ask for it. When there is no desire for it, we would not be asking to be filled. The cost of becoming a child of demonic spirits is eternal life as a child of God in His presence.

Werner assumes that transformation will have a radical effect on society, as transformed individuals through changed relationships and transformed organizations and institutions mediate it. Existing institutions in education, law, medicine, government will then start to work. Humankind will, in the process, be transfigured [to the Antichrist].

From `The Book of est', by Luke Rhinehart: "The problem is that est is not a religion, not an academic course, and not a belief system. Experiencing the training itself is the only way to get what the training offers, but the closest approximation to the training is a dramatization. The training normally lasts fifteen to twenty hours a day. As a result every trainee suffers from periods of `unconsciousness' when he is so bored, angry, involved in his own fantasies, or simply exhausted that he is unable to experience or recall what is happening in the training itself."

The author describes the experience in detail in his book and confirms my letter to my mother. "We breathe deeply. We listen to the long affirmation of life read to us by the trainer. A tape recording begins to play the sounds of waves crashing rhythmically against our beach, and we are asked to play there...however we feel like playing. I began to feel sick to my stomach. There were no thoughts no memories, just nausea, why? The lady next to her threw up all over the place? The whole process is ridiculous. `You're all liars. You've got nothing, NOTHING. And when you've got nothing then you really have something.' `It's doing nothing that works'.

`Truth process' [comes] after the intense emotional confrontations and breakdowns. It is for some a release to be able to stack the chairs at the side of the room and lie on the floor and `go into our space'. There is a good deal of fear in the room as the process begins. There are some 250 trainees lying on the floor, a half dozen sitting in chairs, and a dozen assistants present to hand out tissues or vomit bags where needed."

Taming The Lion

Adelaide Bry who wrote a book, `est', went back after the training to observe as trainer. Here is what she had to say: "Belief is a disease. The truth believed is a lie. What the trainer later called `the roller coaster ride' had begun. It seemed to me that the idea was to reduce us to pulp, to attack us where we're most vulnerable, to eventually have us identify those areas of our lives that don't produce results. "When you reach a critical mass of observation," Werner says, "things can begin to disappear." I looked around and noted that all but one of the exit doors had signs across them saying `NO EXIT'; the other door had an `est' volunteer in front of it to prevent entry from outside. Stewart said, "The truth puts people to sleep. It goes right to what's unconscious in them, and most people are uncomfortable in their unconsciousness, enough just to chance letting some truth strike the truth in them."

"You are going to feel every feeling there is to feel." Stewart's directions continued, and the scene grew noisy; an incredible cacophony of sound (harsh sound) erupted as each one of the two hundred and fifty men and women, lying flat on their backs on the floor of the giant ballroom, went into their `item'. Two hundred and fifty people in every form of emotion, giving free vent to vomiting, shaking, sobbing, hysterical laughing, raging recreating experiences in a safe space."

This author was a trainer and shares: "I stood on the aisle with a pile of vomit bags in my arms. My eyes scanning the couple of a dozen trainees assigned to me, watching for someone's hand to shoot into the air signaling that he wanted to vomit. I had decided to volunteer for the two weekends because I wanted to see what it was like from the other side. `est's meticulous attention to detail paralleled exact instructions. Several est workers proudly told me that est graduates were in great demand on the California job market. A number of businesses, in fact, were reported to be hiring esters.

Incredible! It occurred to me that if Werner actualized his proposal to train millions, it might have a dramatic effect on everyone's job performance. I saw that Werner has created a

Taming The Lion

situation where people clamor to volunteer. It saves the cost of thousands of salaries and it provides est with dedicated people to attend to the myriad details that contribute to est's success. Werner told me that what people really want to do with their lives is to make a contribution to the well being of others.

My feelings about this aspect of `est' are a sense of community and eager commitment. It fulfills a deep need in contemporary American society. Critics of `est' have compared it, disparagingly, with old-time religion. Its sense of service, of mission, and of course its a definition of a way of being and experiencing. And, like many religions, `est' has its own language.

There are the education workshops. Of the 14 percent of 'est' graduates who are educators (teachers, counselors, administrators), 4,000 have responded to 'est's programs to assist them in adapting 'est' to their work. The workshops provide a place for them to share with each other how they've used 'est' professionally in teaching or learning and the results they've obtained. Out of this have come classroom trainings for children (the Watts training reportedly raised reading scores dramatically), in-service training credit for teachers, and courses based on the 'est' experience. I might add that I've adapted some 'est' techniques for use in my therapy practice and have found them valuable," writes the author Adelaide Bry.

Workshops have been conducted for a mixed bag of professional and special-interest groups, including psychotherapists, scientists, clergy, doctors, and nurses, among others. These programs, incidentally, are highly publicized. `est' makes a big point about never advertising, but it is relentless in its efforts to invite graduates to bring newcomers to guest lectures and to attend graduate functions themselves. Almost no event passes without a pitch for at least one other event. Huge numbers of volunteers are continuously involved with mailings and phone calls to solicit attendance. At first I found these tactics offensive, and I no longer do, as I take responsibility for my response to them.

Taming The Lion

There are two teen programs, one a ten-day `live-in', which takes place in a secluded natural setting, and the other a standard training identical to the regular `est' training. "In the teen training we do a breakthrough process, done as an activity until you lose control. The power releases when you lose control, when you are actually driven out of control. At that point trainees have the option of losing control or not, and the 1,000 teenagers who have thus far been through the training and all did lose control.

We transform your teenager or we don't bring him back. So far they've all come back." The cost for all this is $750. The training stripped away the patterns of our old, habitual transactions, unstuck us from our separate niches, rode right through the armor we'd set up to defend ourselves against one another...best of all, it totally erased all fear and anxiety regarding our future relationships together; there is simply no problem that we won't be able to handle. I see him as totally powerful. Over 2,000 children have gone through it to date. Any child between six and twelve, one of whose parents is an 'est' graduate, is qualified to take it. The training is held for fifty children at a time. More than 14 percent of its graduates, a total of almost 11,000, are educators.

`est' is no ordinary California cult. It is a multi million dollar corporation that has doubled in size each year and operates nationwide with the efficiency of a crack brigade. Prominent lawyers, doctors and psychologists, join it; it has trained California schoolchildren under a Federal grant, and a former chancellor of the University of California Medical School, San Francisco, chairs its Advisory Board.

The trainers fall into a very special category. As Werner's emissaries, the fourteen trainers are alter egos if not quite carbon copies and yet each has an individual personality. They are rigorously trained over a long period. Their apprenticeship is to learn to re-create. What they really have to give up is their ego. In regards to `est' and God: Werner has said, "Belief in God is the greatest single barrier to God in the Universe; (it is almost a total barrier to the experience of God. When you think you have experienced God, you haven't). Experiencing God is experiencing God, and that is true religion." A graduate in training with the guest seminar leaders program said to me right after Werner spoke about training forty million people, "Can you imagine what the world out there would be like if forty million people stopped lying to themselves?""

What needs to be remembered about Werner Erhard is his admission of everyone being a liar, including himself. Sixteen years later these types of organizations began approaching members of my family, things changed for me. To just sit by became impossible. Taking a stand activates the Holy Spirit. Information began to flow to me about these establishments and it enabled me to get some answers at least explaining what had happened to me in 1978 at the 'est' training. The book 'Helter Skelter' describes the story about Charles Manson suggested Scientology in his background. It's founder, Ron Hubbard's life, described in the Los Angeles Times in a detailed feature story came to me from a friend. Then at our little bookstore there was one book out of dozens that Hubbard wrote. It held exactly what I wanted to know. Needing information about the process, it was all described in detail by Ron Hubbard himself. It paralleled the `est' seminar, except Erhard processed groups, where Hubbard processed individuals and used methods of exteriorizing (leaving the body) that Hubbard warned against.

In his book Scientology, The Fundamentals of Thought, by L. Ron Hubbard, he states, "Probably the greatest discovery of Scientology and its most forceful contributions to the knowledge of mankind has been the isolation, the description and handling of the human spirit [soul], accomplished in 1952. I established along scientific rather than religious or humanitarian lines that thing which is the person, the personality, is separable from the body and the mind at will and without causing bodily death or mental derangement...Man had not discovered this before because lacking the technologies of Scientology. To the contrary, there has been an awareness of these phenomena for centuries. The entire cult of Communism is based upon the fact that one lives only one life,

Taming The Lion

there is no hereafter and that the individual has no religious significance. Man at large has been close to this state for at least the last century. The state is of a very low order, excluding as it does all self-recognition. In Scientology [the soul] "thetan" [notice that word] has no mass, no wavelength, no energy and no time or location in space except by consideration or postulate. The spirit, then, is not a thing. It is the creator of things.

Hubbard is talking about the soul, the human spirit is embedded in the soul until regenerated by the Holy Spirit through acceptance of Christ Jesus.

One of the goals in processing in Scientology and 'est' is to `exteriorize' the individual [that means to move the soul out of the body, the soul is man's awareness, his consciousness]... since it has been discovered that he is happier and more capable when so situated." Next Hubbard gets into mental imagery and creation... words can be immediately implanted into the reactive mind which become operable under restimulation at later times [hypnosis].. The goal is total knowingness. Exteriorization under duress is sudden and to the patient inexplicable and is in itself very shocking and will cause mental suffering. Exteriorization under duress is the characteristic of death itself... departure of the soul is generally associated with death.. not so in this case."

L. Ron Hubbard's chapter on "Civilization and Savagery" he writes: "The way to paralyze a nation entirely and to make it completely ungovernable would be to forbid education of any kind within its borders. Also to inculcate into every person within it the feeling that he must receive any information from anybody about anything. To conquer a land, there must be some sort of agreement among the people themselves, as well as between the conqueror and the subdued. Only in this way could one have a society, a civilization or, as we say in Scientology, a smoothly running game."

"The goal of Scientology is playing of a better game... The earliest stage is taking over control of the [subject] by repetitive processes up to 75 hours. A possibility of exteriorizing becomes a

Taming The Lion

possibility by observation or because the subject informs the [trainer] that it has happened... A Scientologist, knowing the mind completely, can of course do many `tricks' with the conditions of people to improve them. Aim is civilization without insanity."

In the chapter `The Body'.. Hubbard states: "Biophysics only became feasible when it was discovered in Scientology that a fixed electrical field existed surrounding the body entirely independent of it but can be influenced by the human mind...The complexity of these anchor point can cause an independent series of electronic flows which can occasion much discomfort to the individual. The balance structure of the body and even its joint action and physical characteristics can be changed by changing this electrical field that exists at a distance from, or within, the body. The use of electrical shocks upon a body for any purpose is therefore very dangerous.. was never intended to be therapeutic.. [it] deranges the electronic field in the vicinity of the body.. and causes physical problems.

Hubbard, a world traveler, picked up Eastern philosophies and studied engineering. He took a course nuclear physics. He developed Dianetics, which was targeted by public opinion and is now Scientology, world wide and changed recently to a church status. It is another form of developing the `I Am God' position with deeper implications of the possibility of undesirable spirits taking residence. The God given protections are artificially removed. Occult teachings warn against these types of practices. They can cause a loss of sense of reality. That is what they are deliberately developing in the processing. Reality virtually disappears momentarily.

Scientology runs under many different names hiding their intent. They are making thousands of inroads in all areas of society. Lately even some pastors are resorting to it. Some countries are working hard on keeping the practice away from their public.

In my opinion repeated processing causes diminished controls and loss of protection from the spirit world.

Taming The Lion

"**Be sober, be vigilant; because your adversary the devil, as a roaring lion, walketh about, seeking whom he may devour:**" (1 Peter 5:8)

CHAPTER 12

OVERCOMING THE WICKED

The next nail in the coffin of Mormonism came on a visit to my sister and her husband. Her husband challenged me saying: "You can't buy your way into heaven!" Knowing that, I told him the reason I was giving was in obedience to God. Participating in classes and entertainment and using a facility produces a cost that has to be paid. Since there is no entry fee, people volunteer to pay. There were some who did not have money and others make up for the shortage. "Get your Bible," I told him, "so I can find the Scripture on giving." Not in the habit of carrying my Mormon Bible consisting of four different books and then some, earnestly embarrassed, I could not begin to figure out where to go in his Bible to find anything about tithing to the Lord. There was no way around it, I belonged to the biblically illiterate after many years in Mormonism and listening to preachers on television. Every Sunday, I had attended to Gospel Doctrine classes, studied the Old Testament one year and the New Testament the next and the Book of Mormon. The teachings were verses out of context supporting Mormon doctrine. The information could not become a body of knowledge. They remained fragments because the teachers never read chapters.

Mario Murillo, an evangelist, gave a sermon on that subject. He said: "there are churches that give baby aspirin when two aspirins should be given for adults to cure the fever. He said that is why people never come to the knowledge they need. They starve spiritually. That was never going to happen again and I resolved to begin my own Scripture study program. Right in church, I began to read the Bible during their meetings. At home after work I read Scripture in my own voice unto audiotapes and took them with me to play back to myself while driving. Satan has his plan but so does God. I started from the beginning with the Old Testament. The study did not endanger Mormonism for a while. The Aaronic priesthood is

273

active in the Old Testament just like the Mormons' and King Solomon had 700 wives and 300 Concubines.

What occurred to me over and over and appeared strange was that Mormons including myself disassociated themselves from Mormons verbally. I asked a friend of mine: "why do you say `the Mormons' when you talk about them, when you are the Mormons?" He had never thought about it and did not know why. A member for twenty years, I did not integrate Mormonism with Christianity. It has to be impossible because Mormonism is represented by another spirit. The two spirits cannot live together.

On my visiting route a member came down with cancer and we intensified visits to weekly visits and cared for this woman till she died. She maintained at home with the church's help until time came for a hospice. We visited her up to the end at the cemetery. When I saw her in the casket with her priesthood garment that included a veil over her face, shocked into reality for a moment, I thought about my non-Mormon family at my funeral. That moment helped get me out also.

If one has dead parents and is not sealed to them, there is a twelve-month waiting period after their death to get the sealing done. My husband had not kept up his temple recommend for years because he was out of compliance and not interested. God was intervening by providing a work situation with Sunday work that helped keep him on the fringes of Mormonism. He needed to get a temple pass to get himself sealed to his parents and that meant interviews with the bishop and a higher level official. Before the interview, I told him to be careful how he answered the interrogations in critical areas, such as tithing and attending meetings. Again I had a revelation about myself, I was telling him to lie a little. Shocked at my recommendation, I realized now that I had deteriorated spiritually, sanctification should produce an improved honorable holy character. People go to church for edification.

Taming The Lion

We received justification when Jesus gave His life for our sins and we received Him as our Lord and Savior and repented of our sins. The spiritual baptism of the Holy Spirit by Jesus Christ Himself happens simultaneously. Water baptism follows to make it public that we have received Jesus Christ as our Lord and Savior. The Holy Spirit begins to teach us personally and by the washing of the Word of God we are sanctified. The Holy Spirit feeds on the Word as well.

Mormonism has many opportunities for loving and serving brothers and sisters. Problem was the newborn spirit was starving over time because there was no renewing of the mind through Bible study.

"But he answered and said, It is written, Man shall not live by bread alone, but by every word that proceedeth out of the mouth of God." *(*Matthew 4:4) No revelation or book by other authors can take the place of the Holy Bible, authored by God through God's communication with prophets in the Old Testament and the Holy Spirit's witness to men in the New Testament. Without that witness from God men could not believe the truth.

Gentiles are adopted when they convert to Jesus Christ by receiving circumcision of the heart. **"But he is a Jew, which is one inwardly; and circumcision is that of the heart, in the spirit, and not in the letter; whose praise is not of men, but of God.**" (Romans 2:29)

After this sanctification believers are set apart for a sacred purpose such as a future life with Jesus Christ as their King or becoming a disciple by allowing the Holy Spirit to function through their lives and bringing others into the kingdom. Romans 2:29 to study Scripture daily, praise and worship, and pray daily. These activities in combination build strength to repel demonic forces. Fear cannot be part of the new life.

Through my own daily Bible study, I had finally come to the New Testament. My sinful nature had returned. Given this scripture: "**But we are all as an unclean thing, and all our righteousnesses are as**

filthy rags; and we all do fade as a leaf; and our iniquities, like the wind, have taken us away." (Isaiah 64:6), I came under conviction that I needed to repent.

Mormons don't teach that Jesus will virtually make a new person out of us and teach us personally through the Holy Spirit. Next the Holy Spirit put me in touch with a little book, written by female Christian teacher: `Free To Dream', by Neva Coyle. Neva described how to consecrate your life to God and say `yes God, I want to give myself wholly to you. Take my life, all of it.' My dream had been ministry for years. When I was showing the paintings, I felt that peace in my heart, that all was well between God and myself. It feels like riding a newly purchased car in perfect sunshine and temperature to spend the summer on the beach, knowing every day is going to be fulfilled in perfection. Those years had been the best in my life and I wanted that contentment back.

When I did the art shows I had a part-time job for a Mormon contractor for $5 an hour keeping three sets of books for the whole family on weekends that kept my budget going. I also made jewelry and things that people could purchase at the art shows. I had managed to attend many art shows until one day the contractor laid me off. My career working for the state of Colorado was ready to begin and the art shows ended.

In the Mormon church couples go on missions internationally after they retire using their own funds just like young missionaries. I had a burning desire to do that. It wasn't going to be met. My husband refused to leave the country with me on a mission. I began to wonder why? "Please God, get me out of Mormonism if I am in the wrong place!" I begged. Deep down I was remembering what He had related to me twenty years ago in my Thunderbird in the field before Mormonism. Not only was I related to that I was going to be taken to the cross but that I was going to be used relative to the Gospel as I had been with the paintings. I knew deep within that it was not about the Mormon church whatsoever.

Taming The Lion

"If a man die, shall he live again? all the days of my appointed time will I wait, till my change come. Thou shalt call, and I will answer thee: thou wilt have a desire to the work of thine hands. For now thou numberest my steps: dost thou not watch over my sin? My transgression is sealed up in a bag, and thou sewest up mine iniquity. And surely the mountain falling cometh to nought, and the rock is removed out of his place. The waters wear the stones: thou washest away the things which grow out of the dust of the earth; and thou destroyest the hope of man. Thou prevailest for ever against him, and he passeth: thou changest his countenance, and sendest him away." (Job 14:14-20) **"He leadeth princes away spoiled, and overthroweth the mighty.** *"* (Job 12:19) **"** **"Blessed is the man that endureth temptation: for when he is tried, he shall receive the crown of life, which the Lord hath promised to them that love him.** *"* (James 1:12)

My husband had not followed my advice of bending the truth a little in his temple interview. He told the stake president the truth and reprimanded he came out of that office with: "I quit," on his lips. He had received his pass with strings of having to fulfill duties. With my husband out of the church, we began to experience extraordinary spiritual warfare. He often accompanied me in the car all day and we got into bitter arguments. Convinced that my life had remarkably improved, I had attached the blessings to the LDS Church instead of God. Our Realtor turned out to be Mormon and so did our insurance agent without deliberately seeking them out. We didn't know for years that they were Mormons and that was no coincidence. They just happened out of the blue? I could not believe that. They had been extremely helpful.

All the nice families I watched mature and participated in their weddings, graduations, missions, joys and sorrows were difficult to leave. Never did I have one incident of sexual harassment and I appreciated that. There were many acquaintances that I cherished. Mormonism is a worldwide system and one has access to shelter, food, care and trust anywhere. It is one huge extended family. At fast and testimony day, once a month, I found myself at the podium, telling the congregation what had happened and that I was planning to stay regardless. While talking, I was impressed with a vision in my spirit reassuring me that the LDS body was the body of Jesus. When I came to my seat, I sensed in the spirit what felt like a helmet being placed over my head down to my shoulders. Conveniently, I had forgotten my plea to God to get me out, but ministry continued to preoccupy my mind. God was not about to forget me there. It only takes one prayer once. He had heard my plea. His promises to us stand under any circumstances, hallelujah.

Thank God for people who have the courage to write books about wrong teachings. In a Bible bookstore looking to find a Bible for my previous husband, a Catholic, I came across a little book `The Mormon Illusion' by Floyd McElveen. I bought it to see what it had to say, so I could have answers ready to defend Mormonism. The book had Holy Spirit convicting power. It forced me to decide by asking: "whose side are you on?" It cornered me and put me on the spot. McElveen tackles the problem from within their teachings and basically tears up the Mormon doctrine by comparing it with the Word of God. The veil was finally torn and my eyes opened. But it was only the tip of the iceberg.

When there is divorce in a life, blame is usually on both partners. The feeling that something could have been done different to make it work out in the long run gnaws away in the heart especially when there are children involved. Guilt hangs around like a black cloud because of the Scriptures, we are under the impression that God wanted it different. He ordained one marriage for us.

In His mercy the Holy Spirit took me to my previous husband through an incident with an organization similar to Scientology, involving one of our children, to show me there was no reason for guilt. He showed me that my previous husband liked being a hobo. All he owned, thirty-five years later was a bedroll, a television, an expensive Cadillac, some clothes and cooking utensils. He later confessed to having rejected his Catholic religion long before he met me and still rejected it. He could not describe the triune God, nor did he know that Mary was a virgin when Christ Jesus was conceived in her womb involving the Holy Spirit. He was under the impression that Joseph was the physical father of Jesus. He also admitted that we would have probably killed each other had we stayed together, that had never occurred to me. The Holy Spirit showed me where I would have lived had I stayed with him; I would have still been homeless.

The Scriptures teach on the various vessels (human beings): **"Nevertheless the foundation of God standeth sure, having this seal, The Lord knoweth them that are his. And, Let every one that nameth the name of Christ depart from iniquity. But in a great house there are not only vessels of gold and of silver, but also of wood and of earth; and some to honour, and some to dishonour. If a man therefore purge himself from these, [it is up to us, we have a choice about this] he shall be a vessel unto honour, sanctified, and meet for the master's use, [and] prepared unto every good work."** (2 Timothy 2:19-21) This happened six months before I left the church. My heart had a break through and felt like it had exploded. The guilt was completely taken away and I soared like an eagle for months to cushion the crash I was about to experience. **"Ye have seen what I did unto the Egyptians, and how I bare you on eagles' wings, and brought you unto myself**". (Exodus 19:4)

Not seeing a chance for ministry in Mormonism, I decided to check out Oral Roberts University for educational purposes. It just so happened an International Charismatic Bible Ministry Meeting was going on during our stay in Tulsa. My husband and I signed up to attend for three days. This was in 1991 before the deterioration within the ministries took place. Coming from twenty years of desert into a highly charged charismatic environment with international powerful preachers trying to outdo each other, we were filled with the joy of the Lord much like becoming tipsy from wine for three days straight. Tears of joy were flowing, even after we came home. A lady at work began to cry with me and could not explain it.

Taming The Lion

How sad God must be watching the secular world and its many facets, rejecting his teachings and I should put myself into that same position to become god became real to me.

When I told the bishop that I had no interest in becoming a goddess and why, he admitted he had never analyzed that end of it either. The reason for this is: "**And with all deceivableness of unrighteousness in them that perish; because they received not the love of the truth, that they might be saved. And for this cause God shall send them strong delusion, that they should believe a lie:**" *(*2 Thessalonians 2:10,11)

To have something to read on the way to Oral Robert University, I had taken the book with me: 'The Mormon Illusion'. I could not believe what I was reading aloud to my husband. Floyd McElveen is a Baptist evangelist. He had studied Mormonism for many years to be sure he wasn't missing anything when approached by a Mormon missionary to join. He sat down and wrote his findings. Following are the most important aspects of his discoveries on the discrepancies he found in Mormon doctrines.

Beginning with the Book of Mormon the first problem concerns the rapid increase in population. According to the Book of Mormon in 30 years two nations grew from 28 people or less (see 1 Nephi; 2 Nephi 5:5,6,28). In this time the two nations, which at the greatest possible rate of increase, could have numbered only several hundred, with the majority being women and children). Divided they became fierce enemies called the Nephites and the Lamanites. The second problem concerns the mighty cities built by the Nephites and Jaredites. They "did build many mighty cities" (Ether 9:23; see also Alma 50:15). There are at least 38 names of cities mentioned in the Book of Mormon: Ammonihah, Bountiful, Gideon, Jacobugath, Jerusalem, Manti, Shem, Zarahemla, etc., all in the New World. However, not one of these cities' locations have ever been found in South or Central America. Archaeologists frequently discovered proof that fully contradicts and demolishes the claims of the Book of Mormon. Though scientific research has demonstrated that the American continent was devoid of many domestic animals such as cattle, swine, horses, asses and certain other animals until the Europeans came to America. The Book of Mormon claims these were all here long before Christ. There have been close to 4000 changes to the Book of Mormon since 1830.

One of the primary names of God, Jehovah, means in essence, self-existent one; one who has life originally, permanently, and forever, within Himself. God, then, was never a man, never mortal, but was always God. He is not now an `exalted man', as Mormonism claims. God explicitly declares, "**...for I am God, and not man...**" (Hosea 11:9). Because God plainly declared in Isaiah 43:10 there would be no God after Him, no man will ever now, in the future, or in eternity, become a god. Therefore, the Mormon Creed, their main thrust, "As man is, God once was; as God is, man may be," is untrue according to the Bible. It is not of God. "**Ye are my witnesses, saith the LORD, and my servant whom I have chosen: that ye may know and believe me, and understand that I am he: before me there was no God formed, neither shall there be after me.**" (Isaiah. 43:10)

Mormonism claims God had a beginning. God's Word says He did not. John 1:1 states, "**In the beginning was the Word, and the Word was with God, and the Word was God.**" (Later in John 1:14 we see that "**The Word was made flesh and dwelt among us,**" making Christ and the Word synonymous). John 1:1 teaches us that Christ was the Word and that He was with God and that He was (not became) God. Again, here in the first verse of John's Gospel, we see that God was God from the beginning (which here has the sense of meaning `from all time') and so Jesus Christ was God from the beginning, from all time! Now God has absolutely forbidden the worship of any other god, in biblical passages such as Exodus 34:14, "**For thou shalt worship no other god: for the LORD, whose name is Jealous, is a jealous God:**"

The fact that Jesus permitted encouraged and accepted worship identified Him as God, and there is only one God who has been and will be God, "from everlasting to everlasting." The Mormon belief that "as man is, God once was: as God is, man may be" lends itself to unsaved man's deception that he can somehow earn his salvation, or help earn it. This belief fosters the idea that man can become one of God's sheep by ignoring his sin nature and acting like a sheep, as futile as a pig acting like a sheep to become a sheep. We need to have our nature changed by the new birth, and thus receive a new nature: **"For all have sinned, and come short of the glory of God;"** *(*Romans 3:23)

No church, baptism or great amount of good works can change our nature or pay for past sins. We must turn to Jesus alone for salvation, knowing that His shed blood will cleanse us from all sin. Simultaneously, as we call believing on Him, He will enter our life to change our nature from within. This makes us true children of God. "Nothing in our hands we bring, simply to His Cross we cling."

As we call on Christ, undeserving but believing, He responds with instant salvation. Then as He enters our lives and makes us children of God, Christ from within changes our lives. We receive a new nature, new desires, new love and new power. Behold the mad murderer, Saul, who became the magnificent missionary, Paul, after one vital encounter with the risen Christ on the road to Damascus. If he genuinely accepts the Christ of the Bible, he will soon thirst for an oasis of true Christians, and will leave the Mormon Church. Brigham Young himself unmistakenly and forever clarified what he meant. On February 19, 1854, two years after his initial Adam-God sermon, Brigham Young said, speaking of Christ: "Who did beget him? His Father, and his father is our God, and the Father of our spirits, and he is the framer of the body, the God and Father of our Lord Jesus Christ. Who is he? He is Father Adam." Here Brigham Young identifies Adam as the heavenly Father, God. He is the `Father of our spirits,' and the Father of the Lord Jesus Christ. Clearly and irrefutably, Brigham Young taught that Adam directly, physically had sex relations with Mary and begat Jesus Christ. Thus Brigham Young violated Scripture, denied the virgin birth, and identified the God of Mormonism as Adam!

282

Taming The Lion

Early Mormons had strong 'testimonies' of the truth of Brigham Young's Adam - God doctrine, as Mormons today have strong 'testimonies' that it is a false doctrine. This illustrates the fallacy of 'testimony' compared with the sure Word of God. Mormonism denies there is one God [yet the Book of Mormon contains the following: "..and shall be brought and be arraigned before the bar of Christ the Son, and God the Father, and the Holy Spirit, which is one Eternal God, to be judged according to their works.." (Alma 11:44) which is not only in contradiction to the theology of many gods, but also contradicts that Jesus was a spirit brother of Satan. To be a god in Mormonism, one would have to have all three ingredients separately: the Father, the Son and the Holy Spirit.

The Bible teaches that believers in Christ Jesus are one with the Father, the Son and the Holy Ghost in the same sense God is one in three persons we become part of God as the bride of Christ Jesus who becomes one with her husband. Teachings of Joseph Smith say there are many gods. The Scriptures say: " 1 Corinthians 8:6 **But to us there is but one God, the Father**... " (1 Corinthians 8:6; see also vv.. 4,5); ".. **before me there was no God formed, neither shall there be after me**." (Isaiah 43:10) ".. **for I am God, and there is none else.**" (Isaiah 45:22) (See also Deuteronomy 4:35; 32:39; 2 Samuel 7:22; Psalm 86:10.

In the Doctrine and Covenants, we read that Abraham, Isaac and Jacob "have entered into their exaltation, according to the promises, and sit upon thrones, and are not angels but are gods" (132:37) . In the Pearl of Great Price, Joseph Smith wrote, "So the Gods [plural] went down to organize man in their own image, in the image of the Gods to form they him, male and female, to form they them" (Abraham 4:27).

These are contradictions that can be found in the same book. God has been seen in anthropomorphic or theophanic appearances, as a man, angel, etc., and as incarnate in Christ. He has never been seen in His divine essence. Exodus 33 continues in verse 20, "**And he said, Thou canst not see my face: for there shall no man see me, and live.**" John 1:18 adds, "**No man hath seen God at any time;**

the only begotten Son, which is in the bosom of the Father, he hath declared him". After His resurrection, Jesus appeared to His disciples and said, " "**Behold my hands and my feet, that it is I myself: handle me, and see; for a spirit hath not flesh and bones, as ye see me have.**" (Luke 24:39). Jesus here confirmed that a spirit cannot be seen or touched. "**God is a Spirit:..** " (John 4:24), not has a Spirit, but is a Spirit. A Spirit is invisible as the Bible says God is, and does not have a body of flesh and bone. It is true that we find in Scripture, references to the mouth, arms, eyes, ears, face and hands of God. However, these references are symbolic, not literal. God uses them to communicate truth to us that we can understand.

Deuteronomy 4:24 says, "**For the LORD thy God is a consuming fire..** " "**the blast-furnace God.**" Jeremiah 23:24 says, " Jeremiah 23:24 ".. **Do not I fill heaven and earth? saith the LORD.**" If God were flesh and bone, this might make it a little uncomfortable for the rest of us! In Jeremiah 2:13, God calls Himself the "**fountain of living waters.**" Psalm 91:4, "**He shall cover thee with his feathers, and under his wings shalt thou trust:..**" Surely this verse cannot be taken literally, for our wonderful God is not a chicken or a bird.

Brigham Young, in Journal of Discourses, says, "Adam... is our father and our God and the only God with whom we have to do." Again he says, "Jesus Christ was not begotten by the Holy Ghost." To believe literally that man is made in the image of God could be most confusing. Would God look like a man or a woman? Which race would He resemble in facial characteristics? We are made in the image of God in that we have self-awareness; abstract reasoning power, a spiritual nature and a God-awareness. Mormons love to deny other churches' authority and assert their own, by quoting Hebrews 5:4, "**And no man taketh this honour unto himself, but he that is called of God, as was Aaron.**"

Exodus 28,29 tells exactly how Aaron and his sons were called and consecrated and not one Mormon on earth is called and consecrated in that way. This higher order of the two Mormon

Taming The Lion

priesthoods is "called the Melchizedek Priesthood...because Melchizedek was such a great high priest" (Doctrine and Covenants 107: 2). (See Gen. 14:18; Ps. 110:4; Heb. 5:6; 6:20; 7:1).

The officers of this priesthood include elders, seventies, and high priests. The Mormons believe that, "like God himself, the Melchizedek Priesthood is eternal and everlasting in nature." It is "an everlasting principle, and existed with God from eternity, and will to eternity, without beginning of days or end of years. When Jesus came, He alone was declared "**...Thou art a priest for ever after the order of Melchizedec:**" (Hebrews 7:21). Jesus, "**..because he continueth ever, hath an unchangeable priesthood**" (Hebrews 7:24). According to Greek scholars like Robertson and Thayer, unchangeable means `untransferable'. Jesus alone, for all time, is our Melchizedek priest. For anyone to claim to be a Melchizedek priest today seems exceedingly unwise. Read Hebrews 7. God commanded that the priests were to come through the tribe of Levi, and directly through Aaron and his sons and descendants. Yet most Mormons claim to be either from the tribes of Ephraim or Manasseh-- the wrong tribes!

Forty-five million people have been baptized by proxy. In 1966 "The total microfilm load included 579,679,800 pages of documents. There were more than 5 billion names in the files--the church puts about 4 million dollars a year into the Genealogical Society [which comes from the membership as well as investment income].

Every Christian is now declared to be a priest. "**But ye are a chosen generation, a royal priesthood, an holy nation, a peculiar people; that ye should shew forth the praises of him who hath called you out of darkness into his marvellous light:**" (1 Peter.2:9). After Jesus was crucified, Titus in A.D.70 destroyed all the genealogical records in Jerusalem. All that remained were those recorded in God's Word. God was saying, 'the Messiah has come and He has been genealogically verified. It is finished.'

Taming The Lion

Genealogical records were the means of proving the qualifications of priests. Their bloodlines could be traced all the way back to Aaron. When God instituted the Jewish priesthood, He chose only one of the 12 tribes of Israel, the Levites, to be priests. Within the tribe of Levi, he chose one man, Aaron, as His high priest. All true priests were descendants of Aaron, (see Exodus 28:1; 31:10; Levites 8:2;9 Numbers 3:1-4) . Anyone other than a blood descendant of Aaron, who claimed to be a priest, was a false priest, regardless of how many voices they heard or visions they saw claiming that God had given them the authority of the priesthood. Aaronic descent had to be proven.

When God allowed all these genealogical records to be destroyed, after having miraculously preserved them for centuries, He made it impossible for anyone to trace bloodline descent back to Aaron and thus claim to be an Aaronic priest today is a false priest. Nor has Joseph Smith received this convenient revelation on July 12, 1843. He was killed in 1844. Several Mormon writers claim that Smith had as many as 48 wives. Even the most charitable view could hardly avoid the strong implication that Joseph Smith was living in adultery long before he got his `revelation'.

Jesus Christ taught much about hell. Of the 24 times hell is mentioned in the New Testament, 22 of those times Jesus, the lover of our souls, is the speaker. His description of hell in Luke 16 is very graphic. Jesus told about a man named Lazarus who died and was "carried into Abraham's bosom." A rich man in this actual, factual account also died and went to hell. Jesus does not lie and He said there is an eternal hell for the lost. The Bible definitely, plainly teaches there is a hell, and describes the final form of it in Revelation 20:15; "**And whosoever was not found written in the book of life was cast into the lake of fire**. "

In spite of these plain declarations in the Bible and the Book of Mormon, John A. Widtsoe, a noted Mormon authority and writer and an apostle of the Mormon church, states, "In the Church of Jesus Christ of Latter-day Saints, there is no hell..." In all the Bible, covering many centuries, there is not one command that we should

Taming The Lion

be baptized by proxy for the dead. In Doctrines and Covenants 128:16, Joseph Smith refers to 1 Corinthians 15:29 to support his doctrine of baptizing for the dead: "**Else what shall they do which are baptized for the dead, if the dead rise not at all**?" Why are they then baptized for the dead?" Here is one example where Mormons take a verse out of context. The content of the verse is not talking about the Christians themselves but some other group that was practicing that sort of baptism. A note from the Ryrie Study Bible, Moody Press: "Various interpretations have been given for the difficult expression: 1) It sanctions being baptized vicariously for another in order to assure him a place in heaven - a view that is heretical. 2) It refers to those who were baptized because of the testimony of those who had died." Spirit communication, necromancy is an abomination to God."

The Bible unmistakably teaches there is no chance whatsoever for men to be saved after death. The fate of the lost is then sealed immediately and forever once and for all. "**(…behold, now is the accepted time; behold, now is the day of salvation.)**" (2 Corinthians. 6:2). "**And as it is appointed unto men once to die, but after this the judgment:**" (Hebrews 9:27). There is no salvation for those without Christ, "**He that believeth on the Son hath everlasting life: and he that believeth not the Son shall not see life; but the wrath of God abideth on him.**" (John 3:36).

All men are resurrected; the saved to life, everlasting (see John 6:40) and the unsaved unto damnation (see John 5:29; Rev. 20:3-6). Revelation 20:15 adds the final word on the unsaved; " "**And whosoever was not found written in the book of life was cast into the lake of fire.**" The thief on the cross cried out to Jesus and was instantly saved and assured he would be that very day with Christ in paradise. Paul, the mightiest missionary this world has ever seen, a tremendous apostle, and one of the Holy men through whom God gave His Word, was caught up to the third heaven. . Guess who was already there? That's right, the thief who was unbaptized, had no good works, temple works or religion whatsoever to recommend him! The blood of the Lord Jesus Christ

Taming The Lion

saved him. He was saved instantly and forever because he called believing on Jesus Christ and had his sins washed away and his nature changed by Jesus.

The third heaven is also called paradise! Read it for yourself! "**I knew a man in Christ above fourteen years ago, (whether in the body, I cannot tell; or whether out of the body, I cannot tell: God knoweth;) such an one caught up to the third heaven. And I knew such a man, (whether in the body, or out of the body, I cannot tell: God knoweth;) How that he was caught up into paradise, and heard unspeakable words, which it is not lawful for a man to utter.**" (2 Corinthians 12:2-4).

There is not one indication in all the Bible that there is more than one heaven of God. On the contrary consider this; "**And if I go and prepare a place for you, I will come again, and receive you unto myself; that where I am, there ye may be also.** " (John 14:3) Jesus is here speaking to all truly believing Christians and assuring them that He will come back for all of them and that they will all be together with Him (and surely Jesus will be in the `highest heaven', the only heaven of God) in one place forever! "**For the Lord himself shall descend from heaven with a shout, with the voice of the archangel, and with the trump of God: and the dead in Christ shall rise first: Then we which are alive and remain shall be caught up together with them in the clouds, to meet the Lord in the air: and so shall we ever be with the Lord.**" (1 Thessalonians 4:16,17). There is one heaven, and one hell, and we go to either the one or the other, depending on what we do with Jesus Christ.

According to the Mormons that is the highest heaven and requires being sealed to the opposite sex, temple rituals and a new name to get through the veil. People often ask if there are sexual acts going on in the temple, of course not, people would not come back because Mormons think of themselves as beyond reproach. Lucifer is not that obvious. What is going on, is a simulation of a sexual act at the veil, which candidates at the veil don't realize. Being of a country where expression of love by hugging is not a high priority, I was a bit squeamish about standing knee to knee, embracing and whispering into a man's ear, which I had never seen. When investigating these rituals in Masonic literature, I found this ritual to be simulating a sexual act. Considering that only men participate in Freemasonry it has to relate to love and a spiritual union with another.

Such verses as Jeremiah 1:5 are called upon by the Mormons in support of the doctrine that we existed as spirits before we were born as humans; **"Before I formed thee in the (womb) I knew thee; and before thou camest forth out of the womb I sanctified thee, and I ordained thee a prophet unto the nations."** A tremendous superstructure has been built on this exceedingly skimpy and ambiguous foundation. God talked to a fetus in the womb. God knew Jeremiah and ordained him as a prophet before he was formed in the womb, and He also sanctified him. To Mormons, this whole life is a probationary period, but this interpretation would indicate that Jeremiah had it made before he was even born!

Now look closely at Acts 15:18: **"Known unto God are all his works from the beginning of the world.** Jeremiah is one of God's works. Romans 8:28-30 gives highlights of God's wonderful foreknowledge, without which He would not be God, and all of our security for eternity would be gone. God said in Genesis 2:7, **"And the LORD God formed man of the dust of the ground, and breathed into his nostrils the breath of life; and man became a living soul.** *"* That is when man's life started. He had no life before, anywhere at any time. Notice that God did not put into Adam one of His pre-existent spirit children, which only exist, in Mormon literature. Man got life for the first time direct from God. **"Jesus answered, Verily, verily, I say unto thee, Except a man be born of water and of the Spirit, he cannot enter into the kingdom of God. That which is born of the flesh is flesh; and that which is born of the Spirit is spirit.** *"* (John 3:5,6).

"For as in Adam all die, even so in Christ shall all be made alive. But every man in his own order: Christ the firstfruits; afterward they that are Christ's at his coming." (1 Corinthians

15:22,23). "**I will build my church; and the gates of hell shall not prevail against it.**" If Mormonism is true, what Jesus said was untrue. For Mormons say the gates of hell did prevail against His church, and total apostasy eliminated His true church, His true people, and His true Word off the earth for over a thousand years, to be `restored' by Prophet Smith! Foxe's Book of Martyrs tells how hundreds of thousands died for Jesus Christ, were burned at the stake, tortured unspeakably, and torn apart by wild beasts, all the while proclaiming their undying love to Jesus Christ.

Christ personally called the Twelve Apostles. They were among those who witnessed the living Jesus in His ministry, death and resurrection. As a special sign of their apostleship they worked miracles. (See Matt. 10:7,8; Acts 3:6-8; 5:12-16; 9:37-40; 2 Corinthians 12:12). The LDS church, up to now, has appointed 80 apostles [1977]. The New Testament speaks of "false apostles,"

"**I know thy works, and thy labour, and thy patience, and how thou canst not bear them which are evil: and thou hast tried them which say they are apostles, and are not, and hast found them liars:**" (Revelation 2:2). 1. Corinthians 12:13 says that all Christians are baptized with the Holy Spirit into the body of Christ. This is not speaking of water baptism. The Spirit is deposited in us. Ephesians 5:29-32 and other passages tell us that Christ's body in this sense is His church, and His church is His body! "**For by one Spirit are we all baptized into one body, whether we be Jews or Gentiles, whether we be bond or free; and have been all made to drink into one Spirit.**" (1 Corinthians 12:13)

Serious Christians seek a church that presents Christ most clearly to them and makes His salvation clear. How did the Mormons get so far from the truth of the Word of God, so far that `inspired' Prophet Brigham Young could say, "No man or woman in this dispensation will ever enter the celestial Kingdom of God without the consent of Joseph Smith!" This is a direct challenge to the Word of God and to the Lord Jesus Christ.

Taming The Lion

"**For there is one God, and one mediator between God and men, the man Christ Jesus**" (1 Tim. 2:*5)* " **Neither is there salvation in any other: for there is none other name under heaven given among men, whereby we must be saved.** " (Acts 4:12) His name is Jesus. Mormons should insist that such publications that are often withheld in sacred archives even from the Mormon public should be opened at least to all Mormons.

The Word of God says that we cannot trust our own thoughts because we have "`reprobate' minds" Rom. 1:28, "`carnal' minds" Rom. 8:7, "`vain' minds" Ephesians 4:17, "`defiled' minds" Titus 1:15 and our thoughts continually lean toward evil (see Gen. 6:5; Matt 9:4, 15: 19). The Holy Spirit is not the only powerful spirit in this world. Trusting only in prayer and feeling or experience might deceive you. The mighty evil spirit the Bible calls Satan is posing as an `angel of light', and deceiving all he can to an eternal hell. When we set aside God's prescribed way of finding truth, we are totally without protection and open to Satan's delusions.

Notice Satan's program: "**For such are false apostles, deceitful workers, transforming themselves into the apostles of Christ. And no marvel; for Satan himself is transformed into an angel of light. Therefore it is no great thing if his ministers also be transformed as the ministers of righteousness; whose end shall be according to their works.**" (2 Corinthians 11:13-15). Brilliant doctors and lawyers accept shoddy, unproven and dangerous theories but demand impeccable evidence in their professions, are locked into this system that forces them to accept `facts' like these by their `testimony'. In this way they have confused faith with believing what they know is not true. Biblical faith permits and demands objective, evidential reality, as well as subjective experience. Anything less fosters delusion and dishonesty. Paul declared, "**Through mighty signs and wonders, by the power of the Spirit of God; so that from Jerusalem, and round about unto Illyricum, I have fully preached the gospel of Christ.**" (Romans 15:19), Not one thing needed to be added to the gospel. (See also Galatians 1:8,9).

Taming The Lion

Romans 10:2,3: **"For I bear them record that they have a zeal of God, but not according to knowledge. For they being ignorant of God's righteousness, and going about to establish their own righteousness, have not submitted themselves unto the righteousness of God.** *"* All mankind has received `general salvation' through Adam according to Mormonism, which will get everyone at least into the lowest of the three heavens or degrees of glory. Stephen L. Richards, in his pamphlet, Contributions of Joseph Smith, claims that this salvation is equated with resurrection, for all men will be resurrected--atheists, pagans, unbelievers, etc. It is difficult to fit this belief into John 3:18: **"He that believeth on him is not condemned: but he that believeth not is condemned already, because he hath not believed in the name of the only begotten Son of God."**

John 3:36 tells us there is no salvation of any kind for those who do not believe, only condemnation: John 3:36 **"He that believeth on the Son hath everlasting life: and he that believeth not the Son shall not see life; but the wrath of God abideth on him."**

All men are resurrected, but the saved who believe in Christ are resurrected in the first resurrection. The wicked dead stay buried till the second resurrection. None in this first resurrection is lost. All these were saved through personally receiving Jesus Christ as their Lord and Saviour. The second resurrection takes place at the end of the thousand year Millennium. Satan will be loosed during the latter part of the Millennium to weed out those living who reject Christ. All those weeded anti-Christians and wicked in graves will be resurrected, judged and sentenced in the second resurrection. That is when the Great White Throne Judgment takes place. They rejected Christ Jesus and His salvation. They will be lost (see Rev. 20:5,6). Two resurrections are clearly taught in the Bible.

God cannot accept good works from a bad source, and He declares that all men are sinners, and therefore lost: **"For all have sinned, and come short of the glory of God;** *"* (Romans 3:23). Isaiah said, **".. all our righteousnesses are as filthy rags.** *.."* (Isaiah 64:6) If all our righteousness are as filthy rags to God, what an insult it must be to Him for us to try to buy our salvation with them. Many filthy rags would be even more insulting than a few. God sent Jesus to die in bloody agony on the cross to totally pay for all our sins. How it must hurt Him when we insist on hanging the dirty rags of our good works on the cross to `help Jesus save us' rather than accepting this great gift of salvation. God says in John 1:12, that the problem is that we are not children of God. Men by nature are not children of God! **"But as many as received him, to them gave he power to become the sons of God, even to them that believe on his name:** " Now God would not ask us to become children of God if we already were children of God. He plainly says we have to receive Jesus in order to become children of God. He told religious but lost Nicodemus, **"Ye must be born again**." (John 3:7)

What is going on with those who do not receive the Holy Spirit is in Romans 11:8 **"(According as it is written, God hath given them the spirit of slumber, eyes that they should not see, and ears that they should not hear;) unto this day.** "

We don't have a prayer until we opt in and receive the gift of salvation that Jesus died for. He gives us a new nature as a child of God, and He begins to live His life through us, insuring a changed life. Then and only then, after we are saved, our good works are of any value to God because the Holy Spirit is really the one who produces the fruit not us. Then and only then, after we are saved, for the first time God truly becomes our Father. He is not the Father of all men. He is the Father only of the saved, those born again into the family of God through receiving Christ. Of the unsaved, God says: **"Ye are of your father the devil.**. " (John 8:44). (See 1 John 3:8). By the same token, no one can become a Christian by acting like a Christian. We must be born again, and receive a new nature from God as children of God. Then, we will do good works for God, not in order to become Christians, but because we already are! (See Ephesians 2:10).

God was dealing with me finally, `whose side are you on, now that you know the truth?' There was no question in my mind whom I was desiring to serve, I was always on God's side. All my problems were coming from lack of knowing enough Gospel, relying on people rather than the Bible. In the long walk through Mormonism not once was astrology brought up to be an abomination. It should have been taught that God hates astrology. The reason they do not bring it up is Joseph Smith. He practiced astrology and talking about the subject might leak information into the congregation about his character. Running from demonic forces, I had run right into Satan's arms. Barney Fuller recently authored "The Burning of a Strange Fire" relates the following: "It was a magic book by Francis Barrett and, lo and behold, how thrilled I was when I saw in his list of magic seals the very talisman which Joseph Smith had in his possession at the time of his martyrdom.. To the Egyptians, Jupiter was known as Ammon, but to the Greeks he was Zeus: the ancient sky Father, or Father of the Gods.."

"**But if I cast out devils by the Spirit of God, then the kingdom of God is come unto you**." (Matthew 12:28)

The decision was no problem, whatever had to happen to get right with God had to be done. The problem was waking up to the fact that God does not take us by the hand and lead us. My trust in Him was shaken to the very root. Depending on men's teaching misled me. God leads us through His Word. Without a flight plan I had piloted my plane, and was surprised to land in Los Angeles, when I was heading for Jerusalem. Obedience is to God's truth, his Word, not just obedience to verses and principles taught by preachers. Obedience gives one a feeling of security, but it can become a god in itself.

The Holy Spirit is the teacher and I am in absolute awe of Him. Timing is one point of recognition when He is involved. "**Even the Spirit of truth; whom the world cannot receive, because it seeth him not, neither knoweth him: but ye know him; for he dwelleth with you, and shall be in you**." (John 14:17) According to John 1 the Light is given to all of us but because of the sin factor it is veiled until we receive the Holy Spirit of truth.

Taming The Lion

"**Howbeit when he, the Spirit of truth, is come, he will guide you into all truth: for he shall not speak of himself; but whatsoever he shall hear, that shall he speak: and he will shew you things to come.**" (John 16:13) The Holy Spirit is speaking of Jesus' words:

In John 6:63 Jesus teaches: "**It is the spirit that quickeneth; the flesh profiteth nothing: the words that I speak unto you, they are spirit, and they are life.**"

When we are born again, our encapsulated spirit is resurrected out of our souls and witnessed to by the Holy Spirit. "**And so it is written, The first man Adam was made a living soul; the last Adam [Jesus Christ] was made a quickening spirit.**" (1 Corinthians 15:45). According to the Old Testament when we die, "**Then shall the dust return to the earth as it was: and the spirit shall return unto God who gave it.**" (Ecclesiastes 12:7) After Jesus, the first fruits, of Whom Isaiah spoke and prophesied came this promise: "**For thus saith the high and lofty One that inhabiteth eternity, whose name is Holy; I dwell in the high and holy place, with him also that is of a contrite and humble spirit, to revive the spirit of the humble, and to revive the heart of the contrite ones.**" (Isaiah 57:15) That wasn't all God revived. "**Behold my hands and my feet, that it is I myself: handle me, and see; for a spirit hath not flesh and bones, as ye see me have**". (Luke 24:39). Speaking of Jesus and His resurrection: "**And declared to be the Son of God with power, according to the spirit of holiness, by the resurrection from the dead:**" (Romans 1:4).

God created man to live forever. The sin factor is what caused death, first the spirit and then the body. In John 3:5 "**Jesus answered, Verily, verily, I say unto thee, Except a man be born of water and of the Spirit, he cannot enter into the kingdom of God.**" Now that I'm born again: "**.. the law of the Spirit of life in Christ Jesus hath made me free from the law of sin and death. Romans 8:2 "And grieve not the holy Spirit of God, whereby ye are sealed unto the day of redemption**". (Ephesians 4:30).

Taming The Lion

It is not easy to comprehend this witness in our minds. It is study and research of words and what they truly mean as well as paying attention to the Holy Spirit's unctions to help us do His will instead of ours. To understand the personality of God we need to have an understanding of the whole body of knowledge given in the KJV Bible.

If we do not respond correctly to the Holy Spirit Who is in tune with us and aware of what needs to happen and how to help us, we miss out on opportunities that are blessings from God. The Word is in us but we have to make an effort to bring it into our minds. Since our minds are on a human level, it doesn't stay there automatically. We have to keep putting it there to keep it in front of us and grow spiritually. To see an example of the power of the devil is to decide to read the Bible. More excuses come up to interfere with Bible study than at any other time. Find out how much resistance there is against that decision. The body is at war with the spirit. Satan is in business to derail our efforts to become part of Christ's Body because we become influential to bring more fruit to Christ Jesus.

We do not know what to pray to be in the will of God and God even made that easy:

"And he that searcheth the hearts knoweth what is the mind of the Spirit, because he maketh intercession for the saints according to the will of God. " (Romans 8:27)

In my experience I had the Word in me and needed to bring it to consciousness. I had to find a Bible that I could agree with in regard to that inner knowledge. Dr. John Ankerberg suggested the AMG Bible by a Greek scholar. It worked for me. It had a lexical aid and concordance to define Hebrew and Greek words to the finest degree. There are so many interpretations because people interpret it intellectually and come up with personal interpretations. I relied on preachers and got lost.

For most believers there are connecting points to the Word of God that cause them to believe that it is true because the Bible proves itself. God was testing my personal relationship with Him.

Taming The Lion

Was I really obeying Him because I loved Him, or was I in it to get blessings from Him. We have to get beyond that point and that is the hard part. Job, from the Book of Job in Scripture, is a good example and like Job subject to Satan to a point where Job wasn't sure He was happy with God, he hung in. God turns Satan loose on some of us to show Satan what kind of love we have for Christ Jesus.

God was looking for `unconditional love' from me. He wants us to love Him regardless of what happens to us. It takes that kind of love to endure to the end. The road gets just a little harder as we grow. Walking the path Jesus walked isn't as easy as it sounds. The apostles ran when the going got rough. Without the Holy Spirit to sustain them, they did not have what it takes. The realization that one is on this road `alone' in the flesh, anchored to Jesus Christ and the Holy Spirit is an awakening. Like a parent takes their child so far and then they have to get out of the nest and show what they are made of, so does God move us gradually into more and more spiritual warfare to condition us for ministry if that is His will for our lives.

Satan does not let go easy, because he knows the Scriptures when Jesus reassures that the candle He lights is parallel to the candle lit by man, it will be seen. **"Neither do men light a candle, and put it under a bushel, but on a candlestick; and it giveth light unto all that are in the house."** (Matthew 5:15). We become extremely single-minded about becoming beacons for Christ Jesus.

When one's whole past comes crashing down around, it is virtually a death experience. It was amazing to me how the Holy Spirit is fully prepared to comfort during this crash. He had a whole new environment ready to bridge the gap I was about to experience. Everything was about to be torn away except my relationship with God. Even that intimacy had a close call. For a while I laid the blame on God instead of my own lackadaisical spiritual attitude. Not only was Mormonism taken away, everything I had learned college, my prestigious job of $42,000 a year with travel and fringe benefits, credibility as a person of some wisdom and understanding, self esteem and respect from others: my husband, children, siblings, friends and co-workers and my future all planned in Art at retirement.

God demands that kind of obedience when the time comes, that is what a commitment is about. If a person does not want to make that kind of an offer, it is better not to do it. It is a choice. He does not force us. I walked away from my whole entire past in full knowledge of what Jesus Christ was giving me and that I had to walk into His future all by myself, if I wanted to be a fruit bearing vessel of honor. A preacher compared this point to landing at Hebron `alone'. The climb compared to a steep mountain, a bloody climb that no one wanted to share because of the opposition.

My heart was totally broken when I realized that I had been serving Lucifer. At one point, I felt like a fast train that had hit a concrete wall dead center and disintegrated into a million little pieces. Sitting in the middle of these fragments, I was alive trying to find something that could be salvaged. There was nothing. The investment of twenty years diligently dedicating hours upon hours, dollars upon dollars and most of all emotional turmoil over my family and the broken pieces of my marriage over Mormonism had drawn a total zero. Anger at Satan suddenly burst into a flame that will burn as long as it needs to fuel the energy necessary to serve in ministry. This helped me to understand God's wrath against Satan and it increased my compassion for Jesus Christ and what He endured head on during his three years of ministry. My merciful God was forgiving of my whole past through Christ Jesus and that was awesome and humbling. Having contributed more pain to Christ by being in the wrong places inadvertently was no excuse. God had given me eyes, ears and a mind. " **And we know that we are of God, and the whole world lieth in wickedness.** " *(*1 John 5:19).

Like Jesus on the cross, at some point Satan peels us down to nudeness and all the things that belong to the world have to go eventually and are placed at the foot of the cross. A broken heart hangs around for quite a while and acts as a form of repentance, which in turn leads to healing.

Taming The Lion

Letting go of everything and placing myself at His mercy as a helpless child ready to learn to do it all His way, is not easy. All the books I had read and handles I had developed over time to maintain had wrapped themselves around the wheat like chickweed. Because our minds work by of association, Satan uses Scripture and associates his blasphemy to the truth, so when concepts come up, up comes the lie with it. His aim is to make us entirely ineffective where our discipleship is concerned.

People who have been in jail; come out with a record, same as someone who has been in organizations like Mormonism. There is no credibility. Some people began correcting every sentence relating to the gospel to put me off balance. That was the hardest part to accept. Instead of being this together person I thought I was, I had been a complete joke to everyone but myself.

It became evident, I had to deal with the stages of having contracted a disease which ends in death. Having to be born again became a reality. **"Nicodemus saith unto him, How can a man be born when he is old? can he enter the second time into his mother's womb, and be born? Jesus answered, Verily, verily, I say unto thee, Except a man be born of water and of the Spirit, he cannot enter into the kingdom of God.** " *(*John 3:4,5)

At the International Charismatic Bible Ministries Convention, I met the Happy Church team from Denver, Colorado, Mr. and Mrs. Hickey and began attending. Their ministry was born under the Assembly of God denomination. Years prior, I had seen Marilyn presenting Bible studies on television and had respected her zealous quest for a Christian witness. They had just purchased a thirty- five million dollar shopping center for seven million dollars and were busy developing people. The praise and worship completely foreign to Mormons and healing services were exactly what needed to happen for me. People in her congregation pray for each other and the healing flowed over me like dew from heaven. Marilyn taught at the time the 23rd Psalm, I had met before, twenty years ago: **"The LORD is my shepherd; I shall not want. He maketh me to lie down in green pastures: he leadeth me beside the still waters.**

Taming The Lion

He restoreth my soul: he leadeth me in the paths of righteousness for his name's sake. Yea, though I walk through the valley of the shadow of death, I will fear no evil: for thou art with me; thy rod and thy staff they comfort me. Thou preparest a table before me in the presence of mine enemies: thou anointest my head with oil; my cup runneth over. Surely goodness and mercy shall follow me all the days of my life: and I will dwell in the house of the LORD for ever. *"* (23 Psalm).

In an evening youth program performed by teenagers, full of spirit, they called people forward who needed prayer after the performance. On my knees in a fetal position, I found myself up front. A teenager put his arm around me and asked, what do you need to have prayed over? Sharing with him that I was trying to leave the LDS Church behind, he began praying over me in the spirit: He said: "Mormonism is like being buried in concrete on the bottom of the ocean. The Holy Spirit is going to chip the concrete away, blow by blow and you will be completely free from it." Praise God. Like I mentioned before, the Holy Spirit is ready for whatever needs to happen, all we have to do, is yield to Him so He can cover us with His love.

There was still more to be done. My husband and I, invited to a family reunion of my ex- husband's family, agreed to it on the insistence of one my children. Bringing all the people of my past life back, raised all that pain back into my consciousness and by the time those three days were up, I was a basket case. Marilyn Hickey was planning a healing ministry in Denver the following night. In my heart, I knew it was for me. My husband had to step on it, we traveled from Cleveland to Denver and made it by the opening prayer.

One of the senior pastors prayed and called people forward who had been sexually and spiritually abused. In a forceful, commanding voice he rebuked the spirits and being spiritually sensitive, I could actually feel tentacles curl up on my head. It brought me back to the helmet that I had felt placed on me in the Mormon Church just before I left. It had not left though. This pastor was just the introduction. A lady, who had all gifts of the Spirit active, began her program. Again standing, very soft and gently, I felt enfolded, and in the back of my knees, that sensitive spot was gently touched and I went down into a fetal position again, this time not voluntarily, reminding me of this Scripture: "**That at the name of Jesus every knee should bow, of things in heaven, and things in earth, and things under the earth;**" *(*Philippians 2:10). God could easily make it happen by simply touching that spontaneous reflex He built into the knee. The healing was taking place and whatever had curled up on my head disintegrated. Praise God for His miracles.

In studying the New Testament, what had happened to me was parallel to the healings of Jesus. He rarely healed the same way twice to show us that healing is a spontaneous happening. It is not a formula but a gift and is dependent on our own faith or belief in the existence of the Holy Spirit. Some Ex-Mormon friends wondered how fast I was adjusting. One lady had spent eleven years before she set foot out of the house to mingle with Christians. These experiences cannot be duplicated at will. They are so precious, so gentle, yet so productive, they wipe away all doubt that they could result in failure. We fail God, but He does not fail us. When we do not receive what we ask for, it is because we do not have the faith we think we have. We have to believe the Holy Bible is true before God will reveal His power in our lives. To have that kind of a witness is worth any amount of agony that we might experience in the physical because it anchors us to God.

In fact the physical world as we know it, became completely irrelevant, in light of the future. To have another thousand years with our beautiful Savior Jesus as our King and Lord to live life again and then to have eternal life directly with God fills me daily with unfathomed joy when the thought fleets through my mind. Just think its all true I tell myself and my spirit does somersaults. There is no death. "**So when this corruptible shall have put on incorruption, and this mortal shall have put on immortality, then shall be brought to pass the saying that is written, Death is swallowed up in victory.**" *(*1 Corinthians 15:54).

Taming The Lion

To prove to myself once again that the LDS Church is not in line with the Holy Bible, I wrote the bishop a letter. "My husband has decided to leave the Church and I, being his wife, am under his authority according to the Bible. I have to follow suit." As suspected, he took the bait. The bishop and my `assigned chaperon` Elder friend and another Elder whom, I thought was a Christian, paid me a visit. My husband was there on the couch when the bishop began telling me that my husband was unrighteous and that I needed to get a divorce. It gave me the opening to witness to them, that I believed the Bible to be the true Gospel, not the Book of Mormon and that Jesus Christ is God in the flesh and my shepherd not Joseph Smith but Jesus who gave his blood for my sins.

Something to this order came out of my mouth, my memory is poor, and it may not be exact: "How dare you tell me that my husband is unrighteous, when you are telling me to sin to satisfy the Mormon Doctrine. You are neutralizing what Christ did for us." My `friend' began to cry, when he realized that Mormonism was over for me. From him it was just one more ploy to pull at my heartstrings. I loved the Elder and he knew it. We had been through thick and thin together. We both knew it was over. The bishop asked me to listen to a tape before I pull the curtain on the Church. That tape was the insult of all insults. It was a testimony of a young Christian converted to Mormonism, his glowing report of having found the `True Church of Jesus Christ'. It implied that I had not gotten the message in twenty years, what Mormonism is about. As it turned out, I got the `true' message instead, praise God.

A young man, a member of Happy Church, an Ex-Mormon invited two Mormon missionaries. He wanted me to witness to them. He had another Ex-Mormon come to the meeting with a box full of newsletters and testimonies from other Ex-Mormons. The box represented the door to freedom forever. Satan's number was up, and my walk took a whole new direction from that point forward.

To get into classes in a bible college, recommendations of past service are critical. I wrote a letter to the bishop asking for a recommendation describing my service to the church over the twenty years. He refused to do anything for me. That was my "thank you" from the Mormons. Witnessing to a couple of my friends, one assured me that he hoped I would pass away soon so they could keep my record in tact to insure celestial heaven for me. Another said: "please don't take my little corner of happiness, that is all I have. I would prefer not to know the truth. A third didn't know what to say, when I told him to see what he would say that I was lost, talk me back into the church. They were a poor example of Christ's teachings.

"Like many without family, the families in the Ward had become my family, 200 of them, giving up that kind of a circle was what God expected to see. Love for Christ Jesus has to be greater than the love we feel toward anyone or anything to survive the onslaught of Satan. He hits us where we are most vulnerable. He cuts our hearts to shreds and we have to keep walking regardless, keep loving, keep forgiving and remember the wretched position the Mormons are in. They love the church more than God and will reap hell forever, if they don't come out. They are hopelessly deceived and blinded because they do not embrace the truth. They love the lie instead.

There was no response to my letter to get myself excommunicated. The bishop acted like I did not exist. On January 12, 1992, I wrote the following letter:

Dear Bishop Hillyard,

It is with great regret, that I submit this request for excommunication from the Mormon Church. I have taken this step although I value very much the friendships and associations I developed over twenty years of membership in your church. However, one whom I love more than all of you has said: "**He that loveth father or mother more than me is not worthy of me: and he that loveth son or daughter more than me is not worthy of me.**" (Matthew 10:37)

Taming The Lion

Those who call themselves Christians and believe in the name of Jesus Christ of Nazareth are called to that kind of discipleship. If I am to be true to my Lord, who loved me and gave himself for me, then I must keep His commandments. If I am called to love him more than my own family, how much more am I called to love him more than brothers and sisters at the Mormon Church.

Unfortunately, in spite of my many long standing relationships with members who were family to me and whom I sincerely love, I find that in following Jesus Christ, I must sever my ties with the membership of the church. This is no reflection upon you, or upon the many wonderful things that the Mormons do for each other. It is simply the Jesus of Mormons is not the same as the Jesus of the New Testament.

I began an in depth study of the Holy Bible three years ago and found too many differences between Mormonism and biblical teachings. The departures are too many and too major to keep on the shelf. Over the years of sorting Mormon and Christian teachings I have accumulated that one too many that broke the camel's back. In Hebrews 7:19: **"For the law made nothing perfect, but the bringing in of a better hope did; by the which we draw nigh unto God**.*"* Hebrews 7:20: **"..he {Christ} was made priest:"** Hebrews 7:21: *"***...The Lord sware and will not repent, Thou art a priest for ever after the order of Melchizedec:)**" Hebrews 7:24: **"But this man, because he continueth ever, hath an unchangeable priesthood.***"* Hebrews 7:25: **"Wherefore he is able also to save them to the uttermost that come unto God by him, seeing he ever liveth to make intercession for them.***"* Hebrews 7:28: **"***For the law maketh men high priests which have infirmity; but the word of the oath, which was since the law, maketh the Son, who is consecrated for evermore.***"** Hebrews 8:1,2: **"Now of the things which we have spoken this is the sum: We have such an high priest, who is set on the right hand of the throne of the Majesty in the heavens; A minister of the sanctuary, and of the true tabernacle, which the Lord pitched, and not man.***"* Hebrews 8:6: **"But now hath he obtained a more** excellent ministry, by how much also he is the mediator of a better covenant, which was established upon better promises." Hebrews 8:7: "For if that first covenant had been faultless, then should no place have been sought for the second".

Hebrews 8:13: ".. A new covenant, he hath made the first old. Now that which decayeth and waxeth old is ready to vanish away." Hebrews 9:14: "How much more shall the blood of Christ, who through the eternal Spirit offered himself without spot to God, purge your conscience from dead works to serve the living God?" Romans 10:3,4: "For they being ignorant of God's righteousness, and going about to establish their own righteousness, have not submitted themselves unto the righteousness of God. For Christ is the end of the law for righteousness to every one that believeth."

The Holy Spirit witnessed to me that Christ Jesus is the righteousness. His righteousness has been imputed to us, We become born again as a new person. This birth requires us to die to ourselves and begin living for Jesus requiring only telling others about Him. We lose the desire to be independent and begin longing to be with Him forever and certainly take every precaution not to betray Him again which requires knowing Him through Scripture study. Scripture study is the substance of nourishment of this new person inside us. Like food to the body, Bible verses in context, become food to the spirit in us. Satan will counteract this program with everything he can think of because this is the only narrow road that leads to the Celestial Heaven. The temple has nothing to do with it.

In Hebrews, Scripture clearly states, that the Aaronic priesthood was discontinued when Jesus received the Melchizedec priesthood. I discovered in the book: 'Marvelous Works And A Wonder', one of the missionary books, Chapter 9, page 1, that Joseph Smith said about the messenger who descended from heaven in a cloud: "Upon you my fellow servants, in the name of Messiah, I confer the Priesthood of Aaron, which hold the keys of the ministering of Angels, and of the gospel of Repentance, and of baptism by

Taming The Lion

immersion for the remission of sins; and this shall never be taken again from the earth until the sons of Levi do offer again an offering unto the Lord in righteousness. Jesus stated on the cross: :It is finished."

It sounds to me like Mormons are starting over from the beginning that Jesus Christ did not accomplish what He came to do or else why another offering. Man is filthy rags to God in the flesh. How does man expect to offer anything in righteousness? Man does not have righteousness under any circumstances. Jesus Christ is our righteousness. He is giving us the gift of righteousness through the Holy Spirit. Joseph Smith forbade the Holy Spirit entrance into the church when he prohibited speaking in tongues in the membership. To accept Mormonism is to deny Jesus Christ and the Holy Spirit.

I had made it a point not to read anti Mormon literature, because I loved the church with heart and soul. The Holy Spirit made me choose between Jesus Christ and the LDS Church. Jesus Christ of Nazareth is the one I came to worship when I joined the Mormons. If He does not live there, I had no choice but to move out. I was broken hearted, believe me and feel pretty betrayed. Twenty years serving in the wrong place was hard to accept. Jesus does not and should not come cheap. A young child brought his pet lamb to Jesus when he was born, I guess that is the least we can do too.

Planning to witness for Jesus Christ to every Mormon or prospective Mormon I meet, I hope God has mercy on me and brings many into my path to make up for lost time. I have a great respect for the commitment and sacrifice I saw in Mormons and hope with all my heart they are put where they belong, at the feet of Jesus Christ. Respectfully yours,

The eagle rides the wind and it whips him up high, but gradually he has to come back down to earth and real life is taken back up. Used to being surrounded by people, I could talk to, and not having anyone who understood, became a real problem. Experiencing truth hits every area of one's life, past, present and future and one begins to have many realizations. My marriage was where Satan hit hard and tried to create chaos. My husband and I began blaming each other for being so stupid. We began mistrusting each other. Paranoia, schizophrenia, spells of confusion, thoughts of ending it all, fear of being killed for talking, and relationships with people who were not Christians began to disintegrate seemingly for no reason. Satan was busy discrediting my belief in myself as a wife, mother and friend.

Not being able to share the experience became the biggest problem. There was an Ex-Mormon group in Denver, but it took six months to make a connection with someone in the group. They would not return my calls. The church administration where they were meeting had no clue about them and finally on Christmas there was a break through.

They were a mixed group of various cults and they were undergoing major problems within the group. The group had been taken over by people who thought they could do a better job than the previous leaders and Satan was having a field day causing dissension as he does within Christian ministries in the whole Christian Body. The group disintegrated, and as I suspected God was raising me up into this ministry. My introduction to this type of spiritual warfare was over night and my level of understanding was raised to help me stand steady. The Holy Spirit confirmed that my path had indeed been preparation to become a soldier for Christ Jesus.

What is strange about Mormonism, information that is available to the public does not get to Mormons. `The New World Order' and the whole `End Time Frenzy' was news to me. Not long after the meeting on Oral Robert's Campus, Kenneth Copeland had a crusade at Fort Worth, Texas and I attended. During Gloria Copeland's presentation of the Healing School, she asked people to bear their testimony about healings. There were thousands of people there and we stood in line for hours and praised and worshiped to give a witness. Questioned several times about my testimony related to the Mormon church they finally decided to let me up on stage to give my testimony. Full of the spirit, I began sharing that people should

Taming The Lion

stay out of Mormonism, that I had been delivered out of the church through the Holy Spirit's witness and Copeland's Ministry.

What almost felt like levitation I jumped off the stage light as a feather and somehow landed in Gloria Copeland's lap. She was not happy with my testimony. She said to me, "what did our ministry have to do with you getting out of Mormonism?" I replied: "Your husband kept talking about pulling down strongholds and I guess Mormonism was a stronghold in my life." She was visibly upset. She said that it was impossible that her husband could have had anything to do with my delivery because they believed that we are all one brotherhood and practice love.

People came up and asked me to pray for their Mormon friends and relatives. A black lady from Washington, D.C. said, "I am so glad that you talked about your experience. There are Mormons on my job harassing me to join their church."

Gloria laid hands on thousands of people. My turn came and I went down under the power. The electricity rushing into my body she kept me down longer than the rest, telling me that I was in trouble spiritually because of my testimony about Mormonism. She was right. At dinner break, I decided to go back to the motel. Walking around the building, I fell and broke my foot. In excruciating pain, I tried to walk on it. Only after finding ice and packing could I relieve the pain enough to go back to the Copeland crusade till late that night hoping for a healing. The pain got so bad just sitting, that I had to get back to my rented car. A young woman rushed over to me to help and began to pray over my foot. She got perturbed and blamed me for not having enough faith when my foot did not straighten out. She ran and got a couple of ushers to carry me back to the car. It took from 11pm to 7 am to get to the right gate at the airport. People were giving me wrong directions and I was trying to tackle a suitcase with a broken foot. This was my first lesson in the kind of spiritual warfare I was heading into from that day forward.

Taming The Lion

Back in Denver we went straight to the clinic and got a cast put on. Since it was my right leg, I was hoping to get some sick leave; my job involved driving all day. "No way", said the doctor, "you'll have to manage somehow." The cast was all was up to the kneecap. My husband drove me and together we got through it. I had written the Copeland's several letters and like the Mormons there was no response. They had promised a video of the presentations of people at the Healing School. My testimony had been spliced out.

Oral Roberts University rejected my application because I had no recommendations. God is so good, that also turned out to be a blessing.

The Holy Spirit led me to another book "A Different Gospel" by D.R. McConnell who presented a historical and biblical analysis of the Word Faith Movement that related to Kenneth Copeland's Ministry, which was a clone of Kenneth Hagin's by Copeland's own admission. It became obvious now that God was in the lead and truly birthing my Discernment Ministry. The book revealed that Copeland's teaching of Word Faith was parallel to the teaching of `positive confession' by Norman Vincent Peale. They were advocates of Emerson, a student of Plato, a Greek philosopher and Freemasonry. It was later discovered that Oral Roberts uses Masonic symbols in his insignia revealing that he is most likely a member of the craft. "**Beware lest any man spoil you through philosophy and vain deceit, after the tradition of men, after the rudiments of the world, and not after Christ.**" (Colossians 2:8). Ken was in and out of my waste paper basket for several weeks, I had drawn much strength from his teachings. The scandal about the Word Faith Movement broke not long after that. The Christian Research Institute began running tapes on their incorrect teachings. Copeland confessed that he locked himself up with another preacher's tapes and listened until he could emulate the other preacher word for word, even the voice came through at times. While I was still under that influence I had been so softened by their seed faith message, that I made a loan of eight thousand dollars to hand to a poor person. The Holy Spirit helped me find a way to cut the expense in half but it still cost me four thousand dollars.

"Now the works of the flesh are manifest, which are these; Adultery, fornication, ncleanness, lasciviousness, Idolatry, witchcraft, hatred, variance, emulations, wrath, strife,seditions, heresies,." (Galatians 5:19,20) The dictionary states emulations as ambition or endeavor to equal or excel others (as an achievement), imitation, the use of or technique of an emulator.

Back at Marilyn Hickey's converted shopping center called Happy Church, things were going down hill fast. One night they took a collection for one sprinkler a person. Assuming it could not be more than $25 we were talked into a commitment before we knew how much it would be by a visiting preacher. The price turned out to be $250 and peer pressure got the $250 out of my purse in one night.

Next the Holy Spirit wanted to show me why people come forward and tell people that they are healed. My foot was out of the cast by that time and still very tender, not quite healed. Marilyn was calling healings in feet and I felt a tingle in that foot. Thinking that I was having a healing, I jumped on it walked to the front and realized that my foot was not healed. To save Marilyn's and my face, I continued and began lying about my condition.

The next meeting she asked people who wanted to loose a certain number of pounds in a short time frame, she wanted to pray it off. The Holy Spirit was showing me why many people loose their faith, in this case it was about unanswered prayers. On another occasion we were praising and worshiping and as I tried to raise my hands, as we ought to, I could not get them up. I thought that's strange. Interestingly enough, apparently others experienced the same thing that day and complained to Marilyn about it. She revealed those complaints and stated that the reason for that was the fact that the sanctuary had been a shopping center and that the spirits connected with it were holding our arms down. That was the straw that broke that camel's back.

Taming The Lion

While on the subject of Marilyn Hickey who had a worldwide ministry another episode presented itself from Pakistan. Many years into my ministry online, a gentleman got in touch with me from there. Marilyn had been invited to teach converted Christian pastors over there how to do Christian ministry and run churches. This Christian administrator was well known and popular among Christians in Pakistan. He had been on my website where he found a collection of reports about the Word Faith Movement and became concerned. I shared my experiences with him by email. This happened just before the earthquake in Islamabad not far from where he was located when thousands lost their lives. Marilyn missed the earthquake because they sent her home and never to come back. He sent me a photo of himself laying hands on her because she admitted her own depression and exhaustion. When she got back they kept track of her ministry and found out she was lying about her trip to Pakistan telling people that thousands of Muslims got saved because of her ministry. It confirmed my collection on the web was valid.

After sixty-four years of age, I have come full circle back to Martin Luther with more revelations to come. Lutheran pastors infiltrated due to Satan's final thrust to break up the old traditions to make way for the world church that includes all denominations. The World Council of Churches in Switzerland is ecumenical and gradually has absorbed one denomination after another. It leads to eventual Catholicism for all. The word Catholic means universal.

Satan kept breaking the ground away from under my feet as we ran from one church to another. Many Mormons go through this and return to their church because it is too confusing. The opposition rises as we grow in the gospel right along with our love for Christ Jesus. Satan has no standards and does not care what happens to the individual. Only 25% to 30% of registered Mormons are active Mormons. The rest are on the fringes and often afraid to make the break for Jesus Christ. Their faith is too weak to stand. What they don't realize is unless they renounce Mormonism completely and disconnect the lake if fire is waiting for them at the end of the Millennium.

My husband and I were baptized again to proclaim our allegiance to Christ Jesus of Nazareth and left no doubt in anyone's mind who we belong to. We notified the bishop one more time. That was the catalyst for Satan to release us and we received notice that our names had been removed from the records that included my whole family. It was a relief when the Bishop told me that they would remove every vow and every ordinance we had participated in as well as our whole genealogy. When God states that our past will be pitched into the sea of forgetfulness, He meant it. The false prophets live under God's rule and ultimately have to bow; there is no way of getting around that. Hallelujah.

Most of the Word of God is already fulfilled precept upon precept. Satan's dominion has already been invalidated. Events are moving into place for the final curtain to rise.

We were not excommunicated because they would have had to share my letter with other Elders. They were not about to risk truth on them. The Elders might have left too. The temple vows are no threat compared to the threat of sitting in hell for eternity. God wrote the Bible to serve as a blueprint for creation. He is bound by it. It is absolute and all the rest will happen as it is written. Please take it serious. It is a matter of eternal life with Jesus Christ or hell with demons forever. Don't risk it.

CHAPTER 13

THE MYSTERY OF INIQUITY

Because of modern technology and little resistance from people, the New World Order is taking shape so fast now; it is difficult to keep up with new developments. People behind the scenes are beginning to reap the harvest of many years of diligent effort to bring this new life style about. As the Bible will bear out in the next chapter, the concept of power is experienced in unity and in worship of one leader, and the Antichrist wants the glory. Hitler's power came from the spirit of the people's worship in unity and that is what Satan must have under any circumstances. He has been working on people behind the scenes for centuries.

All the Antichrist spirit has to do now is pull it all together unto one mountain (a king). That is what gave Hitler an eternal reputation of an expression of evil. Even if it was temporary, it fulfilled his purpose. He was satisfied. Cost of lives had no meaning to him. There has to be a reason for having been on this planet somehow. That seems to be at the core of human beings and even the spirit world. Without the unity of Germany he would have remained insignificant. People join because it makes them feel alive to be part of a movement. What could be a loftier goal than a peace movement? That is something we all want. Only the Bible warns us there will never be peace until sin is slain in all of humanity. We can expect complete peace in the glorified state only, even the millennium is going to end in war.

The problem God is having with us begins and ends with the Tower of Babel, which represents having reached heaven in some form independent of God. Too much knowledge without love self-destructs. The atomic bomb is an example. Babylon stands for all that God opposes. He interrupted the construction of this tower and scattered people, gave them new languages to keep them divided. He said that anything would be possible to man if he allowed it to continue. God is testing our motivation all the time. He wants us to seek the truth so we can be saved. Scripture taught out of context creates an incorrect body of understanding in us leading to la la land. Not understanding what we are to do where our eternal future is concerned can have fatal after effects. Because Adam gave our birthright to Satan we have been put out of control. Only the Holy Spirit can change that. Jesus said that His kingdom is not of the world for that reason. We need spirit to Spirit communication.

The global network is three pronged and ultimately pivots into one system: Man (Cain). The three prongs are economic, political and spiritual. God relates through Scripture that our problem is only two pronged: God versus Money, and the gold Jesus Christ wants us to buy from Him versus gold representing the golden calf. Because we want someone to lead us, our problems begin and end with those who are in front of us. If it was just us personally we would have control over our being. Our attention is taken from our eternal Father. Our environment is so full of problems to solve for a reason. The second World War, with the development of the atomic bomb, raised our consciousness to the realization that man's inventions had led to self destruction and something had to be done to get control over nations to keep us all from doom's day.

As the message of the book should convey, Satan has to work behind the scenes to get this tremendous task done. He has to make the goal very plausible and legitimate. What could be more convincing than a goal for peace? To focus all people on one goal, the three areas of existence, political, economic and spiritual, had to undergo major changes.

Control to get movement in society is money. Where the world is concerned an international group of bankers spent large amounts of money on public and private schools to influence people of all ages through education. The film and television industry changed people's thinking from birth to death. The movers flooded churches with new age ideas, so we could all become healthy, wealthy and organized Christians building self esteem and becoming well adjusted capable independent little gods.

Taming The Lion

Economically merchandise from all directions: mail, phone, television, radio and superstores, plunged us into slavery. There was no place for a person to become helpless needing a savior under the power of positive thinking, because it works. Unbelievers and believers saturated with psychic excitement, preoccupied with a smorgasbord of self-transforming and served delusion are distancing themselves from the truth. We delight in numbness to keep from having to participate in the mainstream. The results are unavailability for possible conversion to Christ Jesus. Consciences are gradually put to sleep.

In looking at our political problems, it is not so easy to see what is going on, because the information is not public knowledge and we are dependent on people who do have an inside track. After an experience like Mormonism, testing information against Scripture becomes part of the new curriculum. I acquired quite a library about current events. There is a group of individuals who have come forward with discoveries that they have made in their workplaces or their organizations. They are trying to alert the public. Gary H. Kah is one of them. He wrote "En Route To Global Occupation". His book confirmed many of my suspicions and answered questions like: `why were monopolies re-instituted?' It revealed the big surprise that the United States government does not own the Federal Reserve Banks. A group of secret and general stockholders own it. That was an eye opener. The Federal Reserve Bank of New York is the Federal Reserve and it has banks in other cities. The word `Federal' probably had a lot of people fooled. All moneys are filtered through the bank.

Some of the secret major stockholders are the Rothschild's Bank of London and Berlin, Lazard Brothers Banks of Paris, Israel Moses Seif Banks of Italy; Warburg Bank of Hamburg and Amsterdam, Lehman Brothers of New York, Chase Manhattan Bank of New York and Sachs Bank of New York. A light went on taking me back to President Reagan when he brought `run away' inflation to an almost miraculous halt, or so we thought. He was on the Board of Directors and was quietly replaced when he made recommendations they did not agree with. It was not Reagan but the Federal Reserve who was responsible, which means we are in their hands not the President's. The national debt is out of control for a reason. *"The rich ruleth over the poor, and the borrower is servant to the lender."* (Proverbs 22:7)

To get an idea how we are manipulated, in 1966 it was discovered four of the world's largest oil companies controlled by the Rockefeller family developed a unique situation that later forced gasoline prices suddenly up more than four times hitting the American consumer not only with the purchase of a compact car thinking there would be a shortage forthcoming, but also with gasoline bills not remotely offsetting for the purchase of a foreign car. The OPEC crisis of Arab sheiks plunged the United States into a deep recession but the plan worked to create the Trilateral Commission and we now enjoy three economic superpowers. The Trilaterals are North America, Western Europe and Japan. Today in 2008 the world is going through a similar situation only a whole lot worse. The news is expecting $4.00 a gallon at the pump. A whole number of airlines are bankrupt, merging, raising prices, changing the numbers of flights raising people's ire. Since most people are driving foreign made cars the reason for the present crisis has not been revealed. Exxon raked in $40 billion in 2007 alone. People are under the impression that our leadership is trying to destroy our way of life. These prices increased inflation 10 and 20%. Arabians who run OPEC blame the tax structure by the Federal and State government included in gas prices on high taxes and the factor that the U.S. has not invested in refineries for decades. The Bible states that we will be in a depression during the Tribulation and that seems to be where we are heading. They call it recession today.

The United Nations was not the first attempt at a New World Order. The Council of Foreign Relations (CFR) formed way back on July 29, 1921 involved members of the United Nations who are also participating in ownership of the Federal Reserve: in example Alan Greenspan, Jean J. Kirkpatrick, Richard Cheney and David Rockefeller. CFR advocated building of an international order that

Taming The Lion

became known as the New World Order under a socialist flag. It looks more Communistic than socialists to me because the government owns stock internationally in many corporations. They invest every dollar they can to participate in the high interest earned from people's debts, The Bibles have been rewritten and rewritten, the latest took God's gender out. He is now an 'it' asexual. The thrust is to make the truth disappear. Just today on the news, they put a woman in the loony bin because she told people that God had told her to do something. The teaching of creation is not allowed in schools. Same sex marriages are in. Internet went public in 1996, which has given ministries a vast audience without restrictions to counter act the demonic developments.

Many of the members of the various major organizations involved are Masons. Franklin D. Roosevelt, a 33 degree Mason, formulated our present dollar bill containing the symbol of a pyramid with the all seeing eye of `Osiris' (symbolic of Baal, god of the underworld, worshiped in Solomon's Temple and inviting God's wrath). Osiris is also the object of idolatry in Freemasonry and Mormonism (they don't talk about Osiris but display his eye in their crest and the Egyptian drawings including this god boldly in their combined Bible). The all-seeing eye was popular during the Middle Ages in Europe due to an abundance of Masons. Under the pyramid on our one-dollar bill is a Latin sentence `Novus Ordo Seclorum' which means: The New Order of the Ages.

President Roosevelt first coined the name `United Nations' in 1941 and it was first used officially on January 1, 1942, when 26 states joined pledging themselves to continue their joint war effort. From that concept sprang hundreds of other agencies networking and coordinating their efforts now toward one goal `peace' supposedly. "The Bilderbergers" is not a family but a group of powerful elite people interconnected with NATO, CFR, the Club of Rome and the Trilateral Commission. The Treaty of Rome brought the Common Market into being supported by the Bilderberg meetings. Familiar names included Henry Kissinger and Helmut Schmidt. President Bush added the Skull and Bones, a Masonic

Taming The Lion

Order, to the picture. The Aspen Institute in Colorado connected to the CFR and other organizations, trains people for prospective world government positions.

It becomes obvious quickly that the real goal was `one' totalitarian socialistic worldwide government, based on subordination first of nations on down to individuals and strict control of all aspects of the life of people. The focus is on shifting the nations into a world autocratic authority. It will ultimately come under the control of the Antichrist according to the Bible. The issue is still Cain and Abel. We have a caring Father who had all intentions of giving us the good life but we gave away our birthright to become gods ourselves. We believed the liar in the Garden of Eden was telling the truth exactly the same way we still do today. It comes from some pulpits that we are little gods or have the potential of becoming gods. The truth is, we were created to worship God in deep gratitude for what He has given us: an eternal glorious life, eventually surrounded by exquisite, perfect, beautiful objects and people who are in total agreement. Their goal will be the same, to love and be loved by God the Father, the Son and the Holy Spirit.

According to Scripture, before the seven-year tribulation, the revived Roman Empire consists of seven empires. "**And I stood upon the sand of the sea, and saw a beast rise up out of the sea, having seven heads and ten horns (ten world regional powers}, and upon his horns ten crowns, and upon his heads the name of blasphemy. And the beast, which I saw, was like unto a leopard, and his feet were as the feet of a bear and t he mouth of a lion: and the dragon gave him his power, and his seat, and great authority. And I saw one of his heads as it were wounded to death; and his deadly wound was healed: and all the world wondered after the beast.**" (Revelation 13:1-3)

The Club of Rome is an informal group of scientists, educators, economists and civil servants claiming to be developing solutions for world peace. They developed a model of a global system divided into ten regions worldwide, which is appearing everywhere lately and already used to guide future development. Just recently NAFTA

Taming The Lion

(North American Free Trade Agreement) just so happened to involve Region number 1 of the new world map. On a trip I purchased a road atlas and noticed that it was set up to include Canada and Mexico. The NAFTA (agreement) is not fully disclosed, because there is a lot more involved than a free trade agreement. The Treaty was put together during the Nixon administration and slammed through during President Clinton's leadership with the help of 'Fast Track' an instrument used to prevent the White House from debating or even reading the treaties. NAFTA had 20,000 pages which was impossible to read in fact. That is why it passed not only once but CAFTA passed as well. The House and Senate knew they had a chance to back out of NAFTA but didn't wish to look bad to the rest of the world. Over time certain media, books, Internet websites and blogs are leaking that we have become the North American Union (NAU).

U.S. State Department Chief Geographer William Wood, said, "What we are dealing with is the re-creation of countries." George Demko, a geographer and director of the Rockefeller Center at Dartmouth College, said: "As we're challenging the traditional ideas of state sovereignty, globalizing economies and communications, and breaking up the last empires, the geography of the world is unhooking old connections and hooking up new ones."

The U.S., Canada and Mexico, will break up their government bodies as they knew it when the rest of the information in the agreement is made public. The breakup of the Soviet empire and regional conflicts like Bosnia are related to this new plan. Italian geographer, Fabrizio Eva said, "Borders of present countries, or so-called natural boundaries, will increasingly lose their importance when they correspond to well-recognized linguistic and territorial identities." "A stratified system of governance and power is likely to replace traditional states," stated the Denver Post on August 30, 1992 entitled, "A New North America." This year, the European Community will add Norway, Sweden, Finland and Austria for a total of sixteen countries. Today 2008, the EU is up to twenty-four countries. The question now is how to come up with 10 horns the

Taming The Lion

Bible describes? Easy, there are two European Unions. East and West and the Western European Union has ten members. In all, the EU refuses to get involved in war. That has made them prosper. Their dollar value has risen to more than a 150% where the US dollar keeps falling and its value is 70% today in 2008.

"On April 24, 1994 the central banks of the NAFTA countries created an 8.8 billion U.S. Dollar joint account to be used by all three NAFTA participants when any of their currencies are under pressure. Wall Street Stock Market recently about crashed and the Federal Reserve pumped dollars into it and lowered interest rate to 2% to stabilize it If they merge their money, then a merger of their governments isn't far behind. Can't our military stop this? The answer is 'no'. According to the former president of American Geographers, Saul Cohen, "Many states won't have armies, only police." This is why the U.S. has been handing over more control of our military force to the U.N.." as stated in July 1994, issue of Monetary & Economic Review. Why is the President now involved in local issues such as police? The controls seem to be shifting to the White House and are mandated from the United Nations.

The public is becoming aware that a problem has developed, but the backup system planned behind the scenes is already in place. All the movers have to do now is prove that our leadership is incapable of getting the job done. This is the second President who is producing a gridlock in Washington D.C. and people are falling into the trap that they have rights and can change the leadership themselves instead are playing right into Satan's hands. He is the author of confusion and lies. He keeps people's attention on irrelevant issues and gets his itinerary set up in the meantime.

Today in 2008, again we have had a president George W. Bush who has proven himself to be totally incompetent to run the U.S. The people are under the impression that he has bankrupted the U.S.. In 2001 we were supposedly attacked by a group of ME Muslims who flew large passenger planes into the Twin Towers in New York and supposedly into the Pentagon. After thousands of hours of research by thousands, there are nothing but questions as to what really happened. At first it was feared that some 50,000 people could have been killed referring to the usual traffic in the buildings but the numbers came down to approximately 3,000.plus the passengers in the planes. One aborted plane crashed in Pennsylvania, which is also questionable because there was little debris and no bodies found on the scene.

This incident turned the American way of life upside down and was a major step toward a totalitarian government. It gave them reason to revamp FEMA, FBI, and CIA into one agency called Homeland Security headed by a former Jewish Judge. Thousands of security related changes went into place. The most offensive were long lines at the airports enabling employees to search baggage, clothing, shoes and pocketbooks. After many strange incidences people like sheep submitted to all the government agencies wished to do with them. Behind the scenes there were many small uprisings by young people that were quickly squelched with rubber bullets, tear gas, maze, stun guns and tazers by men in black uniforms with metal shields and helmets covering their whole heads down to the neck.

Of course like Pearl Harbor, the US now had an excuse for war. Even though Iraq had not been involved in the attack nor were they building nuclear weapons President Bush was hell bent going to war with Hussein because his father President Bush Sr. had been ridiculed for not getting the job done. Iraq much like Russia before the wall came down was closed off to the rest of the world. A female reporter finally got past that and filmed her tour. She showed a hotel entrance floor with President Bush Sr's bust in Mosaic tile that people were walking on. It might have been just more propaganda to give reasons for war. Hussein was busy rebuilding Babylon in Iraq from the Old Testament. He thought of himself as Nebuchadnezzar king of Babylon mentioned in the Book of Daniel. He was also part of the brotherhood, a Mason. What the true reason was for this war, only a few know. From a spiritual perspective Satan requires blood sacrifices in return for power. Today they are not easy to come by because these wars are more like civil wars than conventional wars like WWI and WWII.

Another change was that thousands were incarcerated without legal representation and sent to Cuba to American detention facilities. Illegal torture became part of the media dance reminding people that Hitler had returned. Because so many changes were unconstitutional the White House appointees came and went like a revolving door.

The primary elections are about to be completed. The only problem is so far the Democrats are split down the middle because the elite gave the people a black former Muslim and a feminist woman, the former first lady as possible candidates. The Republicans so far have lost the popular vote. The primary election has agreed to a Senator who wants to continue the war for another hundred years in the Middle East. Otherwise he has not presented the public with any other agenda when we have many issues that need discussion.

The recent `people's choice' in California, November 1994 election, to stop supporting illegal immigrants was put on hold immediately by a California judge and treated as a nationally internal issue, when it is not related to Americans other than their pocketbooks and state services. The issue sure seemed to point to future relaxation of entry into the U.S. or maybe total elimination of the border between the U.S. and Mexico. At the same time a protest arose among citizens and Canadian investors in a suburb of Denver, Colorado. Today it is fourteen years later and the US has absorbed some thirty million immigrants from Mexico under the pretense what Americans will not do agricultural jobs. It is called an invasion but there is next to no resistance against it. This influx has caused immense pressure on social services throughout the country. Some American citizens want to know how they can become an illegal immigrant because of all the freebies that they receive from the government. Instead of keeping the dollars earned by the illegals, they send them back to Mexico to the tune of $20 billion a couple of years ago. Mexicans are insisting on making the US a Spanish speaking country. They even voted on it at the White House. Presidential hopefuls Clinton and Obama both voted against English as our native language but lost in the long run. It is absolutely stunning the betrayal of the American people that is going on from the top down. Americans like sheep fall in line with whatever comes down the tube as if they were hypnotized.

Another major development is privatization of government services in many areas. Two of which are roads long paid for by American tax dollars, and the military, The King of Spain, Juan Carlos, has bought a number of federal highways in the U.S. . Toll is expected from people who wish to use the highways. The highways were paid for by the people's money. There is a plan in the making by private companies to build a road from a Mexican port all the way to a Canadian port that will be supported by American tax dollars by means of a membership fee by states that runs into millions of dollars. A law was extended to increase rights of private corporations to take advantage of Eminent domain (taking over private property without consideration of legal rights). For instance in Colorado some approximately 3400 farmers were in jeopardy of losing their properties to make way for this 12 mile wide highway. There are maps today of how many highways will become part of this network for hauling merchandise to global enterprises like WalMart. Not only will these roads turn into toll roads for citizens but the trucks using them will have to pay as well. Here is where computer chips come in. Each national drivers license contains a chip that has all information relating to the person carrying it and will be tied to their money or credit card. By driving through a tollbooth the toll is paid automatically. They will not need people manning tollbooths anymore.

Relating these ten regions to Revelation we have to go to Daniel 2:31-35 NIV **"You looked, O king, and there before you stood a large statue- an enormous, dazzling statue, awesome in appearance (it represented the whole world). The head of the statue was made of pure gold** (Babylon, King over all), **its chest and arms of silver** (Persia, inferior to Babylon), **its belly and**

thighs of bronze (Greece rules over the earth - Greek philosophies), **its legs of iron** (the Roman Empire - the leopard of seven heads including the King who becomes the Antichrist. The iron breaks and crushes everything), **its feet partly of iron and partly of baked clay** (the feet have ten toes that imply the ten world powers. Iron and clay* [* clay: #2635 in the New Strong's Concordance: from an unused root associated to the beautiful tree, (Nebuchadnezzar's kingdom parallel to the tower of Babel which reached into heaven (Dan 4:27) cut down in Daniel 4. The roots (bound in iron and bronze until Micah 4:1-8, the Millennium) go into effect, signifying the remnant of the Israelites getting out of bondage finally. Clay also represents Adam and his progeny as weak earthen vessels). The feet a mix of strong and brittle iron and clay that won't hold as a unity. The feet go and all else tumbles down with it). **While you were watching, a rock was cut out, but not by human hands** (by the Holy Spirit. The rock is Jesus Christ and His Church).

The King James Version: **"Thou, O king, sawest, and behold a great image. This great image, whose brightness was excellent, stood before thee; and the form thereof was terrible. This image's head was of fine gold, his breast and his arms of silver, his belly and his thighs of brass, His legs of iron, his feet part of iron and part of clay. Thou sawest till that a stone was cut out without hands, which smote the image upon his feet that were of iron and clay, and brake them to pieces. Then was the iron, the clay, the brass, the silver, and the gold, broken to pieces together, and became like the chaff of the summer threshing floors; and the wind carried them away, that no place was found for them: and the stone that smote the image became a great mountain, and filled the whole earth."** (Daniel 2:31-35) To become part of the rock we cannot be part of Babylon (spiritual world system or world mentality). The mountain filled the whole earth relates to the Millennium. We will be living like today in families raising children under Christ Jesus as our King. Mind you this was written 537 B.C. and talks about today. The Bible is exciting. It answers every question.

Taming The Lion

"**They are also seven kings. Five have fallen** (includes ancient nations: Babylon, Persia, Egypt, Assyria and Greece), **one is** (Roman Empire was in existence during Apostle John's ministry. It went into suspension in 476 A.D. when the last Roman Emperor was abdicated), **the other has not yet come** (future involving the whole world); **but when he does come, he must remain for a little while** (the Antichrist remains approximately three and a half years). **The beast who once was** (my own opinion `U.N./ VATICAN'), **and now is not, is an eighth king who comes out of the Roman Empire** (representing iron crushing the whole world into worshiping him) **becomes the world ruler for one hour. He is going to his destruction.** `The ten horns you saw are ten kings, who have not yet received a kingdom** (they are supporters of the New World Order and will receive total control over land as a reward), **but who for one hour will receive authority as kings along with the beast. They have one purpose and will give their power and authority to the beast** (Antichrist). **They will make war against the Lamb** (Christ Jesus), **but the Lamb will overcome them because he is Lord of lords and King of kings and with him will be his called, chosen and faithful followers. For God has put it into their hearts to accomplish his purpose by agreeing to give the beast their power to rule, until God's words are fulfilled.**" (Revelation 17:10-14,17 NIV).

Border changes in the U.S. have been forthcoming for a long time. From Roosevelt's plan the Nixon administration further divided the United States into ten federal regions for emergency management and decentralization (FEMA). Every past and present American President since F.D. Roosevelt was a member of the Masonic Lodge, CFR, SB or the Trilateral Commission. Media personalities in all three networks are involved. People like Dan Rather, Harry Reasoner, Bill Moyer (his name and commentary is on the new Bible endorsed by Billy Graham (33 degree Mason) and forty nine other `personalities' of all walks of life called "The Answer"), David Brinkley, Barbara Walters to name a few are members.

Taming The Lion

This elite group of men and women who direct and own financial conglomerates controls the stock market. The previous republican Speaker of the House called President Clinton in 1994 `elitist'. Major magazine publishers like Fortune, Time, Life, Money, People and Sports Illustrated are some, as well as banks and large corporations such as oil companies, department stores and other chain conglomerates. It explains how the censorship works. They control the money therefore have access to management of information which is to get to the public. Public education received extra large donations through the Rockefeller, Carnegie and other Foundations to influence the curriculum into global thinking.

The United States represented peace by not invading without provocation. That image was changed in the Gulf War. Not only was the world made aware of its dependency on the Mideast and the need to unite against a common enemy but it also served as the final step into the One World Order. America now established as the undisputed leader of the world, is the enforcer of the New World Order is but only on the surface. The secret hierarchy of power is in Europe and we are evolving into becoming subservient to Europe because we are in debt to the bankers. There is today some controversy about the US debt. Some believe that the US is the final Antichrist Babylon in conjunction with EU that is taken over the leadership of the world. When president Bush Jr. took office he declared himself the world leader and anyone who was not for him was considered to be the evil axis. Today there are only four countries that are rebelling and they are Venezuela, Cuba, North Korea and Iran.

The police force is in process of merging into an international system. Americans are policing other countries and other countries are policing us. Foreigners have no sympathy for their own countrymen and will enforce orders. Yesterday I was told that U.S. insignia is being removed from American uniforms and army vehicles are painted over to remove American symbols. My grandson enlisted for four years and I noticed on his "American" uniform the same Maltese cross that the Pope and Hitler used.

Taming The Lion

Powerful New Age organizations such as the Lucis Trust and World Union have had a tremendous impact on the public and feed directly into the World Constitution and Parliament Association. It was put in charge of bringing us into the New World Order. Lakewood, Colorado has since 1959 accommodated this large international association sporting many important international men and women. Its large New Age support network is implemented so quickly now; people will not have a chance to realize what is happening. Their plan includes a map of the world divided into ten regions and calls for a new monetary system. Only today news came that millions of American dollars, counterfeited (copied) on the Eastern continent, are so well done that the money will circulate as real money. A perfect reason to pull all the currency is brewing. The Senators are already convinced, more complicated paper money already designed and printed, would not solve the problem. The stage is set with each round. Scripture calls for a cashless society, because there needs to be control over every form of money internationally. Born again Christians will not be able to participate in the system without the mark of the beast. In the New World Order every human being will need the consent of Antichrist to purchase any product or service, make mortgage or loan payments, pay taxes and home insurance. It is obvious now why there needs to be an escape hatch for Christians.

The World Constitution and Parliament Association promotes such programs as "The Children's Peace Circle" a sign of spiritual motivation. In their literature Reverend Jesse Jackson, leader of the Rainbow Coalition and member of the CFR, comes on the pages. Working together with WCPA is the World Council of Churches now spilling into the mainline Catholic and Protestant denominations pushing for unity. Although to pastors it appears to be about uniting Christianity, the underlying theme is the New World Order. Any global effort is suspect to have connections into this network and contributes to the Antichrist. We still have a choice about it. It will become mandatory soon enough. We are to submit to our government and give Caesar what belongs to Caesar, but we do not have to volunteer our services free to further that cause. We cannot take the mark of the beast, which includes '666', not visible because our adversary is an expert at secrecy. That is why we have to be totally familiar with the gospel. We cannot depend on anyone anymore. God is a Father of His Word, the Bible, and will not disappoint or let Christians down. He is in control of all of this. God wants us to try to live outside the system as much as possible. We are considered aliens, as Christians, subject to persecution for marching to a different drummer than the world.

What is most interesting the powerful figures of the Middle East are Freemasons: King Assad of Syria and King Hussein of Jordan belong the Grand Lodge of Jordan and it is under the authority of the Arab Supreme Council. (1994)

The New World does not feel like a threat because it is coming in the name of Democracy and it is wanted. Universal health care is coming. It has to pass because it is the only way of getting every man, woman and child into the records with all their history. Many unsuspecting Christians are involved in pushing this new government.

The constitution is ignored in many decisions and issues. Our Colorado State Representative David Scaggs, quoted in this morning's newspaper (1994), complained to the President that he should consult Congress before he asks permission from the United Nations to get clearance for various actions. Today, 2008, going around the constitution seems to be acceptable. After the 9/11 attacks Congress laid all powers into President Bush Jr's lap and told him whatever he wished to do he could do. It was illegal but is still in effect because we are still at war.

A totalitarian government is in effect since the president stated that the United States is in a perpetual war. John McCain lost the election because he wanted to continue the war if it takes a hundred years. The president elect Obama has half his cabinet in place with long standing politicians of the democratic party that are familiar with, which reflects that the status quo will continue.

Taming The Lion

The fact that Obama replaced the American insignia on his jet with his own, a sun with three curved lines, has many wondering. The Scriptures that came to my mind was: Daniel 7:5 "**And behold another beast, a second, like to a bear, and it raised up itself on one side, and it had three ribs in the mouth of it between the teeth of it: and they said thus unto it, Arise, devour much flesh.**" Whether there is a connection remains to be seen. One thing is clear, the people elected a democratic majority of House of Representatives and the same for the Senate. That means that the time for gridlock in trying to pass new legislation is a thing of the past.

During the two years of following candidates around the country, much was going on behind the scenes. Due to high gasoline prices, a credit card crunch, and the sub-prime mortgage scandal, the whole economy collapsed. The Secretary of the Treasury was appointed from one of the largest collapsing investment firms on Wall Street. Greenspan retired. A Jewish college professor became the Chair of the Federal Reserve. The Secretary of the Treasury, Henry Paulson, is also on the Board of the Federal Reserve.

Too often both of these men appeared on the news channels lowering the interest rate and pumping billions of dollars into Wall Street's Stock market to keep it from collapsing. Paulson approached Congress with a plea that he needed a blank check from the U.S. Treasury to have whatever was needed to keep the credit rating of the U.S. in good standing. After some hot discussions, Paulson walked with a blank check to give to the Federal Reserve, a privately owned banking system. Because we are now global the whole world's economies are unraveling and they finally admitted today that we are in a depression that is much deeper than the one we had in 1929. From what I have learned over the years, I still believe this problem is being manipulated to get a global currency that will include devaluation or better said harmonizing of all currencies.

There are only four countries that are not cooperating: Iran, North Korea, Cuba and Venezuela. North Korea is negotiating with South

Taming The Lion

Korea to make it one country again and has given up to the U.S. Castro in Cuba is ill and will pass on soon. Iran is negotiating as well. Chavez is left in South America. He needs us to buy his fuel. The U,S. is saturated with his gas stations. Obama and Hillary could very well be the kingpins to get the ball rolling in that direction. .

Disarmament is around the corner. The last school shooting involved over thirty people dead. Random shootings are out of control today, which will present a reason for taking the guns. Right now there is a review going on at the supreme court of the Second Amendment. The question being asked is: "Is it being interpreted correctly? Can the general public bear arms or the only the military?" To everyone's surprise so far they ruled that the guns stay with the citizens. Civil war is expected in the U.S. because millions of people have lost their employment and they can only extend unemployment benefits for so long. Reserves are depleted. States like California and Florida have declared a financial state of emergencies due to the looming deficits in their budgets. The usual sources for money are not available anymore. Another stimulus package is on the horizon for January of 2009 but a few hundred dollars for some don't help much. Unsanitary homeless / jobless camps are appearing that can only breed disease. A gun show in Colorado indicated that people are stashing ammunition and guns. The retailers sold everything they had. We could very well be at the brink of losing our freedom to bear arms like most of the rest of the world.

The Bible gives clues about the King who is going to be given authority from all the leaders of the world. "**And out of one of them came forth a little horn, which waxed exceeding great, toward the south, and toward the east, and toward the pleasant land.**"

Daniel 8: "**Until the Ancient of days came, and judgment was given to the saints of the most High; and the time came that the saints possessed the kingdom. Thus he said, The fourth beast shall be the fourth kingdom upon earth, which shall be diverse from all kingdoms, and shall devour the whole earth, and shall**

Taming The Lion

tread it down, and break it in pieces. And the ten horns out of this kingdom are ten kings that shall arise: and another shall rise after them; and he shall be diverse from the first, and he shall subdue three kings. And he shall speak great words against the most High, and shall wear out the saints of the most High, and think to change times and laws: and they shall be given into his hand until a time and times and the dividing of time. *(*Daniel 7:22-25)

Many have written about a possible Antichrist and who it might be. The Bible points out the born again believers will not know who it is but know when we have arrived because the Tribulation happens like a trap when we least expect it. I just heard Rockefeller state that globalism will create PEACE. That is biblical as well and a sign to believers that we have arrived.

One example of a possible Antichrist is described in Dr. Taylor's book 'The Antichrist King - Juan Carlos' by Dr. Charles R. Taylor, published late 1993. It is fully documented. Dr. Taylor stated Prince Juan Carlos I de Borbon y Borbon of Spain was born in Rome, Italy (is a Roman citizen). Tradition from the Middle Ages has it that the Kings of Spain have carried the additional title of `King of Jerusalem'. This knowledge confirmed by a Roman Catholic Church publication indicated on November 27, 1975: `The Tablet' stating: The swearing in of Prince Juan Carlos de Borbon as King of Spain automatically involved revival of an ancient title applied to Spanish Monarchs, `King of Jerusalem'. According to the Spanish Consul General there, Count de Campo Rey said that the title, hereditary in Spanish Royalty since the Middle Ages, `while merely honorific', today was nevertheless `extremely precious'. He said that Popes and Muslim rulers recognized `Catholic Kings' of Spain for centuries as protectors of the Catholic Holy Land interests .."

The connection to Lucifer has come through many writings in France and Spain in 1992 about the Olympic Games in Madrid. They show that King Juan Carlos I ties into the great dragon and witchcraft. Promoting and inviting friends to that type of devilish entertainment won him disdain from some of the dignitaries. King

Taming The Lion

Juan Carlos I is a direct descendant of Louis XIV of the Bourbon Dynasty of France and the Habsburgs of Austria and Germany. Dating back to the Holy Roman Empire crowned by a Pope would be King of the Holy Roman Empire. He is a graduate of Spain's Military, Naval and Air Force Academies and highly qualified to lead. His coronation in Madrid, Spain on November 27, 1975 had sixty-eight foreign dignitaries from sixty-eight countries present. The King is a member of Opus Dei called by critics the `Octopus Dei' or God's Octopus, the Holy Mafia. It exerts immense influence in Spanish economic, academic and political life. Opus Dei has grown into a worldwide organization and is not a Christian movement. In 1972 still a Prince; Juan Carlos of Spain took second place in the pre-Olympic `sailing races' in Kiel, Germany in a craft entitled `The Dragon'. He has such a love for speed some said it's frightening.

Dr. Taylor stated: "As `King of Jerusalem, Defender of Catholic Holy Land interests', he will soon be seen coming on the world scene as the biblical rider on `the white horse' of Revelation 6:2." Dr. Taylor believed that the Rapture will be prior to the King's new throne in Jerusalem as evidenced in Revelation 5:9: "And they sang a new song: `You are worthy to take the scroll and to open its seals, because you were slain, and with your blood you purchased men for God from every tribe and language and people and nation.'" Dr. Taylor went on: "..And will be seen to go forth `conquering and to conquer.' It will be to defend Israel when the `red' Soviets and Muslim forces attack Jerusalem soon after the `peace talks' fail to satisfy the Arab demands for the eastern half of Jerusalem. It includes the Temple Mount. Palestine wants Jerusalem back and call it State of Palestine. Revelation 6:4 states that they shall have `power to take peace from the earth, and that they should kill one another.'

Satan keeps repeating these agreements with Israel prophesied in the Bible and they end up not being the real thing. This is one of them discussed in Taylor's book, THE JERUSALEM COVENANT that declares unequivocally that Jerusalem is and shall be forever the capitol of the State of Israel. Israel restored as a nation, fulfilled many Bible prophecies since May of 1948, but did not have the city of Jerusalem until they won the Six-Day War in 1967. Celebrating that day as JERUSALEM DAY 25 years later on May 31, 1992 Yeshaya Barzel, Director General of the Ministry for Jerusalem Affairs called for a `worldwide celebration to reaffirm the indelible bond between the Jewish people and its eternal spiritual and cultural capitol.' A special `JERUSALEM COVENANT' exemplifying the earlier Covenant drafted, beautifully prepared, signed by 16 of Israel's top officials. Then sent to worldwide Jewish centers for signatures of `many' Dignitaries, returned to Jerusalem and presented to the President of Israel on JERUSALEM DAY (of the Jewish calendar), May 19, 1993. On May 29, 1993, Jerusalem Post stated: `..1500 attended the ceremony, which this year included the signing of the COVENANT OF JERUSALEM. Seventy leaders signed.' This signing must have meant something but it certainly was the covenant believers are waiting for. They made us believe that it relates to this Scripture:

"And he shall confirm the covenant with many for one week: and in the midst of the week he shall cause the sacrifice and the oblation to cease, and for the overspreading of abominations he shall make [it] desolate, even until the consummation, and that determined shall be poured upon the desolate." (Daniel 9:27 KJV).

Evidence that the JERUSALEM COVENANT included the `one week' interpolated into seven years was not included in the Dr. Taylor's book. Israelis hold one week equivalent to seven years, also called the `time of Jacob's trouble,' better known as the Tribulation Period.

Going back into Nehemiah's day when the original Covenant was drawn up it is interesting to note that the Israelites were being restored then: **"And it yieldeth much increase unto the kings whom thou hast set over us because of our sins: also they have dominion over our bodies, and over our cattle, at their pleasure, and we are in great distress**_"_ _(_Nehemiah 9:37) **"And because of**

all this we make a sure [covenant], and write [it]; and our princes, Levites, [and] priests, seal [unto it]. " (Nehemiah 9:38)

Nehemiah in the Old Testament dates back to 425 B.C.. He received permission rebuild the Wall around the Temple in Jerusalem and after completion the people were registered and the Covenant was ratified. Nehemiah's original record on Elephantine Papyri was discovered in 1903 and confirmed the book of Nehemiah as written in the Old Testament. The book completes this history of the restoration of the returned remnant from exile in Babylon. It marks the beginning of Daniel's `seventy weeks' of which one-week is left identifying the seven-year tribulation.

Today in 2008 with President Bush Jr. at the helm this THE JERUSALEM COVENANT is not mentioned anymore. We now are working on a ROADMAP that the parties involved are to agree to in Israel. After much continuous turmoil and even war with Lebanon in Palestine the world got together and devised a ROADMAP that may or may not result in fulfillment of the prophecy in the Bible. Because of so many failures of other prophets I do not like to get into predictions. I am merely reporting what is happening in 2008. Israel still has not been declared a country. It has no borders in essence because it is Palestine. The ROADMAP is supposed to establish a border for Palestinians. It involves giving half of Jerusalem to the Palestinians as well as Gaza, the Westbank, Sumaria and Judaen territories. President Bush is determined to get this agreement accomplished. The signers involved are representatives from Russia, United Nations, the European Union, and the United States. The Bible definitely addresses that there will be no peace in Israel until the Antichrist comes on the scene and offers solutions that will appeal to them enough to sign. The president elect Obama has pledged to complete the Roadmap. That means Jerusalem will be divided as well as displacing thousands of Israelis out of their homes in the various areas promised to the Palestinians. This will do major damage to the tourist industry. Israel will have borders and be considered a country in exchange. Queen Elizabeth II knighted Shimon Peres in November if 2008.

Taming The Lion

The Likud Party headed by Benjamin Netanyahu is expected to be the preferred party for the next election in early 2009. He is not in agreement with the Roadmap.

Changes are manifesting and the new agenda initiated by the Catholic Church and its members. According to the dictionary the meaning of catholic is comprehensive universal: broad in sympathies, tastes and interests. Should we be surprised that the Catholic Church is trying to claim its universal status. Universal means every person coming into a universal religion. The media carries large pictures and write-ups about Catholic Dignitaries and new developments in the Vatican, highly unusual. Every sign of achieving Ecumenism with other denominations is meticulously reported to get readers used to the thrust for global unity. Catholics are becoming part of the political process by identifying with critical issues such as abortion and homosexuality. After all, we are all one in Christ. Reading their scriptural reports proving that they are so fundamental and so right, one is guilt ridden turning it down. We must not forget that they like other cults are not going to publish their beliefs that do not agree with Protestant denominations.

Through the ecumenical World Council of Churches, the Pope and Nobel Prize winner, Mother Teresa, are motivating people of all beliefs to get unified. Like Reagan in Berlin called for the Berlin Wall to come down, so are they calling for all the walls to come down.

Mother Theresa said in a presentation that it is okay for a Buddhist to worship another god as long as the Buddhist loved, when she should be trying to tell him the truth that there is only one way to God and that is through Jesus Christ. It is absurd to think a Buddhist could live under God the Father, the Son and the Holy Ghost, where would he put Buddha? Its obvious someone will have to provide a new idol to make it happen. She has since gone to her heaven and it was revealed that she never became a catholic but was true to her Buddhist religion.

Taming The Lion

The pope used Mother Theresa to get Buddhist to respect the Vatican.. The latest Pope is in the U.S. as I am writing this in April of 2008, having a meeting with President Bush, the United Nation and an Interfaith meeting. That includes Dali Lama and Tutu from Africa. It has become public knowledge that there exists a black pope who serves the Vatican. He runs the Jesuits who are all over the world as well. He stated that people do not have to give up what they believe today that we can all be a happy family simply tolerating and respecting each other's religion. Pope John Paul II who is deceased went so far as kissing the Koran. Islam worships the Queen of Heaven so they have much in common. Mormons wrote an article about Islam and described all their commonalities. They are also holding meetings with Christians and integrating.

Many Baptists with a majority of Freemasons, Presbyterians, Lutherans and hundreds of other organizations have capitulated to ecumenism already. Jesuits infiltrated the Seventh-day Adventist church. The walls are rapidly falling. In spite of incompatibilities it is happening because people feel safer in large numbers. The Pope just had a summit with Muslims. Muslims and Catholics each have a billion members. If everyone is doing it, it feels okay even when it isn't. Judging from the trend, disputing religions will become obsolete. Billy Graham blames Bible illiteracy for this merging of unequally yoked organization. Most people have a Bible in the house, but it stays on the shelf.

Rick Warren of the Purpose Driven Movement has just merged with Reader's Digest to get access to the masses to present his Peace Plan. He has been in the pulpit for many years but admits to not being a fundamental Christian. He is a member of the CFR, which is inappropriate for preachers. Warren has access to all media and has managed to infiltrate most churches with his social gospel. He has trained hundreds of pastors to practice what Warren preaches for the sake of peace.

"Let no man deceive you by any means: for [that day shall not come], except there come a falling away first, and that man of sin be revealed, the son of perdition; Who opposeth and exalteth

336

**himself above all that is called God, or that is worshiped; so that
he as God sitteth in the Temple of God, shewing himself that he
is God. Remember ye not, that, when I was yet with you, I told
you these things? And now ye know what withholdeth that he
might be revealed in his time. For the mystery of iniquity doth
already work: only he (the Holy Spirit) who now letteth [will
let], until he is taken out of the way. And then shall that Wicked
be revealed, whom the Lord shall consume with the spirit of his
mouth, and shall destroy with the brightness of his coming.** " (2
Thessalonians 2:3-8). This Scripture implies the removal of the
restraining power of the Holy Spirit who resides in born again
believers.

End-times downplayed, the rapture was tucked away recently,
because Christians believe that this concept causes complacency.
People are looking to restore old America and Old Time Religion.
The religious right has lost several strong leaders. Senator McCain
decoupled the religious right. The democrats held an interfaith
meeting during the election at the Denver National Democratic
Convention 2008. Any time the movers come up with a common
denominator people are drawn together in unity to practice
ecumenism without fail.

Obama was presented to the public as a Christian, having
attended the Church of Christ for twenty years. By his own
admission he is a Muslim. He proves it by a desire to legalize
abortion, a green light to stem cell research and insisting that
Jerusalem must be divided to get peace. Presently a Senate Bill
2433 is considered called a Global Poverty Act, which is to move
$845 billion to Africa over a thirteen-year period.

Mormonism was like living in a cocoon. Coming out is like
seeing the world for the first time, differences become obvious
immediately. International flags decorate the walls of many
churches. The restoration of America is now the theme of the
Church. It crept in ever so subtly and is now in full swing. The new
religion, although rooted in occult teachings can absorb all religions
because they are offshoots from the same root. The new church will

have a Christian veneer and relate to the notion that we are all one. President Clinton said it, Vice President Gore said it, the majority believes it to be true.

Recently, I came unto this message to the last church. It is about us today 1994. Revelation 3:14 is a message to Laodicea, **"And unto the angel of the church of the Laodiceans write; These things saith the Amen, the faithful and true witness, the beginning of the creation of God; I know thy works, that thou art neither cold nor hot: I would thou wert cold or hot. So then because thou art lukewarm, and neither cold nor hot, I will spue thee out of my mouth. Because thou sayest, I am rich, and increased with goods, and have need of nothing; and knowest not that thou art wretched, and miserable, and poor, and blind, and naked: I counsel thee to buy of me gold tried in the fire, that thou mayest be rich; and white raiment, that thou mayest be clothed, and that the shame of thy nakedness do not appear; and anoint thine eyes with eyesalve, that thou mayest see. As many as I love, I rebuke and chasten: be zealous therefore, and repent. Behold, I stand at the door, and knock: if any man hear my voice, and open the door, I will come in to him, and will sup with him, and he with me. To him that overcometh will I grant to sit with me in my throne, even as I also overcame, and am set down with my Father in his throne. He that hath an ear, let him hear what the Spirit saith unto the churches.** (Revelation 3:14-22)

Joe van Koevering of the ministry `God's News Behind the News' spoke at the International Prophecy Conference 1994 in Tampa, Florida and had the courage to discuss what many have been suspecting and they put it on the back burner, because it is too hard to swallow. Like I said before: truth is a bitter pill. His message called `The Laodicean Lie' refers to the last church before Christ returns.

"And for this cause God shall send them strong delusion, that they should believe a lie: (2 Thessalonians 2:11) Joe continued: "The Spirit of God has put a word in my heart. This message will be extremely different from what I normally share. I'll say some things today that I never said publicly before. Its been difficult to prepare and I did not volunteer to share this message. I have literally been arrested by the Spirit of God to share this word with you.. Many will misunderstand this intent.. I want you to hear my heart today.. three things right up front ..

"First I love America .. there is no land like this great land .. I have nothing but the highest respect and love and deep felt gratitude and appreciation for all who have given their lives. Second, I am not a negative person.. I am an extremely positive person .. Thirdly, and this is the most important of the three .. I am passionately committed to the unity of the Body of Christ .. that we might be made one in Christ is the passion of my ministry .. in attendance we probably have every single denomination in America here today .. I'm going to have to mention several men of God. .. This message is .. not an attack or a witch hunt .. against any man of God .. I respect every servant of the Lord and he is accountable to the Lord Jesus alone. .. The Laodicean Church represents the last church .. Laodicea comes from two Greek words: Lao means people, dicea (dike) means `rights'. Laodicean is people of rights .. a church committed to their personal rights. Self evident rights of the people, sounds like the declaration of independence .. unalienable rights. This church .. the final church prior to the coming of the Lord is in its purest form the church in.. need of nothing and fighting for their Christian religious rights. God says we need to repent. Stay lukewarm, I'm going to spew you out.

The Laodicean Lie will cause you to take your affection off Jesus and onto yourself and unto your rights .. Much is done with the intent to somehow to oppose the New World Order, somehow oppose the Antichrist, somehow go into the tribulation and triumph over him. I have major problems with that. .. Over lunch with a man who travels and talks all over the world in large churches, known the world over, said to me looking me straight in the eye: "Joe, I don't know anybody anymore who believes in the rapture. I'm telling you there is a major shift-taking place in the Christian

Taming The Lion

World right now among the leadership of this church of which you and I are a part. Christ gave His life for the Church. .. Case in point: 1991, Pat Robertson released his book entitled `The New World Order'.

He does an excellent job explaining all the factors behind the move toward new world government .. and how key people have purposely taken us step by step down the road to self destruction for the sole purpose of merging America into the Global New World Order. .. For 230 pages it was great stuff .. he ends up finishing this book with an astonishing conclusion. He just explained how these ruthless men got America to this point of moral, economic, political ruin, so they can usher in the New World Order.. Now suddenly, he is implying that they are now going to see the light. .. find out why: he concludes that if we Christians will just get together, get organized, get our plan of strategy, and unite, we can save America. We can take our votes to the White House, US Senate and US Congress and pressure our leaders with our political power and throw all globalists out of power.

We must rebuild a foundation of a free sovereign America from the grass roots, precinct-by-precinct, city by city and state by state. A 5% swing in the vote means victory .. if properly presented can sweep the One Worlders out of contention .. in a short time. Surely out of 250 million people we can find 5000 men and women for high level presidential appointments, not part of the ruling establishment. .. Indeed there will be a struggle between people of faith and people of the humanistic occultic sphere, but as we think of the New World Order, let us remember the words of Jesus Christ who said: "..**In the world ye shall have tribulation: but be of good cheer; I have overcome the world**." (John 16:33)

Why that scripture? Pat does not believe in a pre-tribulation Rapture, because this verse applies to those who see their church going through the tribulation. Pat defines the Christian's blessed hope quite differently than you and I do. The apostle Paul calls the millennial kingdom the blessed hope and glorious appearing of our Lord Jesus Christ. Instead of our blessed hope being the rapture..

every Christian should be looking for the kingdom age on this earth. The Turning Tide is his next book described as the fall of Liberalism and the rise of common sense.. Today an army of Americans of 80,000,000 strong is on the march and they will not be denied. Question: "Where were they at election of the most liberal leader of America?" Second and much more important is: when he says they are on the march and will not be denied, I must ask myself the question: "denied of what?" and their answer is: "they will not be denied their Christian rights." That is their agenda: The Laodecian Lie. The entire message of the last book is that Pat Robertson's Christian Coalition is going to organize itself politically, oppose the liberal agenda in America, reclaim the White House for the conservatives and thus keep us from entering the New World Order. Texe Marrs exposed Pat Robertson's allegiance to Freemasonry. Where was Pat Robertson in 2008? Today one of the key slogans is "the common good". Thinking today in global terms is relates to the transfer of so-called American wealth to the countries that are supposedly living on $1 a day income. Not only is the U.S. bankrupt due to the many wars she finances, as well as the recent invasion from Mexico of millions of illegals. They receive automatic assistance to a point where the state they settle in goes bankrupt. Millions of Americans are on welfare, Medicare and need help with the many heavy losses due to the increase in hurricanes, tornadoes, fires, floods and unemployment. I myself have been under siege for two years and actually since I retired in 1992. My husband and I were finally out of debt when we retired but were in for a shock where our income was concerned. President Reagan revamped the Social Security system and took away that insurance for retirees who had a government pension even though they contributed to their own SS when they worked in the private sector and their bosses matched the premiums. Not only that, when George, the spouse, passed away, the wife was to receive some of that SS insurance, it disappeared as well. My two youngest sons had built up nice retirements at work and both watched it dwindle to nothing in 2008.

Taming The Lion

My adversary was not done with my finances yet. Five years after George passed away I decided to move closer to my children just in case something went wrong physically. Elderlies are out of luck today. Retirement communities are so expensive that people who have worked all their lives cannot qualify for them. I put my house on the market to sell and borrowed on it to buy a home near my children. The economy collapsed two years ago and is not coming out of it. Home values have dropped one third of their value, below what is owed in mortgages and the banks have no money to lend to buyers if they did wish to purchase a home. Sure enough to be able to handle the payments on my meager income the bank offered a subprime loan. Thinking that it would be short-lived I went with it and am now struggling with a payment that is growing and a principle that is growing instead of declining and no way out but foreclosure. That means that the bank will rape me of everything that I own. At 78 years of age, going back to work is out of the question. Billions are going to CEOs weekly according to the Secretary of the Treasury but nothing is done for the working class who are the ones who pay the taxes ultimately.

Quoting Joe van Koevering: "Today as never in history men and women who agree on certain key principles of Democracy have agreed to overlook the things that keep them apart to concentrate on the things that bring them together. .. Let's not argue about non-important things right now, like Jesus and the Bible but concentrate on key points of Democracy. .. He calls death of liberalism nothing short of an American revolution. This message is not an attack on Pat Robertson. .. I completely disagree with him on the basic premise of his latest book. .. The book is a contradiction of what is going on. The Lord proclaims greater and greater spiritual darkness as we approach the last days. .. The Bible does not talk about a societal or a political or a moral turning tide."

Joe referred to the following Scriptures: "**This know also, that in the last days perilous times shall come. For men shall be lovers of their own selves, covetous, boasters, proud, blasphemers, disobedient to parents, unthankful, unholy, Without natural**

affection, trucebreakers, false accusers, incontinent, fierce, despisers of those that are good, Traitors, heady, highminded, lovers of pleasures more than lovers of God; Having a form of godliness, but denying the power thereof: from such turn away. For of this sort are they which creep into houses, and lead captive silly women laden with sins, led away with divers lusts, Ever learning, and never able to come to the knowledge of the truth. Now as Jannes and Jambres withstood Moses, so do these also resist the truth: men of corrupt minds, reprobate concerning the faith But they shall proceed no further: for their folly shall be manifest unto all men, as theirs also was". (2 Timothy 3:1-9)

"But thou hast fully known my doctrine, manner of life, purpose, faith, longsuffering, charity, patience, Persecutions, afflictions, which came unto me at Antioch, at Iconium, at Lystra; what persecutions I endured: but out of them all the Lord delivered me." (2 Timothy 3:10-11).

How can the Christian leaders justify the agenda that they have in light of these Scriptures. The next question is: "why?" Listen to that person's enemies: in 1993 Firing-line debates sponsored the subject being "Should we fear the religious right?" Among the eight panelist was Pat Robertson (religious right) and Ira Glasser, Executive director of ACLU on the other side. Final conclusion of this debate was that the American should not fear the religious right. Another panel member, a rabbi, suggested that there are 5% committed to the religious right.. this supposed army of Americans 80,000,000 strong simply does not exist. A panelist from the other side.. Mr. Barry Lynn, Theologian of the United Church of Christ said to Pat Robertson referring to the possible hidden agenda of the Christian Coalition: "your national field director of the Christian Coalition, informed a man by the name of Guy Rogers to tell organizers of Christian Coalition to drop redemptive language. Pat's answer was: Barry, a political party or political organization, .. you are right on that one, is interested in seeing certain secular things put into effect. Lower taxes, tax breaks for families, balanced budget and term limits for congress." Mr. Lynn interrupted: "that comes from the Bible does it?" Jesus will one day return again. Christians will have taken the whole earth under our dominion. "How long will that take you ask?" We have 36,600 years to go, writes one of their leaders, until the promise is fulfilled. This world has.. 100 thousands of years.. before the second coming of Christ.

More and more of our Christian leaders are moving over to this position. We who are in this room.. we who still believe in the eminent soon appearing of Jesus Christ to catch us away out of this world. We are now the problem. .. These Christians frown on what we are doing right now (talking about Bible prophecy). We should be going out to prepare the people to reform our nation, after all Jesus is not coming back until we establish God's kingdom on the earth. Stop talking about the rapture and start talking about taking dominion. We are called backward Christian soldiers? .. I am deeply concerned, when I see our Christian leaders, men whom I love and respect, advocating .. reclaiming America. It is rooted in this very theology and reconstructional teachings are sending mixed signals to the church. Many are falling prey to the lies.

A pamphlet: "Reclaiming America" at Coral Ridge Presbyterian Church. In recent months we sensed a hunger among Christians to reclaim our country.. among the featured individuals teaching strategy, is former Vice President Dan Quail. I have great respect for Dr. Kennedy and this is not an attack .. James Kennedy does not believe in the rapture of the church either. "Last Day's Madness" is a book he supports which points to the Rapture, Armageddon and all end time events took place back in the first Century. We must conclude that we are in the kingdom right now and must exert our kingdom dominion. Reconstruction, a little book James Kennedy published ten years ago, which does relate to politics. I am .. alarmed by what I am hearing. What is our agenda? These men are changing the great commission. We still would not reclaim America if they succeeded; the Trilaterals are in both parties. James Kennedy left this planet recently and his family admitted that he had problems with his congregation trying to justify Freemasonry which points to the fact that he was probably involved. He was interested in running for president, had an office in Washington DC. On his website he had an icon portraying the White House with a cross covering it reminding people that state and religion should be one.

We may have the best intention in mind to gather our Christian Coalition to reform; I fear that we are being deceived. We are placing our personal desire for our rights above the desires and purposes of God. .. Several generations ago a certain country faced moral and economic collapse very similar to America right now. And a certain conservative, seemingly moral leader, gained prominence. And with the support of the church and Christian leaders, successfully took power and promised his nation great economical, political and moral reform. Oh that sounds like what we need here in America. I was referring to none other than Adolf Hitler. Bob Rossio in his book Hitler and the New Age, the coming Holocaust, the Extermination of Christendom, says this in his book: "The German Christians were a patriotic group, they loved their country. Hitler used this virtue to confuse and divide them."

Ultimately, they forgot where their true loyalty should rest. .. Only a remnant of ministers opposed Hitler. .. This body counted only 200 pastors out of 18,000 Christian pastors. Is this what Jesus said: "blessed are those who fight for their rights and they shall inherit the earth? Or was it: "blessed are the politically aggressive who shall inherit the earth?" Or one more time: "Blessed are the most organized in Christian Reconstructionism, for they will inherit the earth?" What did Jesus say: "Blessed are the meek, for they shall inherit the earth." Do you love your country more than you love the cross? .. Are we on fire with the flames of revolution and rights? .. It is very subtle and deceptive .. It looks like we are taking a stand for righteousness; it looks so good and sounds so good.

The hearts of people have to change, which is done through the blood of Jesus. **"For I would that ye knew what great conflict I have for you, and for them at Laodicea, and for as many as have not seen my face in the flesh;"** (Colossians 2:1)

345

Taming The Lion

"If ye then be risen with Christ, seek those things which are above, where Christ sitteth on the right hand of God. Set your affection on things above, not on things on the earth. For ye are dead, and your life is hid with Christ in God." Colossians 3:1-3 Amen. "Brethren, if any of you do err from the truth, and one convert him; Let him know, that he which converteth the sinner from the error of his way shall save a soul from death, and shall hide a multitude of sins. (James 5:19-20)

The Holy Spirit took me to Scripture to reassure me that this article needs to be written because it relates to the second commandment: **"*7hou shalt not make unto thee any graven image, or any likeness of any thing that is in heaven above, or that is in the earth beneath, or that is in the water under the earth: Thou shalt not bow down thyself to them, nor serve them: for I the LORD thy God am a jealous God, visiting the iniquity of the fathers upon the children unto the third and fourth generation of them that hate me; And shewing mercy unto thousands of them that love me, and keep my commandments. Thou shalt not take the name of the LORD thy God in vain; for the LORD will not hold him guiltless that taketh his name in vain."** (Exodus 20:4-7)

"Let them alone: they be blind leaders of the blind. And if the blind lead the blind, both shall fall into the ditch." (Matthew 15:14) Yesterday's results (1994) earned a victory for the first time ever, a republican majority in both the House and the Senate in Washington D.C.. Our state of Colorado went republican with few exceptions. Leaders are turning republican from a democratic platform. In my own estimation signs of unity are going to become more evident all the time and we are in for some unexpected events in politics. Today in 2008, Denver Colorado hosted the National Democratic Convention, because it is now a democratic state. This election produced a full house for the democrats in the White House. Their agenda will be on steroids bringing the world together to administer to the "common good of all citizens of the world.."

Taming The Lion

The president elect said today that we have to stop printing money and make painful decisions in budgets to get back on track.

One of the big questions looking at the all the information that comes across my desk every month, and witnessing the changes happening within the church personally, how does it all fit together? What does the Church have to do with the New World Order? The Church has never run well with government in America, because of the separation between Church and State. The only godly part of government over the years has been `In God We Trust' on our dollar bills. In my view government has been instrumental in suppressing religion. In Europe the Church is tax supported and that was a death sentence on the Church. People did not have to be involved in the whole process of making Church happen. Something is happening to the church from the top down. The thrust is coming through conversion of major political figures and political men who would like to get into the White House.

Watching and listening, I see a revolutionary trend in churches in America's young ones, which is gaining momentum quickly. There is real opportunity to take the minds and hearts of people off our Lord Jesus Christ with this excitement of taking back our country. Satan is major on deception. We, as Christians, are in a time of having to be totally awake, objectively looking at what is changing and why. Don't underestimate Lucifer, he is behind movements of people en mass. Jesus walks the road barely traveled.

Not in the habit of watching television, I check in sometimes to listen to trends and came across some information that fits the picture of the strategy of breaking down walls between denominations. In a recent `700 Club' program, Pat Robertson was the host. He confirmed my suspicion was correct: it is going on deliberately. A lady from the audience asked him, "why are the walls between denominations coming down?" He did not respond to her question, but reassured her there was nothing wrong with bringing them down. Next I went to church and picked up a newspaper `Christian Coalition' paid for by the one million members and activists of the Christian Coalition, a citizen organization representing families and children. Stars and stripes, red, white and blue on the front page.

Another page caught my eye: Leadership Training School - A Wake-Up Call for Christians. (sponsored by the Colorado Christian Coalition) calling people into action. "By attending this intensive training seminar you will discover: Many points on 'How to' influence people.." (To win the war? Election? Or what?)

Not surprised a bit, knowing Satan's tactics, he is infecting the powerful new men's movement, 'The Promise Keepers'. Complaints about the movement becoming a political instrument are being aired and 'Chosen Self-Protection' unveiled by Kevin S. Hatcher, founder and chief instructor of 'The Chosen Arts System' intends to teach every interested person the martial arts, 'Christian style'. Kevin equated, "'The Way, The Truth, and the Life are all contained in the name of Jesus who is Christ. It's through faith in the Son of God that we have direct access to the only living God. Every form of martial arts on the market tries to claim that it's a way of life." Are the 233,000 Promise Keepers being sidetracked? Our adversary never sleeps. I noticed gardening; an almost identical plant comes up right next to the authentic one. Only a gardener can tell the difference, a person who knows the plant he or she planted.

"People are looking for help and companionship in life's troubled journey," says the Rev. Joan Campbell, general secretary of the National Council of Churches. "...they were not finding it in churches." What makes the American religious experience unique, however, is the spirited interplay among faiths and the sacred and secular in the broader culture. The U.S. News poll showed 90% describe themselves as not very religious and say that the nation is slipping into deeper moral decline. Billy Graham stated that this is a nation of biblical illiterates. Americans don't know what they believe or why.

"Vatican criticizes literal interpretation of Bible," The Vatican calls literal interpretation of the Bible "a kind of intellectual suicide," was a recent comment in the Rocky Mountain News. How does that stack up with Luke 6:46 if we are not to take the Gospel literally: **"And why call ye me, Lord, Lord, and do not the things which I say?**

How can we do what God or Jesus tell us, if we don't know what it is?

"A Vatican document said fundamentalism "refuses to admit that the inspired Word of God has been expressed in human language... by human authors possessed of limited capacities and resources. The 125-page document, `The Interpretation of the Bible in the Church,' was written by the Pontifical Biblical Commission, a group of scholars who assist the pope in the study of Scripture. People are abandoning the church for fast growing fundamentalist sects especially in Latin America. The fundamentalist approach is dangerous, for it is attractive to people who look to the Bible for ready answers to the problems of life."

No doubt without anyone noticing what is happening to them, they have to bring their flock back to the dark age, when Bible was read to them in a language they could not understand. Martin Luther was the first in Germany to translate the Bible into a language that Germans could read. That also made it possible for English translation so believers could work out their salvation in fear and trembling as it is written.

Revelation Chapters 17 and 18 addresses a powerful global religious system. William R. Goetz writes in his book `Apocalypse Next and the New World Order', ninth printing 1991, he states "I am convinced that the `prostitute' of Revelation is indeed a church, in fact, a powerful global religious system - but I am also quite certain it is not [a].. particular church... I believe the `prostitute church' definitely will contain elements of ...many.. Churches."

"And there came one of the seven angels which had the seven vials, and talked with me, saying unto me, Come hither; I will shew unto thee the judgment of the great whore that sitteth upon many waters: With whom the kings of the earth have committed fornication, and the inhabitants of the earth have

been made drunk with the wine of her fornication. So he carried me away in the spirit into the wilderness: and I saw a woman sit upon a scarlet coloured beast, full of names of blasphemy, having seven heads and ten horns. And the woman was arrayed in purple and scarlet colour, and decked with gold and precious stones and pearls, having a golden cup in her hand full of abominations and filthiness of her fornication: And upon her forehead was a name written, MYSTERY, BABYLON THE GREAT, THE MOTHER OF HARLOTS AND ABOMI-NATIONS OF THE EARTH. And I saw the woman drunken with the blood of the saints, and with the blood of the martyrs of Jesus: and when I saw her, I wondered with great admiration. And the angel said unto me, Wherefore didst thou marvel? I will tell thee the mystery of the woman, and of the beast that carrieth her, which hath the seven heads and ten horns. The beast that thou sawest was, and is not; and shall ascend out of the bottomless pit, and go into perdition: and they that dwell on the earth shall wonder, whose names were not written in the book of life from the foundation of the world, when they behold the beast that was, and is not, and yet is." (Revelation 17:1-8)

"And the woman which thou sawest is that great city, which reigneth over the kings of the earth." (Revelation 17:18)

Most Bible scholars think the city is Rome because it sits on seven hills mentioned in Scriptures about the prostitute. They also believe that the Catholic Church will absorb all the various denominations, since it is the historical Christian Church. Luther was one of the first to break the mold and the Encyclopedia still states that all Christians are Catholics. Watching current religious events brings evidence almost daily that the ecumenical influence is working in most denominations causing a powerful desire to come into unity with the Catholic Church. As Dr. David Breese, Ph.D. spoke at a recent Prophecy Conference, he pointed out that the Church of Jesus Christ is an undetectable Church, invisible and consists of people of all denominations, who will disappear one of these days when Jesus Christ comes like a thief in the night. I do not agree with that statement because cults consider themselves to be denominations as well. They think they believe in Jesus but it is a different Jesus. The Bible tells us to come out of the world system, which includes most worldly churches.

William Goetz in his discussion on Revelation 17 & 18 continued: "A prostitute is a woman who has prostituted her God-given sexuality to sell her body's sexual functions to any number of lovers in direct contrast to a wife who becomes one with her husband in a faithful, pure union. The man/woman relationship frequently found in Scripture is a symbol of a spiritual relationship. For example, the symbol used in Scripture to describe the Church (the body of born-again believers from around the world through the ages since Christ) is that of a bride. In Ephesians 5 and Revelation 19, the Lord Jesus Christ depicted as the Bridegroom, is the One to whom the true Church will be married. We, who are believers, are the Bride of Christ, whose union is not yet been fully consummated. In the Old Testament, God stated through his prophets that he married Israel to Him (Isaiah 54:5- 6) as a wife, with sin and straying was described as `adultery'. Although they departed from God's will he wants to forgive and forget and remarry Israel in spite all that has happened because of the promise He made to Abraham. Gentiles have been included because Israel turned the first invitation down by rejecting Jesus Christ as their Messiah.

Spiritual departure from God symbolized in Scripture with terms like adultery, whoredom, harlotry are associated with a woman, a symbol in Scripture of the church. A good woman, like bride or wife relates to Christ's Church. A bad woman, like a `prostitute', means an evil religious system that deceives the souls of mankind. "For her (the queen, description from the Concordance: #938 in Greek: foundation of power "The Foot". #4433 in Hebrew: ruler. #4446 in Hebrew: they ask her advice) sins are piled up to heaven, and God has remembered her crimes. Give back to her as she has given; pay her back double for what she has done. Mix her a double portion from her own cup. Give her as much torture and grief as the glory

Taming The Lion

and luxury she gave herself. In her heart she boasts, `I sit as queen; I am not a widow, and I will never mourn.'" (Revelation 18:5-7 NIV)

Analyzing the name of the woman riding the beast in Revelation 17:5: "This title was written on her forehead: MYSTERY BABYLON THE GREAT THE MOTHER OF PROSTITUTES AND OF THE ABOMINATIONS OF THE EARTH," the Concordance describes the meaning and it applies to today. Mystery, #3466 in Greek, refers to a secret movement, which operates silently, is imposed by initiations of religious rites to enter into organizations. Members are sworn to secrecy. Baal worship is usually associated with secret organizations, it brings into mechanical, lifeless state. Baal (God's counterpart) is a symbol of idolatry: #1168 in Hebrew, a deity; #1167, a master, hence husband, lord; #1166, has dominion over wife (counterfeit church).

Babylon is interpreted in the Concordance as: #897 in Greek: a type of tyranny and #894 a type of bitterness. Babylon, a function of the Old Testament, #894 in Hebrew, is Babel: confusion (from astrologers and wisemen); #1101, overflow of oil (spiritual term: Holy Spirit) contaminated or mixed with self; #1098, from mixed food (information). Mother of prostitutes: woman, wife also great assembly of prostitutes. #4204 in Greek, pornography traffics people into slavery. She fornicates with kings: #4202 in Greek: idolatry, adultery and incest; #4203 indulge in unlawful lust; #4205 homosexuality; #4097 trafficking merchandise and pierces through. Abominations of the earth: #946 in Greek, a detestation, idolatry; #948 disgusting. The prostitute holds a golden cup: #5552 Greek, made from gold; #5557, related to utility, ornamental or coins; #5530, to entreat or use; #5495, a means of getting what is wanted through loans or employment. The prostitute holds that golden cup in her power as an alternative to God's plan of getting money and it is filled with abominable things. She was drunk with the blood of the saints.

Babylon was the first center of religion where the tower of Babel originated- because there the LORD confused the language of the whole world. From there the LORD scattered them over the face of the whole earth. "

"And Babylon, the glory of kingdoms, the beauty of the Chaldees' excellency, shall be as when God overthrew Sodom and Gomorrah. It shall never be inhabited, neither shall it be dwelt in from generation to generation: neither shall the Arabian pitch tent there; neither shall the shepherds make their fold there. " *(*Isaiah 13:19-20)

So when the prophet John used the term `prostitute' in describing the vision he had received, he was unquestionably writing about a religious system which had prostituted its very existence to that which is totally contradictory to the true purpose God has established for the Church..." and is the substitute for the Bride of Christ. She will spiritually seduce not only kings (that is, she will not only wield control over the leaders of nations) but also mankind in general. But what kind of religion could possibly hold such sway and gain such control over Muslims, Hindus, [nominal] Christians, Buddhists, pagans, atheists and so on? Not one religion like Christianity, or Islam or Confucianism could get all the other religions to join it. Whatever religion it is, it will have to have strong appeal, stronger than the pull of liberal Christianity mingled with Freemasonry.

`Babylon the Great' embodies in itself a world religion, a world empire and a world ruler whom all nations are compelled to worship as supreme. Thus, depraved religion enforced by government decree and a sinful, lustful lifestyle, come to mind when Babylon is mentioned. Nimrod, (whose name meant `we will revolt'), built Babylon. The first united religious act undertaken by mankind was the construction of a tower whose top would `reach into the heavens' see Genesis 11:4. The Tower of Babel was an astrological tower, a ziggurat, built to study stars, cast horoscopes and make predictions. Halley's Bible Handbook declares that idolatrous worship was the whole purpose for the construction of the ziggurats, see Isaiah 47:12-13. It indicated that Babylon `labored with magic spells and many sorceries since her childhood'. Babylon's false religious system appealed to the sensual nature. Being filled with the blood of believers indicates her method of dealing with those who oppose her.

"This calls for a mind with wisdom. The seven heads are seven hills on which the woman sits'. It is believed the seven mountains undoubtedly refer to Rome - a city known around the world to be built upon seven hills. ..and was the center of pagan worship and was even called `Babylon' in Scripture."

New Age philosophies make man the center of the universe instead of God. Man makes up his own rules. Man is capable through the `divine power within him' of whatever he wants or needs. David Weber writing in `The Gospel Truth', explains the buildup to and the rationale the `Instant': "For several months we have been hearing about 1987 - the year of the critical mass - a pivotal year for the New Age program ... Time and Newsweek offering services of Indian guru Maharishi Mahesh Yoga, the founder of Maharishi International University, Fairfield, Iowa, and the inventor of `transcendental meditation'. The global invitation of the Maharishi was to bring peace to all nations that employed his services for a price... This global project was expanded by John Randolph Price to 500 million people meditating on all continents at the same time.. New Agers believe such an event will usher in the New World Order, and reveal the New Age messiah!'

The World Instant of Co-Operation did not achieve its goal... Mega-media rock star famine relief event, `We are the World' was not merely a song. It was a theology - growing out of and promoting such events as `Band-Aid', `USA for Africa',(fund raising effort of the New Age movement..).. John R. Price in his book wrote about `World Healing Day'. that was to trigger a `Planetary Pentecost' that would cause a mass transfiguration and empowerment of millions at once .. a second coming through lifting our consciousness, transforming ourselves as Christ transformed himself.. Such events are now in preparation. A mass spiritual empowerment cannot be organized by human will alone, but since we are co-creators we do our part - God will do His is their mantra.

Taming The Lion

John Denver, the singer and actor.. in Snowmass, Colorado in 1986 .. hosted a New Age 'Choices of the Future' symposium .. speakers: spiritualist Ram Dass, former U.S. Assistant Secretary General Robert Muller, former Colorado Governor Richard Lamm, television mogul Ted Turner and about 1000 others. The plans for the World Instant of Co-Operation were presented. Also, Ted Turner claimed that America must elect a `New Age' president if it wants to survive through the year 2000." They must have been serious. President Clinton was elected a few years later.

Another book is in process by Dave Hunt: "A Woman Rides The Beast" and he confirms the implication of the Catholic Church coming into unity with all religions. We are warned about the churches tragic end. **"The beast and the ten horns you saw will hate the prostitute. They will bring her to ruin and leave her naked; they will eat her flesh and burn her with fire For God has put it into their hearts to accomplish his purpose by agreeing to give the beast their power to rule, until God's words are fulfilled."** (Revelation 17:16,17) We don't have to submit to this desire to be a joiner. By going for the truth we can marry Jesus Christ instead.

"And I heard another voice from heaven, saying, Come out of her, my people, that ye be not partakers of her sins, and that ye receive not of her plagues. For her sins have reached unto heaven, and God hath remembered her iniquities." (Revelation 18:4,5)

The Scripture just given says that we are all part of that system at one point or another and that it is possible to get out. The crimes relate to the blood the woman on the beast is drunk with. Dave Hunt reminds us of the inquisitions (Roman, Medieval and Spanish), which held Europe in their terrible grip. It is estimated the number of Christians condemned exceed three million with 300,000 burned at the stake for their adherence to Christ Jesus.

Pope Pius XII knew of the Nazi Holocaust in spite of complete silence throughout the war on the slaughter of the Jews. Today Pope

Taming The Lion

Pope Benedict XIV wishes to raise his status to sainthood. Had Pope Pius XII protested, as representatives of Jewish organizations and Allied Powers begged him to do, he would have condemned His own church. "In 1936, Bishop Berning of Osnabruch had talked with the Fuehrer for over an hour. Hitler assured his lordship there was no fundamental difference between National Socialism and the Catholic Church. `Had not the church,' he argued, looked on Jews as parasites..?' `I am only doing,' he boasted, `what the Church has done for fifteen hundred years, only more effectively.' Being a Catholic himself, he told Berning, he `admired and wanted to promote Christianity [Catholicism].'"

"Finally, the angel reveals to John that the woman "is that great city, which reigneth over the kings of the earth (v 18). Is there such a city? Yes, and again only one: Vatican City. One of the eighteenth-century historians counted 95 popes who claimed to have divine power to depose kings and emperors. Historian Walter James wrote that Pope Innocent III (1198-1216) "held Europe in his net." Gregory IX (1227-1241) thundered that the Pope was Lord and Master of everyone and everything. Popes crowned and deposed kings and emperors, exacting obedience by threatening excommunication. Pope Nicholas I boasted: "Fear then our wrath and the thunders of our vengeance; for Jesus Christ has appointed us [the popes]. absolute judges of all men; and kings .. are submitted to our authority." In commanding one king to destroy another, Nicholas wrote, "We order you, in the name of religion, to invade his states, burn his cities, and massacre his people.," Dave continued.

"Eminent Catholic historian Ignaz von Dollinger writes, "Pope Clement IV, in 1265, after selling millions of South Italians to Charles Anjou for a yearly tribute of eight hundred ounces of gold, declared that he would be excommunicated if the first payment was deferred.." Catholic Professor Carrerio boasted that the popes had "put down from their thrones great kings and yet mightier emperors, and set others in their place, to whom the greatest kingdoms have long paid tribute, as they do to no other, and who dispense such riches.. that no king or emperor has ever had.."

Dave Hunt, a Catholic Apologist, further states: "The qualifying data that John gives us under the inspiration of the Holy Spirit for identifying this woman/city, is specific, conclusive and irrefutable. There is no city upon earth, past or present, which meets all of these criteria except Catholic Rome and Vatican City. Pray for the 980 million Catholics who are deceived into trusting their church instead of Christ for salvation."

Catholic Apologist Karl Keting confirms that Rome was known as Babylon and cites the Catholic Encyclopedia: "It is within the city of Rome, called the city of seven hills, that the entire area of Vatican State proper is now confined."

The Pope, John Paul II, on his visit to Denver in 1993 spent the last day adoring the Virgin Mary carried as a beautiful Icon of her. Painted specifically for this occasion of her, Jesus was displayed in her arms. The story about the Pope's life saving experience in connection with a medallion of the Virgin Mary was told. He wears it around his neck. A bullet targeted for him hit this medallion instead and saved his life. He is looking forward to another vision and message from the Virgin Mary to guide his actions, which leads me to the False Prophet who appears to stand by the Antichrist and helps him make it all happen.

A recent book "The False Prophet" by Ken Klein tries to deal with this issue from a different perspective than most people who try to deal with Revelation. It requires a shift in thinking because we think of a false prophet as a man rather than a nation or in this case two nations (two horns).. Ken points to the United States and Great Britain as the False Prophet implementing and setting the stage via the economic collapse (bankruptcy of the United States). The U.S. will be forced to give up its lands to the international world bankers. The Antichrist's reward to others who support his control will be land according to Scripture. Ken spent seven years researching and writing about the CFR and the Round Table of the ruling class of

Taming The Lion

England and how the indebtedness was deliberately manipulated to put us into this vulnerable position subject to the world bankers. Great Britain had much to do with propagating Anglicized Hinduism and launching worldwide cultural warfare through philosophers like Henry David Thoreau, Ralph Waldo Emerson and Charles Darwin.

Ken reveals the division between the Pope and the Church of England, the King of England Henry VIII would not submit to the Pope over a divorce from his wife. The King became independent of the Vatican, which ultimately led to the first Amendment in the US Constitution. The book is full of relative information. It confirms other readings. I disagree with his theory about the False Prophet. In my logic God usually has a person to identify and confirm a personage of importance as in the days of Jesus Christ. John the Baptist identified Him as the Christ. There will have to be a highly respected and honored person from a spiritual point of view, who will confirm that the Antichrist is God and should be received. To prove that the False Prophet is humanly divine, he will be endowed with power to perform supernatural events with the power in this case coming from Satan with the sanction of God to fulfill His prophecies in the Holy Bible.

Characteristics of the False Prophet stated in Scripture are defined as: #5578 in Greek, a religious impostor or pretender, untrue, erroneous, deceitful, wicked and a foreteller or inspired speaker. Because of his powers, he leads many into captivity. **"And I beheld another beast coming up out of the earth; and he had two horns like a lamb, and he spake as a dragon. And he exerciseth all the power of the first beast before him, and causeth the earth and them which dwell therein to worship the first beast, whose deadly wound was healed. And he doeth great wonders, so that he maketh fire come down from heaven on the earth in the sight of men, And deceiveth them that dwell on the earth by the means of those miracles which he had power to do in the sight of the beast; saying to them that dwell on the earth, that they should make an image to the beast, which had the** wound by a sword, and did live. And he had power to give life unto the image of the beast, that the image of the beast should both speak, and cause that as many as would not worship the image of the beast should be killed. And he causeth all, both small and great, rich and poor, free and bond, to receive a mark in their right hand, or in their foreheads: And that no man might buy or sell, save he that had the mark, or the name of the beast, or the number of his name." (Revelation 13:11-17).

2 Chronicles 18:19-22 states: "And the LORD said, Who shall entice Ahab king of Israel, that he may go up and fall at Ramothgilead? And one spake saying after this manner, and another saying after that manner. Then there came out a spirit, and stood before the LORD, and said, I will entice him. And the LORD said unto him, Wherewith? And he said, I will go out, and be a lying spirit in the mouth of all his prophets. And the LORD said, Thou shalt entice him, and thou shalt also prevail: go out, and do even so. Now therefore, behold, the LORD hath put a lying spirit in the mouth of these thy prophets, and the LORD hath spoken evil against thee."

Relating the Old Testament to Revelation 16:13 "And I saw three unclean spirits like frogs come out of the mouth of the dragon, and out of the mouth of the beast, and out of the mouth of the false prophet." "And the beast was taken, and with him the false prophet that wrought miracles before him, with which he deceived them that had received the mark of the beast, and them that worshiped his image(#1504, i- kon a likeness, i.e. statue, profile, or representation, resemblance). *These both* (#1417, a primary numeral `two' both, twain, two) were cast alive into a lake of fire burning with brimstone." Revelation 19:20 *In* my opinion the false prophet will be a highly honored religious man of equal power as the Antichrist.

Many think that we are closer to the end then we would like to believe. We are not ready because so many people, especially our relatives are still lost in spite of the efforts of many to spread the word. They have been turned off because the gospel has been misrepresented and used commercially. That is why we are told in Scripture not to trust in the flesh. The gospel was written down to make it available to each one of us in purity. God gave us the Holy Spirit to help interpret as we grow in spirituality.

"**Little children, it is the last time: and as ye have heard that Antichrist shall come, even now are there many Antichrists; whereby we know that it is the last time. They went out from us, but they were not of us; for if they had been of us, they would no doubt have continued with us: but they went out, that they might be made manifest that they were not all of us. But ye have an unction from the Holy One, and ye know all things. I have not written unto you because ye know not the truth, but because ye know it, and that no lie is of the truth. Who is a liar but he that denieth that Jesus is the Christ? He is Antichrist, that denieth the Father and the Son. Whosoever denieth the Son, the same hath not the Father: (but) he that acknowledgeth the Son hath the Father also. Let that therefore abide in you, which ye have heard from the beginning. If that which ye have heard from the beginning shall remain in you, ye also shall continue in the Son, and in the Father. And this is the promise that he hath promised us, even eternal life. These things have I written unto you concerning them that seduce you.**" (1 John 2:18-26)

"**Finally, my brethren, rejoice in the Lord. To write the same things to you, to me indeed is not grievous, but for you it is safe. Beware of dogs, beware of evil workers, beware of the concision. For we are the circumcision, which worship God in the spirit, and rejoice in Christ Jesus, and have no confidence in the flesh. Though I might also have confidence in the flesh. If any other man thinketh that he hath whereof he might trust in the flesh, I more: Circumcised the eighth day, of the stock of Israel, of the tribe of Benjamin, an Hebrew of the Hebrews; as touching the law, a Pharisee; Concerning zeal, persecuting the church; touching the righteousness which is in the law, blameless. But what things were gain to me, those I counted loss for Christ.**

Taming The Lion

"Yea doubtless, and I count all things but loss for the excellency of the knowledge of Christ Jesus my Lord: for whom I have suffered the loss of all things, and do count them but dung, that I may win Christ, And be found in him, not having mine own righteousness, which is of the law, but that which is through the faith of Christ, the righteousness which is of God by faith: That I may know him, and the power of his resurrection, and the fellowship of his sufferings, being made conformable unto his death; If by any means I might attain unto the resurrection of the dead. Not as though I had already attained, either were already perfect: but I follow after, if that I may apprehend that for which also I am apprehended of Christ Jesus. Brethren, I count not myself to have apprehended: but this one thing I do, forgetting those things which are behind, and reaching forth unto those things which are before, I press toward the mark for the prize of the high calling of God in Christ Jesus. (Philippians 3:1-14)

"Humble yourselves therefore under the mighty hand of God, that he may exalt you in due time: Casting all your care upon him; for he careth for you. Be sober, be vigilant; because your adversary the devil, as a roaring lion, walketh about, seeking whom he may devour: Whom resist steadfast in the faith, knowing that the same afflictions are accomplished in your brethren that are in the world." (1 Peter 5:6-9)

"Blessed be the God and Father of our Lord Jesus Christ, which according to his abundant mercy hath begotten us again unto a lively hope by the resurrection of Jesus Christ from the dead, To an inheritance incorruptible, and undefiled, and that fadeth not away, reserved in heaven for you, Who are kept by the power of God through faith unto salvation ready to be revealed in the last time." (1 Peter 1:3-5)

Speaking of Christ Jesus, "Who is the image of the invisible God, the firstborn of every creature: For by him were all things created, that are in heaven, and that are in earth, visible and invisible, whether they be thrones, or dominions, or principalities, or powers: all things were created by him, and for him: And he is before all things, and by him all things consist. And he is the head of the body, the church: who is the beginning, the firstborn from the dead; that in all things he might have the preeminence. For it pleased the Father that in him should all fullness dwell; And, having made peace through the blood of his cross, by him to reconcile all things unto himself; by him, I say, whether they be things in earth, or things in heaven. And you, that were sometime alienated and enemies in your mind by wicked works, yet now hath he reconciled In the body of his flesh through death, to present you holy and unblameable and unreproveable in his sight: If ye continue in the faith grounded and settled, and be not moved away from the hope of the gospel, which ye have heard, and which was preached to every creature which is under heaven; whereof I Paul am made a minister;" (Colossians 1:15-23)

"To whom God would make known what is the riches of the glory of this mystery among the Gentiles; which is Christ in you, the hope of glory: Whom we preach, warning every man, and teaching every man in all wisdom; that we may present every man perfect in Christ Jesus: Whereunto I also labour, striving according to his working, which worketh in me mightily." (Colossians 1:27-29)

"Beware lest any man spoil you through philosophy and vain deceit, after the tradition of men, after the rudiments of the world, and not after Christ. For in him dwelleth all the fulness of the Godhead bodily. And ye are complete in him, which is the head of all principality and power:" (Colossians 2:8-10)

"In him you were also circumcised in the heart, in the putting off our sinful nature with His help, not with a circumcision done by the hands of men but with the circumcision done by Christ, having been buried with Him in baptism and raised with Him through your faith in the power of God, who raised Him [Christ Jesus] from the dead. [If God can raise people from the dead, He can certainly help us move the sin out]. When you were dead in your sins and in the uncircumcision of your sinful nature, God made you alive with Christ. He forgave us all our sins, having canceled the written code [thou shalt not do this or that], with its regulations, that was against us and that stood opposed to us; he took it away, nailing it to the cross. And having disarmed the powers and authorities [Satan cannot accuse us anymore when we stop sinning], he made a public spectacle of them, triumphing over them by the cross. Therefore do not let anyone judge you by what you eat or drink, or with regard to a religious festival, a New Moon celebration or a Sabbath day. These are a shadow of the things that were to come; the reality, however, is found in Christ [if we love Him we want to do Him honor and behave the way He thinks its proper to behave]. Do not let anyone who delights in false humility and the worship of angels disqualify you for the prize. Such a person goes into great detail about what he has seen, and his unspiritual mind puffs him up with idle notions. He has lost connection with the Head, from whom the whole body, supported and held together by its ligaments and sinews, grows as God causes it to grow."

"Since you died with Christ to the basic principles of this world, why, as though you still belonged to it, do you submit to its rules: `Do not handle! Do not taste! Do not touch!'? These [rules] are all destined to perish with use, because they are based on human commands and teachings. Such regulations indeed have an appearance of wisdom, with their self-imposed worship [worship should be a bubbling from a heart full of joy, gratitude and expectation for the future - the millennium and eternity with our gracious God the Father, the Son and Holy Spirit], their false humility and their harsh treatment of the body, but they lack any value in restraining sensual indulgence."

"Since, then, you have been raised with Christ, set your hearts on things above, where Christ is seated at the right hand of God. Set your minds on things above, not on earthly things. For you died, and your life is now hidden with Christ in God.

Taming The Lion

When Christ, who is your life, appears, then you also will appear with him in glory. Put to death, therefore, whatever belongs to your earthly nature: sexual immorality, impurity, lust, evil desires and greed, which is idolatry. Because of these, the wrath of God is coming [on those who are disobedient]. You used to walk in these ways, in the life you once lived. But now you must rid yourselves of all such things as these: anger, rage, malice, slander and filthy language from your lips. Do not lie to each other, since you have taken off your old self with its practices and have put on the new self, which is being renewed in knowledge in the image of its Creator. Here there is no Greek or Jew, circumcised or uncircumcised, barbarian, Scythian, slave or free, but Christ is all, and is in all . Therefore, as God's chosen people, holy and dearly loved, clothe yourselves with compassion, kindness, humility, gentleness and patience [an action by you]. Bear with each other and forgive whatever grievances you may have against one another . Forgive as the Lord forgave you. And over all these virtues put on love, which binds them all together in perfect unity. Let the peace of Christ rule in your hearts, since as members of one body you were called to peace. And be thankful. Let the word of Christ dwell in you richly as you teach and admonish one another with all wisdom, and as you sing psalms, hymns and spiritual songs with gratitude in your hearts to God. And whatever you do, whether in word or deed, do it all in the name of the Lord Jesus, giving thanks to God the Father through him." (Colossians 2:8-3:17 NIV).

His covenant (promise) to us that He will come back and establish Himself here on earth can be tracked in the following Scriptures: Gen. 9:13, 17:3, 17:7, 17:13; 2 Sam. 7:13,16; Psalms 105:9,10; Isa. 59:20,21; Jeremiah 31:31-34,32:40; Ezekiel 37:26; Isaoah 54:10; Romans 11:26,27; Isaiah 42:6; Luke 22:20; Hebrews 8:8-12; and Hebrews 10:16-17. The promise was sealed in His blood. "**Saying, This is the blood of the testament which God hath enjoined unto you**." (Hebrews 9:20)

Taming The Lion

"For nearly 2000 years, Jesus has been in heaven `preparing a place for us'. In God's time, Jesus descends from heaven with a shout with the voice of the Archangel, and with the trump of God. We who are alive and remain shall be caught up together with them in the clouds to meet the Lord in the air: so shall we ever be with the Lord.

This catching away, called by many "the Rapture" is pictured in the Jewish marriage custom. The groom comes to the bride's home and brings her back to the wedding ceremony that is held at his father's house. This is the same house where he has also prepared a home for her. Although we, the Bride of Christ, have known for nearly 2000 years that Jesus would return for us, we have only been able to say, "He's coming back - maybe in my lifetime.." As the listening Bride should react when we hear the call, ahead of Jesus's arrival, "The Bridegroom is coming."

The wedding celebration of seven days (seven-year tribulation is carried on by the guests while the Bride and Groom spend this time in seclusion. At the end of the seven days the Groom brings His Bride out and her veil is removed for the first time, so all guests can see her beauty... **"Let us be glad and rejoice, and give honour to him: for the marriage of the Lamb is come, and his wife hath made herself ready. And to her was granted that she should be arrayed in fine linen, clean and white: for the fine linen is the righteousness of saints. And he saith unto me, Write, Blessed are they which are called unto the marriage supper of the Lamb. And he saith unto me, These are the true sayings of God."** (Revelation 19:7-9) Amen

The saints that are overcome by the Antichrist called the tribulation saints are the believers depicted by the five virgins who did not have oil in their lamps when Jesus came to get the Bride. Note they were virgins which meant they had salvation but did not have the Word of God in their hearts, therefore had to die for their faith when the Antichrist murdered them because they would not take the mark of the beast.

Taming The Lion

CHAPTER 14

THOU SHALT NOT BE ASHAMED

To conclude this true story, I pray for God's precious touch and blessing upon every life that touches this story. To help them see, I hope He pores His grace upon them in their walk and mightily increases their `Faith'.

To me the most startling remark in the gospel was when Jesus stated: "**Because strait is the gate, and narrow is the way, which leadeth unto life, and few there be that find it**." (Matthew 7:14). How can that be when there are a billion plus Catholics alone and many millions in other denominations laboring hard in this present age to present themselves worthy to God? And in addition to that, Jesus has been calling people to Himself since He was here. The reason is, that the truth is too simple. We want life to be a challenge. We want it to be complicated and competitive. For us to come into perfect standing with God is through His Son Jesus Christ.

The message of righteousness (rightness) without working for it just does not get through to us. We are brought up to be a good little girl or boy and we believe that God has the same agenda and many run from God because they feel defeated. "I'll never make it," was my son's reply. That is why God is doing it different. He tells us we don't have to make it. He is giving us a clean slate when we come to him. He wipes the whole past away and Jesus, between God, and us, prays for us to continue to keep us clean and perfect because He purchased us just the way we are. Not one hair needed to be rearranged. Jesus paid the price with His blood just the way we are. He moved our status from that of slavery to becoming sons of God and brothers of Jesus Christ, in line to share His inheritance in future times. Not only that, we will be alive forever from that moment and delivered from the plans God has for Satan and all those who do not accept this simple message.

Taming The Lion

God is our Father, He created us, He wants us to come back to his wonderful original creation. After all He created everything for His children. Thousands of different flowers, animals, mountains, oceans and all the marvelous natural wonders. His intent was to set this miracle of life and us in a right world, without a threat of death and tribulation. People are proving today that it takes more than brains to keep people from doing evil. Only God knows the answers and He wants to prove it to us in the Millennium. The thousand years that follow the events of the Tribulation prophesied in the Book of Daniel and Revelation are called the Millennium.

The challenge God faces daily is the free choice He gave us. Our minds think that we can do it better somehow. What God's proposition is: `give me an opportunity to prove that I know what I'm doing, you don't have to accept it if you are not convinced.' At the end of the Millennium God gives us another opportunity to say `no'. God does not want anyone in His kingdom who does not wholeheartedly love Him, God the Father, God the Son and God the Holy Spirit, who are one God in three persons. All three are involved in our wellbeing. God is love, a love that is far greater than a pure hearted mother's love for her newborn infant. His goal is to live surrounded by that kind of love within His family. Why would anyone refuse such an offer?

Satan is the troublemaker and to satisfy his demands Jesus went to the cross. Satan demands blood even though blood is what is needed to live for humans. Satan's world is still run under the rule of an eye for an eye. When we sin he has a right to punish us. Without Jesus Christ we have no defense against him.

Jesus died so we could be set free from the law of sin and death. God came down in the person of Jesus Christ to make sure that the price for all sin would be paid once and for all time. Little of this truth is coming from the pulpits because the men don't understand it themselves and they labor under the impression that they are somehow elect and special, which is far from the truth. According to God, thoughts of lust are even sin and when one sin is committed, it is the same as committing them all. We can't win without Jesus

Taming The Lion

Christ. The reason for this attitude from God is to make sure not one tittle goes wrong. We can rest assured that all will go according to schedule.

We hear this word salvation in connection with the gospel. What does it mean, have you ever thought about it? The Greek word is Soterion: #4992 the word stands for the Savior, Christ `soter' derived from #4990 and #4991 In Ephesians it is described as a helmet. Think about motorcycle riding what is a helmet to do, but to save a person from death. #4990 -A savior and deliverer, preserver. Used of God, of Christ and His return to receive His believers (His Church) to Himself. #4991 of spiritual and eternal deliverance, of the present experience of God's power to deliver, .. Inclusively of all the blessing of God and .. as to what He bestows, according to the Lexical Aids to the New Testament. It is as simple as that. The Gospel is of the Grace of God or the gift of God. When you accept Christ as personal Savior, you are given everlasting life in Heaven. When you accept the Gospel of the Kingdom, which is taught from the pulpits, we are told to fulfill the laws so we could be given everlasting life and also become heir of the world. That is the difference between the Gospel of the Kingdom and the Gospel of the Grace of God.

"A saint is not some arbitrarily chosen person, about which a committee meets to discuss his qualifications, and by a vote of five to four makes him a saint. No one is made a saint by the democratic vote of anybody. A saint is someone who has the imputed righteousness of Jesus Christ," according to Dr. David Breese, a worldwide conservative evangelist and the Gospel backs this up. What does the word `imputed' mean? "**But for us also, to whom it shall be imputed, if we believe on him that raised up Jesus our Lord from the dead**;" (Romans 4:24) To further investigate the word `imputed' we find in the Concordance and Lexical Aid: #3049 in Greek: Logizomal; derived from logos, reason, word and account. Actually the word means to put together with one's mind. God placed something to our [bank] account, for lack of a word. Another word may be [sin] account, to give us freedom from guilt

368

Taming The Lion

[because the debt has been paid on the cross]." We have to truly believe it, that is what 'faith' is. The goal is to believe that to a point where nobody can shake it and an effort needs to be made to get to know God Himself, which is possible.

In conclusion I wish to discuss the 'End of the Age'. It relates to the conclusion of this dispensation. The original book was self-published in 1994. I have added and subtracted from that book and this last chapter was written in 2008.

No doubt there is an endtime frenzy going on. Many strange stories are coming my way, which encouraged me to study it out myself and share my findings with the readers. The fact that Christians will be increasingly persecuted, put to death and hated by all nations, confirms integration into mainline religions. Many will turn away from the 'Faith' due to false prophets and fear. Love grows cold (see Matthew 24:9) Preliminary signs will be continuously increasing until the end of the age.

The precursors are the following: many come in the name of Jesus, rumors of wars, nation rising against nation, famines and increased earthquakes (see Matthew 24:3) The Gospel will be preached to the whole world (all nations) and then the end will come. Christians are expected to stand firm to the end [end in the concordance is #5056: to conclusion until the debt is discharged, Satan and his cohorts get back double of what they have done]. Preliminaries are likened to labor pains of a woman in travail getting ready to deliver a child.

The secret power of lawlessness has been at work since the beginning with increasing magnitude and will be totally revealed. A royal king will tell the world that he will bring peace and three and a half years into the tribulation Satan will enter his body. Many evangelists are talking about a revival leading to restoration when in effect our environment has so deteriorated, that we are physically unable to absorb more pressure. There are days when I get physically ill from breathing city air. Its effects are so poisonous. A reporter said today on the news that the trees are dying at a rate three times faster than normal. That in itself is a major sign that time is short. People do not have the answers to problems.

With that fact established, Scriptures tells us: "**Let no man deceive you by any means: for that day shall not come, except there come a falling away first, and that man of sin be revealed, the son of perdition;**" (2 Thessalonians 2:3) Apostasy is to be expected, which does not mean the churches will become empty. It means the truth will not be preached.

"**The fear of the LORD is the beginning of knowledge: but fools despise wisdom and instruction.**" Proverbs 1:7 God warns us thus: "**My people are destroyed for lack of knowledge: because thou hast rejected knowledge, I will also reject thee, that thou shalt be no priest to me: seeing thou hast forgotten the law of thy God, I will also forget thy children**." (Hosea 4:6) Hosea is from the Old Testament and God is talking to the Jews who are an example of what happens when we ignore God. God is telling us to stick as close to his prophecy, the Holy Bible, as possible. Men's preaching cannot be trusted. The book is full of examples. "**Therefore wait ye upon me, saith the LORD, until the day that I rise up to the prey: for my determination is to gather the nations, that I may assemble the kingdoms, to pour upon them mine indignation, even all my fierce anger: for all the earth shall be devoured with the fire of my jealousy**." (Zephaniah 3:8) This prophecy relates to the coming Tribulation period climaxing at Armageddon.

Don't let anyone talk you into believing that there is no rapture. When people say that, they are denying the first resurrection. The Bible is absolute and will come true. Some people think because there is no mention of His church in the Book of Revelation, 4:1-22 that the rapture occurs before the tribulation begins. Looking at the last message to the Church of Laodicea, he clearly warns people that he is going to spit them out of his mouth because they are lukewarm. They don't really hear what God wants them to do. He wants Christians to be on fire for Him, to tell it to as many as possible, not on fire for other agendas.

Taming The Lion

The apostle Peter, who walked with Jesus personally had this to say: **"The elders which are among you I exhort, who am also an elder, and a witness of the sufferings of Christ, and also a partaker of the glory that shall be revealed: Feed the flock of God which is among you, taking the oversight thereof, not by constraint, but willingly; not for filthy lucre, but of a ready mind; Neither as being lords over God's heritage, but being ensamples to the flock. And when the chief Shepherd shall appear, ye shall receive a crown of glory that fadeth not away. Likewise, ye younger, submit yourselves unto the elder. Yea, all of you be subject one to another, and be clothed with humility: for God resisteth the proud, and giveth grace to the humble. Humble yourselves therefore under the mighty hand of God, that he may exalt you in due time: Casting all your care upon him; for he careth for you. Be sober, be vigilant; because your adversary the devil, as a roaring lion, walketh about, seeking whom he may devour: Whom resist stedfast in the faith, knowing that the same afflictions are accomplished in your brethren that are in the world. But the God of all grace, who hath called us unto his eternal glory by Christ Jesus, after that ye have suffered a while, make you perfect, stablish, strengthen, settle you. To him be glory and dominion for ever and ever. Amen."** (1 Peter 5:1-11)

His last words to the church were: **"As many as I love, I rebuke and chasten: be zealous therefore, and repent. Behold, I stand at the door, and knock: if any man hear my voice, and open the door, I will come in to him, and will sup with him, and he with me. To him that overcometh will I grant to sit with me in my throne, even as I also overcame, and am set down with my Father in his throne"** (Revelation 3:19-22).

The tribulation, including the first resurrection, Armageddon, the second coming, the Millennium, the second resurrection and the great white throne judgment in total are considered to be `. The Lord's Day.' It will come unexpectedly to those who are not interested and are walking in darkness because of it. Unbelievers are

371

morally asleep. Believers will be fully awake and aware of what is going on. The Day of the Lord will not be a surprise to believers. Scripture predicts this lack of discernment in unbelievers or people who live on Scripture out of context. Here is proof: "**And take heed to yourselves, lest at any time your hearts be overcharged with surfeiting, and drunkenness, and cares of this life, and so that day come upon you unawares**." (Luke 21:34)

Why is the seven-year tribulation approaching? "**Seventy weeks are determined upon thy people and upon thy holy city, to finish the transgression, and to make an end of sins, and to make reconciliation for iniquity, and to bring in everlasting righteousness, and to seal up the vision and prophecy, and to anoint the most Holy. Know therefore and understand, that from the going forth of the commandment to restore and to build Jerusalem unto the Messiah the Prince shall be seven weeks, and threescore and two weeks: the street shall be built again, and the wall, even in troublous times. And after threescore and two weeks shall Messiah be cut off, but not for himself: and the people of the prince that shall come shall destroy the city and the sanctuary; and the end thereof shall be with a flood, and unto the end of the war desolations are determined. And he shall confirm the covenant with many for one week: and in the midst of the week he shall cause the sacrifice and the oblation to cease, and for the overspreading of abominations he shall make it desolate, even until the consummation, and that determined shall be poured upon the desolate.**" (Daniel 9:24-27)

Another reason for the tribulation is the cup of iniquity. "**Babylon hath been a golden cup in the LORD'S hand, that made all the earth drunken: the nations have drunken of her wine; therefore the nations are mad.**" (Jeremiah 51:7) "**Ye cannot drink the cup of the Lord, and the cup of devils: ye cannot be partakers of the Lord's Table, and of the table of devils.**" (1 Corinthians 10:21) The Old Testament is a forerunner of the New Testament and from the Old, we can understand end time happenings. God is planning to burn the weeds [people who reject Jesus Christ as their savior] on this earth. Scripture states that the weeds will be bundled up and wheat will be laid into a barn [a holding place of safety from the elements].

Pointing to the rapture Jesus lectured: "**Heaven and earth shall pass away, but my words shall not pass away. But of that day and hour knoweth no man, no, not the angels of heaven, but my Father only. But as the days of Noe were, so shall also the coming of the Son of man be. For as in the days that were before the flood they were eating and drinking, marrying and giving in marriage, until the day that Noe entered into the ark, And knew not until the flood came, and took them all away; so shall also the coming of the Son of man be. Then shall two be in the field; the one shall be taken, and the other left. Two women shall be grinding at the mill; the one shall be taken, and the other left** ". (Matthew 24:35-41)

Looking at Sodom and Gomorrah in Genesis 18:20-26: "**And the LORD said, Because the cry of Sodom and Gomorrah is great, and because their sin is very grievous; I will go down now, and see whether they have done altogether according to the cry of it, which is come unto me; and if not, I will know. And the men turned their faces from thence, and went toward Sodom: but Abraham stood yet before the LORD. And Abraham drew near, and said, Wilt thou also destroy the righteous with the wicked? Peradventure there be fifty righteous within the city: wilt thou also destroy and not spare the place for the fifty righteous that are therein? That be far from thee to do after this manner, to slay the righteous with the wicked: and that the righteous should be as the wicked, that be far from thee: Shall not the Judge of all the earth do right? And the LORD said, If I find in Sodom fifty righteous within the city, then I will spare all the place for their sakes.** "

Genesis 19:9 "**And they said, Stand back. And they said again, This one fellow came in to sojourn, and he will needs be a judge: now will we deal worse with thee, than with them. And they** pressed sore upon the man, even Lot, and came near to break the door." "And the men said unto Lot, Hast thou here any besides? son in law, and thy sons, and thy daughters, and whatsoever thou hast in the city, bring them out of this place: For we will destroy this place, because the cry of them is waxen great before the face of the LORD; and the LORD hath sent us to destroy it. And Lot went out, and spake unto his sons in law, which married his daughters, and said, Up, get you out of this place; for the LORD will destroy this city. But he seemed as one that mocked unto his sons in law. And when the morning arose, then the angels hastened Lot, saying, Arise, take thy wife, and thy two daughters, which are here; lest thou be consumed in the iniquity of the city. And while he lingered, the men laid hold upon his hand, and upon the hand of his wife, and upon the hand of his two daughters; the LORD being merciful unto him: and they brought him forth, and set him without the city. And it came to pass, when they had brought them forth abroad, that he said, Escape for thy life; look not behind thee, neither stay thou in all the plain; escape to the mountain, lest thou be consumed. " (Genesis 19:9,12-17)

Their survival depended on a personal relationship with God who sent angels. It also depended on hearing exactly what the advice was on how to get out to the point of 'not turning their heads'. The Lord rained down burning sulfur on Sodom and Gomorrah and Lot and his children were rescued out of the catastrophe. Lot's wife looked back, when she was told not to and did not make it. Scriptures of the New Testament refer to this story: "**And turning the cities of Sodom and Gomorrha into ashes condemned them with an overthrow, making them an ensample unto those that after should live ungodly; And delivered just Lot, vexed with the filthy conversation of the wicked: (For that righteous man dwelling among them, in seeing and hearing, vexed his righteous soul from day to day with their unlawful deeds;) The Lord knoweth how to deliver the godly out of temptations, and to reserve the unjust unto the day of judgment to be punished." ** (2 Peter 2:6-9)

374

Taming The Lion

Jesus Christ himself opens the first seal initiating the seven-year tribulation at a time when the world leaders have everything in place to fulfill the final part of Bible prophecy. The seven year period includes the thousand year Millennium (God counts a day for a thousand years) supervised by Jesus Christ with an iron scepter (see Rev. 2:27). It is a time of separating good from evil physically. Even that late Jesus still asks us to come out: "**Behold, I stand at the door, and knock: if any man hear my voice, and open the door, I will come in to him, and will sup with him, and he with me.**" (Revelation 3:20)

Before it's too late people will still be saved because they will come under such physical pressure, they will be calling on God to help them. There will be a lot more tribulation saints than raptured believers. The Bible relates stories to teach us the meaning of what God has in mind. Being under the blood of Christ Jesus will have its problems, but we are to comfort each other with the teaching of the rapture. Believers will be removed before that critical point when the dragon (Satan) is thrown to earth and released into a fatally wounded royal world leader. Scriptures relating to it make it very clear that Holy Spirit filled believers will not be present in the tribulation.

Scripture gives many clues to believers. The `fig tree' was symbolic of Israel in Matthew 21:19. Jesus cursed this tree for not bearing fruit [believing that Jesus was their Messiah]. The tree withered. In Matthew 24:32, Jesus taught that summer is near when the fig tree comes back to life. He meant, tribulation is close when the Jews return to Israel to revitalize the land. God is drawing the Jews back home since 1948 and some are very anxious to rebuild the Temple in Jerusalem. A Muslim Temple is on the mount now and the struggle and turmoil in Jerusalem is over who is going to control Jerusalem, especially the temple mount. It is now realized that no-one knows for sure exactly where Solomon's Temple was originally located and Jews involved in this issue are coming around to thinking that building the third temple would be appropriate next to the Islamic Temple.

Taming The Lion

Christian teachers who go to Israel often claim Jerusalem is the most heathen city on earth. Israelis dedicated to the Old Testament who still pray on the Wall are approximately 2%. The Palestinians just recently got back into the West bank and their leader has voiced the desire to control Jerusalem. The Pope is now getting involved, befriending the Jews by apologizing for not stopping Adolf Hitler from the holocaust. Hitler was Catholic and Pope Pius XII could have intervened and did nothing.

The most obvious clues are movements that have covered the world with a net-like network, where each knot in the net is a related organization based in religion, economics or politics and they are interconnected to achieve one goal: A New World Order served by politicians and evangelists of all denominations. Peace and unity is the goal. What has amazed me, it is reaching every person on this planet in some form. The same year Jerusalem was reborn as a Jewish state, the World Council of Churches was founded in Amsterdam. It has become an assembly of all major religions, including Buddhism, Islam, Hinduism, New Age, most Christian denominations and many others. The council promotes world-wide annual meetings to work out differences among the many different denominations and they are making so much headway that one by one churches are clamoring for membership in this ecumenical movement. The council maintains an their ecumenical institute in Geneva Switzerland in which nearly every major U.S. Protestant denomination participates to bring unity among all religious people. The Catholic Church was instrumental in founding this organization behind the scenes.

So much has been done behind the scenes that many people are not aware of. Only through working in my discernment ministry did I get to this kind of information. Since grassroots are the movers where political agenda is concerned, the politicians are engaging the religious movements to get motion toward the final goal. The two underlying forces in juxta position, good and evil, are God versus Mammon or God versus the rich, and gold (only purchased from Jesus) versus golden (artificial substitutes).

Taming The Lion

Parallel to the days of Moses, when God used him to lead the Israelites from slavery to the Promised Land out of Egyptian oppression, God is going to use Jesus Christ to do it again. The Israelites were in slavery, building the pyramids (tombs) for Egyptian rulers, Moses was to lead them out by means of astonishing miracles. Moses eventually could not control the Israelites nor himself and they all died in the wilderness. Joshua received the honor to take the next generation of Israelites to the Promised Land across the Jordan and made it through.

God's plan is fascinating. The seven-year tribulation begins with two witnesses in sackcloths walking through Jerusalem for three and a half years, warning people of the impending tyranny of the Antichrist if they do not accept Jesus Christ.

"And there was given me a reed like unto a rod: and the angel stood, saying, Rise, and measure the temple of God, and the altar, and them that worship therein. But the court which is without the temple leave out, and measure it not; for it is given unto the Gentiles: and the holy city shall they tread under foot forty and two months. And I will give power unto my two witnesses, and they shall prophesy a thousand two hundred and threescore days [3.5 years], clothed in sackcloth. These are the two olive trees, and the two candlesticks standing before the God of the earth. And if any man will hurt them, fire proceedeth out of their mouth, and devoureth their enemies: and if any man will hurt them, he must in this manner be killed. These have power to shut heaven that it rain not in the days of their prophecy: and have power over waters to turn them to blood, and to smite the earth with all plagues, as often as they will. And when they shall have finished their testimony, the beast that ascendeth out of the bottomless pit shall make war against them, and shall overcome them, and kill them."

"And their dead bodies shall lie in the street of the great city, which spiritually is called Sodom and Egypt, where also our Lord was crucified. And they of the people and kindreds and tongues and nations shall see their dead bodies three days and

an half, and shall not suffer their dead bodies to be put in graves. And they that dwell upon the earth shall rejoice over them, and make merry, and shall send gifts one to another; because these two prophets tormented them that dwelt on the earth. And after three days and an half the Spirit of life from God entered into them, and they stood upon their feet; and great fear fell upon them which saw them. And they heard a great voice from heaven saying unto them, Come up hither. And they ascended up to heaven in a cloud; and their enemies beheld them. And the same hour was there a great earthquake, and the tenth part of the city fell, and in the earthquake were slain of men seven thousand: and the remnant were affrighted, and gave glory to the God of heaven. " (Revelation 11:1-13)

The question now is: "who are these two witnesses?" "**And two olive trees by it, one upon the right [side] of the bowl, and the other upon the left [side] thereof. Zechariah 4:3 "Then answered I, and said unto him, What [are] these two olive trees upon the right [side] of the candlestick and upon the left [side] thereof?** " (Zechariah 4:11)

And as it is appointed unto men once to die, but after this the judgment: (Hebrews 9:27) Because of Hebrews 9:27 they were prophets who lived on the earth and did not die when they departed. Here is evidence of two who are with Jesus in bodily form. Mathew 17:1-4 "**And after six days Jesus taketh Peter, James, and John his brother, and bringeth them up into a high mountain apart, And was transfigured before them: and his face did shine as the sun, and his raiment was white as the light. And behold, there appeared unto them Moses and Elijah talking with him. Then answered Peter, and said unto Jesus, Lord, it is good for us to be here: if thou wilt, let us make here three tabernacles; one for thee, and one for Moses, and one for Elijah.**"

Transfiguration is described as # 3339. Metamorphoo; denoting change of condition.. Used of Jesus involving the miracle of transformation from an earthly form into a supernatural, which is denoted by the radiance of the garments, also the countenance, suggesting what the bodies of the righteous may be like in the age to come 1Cor. 15:51f.

What Jesus was teaching in this miracle was that Moses and Elijah where still alive and are the only two that are qualified to become the two anointed in the streets of Jerusalem. Moses and Elijah both did powerful miracles. Moses had power from God to part the sea and bring about many other miracles and Elijah called fire from heaven. Elijah was translated when he was taken up: "**And it came to pass, as they still went on, and talked, that, behold, [there appeared] a chariot of fire, and horses of fire, and parted them both asunder; and Elijah went up by a whirlwind into heaven.**" (2 Kings 2:11)

Moses was said to have died, it was written but they never found his remains. "**Nevertheless death reigned from Adam to Moses, even over them that had not sinned after the similitude of Adam's transgression, who is the figure of him that was to come.**" (Romans 5:14) "**Yet Michael the archangel, when contending with the devil he disputed about the body of Moses, durst not bring against him a railing accusation, but said, The Lord rebuke thee.**" (Jude 1:9) The fact that the archangel Michael brought Moses's body to heaven (the rest of the dead are still in graves on earth. Their bodies have not been resurrected at the beginning of the Tribulation. The Rapture is simultaneous with the Tribulation. The two are mutually exclusive and prove where Moses's body is located: in heaven confirming the two witnesses are Moses and Elijah.

There was a time when I thought Joshua and Zerubbabel were the two witnesses but more research proved that to be incorrect. "**The hands of Zerubbabel have laid the foundation of this house; his hands shall also finish it; and thou shalt know that the LORD of hosts hath sent me unto you. For who hath despised the day of small things? for they shall rejoice, and shall see the plummet in the hand of Zerubbabel with those seven; they are the eyes of the LORD, which run to and fro through the whole earth. Then answered I, and said unto him, What are these two olive trees** upon the right side of the candlestick and upon the left side thereof? And I answered again, and said unto him, What be these two olive branches which through the two golden pipes empty the golden oil out of themselves? And he answered me and said, Knowest thou not what these be? And I said, No, my lord. Then said he, These are the two anointed ones, that stand by the Lord of the whole earth." (Zechariah 4:9-14)

In Zechariah we are told that Zerubbabel is chosen by God to finish the temple. Since Zerubbabel previously participated in the actual construction of the house of the Lord, we must keep Zerubbabel in that frame of reference. He had little to do with building the temple built without hands of which Christ Jesus is the cornerstone and capstone. If Zachariah 4:9 is literal he will be in the first resurrection / rapture coming out of his grave to fulfill that Scripture. That, of course, points to a Rapture that is prior to the revealing of the Antichrist in God's temple.

"Hear now, O Joshua the high priest, thou, and thy fellows that sit before thee: for they are men wondered at: for, behold, I will bring forth my servant the BRANCH. For behold the stone that I have laid before Joshua; upon one stone shall be seven eyes: behold, I will engrave the graving thereof, saith the LORD of hosts, and I will remove the iniquity of that land in one day. In that day, saith the LORD of hosts, shall ye call every man his neighbour under the vine and under the fig tree." (Zechariah 3:8-10).

A commentary by Jamiesson, Fauset and Brown proves that Zechariah 3:8-10 is about the future and expresses ground for encouragement to the Jews in building the temple [although this temple will be occupied by Antichrist. Joshua brought the Jews to the promised land out of the wilderness]. The hand of Zerubbabel will finish the temple. (Jehovah) have laid the (foundation) stone as the chief architect, before (in the presence of) Joshua, by "the hand of Zerubbabel" (Zechariah 4:10; Ezra 3:8-13), so that your labor in building shall) not be vain. Antitypically, the (foundation) stone alluded to is Christ, before called "the Branch." Lest any should think from that term that His kingdom is weak, He now calls it "the stone," because of its solidity and strength whereby it is to be the foundation of the Church, and shall crush all the world kingdoms (Psalm 118:22; compare Isa 28:16; Daniel 2:45; Matthew 21:42; 1Corinthians 3:11; 1Peter 2:6-7). The angel pointing to the chief stone lying before Him, intimates that a deeper mystery than the material temple is symbolized as well.

The word remove relates to iniquity of that land in one day--that is, the iniquity and its consequences, namely the punishment to which the Jews heretofore had been subjected (Hag 1:6,9-11). The remission of sin is the fountain of every other blessing. The "one day" of its removal is primarily the day of national atonement celebrated after the completion of the temple (Le 23:27) on the tenth day of the seventh month.

Antitypically, the atonement by Messiah for all men, once for all ("one day") offered, needing no repetition like the Mosaic sacrifices (Heb 10:10,12,14).

No doubt Haggai 2:22,23 is referring to the tribulation: "**And I will overthrow the throne of kingdoms, and I will destroy the strength of the kingdoms of the heathen; and I will overthrow the chariots, and those that ride in them; and the horses and their riders shall come down, every one by the sword of his brother. In that day, saith the LORD of hosts, will I take thee, O Zerubbabel, my servant, the son of Shealtiel, saith the LORD, and will make thee as a signet: for I have chosen thee, saith the LORD of hosts.**"

"**Yet now be strong, O Zerubbabel, saith the LORD; and be strong, O Joshua, son of Josedech, the high priest; and be strong, all ye people of the land, saith the LORD, and work: for I am with you, saith the LORD of hosts: According to the word that I covenanted with you when ye came out of Egypt, so my spirit remaineth among you: fear ye not. For thus saith the LORD of hosts; Yet once, it is a little while, and I will shake the heavens, and the earth, and the sea, and the dry land; And I will** shake all nations, and the desire of all nations shall come: and I will fill this house with glory, saith the LORD of hosts." (Haggai 2:4-7) "And the LORD stirred up the spirit of Zerubbabel the son of Shealtiel, governor of Judah, and the spirit of Joshua the son of Josedech, the high priest, and the spirit of all the remnant of the people; and they came and did work in the house of the LORD of hosts, their God," (Haggai 1:14).

"God is constantly reassuring us that He helps us stand firm: "Now he which stablisheth us with you in Christ, and hath anointed us, is God; Who hath also sealed us, and given the earnest of the Spirit in our hearts." (2 Corinthians 1:21-22)

About the coming King of Jerusalem: "And he shall confirm the covenant with many for one week: and in the midst of the week he shall cause the sacrifice and the oblation to cease, and for the overspreading of abominations he shall make it desolate, even until the consummation, and that determined shall be poured upon the desolate." (Daniel 9:27)

During the seven-year tribulation that comes like a thief in the night when least expected, Jesus Himself opens seven seals in the spirit realm. Each seal marks certain events over the seven year period. With the first seal opened the earth will be smitten with fire mixed with blood and one third of the trees and grass will be destroyed. These indications more evident every day: 130,000 acres burned this year, a whole group of people lost their lives in trying to extinguish the fires and Europe is experiencing an unusually hot summer with the same effects. Natural disasters are of increased intensity as we move in time. An Angel tells people to fear God and worship Him. The second seal opened signifies war and more natural disasters. A blazing object as big as a mountain will fall into the sea killing one third of the fish and one third of all ships are destroyed. A second Angel proclaims that Babylon, the counterfeit religious system, will fall. The third phase brings famine as a result of the natural disasters and war.

Taming The Lion

"And at the time of the end shall the king of the south push at him: and the king of the north shall come against him like a whirlwind, with chariots, and with horsemen, and with many ships; and he shall enter into the countries, and shall overflow and pass over. He shall enter also into the glorious land, and many countries shall be overthrown: but these shall escape out of his hand, even Edom, and Moab, and the chief of the children of Ammon. He shall stretch forth his hand also upon the countries: and the land of Egypt shall not escape. But he shall have power over the treasures of gold and of silver, and over all the precious things of Egypt: and the Libyans and the Ethiopians shall be at his steps. But tidings out of the east and out of the north shall trouble him: therefore he shall go forth with great fury to destroy, and utterly to make away many. And he shall plant the tabernacles of his palace between the seas in the glorious holy mountain; yet he shall come to his end, and none shall help him." (Daniel 11:40-45)

The third seal opened promises inflation that causes prices to skyrocket as in Hitler's take-over. Inflation drove people to accept his offer to fix the economy just as the Antichrist will make an offer to the people. More natural disasters, another blazing star falls and creates calamity in rivers causing one third of drinking water to contaminate and people die. A third Angel proclaims: "If anyone receives the mark of the beast, God will torment him with burning sulphur. This calls for patience and endurance on the part of those who don't plan to take the mark.

By now twenty five percent of the population has died from hunger, plagues, swords [war] and possessed animals [there is evidence of these predictions in Africa recently when a revolt caused thousands to leave their villages and suffer and die from plagues and starvation]. Lights, the sun and the moon have lost one third of their light causing days to shorten by one third. A fourth Angel throws the sickle in to reap a harvest [In my opinion this relates to the rapture because of other events coinciding and people are coming to the Lord in fear and trembling]. The Holy Spirit is about to be removed. The climax of the One World Order apexes in the Antichrist's hour of power, is about to arrive." "**But if our gospel be hid, it is hid to them that are lost: And even if our gospel is veiled, it is veiled to those who are perishing." 2 Corinthians 4:3 "For we are unto God a sweet savour of Christ, in them that are saved, and in them that perish:"** *(*2 Corinthians 2:15)

"**I know thy works: behold, I have set before thee an open door, and no man can shut it: for thou hast a little strength, and hast kept my word, and hast not denied my name. Behold, I will make them of the synagogue of Satan, which say they are Jews, and are not, but do lie; behold, I will make them to come and worship before thy feet, and to know that I have loved thee. Because thou hast kept the word of my patience, I also will keep thee from the hour of temptation, which shall come upon all the world, to try them that dwell upon the earth. Behold, I come quickly: hold that fast which thou hast, that no man take thy crown. Him that overcometh will I make a pillar in the temple of my God, and he shall go no more out: and I will write upon him the name of my God, and the name of the city of my God, which is new Jerusalem, which cometh down out of heaven from my God: and I will write upon him my new name.** *"* (Revelation 3:8-12)

"**But of the times and the seasons, brethren, ye have no need that I write unto you. For yourselves know perfectly that the day of the Lord so cometh as a thief in the night. For when they shall say, Peace and safety; then sudden destruction cometh upon them, as travail upon a woman with child; and they shall not escape. But ye, brethren, are not in darkness, that that day should overtake you as a thief. Ye are all the children of light, and the children of the day: we are not of the night, nor of darkness. Therefore let us not sleep, as do others; but let us watch and be sober. For they that sleep sleep in the night; and they that be drunken are drunken in the night. But let us, who are of the day, be sober, putting on the breastplate of faith and** love; and for an helmet, the hope of salvation. For God hath not appointed us to wrath, but to obtain salvation by our Lord Jesus Christ, Who died for us, that, whether we wake or sleep, we should live together with him." (1 Thessalonians 5:1-10)

"And his [the Antichrist] power shall be mighty, but not by his own power: and he shall destroy wonderfully, and shall prosper, and practise, and shall destroy the mighty and the holy people [Israelites]." (Daniel 8:24) "Neither shall he regard the God of his fathers, nor the desire of women, nor regard any god: for he shall magnify himself above all. But in his estate shall he honour the God of forces: and a god whom his fathers knew not shall he honour with gold, and silver, and with precious stones, and pleasant things." (Daniel 11:37-38)

" And then shall that Wicked be revealed, whom the Lord shall consume with the spirit of his mouth, and shall destroy with the brightness of his coming: Even him, whose coming is after the working of Satan with all power and signs and lying wonders, And with all deceivableness of unrighteousness in them that perish; because they received not the love of the truth, that they might be saved. And for this cause God shall send them strong delusion, that they should believe a lie: That they all might be damned who believed not the truth, but had pleasure in unrighteousness." (2 Thessalonians 2:8-12)

"For the secret power of lawlessness is already at work [when the apostles wrote this some 1900 and some odd years ago]; but the one who now holds it back [the Holy Spirit in believer's hearts] will continue to do so till he is taken out of the way. And then the lawless one will be revealed, whom the Lord Jesus will overthrow with the breath of his mouth and destroy by the splendour of His (Jesus's) coming." (2 Thessalonians 2:7,8 NIV) The Ryrie Study Bible shows the following note on page 1644: 2:7 `The one who now holds it [lawlessness] back will continue to do so till. Antichrist is now being held back by a restrainer. Some understand this to be God indwelling His church by the Holy Spirit, while others see human government as the restraint. According to the former view, the removal will be at the rapture of the church (see 1 Thessalonians 4:13-18); according to the latter, at the overthrow of human government by Antichrist.' 2:8 `..The Day of the Lord will not begin until the Antichrist is revealed. Half way through the tribulation the King of Jerusalem is mortally wounded. The dragon spirit, (another word for Satan) will give the beast [Antichrist] his power. In Revelation 13:3 the [seemingly] fatal wound had been healed. Apparently Satan will miraculously restore Antichrist by imitating the resurrection of Christ. No wonder the world will acclaim Antichrist' [as the Messiah]. Remember it will only seem that way. Satan does not have resurrection power like Jesus Christ did.

The reason I came to the conclusion that the rapture is just before Antichrist is exposed is not only the progression of events of the seven seals, the seven trumpets, the seven angels, the seven bowls, the sign in heaven to the Israelites at midpoint and the removal of the restrainer, but also the following Scripture: "**For he will finish the work, and cut [it] short in righteousness: because a short work will the Lord make upon the earth.**" (Romans 9:28). Could it be that the reference to the `wrath of God' that born again Christians are excluded from: "**For God hath not appointed us to wrath, but to obtain salvation by our Lord Jesus Christ,**" *(*1 Thessalonians 5:9) We assume that means the whole seven-year tribulation. "**And to wait for his Son from heaven, whom he raised from the dead, even Jesus, which delivered us from the wrath to come.** *(*1 Thessalonians 1:10) "**Wherefore gird up the loins of your mind, be sober, and hope to the end for the grace that is to be brought unto you at the revelation of Jesus Christ;** *(*1 Peter 1:13) "**Looking for and hasting unto the coming of the day of God, wherein the heavens being on fire shall be dissolved, and the elements shall melt with fervent heat?**" (2 Peter 3:12)

The winepress is mentioned in conjunction with His wrath, as noted in the following verses refer to the latter part of the tribulation right after the harvest of believers: "**And the angel thrust in his sickle into the earth, and gathered the vine of the earth, and cast**

386

Taming The Lion

it into the great winepress of the wrath of God. And the winepress was trodden without the city, and blood came out of the winepress, even unto the horse bridles, by the space of a thousand and six hundred furlongs." (Revelation 14:19-20).

"And out of his mouth goeth a sharp sword, that with it he should smite the nations: and he shall rule them with a rod of iron: and he treadeth the winepress of the fierceness and wrath of Almighty God*"* *(*Revelation 19:15) Another significant account of this period is in Isaiah: "**I the LORD do keep it; I will water it every moment: lest any hurt it, I will keep it night and day. Fury is not in me: who would set the briers and thorns against me in battle? I would go through them, I would burn them together. Or let him take hold of my strength, that he may make peace with me; and he shall make peace with me. He shall cause them that come of Jacob to take root: Israel shall blossom and bud, and fill the face of the world with fruit. Hath he smitten him, as he smote those that smote him? or is he slain according to the slaughter of them that are slain by him? In measure, when it shooteth forth, thou wilt debate with it: he stayeth his rough wind in the day of the east wind. By this therefore shall the iniquity of Jacob be purged; and this is all the fruit to take away his sin; when he maketh all the stones of the altar as chalkstones that are beaten in sunder, the groves and images shall not stand up.*"***

"**Yet the defenced city shall be desolate, and the habitation forsaken, and left like a wilderness: there shall the calf feed, and there shall he lie down, and consume the branches thereof. When the boughs thereof are withered, they shall be broken off: the women come, and set them on fire: for it is a people of no understanding: therefore he that made them will not have mercy on them, and he that formed them will shew them no favour. And it shall come to pass in that day, that the LORD shall beat off from the channel of the river unto the stream of Egypt, and ye shall be gathered one by one, O ye children of Israel. And it shall come to pass in that day, that the great**

trumpet shall be blown, and they shall come which were ready to perish in the land of Assyria, and the outcasts in the land of Egypt, and shall worship the LORD in the holy mount at Jerusalem."

"Woe to the crown of pride, to the drunkards of Ephraim, whose glorious beauty is a fading flower, which are on the head of the fat valleys of them that are overcome with wine! Behold, the Lord hath a mighty and strong one, which as a tempest of hail and a destroying storm, as a flood of mighty waters overflowing, shall cast down to the earth with the hand. The crown of pride, the drunkards of Ephraim, shall be trodden under feet: " (Isaiah 27:3-28:3)

At midpoint of the seven years, a sign appears in heaven. A woman clothed with the sun, standing on the moon wearing a crown of twelve stars, crying in labor pains. **"And she brought forth a man child, who was to rule all nations with a rod of iron: and her child was caught up unto God, and to his throne.** *"* (Revelation 12:5) Later the rest of her offspring, children of light, Israel, flee with the woman to a lonely wasteland: wilderness prepared by God to feed and hide His children for three and a half years.

This does not relate to the 144,000 Israelites [twelve tribes, twelve thousand of each tribe] because of the timing. The elect are sealed and martyred and resurrected during the second part of the tribulation. Analyzing this woman in the Lexical Aids and Concordance in Greek language, she was a wonder: #4592, miracle with an ethical end and purpose. Indicates grace and power of the doer or of his immediate connection with a higher spiritual world, or a sign or mark in heaven: #3772, elevation, happiness, power, eternity, where God lives, Paul was raptured to this heaven and returned; #3735, a mountain lifting itself. Woman, #1135, wife; #1096, come into being to be married, assembled to come together.

Clothed with the sun: #2246 helios, light; #138, take for oneself, to be called; #142, raise up, to take up, to be lifted up as the Lord's ascension, sail away. #5375 Hebrew: expiate sin, Lexical Aid: basic meaning is to lift up. To take away, to declare independence, be free, clear conscience, taking away of sin. Moon: #4582, brilliancy, under her feet: #4228, footstool. Her crown, #4735, symbolic of high honor (royalty). Lexical Aid: a crown of victory, nuptial joy. Twelve stars, [in my opinion the 12 Apostles] #792, #4766, spread light; #4731, steadfast; #2476, stood. Woman with child: #5605, per Lexical Aids: to be in pains, as when a woman is travail applied spiritually to the Church with respect to bringing it to actual fruition and the grief, distress, woe connected with childbirth. #5088 produced from seed, brings forth to be born as Jesus was born.

"That was the true Light, which lighteth every man that cometh into the world. He was in the world, and the world was made by him, and the world knew him not. He came unto his own, and his own received him not. But as many as received him, to them gave he power to become the sons of God, even to them that believe on his name: Which were born, not of blood, nor of the will of the flesh, nor of the will of man, but of God. And the Word was made flesh, and dwelt among us, (and we beheld his glory, the glory as of the only begotten of the Father,) full of grace and truth." (John 1:9-14).

This wonder will be a sign for the 144,000 to gather in Jerusalem once and for all. If they don't come back to Jerusalem, it will be too late. **"Therefore will he give them up, until the time that she which travaileth hath brought forth: then the remnant of his brethren shall return unto the children of Israel."** (Micah 5:3) To shed more light on the sequence of events Jesus was talking to the Sadducees (teachers of the Old Testament laws) " **And when ye shall see Jerusalem compassed with armies, then know that the desolation thereof is nigh. Then let them which are in Judaea flee to the mountains; and let them which are in the midst of it depart out; and let not them that are in the countries enter thereinto. For these be the days of vengeance, that all things which are written may be fulfilled."**

Taming The Lion

"But woe unto them that are with child, and to them that give suck, in those days! for there shall be great distress in the land, and wrath upon this people. And they shall fall by the edge of the sword, and shall be led away captive into all nations: and Jerusalem shall be trodden down of the Gentiles, until the times of the Gentiles be fulfilled. And there shall be signs in the sun, and in the moon, and in the stars; and upon the earth distress of nations, with perplexity; the sea and the waves roaring; Men's hearts failing them for fear, and for looking after those things which are coming on the earth: for the powers of heaven shall be shaken. And then shall they see the Son of man coming in a cloud with power and great glory. And when these things begin to come to pass, then look up, and lift up your heads; for your redemption draweth nigh." (Luke 21:20-28)

More about the rapture from the apostle Paul: "But I would not have you to be ignorant, brethren, concerning them which are asleep, that ye sorrow not, even as others which have no hope. For if we believe that Jesus died and rose again, even so them also which sleep in Jesus will God bring with him. For this we say unto you by the word of the Lord, that we which are alive and remain unto the coming of the Lord shall not prevent them which are asleep. For the Lord himself shall descend from heaven with a shout, with the voice of the archangel, and with the trump of God: and the dead in Christ shall rise first: Then we which are alive and remain shall be caught up together with them in the clouds, to meet the Lord in the air: and so shall we ever be with the Lord. Wherefore comfort one another with these words." (1 Thessalonians 4:13-18)

To confirm this promise, the apostle Paul stated: "But now is Christ risen from the dead, and become the firstfruits of them that slept. For since by man came death, by man came also the resurrection of the dead. For as in Adam all die, even so in Christ shall all be made alive. But every man in his own order: Christ the firstfruits; afterward they that are Christ's at his coming." (1 Corinthians 15:20-23)

Taming The Lion

War in heaven begins between Michael and his Angels and the Dragon [according to the Lexical Aid: #8577 in Hebrew: imagery used to show the Lord's power over political enemies]. The dragon and **"And his tail drew the third part of the stars of heaven, and did cast them to the earth: and the dragon stood before the woman which was ready to be delivered, for to devour her child as soon as it was born.** *"* (Revelation 12:4)

Basically God takes the controls off and allows the Antichrist full play for one hour in regard to tribulation saints and Israelis. This event culminates with the following verse about the witnesses: **"And when they shall have finished their testimony, the beast that ascendeth out of the bottomless pit shall make war against them, and shall overcome them, and kill them"** (Revelation 11:7)

The beast I saw resembled a leopard [ruler of Greek Empire (Asia Minor, Syria, Egypt and Macedonia0], but had feet like those of a bear [Medo-Persian Empire] and a mouth like that of a lion [& eagle, Babylon]. The dragon gave the beast his power and his throne and great authority. One of the heads [of the Roman Empire] of the beast seemed to have had a fatal wound, but the fatal wound had been healed. The whole world was astonished and followed the beast. Men worshiped the dragon because he had given authority to the beast, and they also worshiped the beast and asked, Who is like the beast? Who can make war against him? [because there is unity and he is in total control of the world]'" (Revelation 13:2-4 NIV)

The two witnesses had power to stop the rain, turn water to wine and wrought miracles. People hated them and persecuted them. The Gentiles had trampled the holy city for three and a half years. The temple had been rebuilt and only Jews were allowed in the inner court. The whole world saw the witnesses lay dead in the street and people celebrated their death and did not want to bury them. **"And after three days and an half the Spirit of life from God entered into them, and they stood upon their feet; and great fear fell upon them which saw them. And they heard a great voice from heaven saying unto them, Come up hither. And they ascended up to heaven in a cloud; and their enemies beheld them. And the**

same hour was there a great earthquake, and the tenth part of the city fell, and in the earthquake were slain of men seven thousand: and the remnant were affrighted, and gave glory to the God of heaven. The second woe is past; and, behold, the third woe cometh quickly. " (Revelation 11:11-14)

The dragon is furious and knows he only has a short time, three and a half years. The dragon gives the body of the wounded king his power. He goes after the woman with floodwaters and most of her offspring is with her. He does not succeed. The devil makes war with that remnant and they are martyred. Satan cannot really kill Christians, only put their bodies temporarily to sleep, while their spirits are very much alive.

Jesus advises the following: "when you see Jerusalem surrounded by armies, will know that the beast which comes out of the sea is about to be exposed." According to the Concordance: the beast #2342 in Greek, a dangerous, venomous trap. The sea represents all nations or the New World Order developed over many years, run by ungodly men, a final world power dominating federated nations. It has within it the mystery of iniquity. The New World Order is described as being terrifying and very powerful. It crushes whatever stands in its way. It is based on the concept of the tower of Babel [Unity brought about by the `Mystery Babylon' who sits on the beast, who advises the leaders of the world to unify]. It is history repeating itself. The tower of Babel was built soon after the flood that drowned all people except Noah and his family. "**Therefore is the name of it called Babel; because the LORD did there confound the language of all the earth: and from thence did the LORD scatter them abroad upon the face of all the earth.**" (Genesis 11:9)

Why did he scatter civilization? "**And the LORD said, Behold, the people is one, and they have all one language; and this they begin to do: and now nothing will be restrained from them, which they have imagined to do.** " (Genesis 11:6) God is telling us here that He does not support a global World Order that all is one being. Civilization has made a full circle.

Taming The Lion

The mother of prostitutes and of the abominations of the earth is a large concept of which only a fragment can be discussed. The virgin Mary in the Bible contained within her Jesus Christ and symbolizes the Church of Christ Jesus held together by the Holy Spirit for the Glory of God. The Church is considered to be the bride of Christ [a virgin] because she is betrothed to one husband [Christ Jesus] forever. The reason the Church is a virgin and uncontaminated is the new birth of each 'born again' [regenerated] person when he or she repents and comes to Christ Jesus for forgiveness. God sees the Church perfect because God looks at Jesus Christ who stands between us and God, and Jesus looks to the Holy Spirit to perfect us believers for the wedding.

In contrast to the virgin God speaks of, the mother of harlots, a prostitute who goes to bed with many, pretends to be the queen of heaven. This relates to the last church contaminated with myriads of false teachings and merging with all religions and mentioned in Revelation 3:16, "So, because you are lukewarm- neither hot nor cold- I am about to spit you out of my mouth" right after the takeover of the Beast [#500 in Greek according to the Lexical Aid: Antichristos .the Beast will attempt to assert the fulfillment of God's Word in himself and will seek to establish his own throne. A false Christ]. "**And for this cause God shall send them strong delusion, that they should believe a lie:**" (2 Thessalonians 2:11)

"There is a voice of the howling of the shepherds [evangelists]; for their glory is spoiled: a voice of the roaring of young lions; for the pride of Jordan is spoiled. Thus saith the LORD my God; Feed the flock [believers] of the slaughter; Whose possessors slay them, and hold themselves not guilty: and they that sell them say, Blessed be the LORD; for I am rich: and their own shepherds pity them not. For I will no more pity the inhabitants of the land, saith the LORD: but, lo, I will deliver the men every one into his neighbour's hand, and into the hand of his king: and they shall smite the land, and out of their hand I will not deliver them." (Zechariah 11:3-6).

Taming The Lion

God is saying here that our only hope is Jesus Christ with the help of the Holy Spirit because the shepherds rejected Jesus Christ for money. In Judas's case thirty pieces of silver.

"No man can serve two masters: for either he will hate the one, and love the other; or else he will hold to the one, and despise the other. Ye cannot serve God and mammon." (Matthew 6:24) **"Let them alone: they be blind leaders of the blind. And if the blind lead the blind, both shall fall into the ditch**." (Matthew 15:14)

The `Beast' has permission from God to attack anyone who is not in the Book of Life [the Savior Jesus Christ's book). People are astonished when they see the beast for the first time and the woman who rides the beast, because it is the counterfeit church, the harlot. The false prophet is exposed at the same time. He comes out of the earth after the beast. A man in sheep's clothing or of the cloth but speaks like a devil. He is the beast's mouthpiece and of equal authority and performs major miracles falsely persuading the world that he is a prophet from God and should be totally believed. His signs and wonders delude everyone who does not have Christ and even some lukewarm Christians.

He makes fire come out of heaven, simulating the Holy Spirit and seemingly raises the king from death. He deceives those who are perishing who refused to love God's truth and be saved. He sends delusion on people's minds and all inhabitants of the earth will worship the beast (Antichrist). The false prophet overrides God's first commandment, that we shall not make or worship graven images. He orders an image of the king to be built. The king proclaimed himself to be God and has taken possession of the Jewish temple. The false prophet breathes life into the image and it begins to talk and live. By now people are certainly convinced the beast and false prophet are straight from God. All who refuse to fall down on their face and worship this image are killed. The rest receive the mark of the beast, which includes `666' on their hand or forehead. The world leaders give their authority to the Antichrist and give him complete authority for one hour and he recreates the world system, giving land to ten kings as a reward. He tries to change laws and time. Men worship him because he represents peace and safety. He received authority to rule for three and a half years, blasphemes God and receives permission to make war on the tribulation saints and overcomes them. Patient endurance and keeping the faith is a must for born again believers. The tribulation saints were those who did not take the mark, They will be slain along with the counterfeit church `Mystery Babylon'.

"And after these things I saw another angel come down from heaven, having great power; and the earth was lightened with his glory. And he cried mightily with a strong voice, saying, Babylon the great is fallen, is fallen, and is become the habitation of devils, and the hold of every foul spirit, and a cage of every unclean and hateful bird. For all nations have drunk of the wine of the wrath of her fornication, and the kings of the earth have committed fornication with her, and the merchants of the earth are waxed rich through the abundance of her delicacies. And I heard another voice from heaven, saying,"

"Come out of her, my people, that ye be not partakers of her sins, and that ye receive not of her plagues. For her sins have reached unto heaven, and God hath remembered her iniquities. Reward her even as she rewarded you, and double unto her double according to her works: in the cup which she hath filled fill to her double. How much she hath glorified herself, and lived deliciously, so much torment and sorrow give her: for she saith in her heart, I sit a queen, and am no widow, and shall see no sorrow. Therefore shall her plagues come in one day, death, and mourning, and famine; and she shall be utterly burned with fire: for strong is the Lord God who judgeth her." (Revelation 18:1-8)

A star fell and became a means to open abyss [deep hole] creating a fiery furnace in the ground [just past the midpoint of tribulation]. Smoke rose out of the earth, which darkens the sun. Locust like humans [airplanes] with iron wings, noisy, tortured unsaved people for five months. All those who took the mark of the beast suddenly developed painful sores and boils over their bodies. Angels are harvesting unbelievers by crushing them. During the sixth period of the tribulation, earthquakes are added, the sun looses its light, the moon becomes red, stars fall to the ground, the sky rolls up, mountains flatten, people get so frightened, they wish they could die and won't be able to.

Jesus appears in the clouds with a trumpet to gather his elect (original chosen Israelites) 144,000 Israelites, 12,000 men from every tribe. They receive a mark of ownership from Jesus Christ (see Matthew 24:29,30). All nations will mourn when they see Jesus coming in the clouds to the Mount of Olives.

Millions of troops engage in war, one third of mankind is killed by fire [Angels release fire], smoke and sulfur. The remaining two thirds did not repent and continue idolatry, murder, magical arts, sexual sins and did not stop worshiping demons [note there are no tribulation saints at this point]. The sea turns into blood and so do rivers. The sun scorches the people, but they still refuse to repent. The throne of the beast is plunged into darkness. Rivers dry up and three evil spirits enter the beast [Antichristos], the dragon [political enemies of the Lord], the false prophet, to lie to the world population and talk all leaders into gathering at Armageddon. The ten kings [presidents] received authority back because they worshiped the Antichrist.

"**And knew not until the flood came, and took them all away; so shall also the coming of the Son of man be. Then shall two be in the field; the one shall be taken, and the other left**." (Matthew 24:39-40) Jesus appears in the clouds just before Armageddon after the seventh seal. "**Behold, I come as a thief. Blessed is he that watcheth, and keepeth his garments, lest he walk naked, and they see his shame.**" (Revelation 16:15) **"For what is our hope, or joy, or crown of rejoicing? Are not even ye in the presence of our Lord Jesus Christ at his coming?"** (1 Thessalonians 2:19)

People who are repenting just before Armageddon and call on the name of Jesus Christ will be heard and saved during the final period of the tribulation and a multitude do take advantage of that opportunity. They will be purified and made spotless during the Millennium. Then there is silence in heaven (quiet before the storm). An Angel took a censer filled with fire, hurled it to the earth causing earthquakes. An Angel was told to eat the little scroll, no more delay. Let the wicked remain wicked. It's over. Lightning and earthquakes become the backdrop of Christ Jesus's second coming when He comes in His glory, accompanied by the 144,000 Israelis. He puts his feet on mount Olive and the mountains splits in half and the halves move away from each creating a shelter for the remnant. He tells them to flee to the mountains. Armageddon proceeds.

"And I saw an angel standing in the sun; and he cried with a loud voice, saying to all the fowls that fly in the midst of heaven, Come and gather yourselves together unto the supper of the great God; That ye may eat the flesh of kings, and the flesh of captains, and the flesh of mighty men, and the flesh of horses, and of them that sit on them, and the flesh of all men, both free and bond, both small and great. And I saw the beast, and the kings of the earth, and their armies, gathered together to make war against him that sat on the horse, and against his army. And the beast was taken, and with him the false prophet that wrought miracles before him, with which he deceived them that had received the mark of the beast, and them that worshiped his image. These both were cast alive into a lake of fire burning with brimstone. And the remnant were slain with the sword of him that sat upon the horse, which sword proceeded out of his mouth: and all the fowls were filled with their flesh." (Revelation 19:17-21). This is considered to be Satan's last supper.

"And I saw an angel come down from heaven, having the key of the bottomless pit and a great chain in his hand. And he laid hold on the dragon, that old serpent, which is the Devil, and Satan, and bound him a thousand years, And cast him into the bottomless pit, and shut him up, and set a seal upon him, that he should deceive the nations no more, till the thousand years

should be fulfilled: and after that he must be loosed a little season." (Revelation 20:1-3)

To confirm what is to transpire we read: "**Behold, the day of the LORD cometh, and thy spoil shall be divided in the midst of thee. For I will gather all nations against Jerusalem to battle; and the city shall be taken, and the houses rifled, and the women ravished; and half of the city shall go forth into captivity, and the residue of the people shall not be cut off from the city. Then shall the LORD go forth, and fight against those nations, as when he fought in the day of battle."**

"**And his feet shall stand in that day upon the mount of Olives, which is before Jerusalem on the east, and the mount of Olives shall cleave in the midst thereof toward the east and toward the west, and there shall be a very great valley; and half of the mountain shall remove toward the north, and half of it toward the south. And ye shall flee to the valley of the mountains; for the valley of the mountains shall reach unto Azal: yea, ye shall flee, like as ye fled from before the earthquake in the days of Uzziah king of Judah: and the LORD my God shall come, and all the saints with thee. And it shall come to pass in that day, that the light shall not be clear, nor dark: But it shall be one day which shall be known to the LORD, not day, nor night: but it shall come to pass, that at evening time it shall be light.**

"**And it shall be in that day, that living waters shall go out from Jerusalem; half of them toward the former sea, and half of them toward the hinder sea: in summer and in winter shall it be. And the LORD shall be king over all the earth: in that day shall there be one LORD, and his name one. All the land shall be turned as a plain from Geba to Rimmon south of Jerusalem: and it shall be lifted up, and inhabited in her place, from Benjamin's gate unto the place of the first gate, unto the corner gate, and from the tower of Hananeel unto the king's winepresses. And men shall dwell in it, and there shall be no more utter destruction; but Jerusalem shall be safely inhabited.**

And this shall be the plague wherewith the LORD will smite all the people that have fought against Jerusalem; Their flesh shall consume away while they stand upon their feet, and their eyes shall consume away in their holes, and their tongue shall consume away in their mouth.

"And it shall come to pass in that day, that a great tumult from the LORD shall be among them; and they shall lay hold every one on the hand of his neighbour, and his hand shall rise up against the hand of his neighbour. And Judah also shall fight at Jerusalem; and the wealth of all the heathen round about shall be gathered together, gold, and silver, and apparel, in great abundance. And so shall be the plague of the horse, of the mule, of the camel, and of the ass, and of all the beasts that shall be in these tents, as this plague. And it shall come to pass, that every one that is left of all the nations which came against Jerusalem shall even go up from year to year to worship the King, the LORD of hosts, and to keep the feast of tabernacles.

"And it shall be, that whoso will not come up of all the families of the earth unto Jerusalem to worship the King, the LORD of hosts, even upon them shall be no rain. And if the family of Egypt go not up, and come not, that have no rain; there shall be the plague, wherewith the LORD will smite the heathen that come not up to keep the feast of tabernacles. This shall be the punishment of Egypt, and the punishment of all nations that come not up to keep the feast of tabernacles. In that day shall there be upon the bells of the horses, HOLINESS UNTO THE LORD; and the pots in the LORD'S house shall be like the bowls before the altar. Yea, every pot in Jerusalem and in Judah shall be holiness unto the LORD of hosts: and all they that sacrifice shall come and take of them, and seethe therein: and in that day there shall be no more the Canaanite in the house of the LORD of hosts." (Zechariah 14:1-21)

"But now thy kingdom shall not continue: the LORD hath sought him a man after his own heart, and the LORD hath commanded him to be captain over his people, because thou hast not kept that which the LORD commanded thee." 1 Samuel 13:14 "But the judgment shall sit, and they shall take away his dominion, to consume and to destroy it unto the end. And the kingdom and dominion, and the greatness of the kingdom under the whole heaven, shall be given to the people of the saints of the most High, whose kingdom is an everlasting kingdom, and all dominions shall serve and obey him." *(Daniel 7:26-27)*

The Book of Micah gives some clues about the Millennium. "**But in the last days it shall come to pass, that the mountain of the house of the LORD shall be established in the top of the mountains, and it shall be exalted above the hills; and people shall flow unto it. And many nations shall come, and say, Come, and let us go up to the mountain of the LORD, and to the house of the God of Jacob; and he will teach us of his ways, and we will walk in his paths: for the law shall go forth of Zion, and the word of the LORD from Jerusalem. And he shall judge among many people, and rebuke strong nations afar off; and they shall beat their swords into plowshares, and their spears into pruninghooks: nation shall not lift up a sword against nation, neither shall they learn war any more.** *"*

"**But they shall sit every man under his vine and under his fig tree; and none shall make them afraid: for the mouth of the LORD of hosts hath spoken it. For all people will walk every one in the name of his god, and we will walk in the name of the LORD our God for ever and ever. In that day, saith the LORD, will I assemble her that halteth, and I will gather her that is driven out, and her that I have afflicted; And I will make her that halted a remnant, and her that was cast far off a strong nation: and the LORD shall reign over them in mount Zion from henceforth, even for ever. And thou, O tower of the flock, the strong hold of the daughter of Zion, unto thee shall it come, even the first dominion; the kingdom shall come to the daughter of Jerusalem.**" (Micah 4:1-8)

Taming The Lion

Isaiah confirms this: "**And it shall come to pass in the last days, that the mountain of the LORD'S house shall be established in the top of the mountains, and shall be exalted above the hills; and all nations shall flow unto it.** And many people shall go and say, Come ye, and let us go up to the mountain of the LORD, to the house of the God of Jacob; and he will teach us of his ways, and we will walk in his paths: for out of Zion shall go forth the law, and the word of the LORD from Jerusalem. And he shall judge among the nations, and shall rebuke many people: and they shall beat their swords into plowshares, and their spears into pruninghooks: nation shall not lift up sword against nation, neither shall they learn war any more. O house of Jacob, come ye, and let us walk in the light of the LORD.**" (Isaiah 2:2-5)

"**And I will set my glory among the heathen, and all the heathen shall see my judgment that I have executed, and my hand that I have laid upon them. So the house of Israel shall know that I am the LORD their God from that day and forward. And the heathen shall know that the house of Israel went into captivity for their iniquity: because they trespassed against me, therefore hid I my face from them, and gave them into the hand of their enemies: so fell they all by the sword. According to their uncleanness and according to their transgressions have I done unto them, and hid my face from them.**" Ezekiel 39:21-24 "**Neither will I hide my face any more from them: for I have poured out my spirit upon the house of Israel, saith the Lord GOD.**" (Ezekiel 39:29)

"**And the nations were angry, and thy wrath is come, and the time of the dead, that they should be judged, and that thou shouldest give reward unto thy servants the prophets, and to the saints, and them that fear thy name, small and great; and shouldest destroy them which destroy the earth.**" Revelation 11:18 "**And before him shall be gathered all nations: and he shall separate them one from another, as a shepherd divideth his sheep from the goats:**" (Matthew 25:32)

Taming The Lion

"And I saw a great white throne, and him that sat on it, from whose face the earth and the heaven fled away; and there was found no place for them. And I saw the dead, small and great, stand before God; and the books were opened: and another book was opened, which is the book of life: and the dead were judged out of those things which were written in the books, according to their works. And the sea gave up the dead, which were in it; and death and hell delivered up the dead, which were in them: and they were judged every man according to their works. And death and hell were cast into the lake of fire. This is the second death. And whosoever was not found written in the book of life was cast into the lake of fire."(Revelation 20:11-15)

"Behold, I shew you a mystery; We shall not all sleep, but we shall all be changed, In a moment, in the twinkling of an eye, at the last trump: for the trumpet shall sound, and the dead shall be raised incorruptible, and we shall be changed. For this corruptible must put on incorruption, and this mortal must put on immortality. So when this corruptible shall have put on incorruption, and this mortal shall have put on immortality, then shall be brought to pass the saying that is written, Death is swallowed up in victory. O death, where is thy sting? O grave, where is thy victory? The sting of death is sin; and the strength of sin is the law." (1 Corinthians 15:51-56)

Basically there are two groups of people, believers and unbelievers. All are immortal. The fate of believers: 'we, the believers' will be changed to an eternal imperishable state and the unbeliever goes into an eternal existence in the lake of fire.

"And the seventh angel sounded; and there were great voices in heaven, saying, The kingdoms of this world are become the kingdoms of our Lord, and of his Christ; and he shall reign for ever and ever." (Revelation 11:15)

The following verses describe believer's eternal existence: "And I saw a new heaven and a new earth: for the first heaven and the first earth were passed away; and there was no more sea.

Taming The Lion

And I John saw the holy city, new Jerusalem, coming down from God out of heaven, prepared as a bride adorned for her husband. And I heard a great voice out of heaven saying, Behold, the tabernacle of God is with men, and he will dwell with them, and they shall be his people, and God himself shall be with them, and be their God. And God shall wipe away all tears from their eyes; and there shall be no more death, neither sorrow, nor crying, neither shall there be any more pain: for the former things are passed away."

"And he that sat upon the throne said, Behold, I make all things new. And he said unto me, Write: for these words are true and faithful. And he said unto me, It is done. I am Alpha and Omega, the beginning and the end. I will give unto him that is athirst of the fountain of the water of life freely. He that overcometh shall inherit all things; and I will be his God, and he shall be my son. But the fearful, and unbelieving, and the abominable, and murderers, and whoremongers, and sorcerers, and idolaters, and all liars, shall have their part in the lake which burneth with fire and brimstone: which is the second death. " (Revelation 21:1-8)

If you are curious what a glorified state is, the apostle John defines it: "And the glory which thou gavest me I have given them; that they may be one, even as we are one: I in them, and thou in me, that they may be made perfect in one; and that the world may know that thou hast sent me, and hast loved them, as thou hast loved me." (John 17:22,23)

The New International Version states it slightly different implying 'complete unity' with the world church, which is causing confusion today. Evangelist use this verse to move into the unification of all religions. The unity is in Jesus Christ, a one to one relationship, that we may be made perfect in one. See John 17:22,23 NIV: "I have given them the glory that you gave me, that they may be one as we are one: I in them and you in me. May they be brought to complete unity to let the world know that you sent me and have loved them even as you have loved me."

Taming The Lion

"And the seventh angel sounded; and there were great voices in heaven, saying, The kingdoms of this world are become the kingdoms of our Lord, and of his Christ; and he shall reign for ever and ever." (Revelation 11:15)

While the exact words of your prayer to God are not of vital importance (since God sees and knows the attitude of your heart), the following is the kind of prayer that you could pray in calling upon God for salvation: "Dear Lord Jesus: I realize that I need You. I admit that I have sinned and that I deserve Your just, eternal punishment for that sin. But I am sorry for my sin and am sincerely willing to turn from it. I renounce Satan and all his works by the authority of Your Son Jesus Christ of Nazareth given to me while praying this prayer. I believe that You died and rose again to pay sin's penalty on my behalf. I come to You and open my heart to You. I ask You to come into my life, forgive me for all my sin, cleanse me from it, and make me Your child. I invite You to take control of my life and to cause me to be the kind of person that You want me to be. And I thank You for doing this - because You have promised that whoever calls upon You, as I have done now, shall be saved. I pray this in the name of Your Son, the Lord Jesus Christ of Nazareth. Amen"

www.ingramcontent.com/pod-product-compliance
Lightning Source LLC
Chambersburg PA
CBHW052028090426
42739CB00010B/1821